Fodor's 18th Edition

San Diego

The Guide
for All Budgets

Completely
Updated

Where to Stay, Eat,
and Explore

On and Off
the Beaten Path

When to Go,
What to Pack

Maps, Travel Tips,
and Web Sites

Fodor's Travel Publications • New York, Toronto, London, Sydney, Auckland
www.fodors.com

Fodor's San Diego

EDITOR: Emmanuelle Morgen

Editorial Contributors: Rob Aikins, Lenore Greiner, Satu Hummasti, David Nelson, Bobbi Zane

Editorial Production: Ira-Neil Dittersdorf

Maps: David Lindroth, *cartographer;* Rebecca Baer and Robert P. Blake, *map editors*

Design: Fabrizio La Rocca, *creative director;* Guido Caroti, *art director;* Jolie Novak, *senior picture editor;* Melanie Marin, *photo editor*

Cover Design: Pentagram

Production/Manufacturing: Yexenia (Jessie) Markland

Cover Photo (SeaWorld): James Lemass

Copyright

Eighteenth Edition

ISBN 1–4000–1050–0

ISSN 1053–5950

Important Tip

Although all prices, opening times, and other details in this book are based on information supplied to us at press time, changes occur all the time in the travel world, and Fodor's cannot accept responsibility for facts that become outdated or for inadvertent errors or omissions. So **always confirm information when it matters,** especially if you're making a detour to visit a specific place.

Special Sales

Fodor's Travel Publications are available at special discounts for bulk purchases for sales promotions or premiums. Special editions, including personalized covers, excerpts of existing guides, and corporate imprints, can be created in large quantities for special needs. For more information, contact your local bookseller or write to Special Markets, Fodor's Travel Publications, 280 Park Avenue, New York, NY 10017. Inquiries from Canada should be directed to your local Canadian bookseller or sent to Random House of Canada, Ltd., Marketing Department, 2775 Matheson Boulevard East, Mississauga, Ontario L4W 4P7. Inquiries from the United Kingdom should be sent to Fodor's Travel Publications, 20 Vauxhall Bridge Road, London SW1V 2SA, England.

PRINTED IN THE UNITED STATES OF AMERICA

10 9 8 7 6 5 4 3 2 1

CONTENTS

Maps

ON THE ROAD WITH FODOR'S

A TRIP TAKES YOU OUT OF YOURSELF. Concerns of life at home completely disappear, driven away by more immediate thoughts—about, say, what marvels will beguile the next day, or where you'll have dinner. That's where Fodor's comes in. We make sure that you know all your options, so that you don't miss something that's around the next bend just because you didn't know it was there. Mindful that the best memories of your trip might have nothing to do with what you came to San Diego to see, we guide you to sights large and small all over town. You might set out to see every animal in the San Diego Zoo, but back at home you find yourself unable to forget peering into tide pools in La Jolla Cove and strolling around the colorful streets of Old Town.

About Our Writers

Our success in showing you every corner of San Diego is a credit to our extraordinary writers.

Rob Aikins has lived in the North Coast community of Encinitas for 15 years, not counting his surf forays into Mexico and Central America. He writes about music, art, and sports for national and local publications and Web sites. His byline has appeared in *SLAMM, San Diego Reader, San Diego Union-Tribune,* and MTVonline among others.

Lenore Greiner grew up in the San Francisco Bay Area but transplanted herself to San Diego 11 years ago after vacationing in Coronado. Her travel articles have appeared in *Newsday,* the *San Francisco Examiner/Chronicle,* Delta Airlines' *Sky,* Air New Zealand's *Pacific Way, Woman,* and *Healing Retreats & Spas.*

Dining writer **David Nelson** has known San Diego since childhood and has lived there for more than 20 years. Respected for his extensive knowledge of food lore, cooking techniques, and the restaurant industry, he was a columnist for the former San Diego edition of the *Los Angeles*

Times for a dozen years. He now writes restaurant reviews and travel pieces for a number of southern California publications.

Longtime southern Californian **Bobbi Zane** makes her home in the mountain hamlet of Julian. Bobbi's byline has appeared in the *Los Angeles Times, Los Angeles Daily News,* and *Orange County Register.*

How to Use this Book

Up front is **Smart Travel Tips A to Z,** loaded with tips, Web sites, and contact information. **Destination: San Diego** helps get you in the mood for your trip. The Exploring chapter is divided into neighborhood sections arranged in logical geographical order; each recommends a good tour and lists local sights alphabetically. The chapters that follow Exploring are arranged alphabetically.

Icons and Symbols

★ Our special recommendations
✕ Restaurant
📷 Lodging establishment
🐤 Good for kids (rubber duck)
✉ Address
☎ Telephone number
🕐 Opening and closing times
💰 Admission prices (those we give apply to adults; substantially reduced fees are almost always available for children, students, and senior citizens)

Don't Forget to Write

Your experiences—positive and negative—matter to us. We follow up on all suggestions. Contact the San Diego editor at editors@fodors.com or c/o Fodor's, 280 Park Avenue, New York, New York 10017. And have a fabulous trip!

Karen Cure
Editorial Director

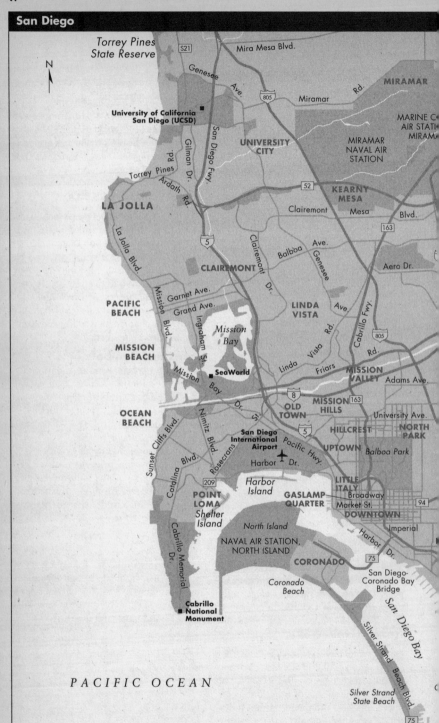

Torrey Pines State Reserve

N

Mira Mesa Blvd.

S21

Genesee Ave.

805

Miramar Rd.

MIRAMAR

University of California San Diego (UCSD)

MARINE C• AIR STATIO MIRAMA

UNIVERSITY CITY

MIRAMAR NAVAL AIR STATION

Gilman Dr.

San Diego Fwy.

Torrey Pines Rd.

Ardath Rd.

52

KEARNY MESA

Clairemont Mesa Blvd.

LA JOLLA

163

La Jolla Blvd

5

Clairemont Dr.

CLAIREMONT

Balboa Ave.

Genesee

Aero Dr.

PACIFIC BEACH

Garnet Ave.

Grand Ave.

Ingraham St.

Mission Blvd.

Mission Bay

LINDA VISTA

Ave.

Vista Rd.

Cabrillo Fwy.

805

MISSION BEACH

Mission Bay

SeaWorld

Linda Vista Rd.

Friars Rd.

MISSION VALLEY

Adams Ave.

OCEAN BEACH

Sunset Cliffs Blvd.

Nimitz Blvd.

Mission St.

Dr.

8

OLD TOWN

MISSION HILLS

163

University Ave.

Catalina Blvd.

Rosecrans

San Diego International Airport

5

HILLCREST

NORTH PARK

Pacific Hwy.

UPTOWN

Balboa Park

Harbor Dr.

209

POINT LOMA

Harbor Island

LITTLE ITALY

Broadway

94

Cabrillo Memorial Dr.

Shelter Island

GASLAMP QUARTER

Market St.

DOWNTOWN

North Island

Imperial

Harbor Dr.

NAVAL AIR STATION, NORTH ISLAND

CORONADO

75

San Diego-Coronado Bay Bridge

Cabrillo National Monument

Coronado Beach

San Diego Bay

PACIFIC OCEAN

Silver Strand State Beach

Silver Strand Beach Blvd.

75

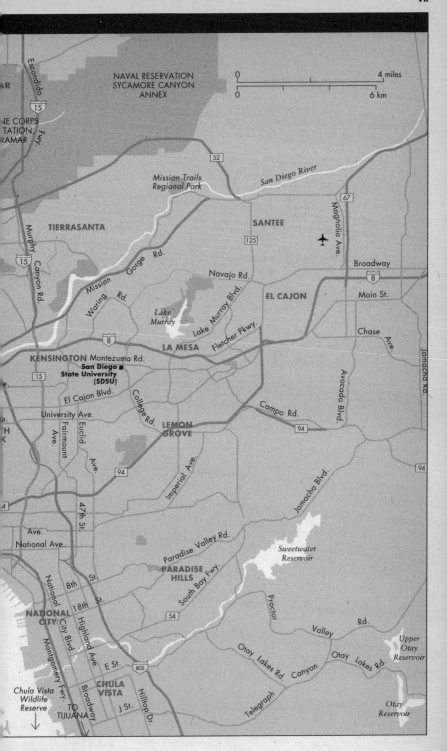

NAVAL RESERVATION
SYCAMORE CANYON
ANNEX

0   4 miles

0   6 km

Escondido Fwy.

15

NE CORPS
TATION,
RAMAR

San Diego River

52

Mission Trails
Regional Park

67

Murphy Canyon Rd.

15

TIERRASANTA

SANTEE

Magnolia Ave.

Mission Gorge Rd.

125

Navajo Rd.

Broadway

8

Waring Rd.

Lake Murray Blvd.

EL CAJON

Main St.

Lake
Murray

8

Fletcher Pkwy.

LA MESA

Chase Ave.

KENSINGTON   Montezuma Rd.

San Diego
State University
(SDSU)

15

College Rd.

Avocado Blvd.

Jamacha Rd.

El Cajon Blvd.

University Ave.

LEMON
GROVE

Campo Rd.

94

Fairmount Ave.

Euclid Ave.

94

Imperial Ave.

94

47th St.

Jamacha Blvd.

4

Ave.

National Ave.

Paradise Valley Rd.

Sweetwater
Reservoir

PARADISE
HILLS

South Bay Fwy.

Proctor

National City Blvd.

8th St.

18th St.

54

Valley   Rd.

Upper
Otay
Reservoir

NATIONAL
CITY

Highland Ave.

Otay Lakes Rd.

Canyon

Otay Lakes Rd.

805

E St.

Montgomery Fwy.

Broadway

CHULA
VISTA

Telegraph

Otay
Reservoir

Chula Vista
Wildlife
Reserve

TO
TIJUANA

Hilltop Dr.

J St.

↓

San Diego Trolley System

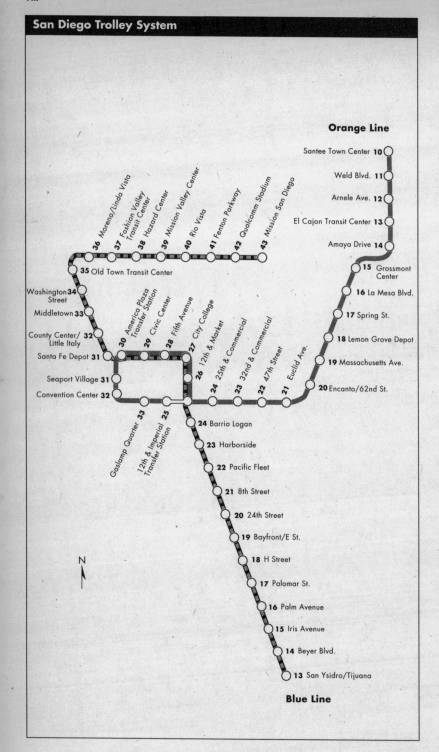

Orange Line

Santee Town Center **10**
Weld Blvd. **11**
Arnele Ave. **12**
El Cajon Transit Center **13**
Amaya Drive **14**
15 Grossmont Center
16 La Mesa Blvd.
17 Spring St.
18 Lemon Grove Depot
19 Massachusetts Ave.
20 Encanto/62nd St.

36 Moreno/Linda Vista
37 Fashion Valley Transit Center
38 Hazard Center
39 Mission Valley Center
40 Rio Vista
41 Fenton Parkway
42 Qualcomm Stadium
43 Mission San Diego

35 Old Town Transit Center

Washington Street **34**
Middletown **33**
County Center/ Little Italy **32**
Santa Fe Depot **31**
Seaport Village **31**
Convention Center **32**

30 America Plaza Transfer Station
29 Civic Center
28 Fifth Avenue
27 City College
26 12th & Market
25 25th & Commercial
24
23 32nd & Commercial
22 47th Street
21 Euclid Ave.

Gaslamp Quarter **33**
12th & Imperial Transfer Station **25**

24 Barrio Logan
23 Harborside
22 Pacific Fleet
21 8th Street
20 24th Street
19 Bayfront/E St.
18 H Street
17 Palomar St.
16 Palm Avenue
15 Iris Avenue
14 Beyer Blvd.
13 San Ysidro/Tijuana

Blue Line

N

ESSENTIAL INFORMATION

ADDRESSES

Downtown San Diego streets are on a grid divided largely in alphabetical and numerical order. Numbered avenues and streets run on the north–south axis. East–west streets are alphabetical. North of Ash Street, streets continue as Beech, Cedar, Date, through Upas Street. Below Ash Street is A Street, followed by B Street, etc., with a few named streets in place of letters.

AIR TRAVEL TO AND FROM SAN DIEGO

Although expansion has eased congestion, the San Diego International Airport remains too small to accommodate projected traffic. Small problems can cause congestion and delays. Most international flights depart from and arrive at the Los Angeles International Airport (LAX); ground and air shuttle service is available between LAX and San Diego.

BOOKING

When you book **look for nonstop flights** and **remember that "direct" flights stop at least once.** Try to avoid connecting flights, which require a change of plane. Two airlines may operate a connecting flight jointly, so ask if your airline operates every segment of the trip; you may find that the carrier you prefer flies you only part of the way. To find more booking tips and to check prices and make on-line flight reservations, log on to www.fodors.com.

CARRIERS

All major and some regional U.S. carriers serve San Diego International Airport. British Airways, Aero Mexico, and Air Canada are the only international carriers to San Diego. All others will require a connecting flight, usually in Los Angeles. Other connection points are Chicago, Dallas, and San Francisco.

➤ MAJOR AIRLINES: AeroMexico (☎ 800/237–6639, WEB www.aeromexico. com) Air Canada (☎ 888/247–2262, WEB www.aircanada.ca). America West (☎ 800/235–9292, WEB www. americawest.com). American (☎ 800/ 433–7300; 0345/789789 in the U.K., WEB www.americanairlines.com). British Airways (☎ 800/247–9297; 0345/222111 in the U.K., WEB www. british-airways.com). Continental (☎ 800/231–0856, WEB www.continental. com). Delta (☎ 800/221–1212; 0800/ 414767 in the U.K., WEB www.delta. com). Hawaiian Airlines (☎ 800/367– 5320, WEB www.hawaiianair.com). Northwest (☎ 800/225–2525, WEB www.nwa.com). Southwest (☎ 800/ 435–9792, WEB www.iflyswa.com). United (☎ 800/538–2929; 0800/ 888555 in the U.K., WEB www.ual. com). US Airways (☎ 800/428–4322, WEB www.usairways.com). Virgin Atlantic (☎ 01293/747747 in the U.K.) via Los Angeles.

➤ SMALLER AIRLINES: Alaska Airlines (☎ 800/426–0333, WEB www. alaska-air.com). Frontier (☎ 800/ 432–1359, WEB www.frontierairlines. com).

CHECK-IN AND BOARDING

Coastal fog can delay landings and take-offs, and a delayed flight or two can jam the small boarding areas. During inclement weather **call your airline** to see if there are delays.

Always **ask your carrier about its check-in policy.** Plan to arrive at the airport about two hours before your scheduled departure time for domestic flights and 2½ to 3 hours before international flights.

Assuming that not everyone with a ticket will show up, airlines routinely overbook planes. When everyone does, airlines ask for volunteers to give up their seats. In return, these volunteers usually get a certificate for a free flight and are rebooked on the next flight out. If there are not enough volunteers, the airline must choose who will be denied boarding. The first to get bumped are passengers who checked in late and those flying on discounted tickets, so **get to the gate and check in as early as possible,** especially during peak periods.

Always **bring a government-issued photo I.D. to the airport;** even when it's not required, a passport is best.

CUTTING COSTS

The least expensive airfares to San Diego are priced for round-trip travel and usually must be purchased in advance. Airlines generally allow you to change your return date for a fee; most low-fare tickets, however, are nonrefundable.

It's smart to **call a number of airlines,** and when you are quoted a good price, **book it on the spot**—the same fare may not be available the next day. Always **check different routings** and look into using alternate airports, such as LAX or Orange County. Ask about off-peak flights, which may be significantly less expensive than others. Travel agents, especially low-fare specialists (☞ Discounts and Deals), are helpful.

Consolidators are another good source. They buy tickets for scheduled international flights at reduced rates from the airlines, then sell them at prices that beat the best fare available directly from the airlines. Sometimes you can even get your money back if you need to return the ticket. Carefully read the fine print detailing penalties for changes and cancellations, purchase the ticket with a credit card, and **confirm your consolidator reservation with the airline.**

When you **fly as a courier,** you trade your checked-luggage space for a ticket deeply subsidized by a courier service. There are restrictions on when you can book and how long you can stay. Some courier companies list with membership organizations, such as the Air Courier Association and the International Association of Air Travel Couriers; these require you to become a member before you can book a flight.

➤ CONSOLIDATORS: **Cheap Tickets** (☎ 800/377–1000 or 888/922–8849, WEB www.cheaptickets.com). **Discount Airline Ticket Service** (☎ 800/576–1600). **Unitravel** (☎ 800/325–2222, WEB www.unitravel.com). **Up & Away Travel** (☎ 212/889–2345, WEB www.upandaway.com). **World Travel Network** (☎ 800/409–6753).

ENJOYING THE FLIGHT

State your seat preference when purchasing your ticket, and then repeat it when you confirm and when you check in. For more legroom, you can request one of the few emergency-aisle seats at check-in, if you are capable of lifting at least 50 pounds—a Federal Aviation Administration requirement of passengers in these seats. Seats behind a bulkhead also offer more legroom, but they don't have under-seat storage. Don't sit in the row in front of the emergency aisle or in front of a bulkhead, where seats may not recline.

Ask the airline whether a snack or meal is served on the flight. If you have dietary concerns, **request special meals when booking.** These can be vegetarian, low-cholesterol, or kosher, for example. It's a good idea to pack some healthy snacks and a small (plastic) bottle of water in your carry-on bag. On long flights, try to maintain a normal routine, to help fight jet lag. At night, **get some sleep.** By day, **eat light meals, drink water** (not alcohol), and **move around the cabin** to stretch your legs. For additional jet-lag tips consult *Fodor's FYI: Travel Fit & Healthy* (available at bookstores everywhere).

Smoking policies vary from carrier to carrier. Many airlines prohibit smoking on all of their flights; others allow smoking only on certain routes or certain departures. Ask your carrier about its policy.

FLYING TIMES

Flying time to San Diego is 5 hours from New York, 3½ hours from Chicago, 3 hours from Dallas, ¾ hour from Los Angeles, 10–11 hours from London.

HOW TO COMPLAIN

If your baggage goes astray or your flight goes awry, complain right away.

Most carriers require that you **file a claim immediately.** The Aviation Consumer Protection Division of the Department of Transportation publishes *Fly-Rights,* which discusses airlines and consumer issues and is available on-line. At the Web site PassengerRights.com, you can compose a letter of complaint and distribute it electronically.

➤ AIRLINE COMPLAINTS: **Aviation Consumer Protection Division** (✉ U.S. Department of Transportation, Room 4107, C-75, Washington, DC 20590, ☎ 202/366–2220, WEB www. dot.gov/airconsumer). **Federal Aviation Administration Consumer Hotline** (☎ 800/322–7873).

RECONFIRMING

Check the status of your flight before you leave for the airport. You can do this on your carrier's Web site, by linking to a flight-status checker (many Web booking services offer these), or by calling your carrier or travel agent.

AIRPORTS AND TRANSFERS

The major airport is **San Diego International Airport,** called Lindbergh Field locally. The airport's three-letter code is SAN. If you need travel assistance at the airport, Travelers Aid has three information booths, one in Terminal One (east) and two in Terminal Two (west), open daily 8 AM–11 PM. Because of congestion, delays of 20–30 minutes in baggage claim are not unusual.

Major airlines depart and arrive at Terminal One and Terminal Two; commuter flights identified on your ticket with a 3000 sequence flight number depart from the commuter terminal. A red shuttle bus travels between terminals.

➤ AIRPORT INFORMATION: **San Diego International Airport** (☎ 619/231–2100, WEB www.portofsandiego.org).

AIRPORT TRANSFERS

Ground transportation services include shuttle vans, buses, and taxis. All services operate from one of three islands in front of the terminals. Only Cloud 9 can accommodate wheelchairs. The cheapest and sometimes most convenient shuttle is the San Diego Transit Flyer, red- and blue-striped express buses equipped with luggage racks that cruise the airport's terminals at 10- to 15-minute intervals between 5 AM and 1 AM. These buses will drop you at most downtown businesses and hotels. The fare is $2.25, including transfer to local transit buses and the San Diego Trolley, and you should **have exact fare handy.** If you're heading to North County, the Flyer can drop you off at the Santa Fe Terminal, from which you can take the Coaster commuter train as far north as Oceanside for $3.75–$4.75.

Limousine rates vary and are per hour, per mile, or both, with some minimums established. Most offer bilingual guide service.

Taxi fare is $7–$9 plus tip to most downtown hotels. Fare to Coronado runs about $15 plus tip.

If you rent a car at the airport, take Harbor Drive, at the perimeter of the airport, to downtown, which is 3 mi east. Take Harbor Drive west to reach Shelter Island and Point Loma. To reach I–5 and I–8, take Harbor Drive west to Nimitz Boulevard, then right on Rosecrans Street. You can reach La Jolla and North County via I–5 North. I–8 East leads to Hotel Circle, Fashion Valley, Mission Valley, and Qualcomm Stadium. To reach Mission Bay continue on Nimitz Boulevard, which intersects with Sunset Cliffs Boulevard. To reach Coronado take Harbor Drive east and turn left on Grape Street to reach I–5 South. Take the Hwy. 75 exit to cross the San Diego–Coronado Bay Bridge.

➤ TAXIS AND SHUTTLES: **Cloud 9 Shuttle** (☎ 800/974–8885 San Diego County, 858/974–8885 elsewhere, WEB www.cloud9shuttle.com). **LJL Transportation/La Jolla Limousines** (☎ 619/232–6533). **Premier Ride** (☎ 619/234–7433). **San Diego Transit** (☎ 619/233–3004, WEB www.sdcommute.com).

BOAT AND FERRY TRAVEL

If you're arriving in San Diego by private boat, keep in mind that many hotels, marinas, and yacht clubs rent slips short-term. Call ahead as available space is limited.

The small Coronado ferry is fun to ride, but doesn't offer practical transportation to and from downtown.

FARES AND SCHEDULES

➤ BOAT AND FERRY INFORMATION: **San Diego–Coronado Ferry** (☎ 619/234–4111).

➤ MARINAS: **Best Western Island Palms Hotel & Marina** (✉ 2051 Shelter Island Dr., ☎ 619/222–0561). **Dana Inn & Marina** (✉ 1710 W. Mission Bay Dr., ☎ 619/222–6440). **Hyatt Regency Islandia** (✉ 1441 Quivira Rd., ☎ 619/224–1234). **Shelter Pointe Hotel and Marina** (✉ 1551 Shelter Island Dr., ☎ 619/224–7547). **San Diego Marriott Hotel and Marina** (✉ 333 W. Harbor Dr., ☎ 619/234–1500). **Sheraton San Diego Hotel and Marina** (✉ 1380 Harbor Island Dr., ☎ 619/291–2900). Both the **San Diego Yacht Club** (✉ 1011 Anchorage La., ☎ 619/221–8400) and the **Southwestern Yacht Club** (✉ 2702 Qualtrough St., ☎ 619/222–0438) have reciprocal arrangements with other yacht clubs.

BUSINESS HOURS

Most banks are open weekdays 10–4. Some open for several hours on Saturday. Most other businesses are open Monday–Saturday 9 or 10 AM to 6 or 9 PM. Many others are also open Sunday from noon to 5 or 6.

MUSEUMS AND SIGHTS

Most museums are open Tuesday through Sunday 10 to 5. Major attractions are open daily 9 to 5, later in summer.

PHARMACIES

Most pharmacies in malls are open daily from 8 or 9 AM to 9 PM; some may close at 6 PM on Sunday.

SHOPS

Mall and shopping center stores are open daily from 9 or 10 AM to 9 PM; some close at 6 PM on Sunday. Shops and boutiques in neighborhoods such as Hillcrest and La Jolla keep somewhat erratic hours, so it's a good idea to call first. Shops in rural areas such as Julian may close mid-week.

BUS TRAVEL TO AND FROM SAN DIEGO

Greyhound operates 26 buses a day between San Diego and Los Angeles, connecting with buses to all major U.S. cities. Many buses are express or nonstop; others make stops at coastal towns en route. Smoking is prohibited on all buses.

FARES AND SCHEDULES

One-way fare to Los Angeles is $13, round-trip is $22. You can buy tickets at the depot or in advance by phone.

RESERVATIONS

Boarding is on a first-come first-served basis.

➤ BUS INFORMATION: **Greyhound** (✉ 120 W. Broadway, ☎ 619/239–8082 or 800/231–2222).

BUS TRAVEL WITHIN SAN DIEGO

Also see *Trolley Travel.*

San Diego County is served by a coordinated, efficient network of bus and rail routes that includes service to Oceanside in the north, the Mexican border at San Ysidro, and points east to the Anza-Borrego Desert. There are two major transit agencies, San Diego Transit and North County Transit District (NCTD), plus some smaller ones which connect to cities such as Chula Vista, National City, and Campo. Smoking is prohibited on all forms of public transport in California.

San Diego Transit Buses connect with the San Diego Trolley light rail system at the San Diego Zoo, Balboa Park, Lindbergh Field, Mission Beach, Pacific Beach, La Jolla, and regional shopping centers.

NCTD routes serve from Del Mar North to San Clemente, inland to Fallbrook, Pauma Valley, Valley Center, Ramona, and Escondido, with transfer points within the city of San Diego. NCTD also offers special express-bus service to Qualcomm Stadium for select major sporting events. Northeast Rural Bus System serves backcountry areas such as Ramona, Julian, and Borrego Springs.

In Coronado the ATV Van Co. operates a bus service. The staff at the downtown Transit Store can help plan your travel.

FARES AND SCHEDULES

San Diego Transit fares range from $1.75 to $2. NCTD fares are $1.50. Community and rural bus routes charge from $1 to $3.75. Discounted fares of $.75 are available for seniors and for people with disabilities. Most transfers are free; request one when boarding. Schedules are posted at each stop, and the buses usually are on time.

➤ BUS INFORMATION: **Chula Vista Transit** (☎ 619/233–3004). **National City Transit** (☎ 619/474–7505) for National City. **North County Transit District** (☎ 800/266–6883). **Northeast Rural Bus System** (☎ 760/767–4287). **San Diego Transit** (☎ 619/233–3004; 619/234–5005 TTY/TDD, WEB www.sdcommute.com) for city transit and San Diego Trolley. **Southeast Rural Bus System** (☎ 619/478–5875). **Transit Store** (✉ 102 Broadway, ☎ 619/234–1060).

PAYING

You must have exact change in coins and/or bills. Pay upon boarding; Day Tripper tickets must be purchased in advance.

CAMERAS AND PHOTOGRAPHY

Must-have photos for most visitors to San Diego are of Shamu the whale at Sea World and the San Diego Zoo's giant pandas. But there are also dramatic views of the harbor from the Coronado Bridge and of the ocean from the bluffs at La Jolla Cove. The *Kodak Guide to Shooting Great Travel Pictures* (available at bookstores everywhere) is loaded with tips.

➤ PHOTO HELP: **Kodak Information Center** (☎ 800/242–2424, WEB www.kodak.com).

EQUIPMENT PRECAUTIONS

Don't pack film and equipment in checked luggage, where it is much more susceptible to damage. X-ray machines used to view checked luggage are becoming much more powerful and therefore are much more

likely to ruin your film. Try to **ask for hand inspection of film,** which becomes clouded after repeated exposure to airport X-ray machines, and **keep videotapes and computer disks away from metal detectors.** Always **keep film, tape, and computer disks out of the sun.** Carry an extra supply of batteries, and **be prepared to turn on your camera, camcorder, or laptop** to prove to airport security personnel that the device is real.

CAR RENTAL

A car is essential for San Diego's sprawling freeway system and comes in handy for touring Baja California (though the trolley serves the border at Tijuana). Rates in San Diego fluctuate with seasons and demand, but generally begin at $30 a day and $230 a week for an economy car with air-conditioning, automatic transmission, and unlimited mileage. This does not include tax on car rentals, which is 7.5%.

➤ MAJOR AGENCIES: **Alamo** (☎ 800/327–9633; WEB www.alamo.com). **Avis** (☎ 800/331–1212; 800/879–2847 in Canada; 02/9353–9000 in Australia; 09/526–2847 in New Zealand; 0870/606–0100 in the U.K.; WEB www.avis.com). **Budget** (☎ 800/527–0700; 0870/156–5656 in the U.K.; WEB www.budget.com). **Dollar** (☎ 800/800–4000; 0124/622–0111 in the U.K.; where it's affiliated with Sixt; 02/9223–1444 in Australia; WEB www.dollar.com). **Hertz** (☎ 800/654–3131; 800/263–0600 in Canada; 020/8897–2072 in the U.K.; 02/9669–2444 in Australia; 09/256–8690 in New Zealand; WEB www.hertz.com). **National Car Rental** (☎ 800/227–7368; 020/8680–4800 in the U.K.; WEB www.nationalcar.com).

CUTTING COSTS

For a good deal, **book through a travel agent who will shop around.** Also, **price local car-rental companies**—whose prices may be lower still, although their service and maintenance may not be as good as those of major rental agencies—and **research rates on-line.** Remember to ask about required deposits, cancellation penalties, and drop-off charges if you're planning to pick up the car in one city and leave it in another. If you're traveling during a holiday period, also make sure that a confirmed reservation guarantees you a car.

Do **look into wholesalers,** companies that do not own fleets but rent in bulk from those that do and often offer better rates than traditional car-rental operations. Prices are best during off-peak periods. Rentals booked through wholesalers often must be paid for before you leave home.

➤ LOCAL AGENCIES: **Enterprise** (✉ 1465 C St., 92101, ☎ 619/696–5000) picks up at area hotels; **Red & Blue Payless San Diego** (✉ 2727 Kettner Blvd., 92101, ☎ 619/297–7071).

INSURANCE

When driving a rented car you are generally responsible for any damage to or loss of the vehicle. You may also be liable for any property damage or personal injury that you may cause while driving. Before you rent, see what coverage you already have under the terms of your personal auto-insurance policy and credit cards.

For about $15 to $20 a day, rental companies sell protection, known as a collision- or loss-damage waiver (CDW or LDW), that eliminates your liability for damage to the car; it's always optional and should never be automatically added to your bill. In most states you don't need a CDW if you have personal auto insurance or other liability insurance. Some states, including California, have capped the price of the CDW and LDW. However, **make sure you have enough coverage to pay for the car.** If you do not have auto insurance or an umbrella policy that covers damage to third parties, purchasing liability insurance and a CDW or LDW is highly recommended.

REQUIREMENTS AND RESTRICTIONS

In California you must be 21 to rent a car. Some agencies will not rent to those between 21 and 24; check when you book. Children age six and under, and weighing less than 60 pounds, must be placed in child safety seats.

SURCHARGES

Before you pick up a car in one city and leave it in another, **ask about drop-off charges or one-way service fees,** which can be substantial. Note, too, that some rental agencies charge extra if you return the car before the time specified in your contract. To avoid a hefty refueling fee, **fill the tank just before you turn in the car,** but be aware that gas stations near the rental outlet may overcharge. It's almost never a deal to buy the tank of gas in the car when you rent it; the understanding is that you'll return it empty, but some fuel usually remains.

Surcharges may apply if you're under 25. You'll pay extra for child seats (about $6 a day), which are compulsory for children age six and under, and for additional drivers (about $5 per day).

CAR TRAVEL

Interstate 5 stretches from Canada to the Mexican border and bisects San Diego. Interstate 8 provides access from Yuma, Arizona, and points east. Drivers coming from Nevada and the mountain regions beyond can reach San Diego on I–15. To avoid traffic on I–5 and on I–15 between I–805 and Escondido **steer clear of rush-hour periods.**

Your driver's license may not be recognized outside your home country. International driving permits (IDPs) are available from the American and Canadian automobile associations and, in the United Kingdom, from the Automobile Association and Royal Automobile Club. These international permits, valid only in conjunction with your regular driver's license, are universally recognized; having one may save you a problem with local authorities.

EMERGENCY SERVICES

Dial 911 to report accidents on the road and to reach police, the highway patrol, or the fire department. Emergency phone boxes can be found along most Interstate highways.

GASOLINE

The cost of gas varies widely depending on location, oil company, and whether you use the full-serve or self-serve aisle. Prices on the West Coast tend to be higher than those in most of the country, and in San Diego prices run about 15% higher than in many other California cities. At press time, regular unleaded gasoline at self-serve stations costs about $1.25 a gallon.

PARKING

Balboa Park, Cabrillo National Monument, and Mission Bay all have huge free parking lots and it's rare not to find a space, though it may seem as if you've parked miles from your destination. Lots downtown are plentiful and cost $3–$35 per day. Old Town has large lots off the Transit Center. Parking is more of a problem in La Jolla and Coronado, where you generally need to rely on hard-to-find street spots or expensive by-the-hour parking lots.

Parking at meters costs $1 an hour; enforcement is 8 AM–6 PM except Sunday. Be extra careful around rush hour, when certain street-parking areas become tow-away zones. In the evenings and during events it can be difficult to locate parking spaces downtown. Car renters are liable for parking tickets and towing charges incurred.

ROAD CONDITIONS

Highways are generally in good condition in the San Diego area. Traffic is particularly heavy on I–5, I–8, I–805, and I–15 during morning and afternoon rush hours 6–8:30 AM and 3:30–6 PM. Before venturing into the mountains, check on road conditions; mountain driving can be dangerous. Listen to radio traffic reports for information on the lines waiting to cross the border to Mexico.

➤ MAPS: **AAA San Diego** (✉ 815 Date St., ☎ 619/233–1000).

RULES OF THE ROAD

Speed limits are 35 mph on city streets and 65 mph on freeways, unless otherwise indicated. Seat belts are required at all times and tickets are given for failing to comply. Right turns are permitted at red lights after stopping unless otherwise indicated. Driving with a blood-alcohol level higher than 0.08 will result in arrest and seizure of driver's license. The law is strictly enforced, and fines are severe.

Always **strap children age six and under, and weighing 60 pounds or less, into approved child-safety seats.** Children must wear seat belts regardless of where they're seated (studies show that children are safest in the rear rather than the front seats). In San Diego, be alert for one-way streets, "no left turn" intersections, and blocks closed to car traffic.

Many California freeways have High Occupancy Vehicle lanes, usually restricted to vehicles carrying two or more persons. There is no law against using radar detectors, but they're not common.

CHILDREN IN SAN DIEGO

San Diego is a family-oriented destination, with many attractions geared to kids. Expect to find strollers for rent, diaper-changing facilities, kids' menus, and special activities for kids at most major attractions.

The monthly *San Diego Family Magazine* is filled with listings of events and resources; it is available by mail for $3.50, which covers postage and handling, or free in San Diego at Longs Drug Stores, Toys R Us, and local libraries. If you are renting a car, don't forget to **arrange for a car seat** when you reserve. For general advice about traveling with children, consult *Fodor's FYI: Travel with Your Baby* (available in bookstores everywhere).

➤ LOCAL INFORMATION: *San Diego Family Magazine* (✉ Box 23960, San Diego 92193, ☎ 619/685–6970, WEB www.sandiegofamily.com). *San Diego Parent Magazine* (✉ 3160 Camino del Rio S, Suite 315, San Diego 92108, ☎ 619/624–2770). Fodor's by-parents, for-parents *Where Should We Take the Kids? California* (☎ 800/533–6478 or in bookstores); $17.

BABY-SITTING

Many agencies specialize in on-and-off-site group and individual child care for conventions, tourists, and special events. They are licensed, bonded, and insured. Hotel concierges can usually recommend a reliable baby-sitting service.

➤ AGENCIES: **Panda Services** (✉ 7677 Ronson Rd. #202, San Diego 92111, ☎ 858/292–5503) will provide sitters to hotels. **KiddieCorp, Inc.** (✉ 10455 Sorrento Valley Rd. #200, San Diego 92121, ☎ 800/942–9947) provides child care for conventions and special events. **Marion's Child Care** (✉ 4328 60th St., San Diego 92115, ☎ 619/ 582–5029) provides baby-sitters to area hotels.

FLYING

If your children are two or older, **ask about children's airfares.** As a general rule, infants under two not occupying a seat fly at greatly reduced fares or even for free. When booking, **confirm carry-on allowances** if you're traveling with infants. In general, for babies charged 10% of the adult fare you are allowed one carry-on bag and a collapsible stroller; if the flight is full, the stroller may have to be checked or you may be limited to less.

Experts agree that it's a good idea to use safety seats aloft for children weighing less than 40 pounds. Airlines set their own policies: U.S. carriers usually require that the child be ticketed, even if he or she is young enough to ride free, since the seats must be strapped into regular seats. Do **check your airline's policy about using safety seats during takeoff and landing.** Safety seats are not allowed everywhere in the plane, so get your seat assignments as early as possible.

When reserving, **request children's meals or a freestanding bassinet** (not available at all airlines) if you need them. But note that bulkhead seats, where you must sit to use the bassinet, may lack an overhead bin or storage space on the floor.

FOOD

Most San Diego restaurants make at least some accommodation for kids: child-size portions, seats for children, amusements such as crayons and coloring paper, or, at a minimum, friendliness. The Gaslamp Quarter and La Jolla both have a Hard Rock Cafe, which is a big hit with kids and teenagers. Of the places reviewed in the Dining chapter, The Cheesecake Factory, The Fish Market, Ghirardelli Soda Fountain & Chocolate Shop,

Hob Nob Hill, Ricky's Family Restaurant, and Blumberg's are particularly suited to families; your children's din will blend right in.

LODGING

Most hotels in San Diego allow children under a certain age to stay in their parents' room at no extra charge, but others charge for them as extra adults; be sure to **find out the cutoff age for children's discounts.** Kids will find plenty to keep them busy at any of San Diego's waterfront hotels, including the Hotel Del Coronado, the Dana Inn, and Bahia Resort Hotel on Mission Bay.

➤ BEST CHOICES: **Bahia Resort Hotel** (✉ 998 W. Mission Bay Dr., ☎ 858/ 488–0551). **Dana Inn and Marina** (✉ 1710 W. Mission Bay Dr., ☎ 619/ 222–6440). **Hotel Del Coronado** (✉ 1500 Orange Ave., Coronado, ☎ 619/435–6611).

SIGHTS AND ATTRACTIONS

All of San Diego's top attractions are designed for family entertainment. Places that are especially appealing to children are indicated by a rubberduckie icon (🐤) in the margin.

The San Diego Zoo has a Children's Zoo filled with pettable goats, lambs, bunnies, and guinea pigs; diapered baby primates are often on display in the nursery. SeaWorld SanDiego always makes a big splash with the kids, many of whom race for frontrow seats at the Shamu show. Handson activities include Shamu's Happy Harbor, Forbidden Reef, and California Tide Pools.

All attractions at Legoland California are designed to entertain and delight youngsters. Colorful plastic building blocks are climb-on or crawl-through. Expect long lines at the driving school, the pedal boats, and for the Power Tower.

CONCIERGES

Concierges, found in many hotels, can help you with theater tickets and dinner reservations: a good one with connections may be able to get you seats for a hot show or prime-time dinner reservations at the restaurant of the moment. You can also turn to your hotel's concierge for help with travel arrangements, sightseeing plans, services ranging from aromatherapy to zipper repair, and emergencies. Always, **always tip** a concierge who has been of assistance (☞ Tipping).

CONSUMER PROTECTION

Whether you're shopping for gifts or purchasing travel services, **pay with a major credit card** whenever possible, so you can cancel payment or get reimbursed if there's a problem (and you can provide documentation). If you're doing business with a particular company for the first time, **contact your local Better Business Bureau and the attorney general's offices** in your state and (for U.S. businesses) the company's home state as well. Have any complaints been filed? Finally, if you're buying a package or tour, always **consider travel insurance** that includes default coverage (☞ Insurance).

➤ BBBs: **Council of Better Business Bureaus** (✉ 4200 Wilson Blvd., Suite 800, Arlington, VA 22203, ☎ 703/276–0100, FAX 703/525–8277, www.bbb.org). **Better Business Bureau** (✉ 5050 Murphy Canyon Rd., Suite 110, San Diego, CA 92123, ☎ 858/637–6199, FAX 858/496–2141, WEB www.sandiegobbb.org).

CRUISE TRAVEL

Several cruise-ship lines make San Diego a port of call. Holland America and Royal Caribbean use San Diego as a regular point of embarkation for seasonal cruises to Alaska, the Mexican Riviera, and the Panama Canal. Other lines including Princess, Celebrity, Cunard, and Norwegian Cruise Line originate repositioning cruises from San Diego throughout the year. To learn how to plan, choose, and book a cruise-ship voyage, check out Cruise How-to's on www.fodors.com.

➤ CRUISE LINES: **Carnival** (☎ 800/327–95021, WEB www.carnival.com). **Celebrity** (☎ 800/437–3111, WEB www.celebrity-cruises.com). **Cunard** (☎ 800/528–6273, WEB www.cunardline.com). **Holland America** (☎ 800/426–0327, WEB hollandamerica.com). **Norwegian Cruise Line** (☎ 800/327–7030, WEB www.ncl.com). **Princess** (☎ 800/774–6237, WEB www.princess.com). **Seabourn** (☎ 800/929–9391, WEB www.seabourn.com).

CUSTOMS AND DUTIES

When shopping in Mexico, **keep receipts** for all purchases. Upon reentering the country, **be ready to show customs officials what you've bought.** If you feel a duty is incorrect, appeal the assessment. If you object to the way your clearance was handled, note the inspector's badge number. In either case, first ask to see a supervisor. If the problem isn't resolved, write to the appropriate authorities, beginning with the port director at your point of entry. Customs officers operate at the San Ysidro border crossing, San Diego International Airport, and in the bay at Shelter Island.

➤ INFORMATION: **San Ysidro Port of Entry** (✉ 720 E. San Ysidro Blvd., 92173, ☎ 619/690–8800, FAX 619/662–7374). **San Diego Customs Management Center** (✉ 610 W. Ash St., Ste. 1200, San Diego 92101, ☎ 619-557–5455, FAX 619/557–5394, WEB www.customs.gov).

IN AUSTRALIA

Australian residents who are 18 or older may bring home A$400 worth of souvenirs and gifts (including jewelry), 250 cigarettes or 250 grams of tobacco, and 1,125 ml of alcohol (including wine, beer, and spirits). Residents under 18 may bring back A$200 worth of goods. Prohibited items include meat products. Seeds, plants, and fruits need to be declared upon arrival.

➤ INFORMATION: **Australian Customs Service** (Regional Director, ✉ Box 8, Sydney, NSW 2001, ☎ 02/9213–2000 or 1300/363263; 1800/020504 quarantine-inquiry line, FAX 02/9213–4043, WEB www.customs.gov.au).

IN CANADA

Canadian residents who have been out of Canada for at least seven days may bring in C$750 worth of goods duty-free. If you've been away fewer than seven days but more than 48 hours, the duty-free allowance drops to C$200; if your trip lasts 24 to 48 hours, the allowance is C$50. You may not pool allowances with family members. Goods claimed under the C$750 exemption may follow you by mail; those claimed under the lesser exemptions must accompany you.

Alcohol and tobacco products may be included in the seven-day and 48-hour exemptions but not in the 24-hour exemption. If you meet the age requirements of the province or territory through which you reenter Canada, you may bring in, duty-free, 1.5 liters of wine *or* 1.14 liters (40 imperial ounces) of liquor *or* 24 12-ounce cans or bottles of beer or ale. If you are 19 or older you may bring in, duty-free, 200 cigarettes and 50 cigars. Check ahead of time with the Canada Customs and Revenue Agency or the Department of Agriculture for policies regarding meat products, seeds, plants, and fruits.

You may send an unlimited number of gifts (only one gift per recipient, however) worth up to C$60 each duty-free to Canada. Label the package UNSOLICITED GIFT—VALUE UNDER $60. Alcohol and tobacco are excluded.

➤ INFORMATION: **Canada Customs and Revenue Agency** (✉ 2265 St. Laurent Blvd. S, Ottawa, Ontario K1G 4K3, ☎ 204/983–3500; 506/636–5064; 800/461–9999, WEB www.ccra-adrc.gc.ca/).

IN NEW ZEALAND

All homeward-bound residents may bring back NZ$700 worth of souvenirs and gifts; passengers may not pool their allowances, and children can claim only the concession on goods intended for their own use. For those 17 or older, the duty-free allowance also includes 4.5 liters of wine or beer; one 1,125-ml bottle of spirits; and either 200 cigarettes, 250 grams of tobacco, 50 cigars, *or* a combination of the three up to 250 grams. Meat products, seeds, plants, and fruits must be declared upon arrival to the Agricultural Services Department.

➤ INFORMATION: **New Zealand Customs** (Head Office: ✉ The Customhouse, 17–21 Whitmore St., Box 2218, Wellington, ☎ 09/300–5399 or 0800/428–786, WEB www.customs.govt.nz).

IN THE U.K.

From countries outside the European Union, including the U.S., you may bring home, duty-free, 200 cigarettes or 50 cigars; 1 liter of spirits or 2 liters of fortified or sparkling wine or liqueurs; 2 liters of still table wine; 60 ml of perfume; 250 ml of toilet water; plus £145 worth of other goods, including gifts and souvenirs. Prohibited items include meat products, seeds, plants, and fruits.

➤ INFORMATION: **HM Customs and Excise** (✉ Portcullis House, 21 Cowbridge Rd. E, Cardiff CF11 9SS, ☎ 029/2038–6423 or 0845/010–9000, WEB www.hmce.gov.uk).

IN THE U.S.

U.S. residents who have been out of the country for at least 48 hours may bring home, for personal use, $400 worth of foreign goods duty-free, as long as they haven't used the $400 allowance or any part of it in the past 30 days. This exemption may include 1 liter of alcohol (for travelers 21 and older), 200 cigarettes, and 100 non-Cuban cigars. Family members from the same household who are traveling together may pool their $400 personal exemptions. For fewer than 48 hours, the duty-free allowance drops to $200, which may include 50 cigarettes, 10 non-Cuban cigars, and 150 milliliters of alcohol (or perfume containing alcohol). The $200 allowance cannot be combined with other individuals' exemptions, and if you exceed it, the full value of all the goods will be taxed. Antiques, which the U.S. Customs Service defines as objects more than 100 years old, enter duty-free, as do original works of art done entirely by hand, including paintings, drawings, and sculptures.

You may also send packages home duty-free, with a limit of one parcel per addressee per day (except alcohol or tobacco products or perfume worth more than $5). You can mail up to $200 worth of goods for personal use; label the package PERSONAL USE and attach a list of its contents and their retail value. If the package contains your used personal belongings, mark it PERSONAL GOODS RETURNED to avoid paying duties. You may send up to $100 worth of goods as a gift; mark the package UNSOLICITED GIFT. Mailed items do not affect your duty-free allowance on your return.

> **INFORMATION: U.S. Customs Service** (for inquiries, ✉ 1300 Pennsylvania Ave. NW, Washington, DC 20229, 🌐 www.customs.gov, ☎ 202/354–1000; for complaints, ✉ Customer Satisfaction Unit, 1300 Pennsylvania Ave. NW, Room 5.5A, Washington, DC 20229; for registration of equipment, ✉ Office of Passenger Programs, 1300 Pennsylvania Ave. NW, Room 5.4D, Washington, DC 20229, ☎ 202/927–0530).

DINING

San Diego restaurants tend to be casual, and the service easygoing and friendly. Many have ocean-view settings. You can find just about any kind of cuisine in San Diego, although Italian restaurants predominate in the Gaslamp Quarter and other areas popular with visitors. Fresh seafood is available along the waterfront and in North County beach communities. Those interested in small, off-beat, and ethnic eateries can find them in the Kearney Mesa area. In general, when you order a regular coffee, you get coffee with milk and sugar. The restaurants we list are the cream of the crop in each price category.

RESERVATIONS AND DRESS

Reservations are always a good idea; we mention them only when they're essential or not accepted. Book as far ahead as you can, and reconfirm as soon as you arrive. (Large parties should always call ahead to check the reservations policy.) We mention dress only when men are required to wear a jacket or a jacket and tie.

SPECIALTIES

Because of its multi-ethnic population, you can find cuisine from nearly every part of the world in San Diego. A local specialty is the fish taco, sold at the chain restaurant Rubio's as well as at beach-side taco stands and in a few restaurants.

WINE, BEER, AND SPIRITS

Alcohol may be served between the hours of 6 AM and 2 AM. The legal age to buy alcoholic beverages in California is 21. Alcoholic beverages can be purchased in liquor stores, supermarkets, and some convenience stores.

DISABILITIES AND ACCESSIBILITY

San Diego ranks as one of the most accessible cities in the United States for people using wheelchairs. Although the Old Town district has some moderately uneven streets, curb cuts and smooth sidewalks are decidedly the rule rather than the exception for the city as a whole. The extensive network of walkways in Balboa Park affords views that are both lovely and negotiable. Most major attractions, shopping malls, tour services and casinos are accessible. Special beach wheelchairs are available. The Access Center of San Diego has a comprehensive guide to hotels, motels, attractions, and restaurants with access for people with disabilities. Accessible San Diego has a visitor information center and telephone hot line, makes hotel referrals, and provides guides to San Diego's attractions for visitors with mobility problems.

> LOCAL RESOURCES: **Access Center of San Diego** (✉ Information and Referrals, 1295 University Ave., Suite 10, San Diego 92103, ☎ 619/293–3500; 619/293–7757 TDD). **Accessible San Diego** (✉ Executive Complex, 1010 2nd Ave., Suite 110A, San Diego 92101, ☎ 858/279–0704, 🌐 www.accessandiego.org). **MTS Access** (✉ 4970 Market St., San Diego 92102, ☎ 888/517–9627, 🌐 www.commute.com).

LODGING

Despite the Americans with Disabilities Act, the definition of accessibility seems to differ from hotel to hotel. Some properties may be accessible by ADA standards for people with mobility problems but not for people with hearing or vision impairments, for example.

If you have mobility problems, ask for the lowest floor on which accessible services are offered. If you have a hearing impairment, check whether the hotel has devices to alert you visually to the ring of the telephone, knock at the door, and a fire/emergency alarm. Some hotels provide these devices without charge. Discuss your needs with hotel personnel if this equipment isn't available, so that a staff member can personally alert you in the event of an emergency.

If you're bringing a guide dog, get authorization ahead of time and write down the name of the person you spoke with.

The downtown San Diego Marriott Hotel and Marina has 40 rooms designed for people who use wheelchairs. Comfort Inn and Suites in Mission Valley has two rooms with wheelchair-accessible showers, and rooms with text telephones and raised Braille signage. Holiday Inn on the Bay has 10 rooms with wheelchair-accessible showers, plus a lift-equipped airport shuttle, text telephones, and Braille signage.

➤ BEST CHOICES: **Comfort Inn and Suites** (2485 Hotel Circle Pl., ☎ 619/688–4017). **San Diego Marriott Hotel and Marina** (333 W. Harbor Dr., ☎ 619/234–1500). **Holiday Inn on the Bay** (1355 N. Harbor Dr., ☎ 619/232–3861).

RESERVATIONS

When discussing accessibility with an operator or reservations agent, **ask hard questions.** Are there any stairs, inside *or* out? Are there grab bars next to the toilet *and* in the shower/tub? How wide is the doorway to the room? To the bathroom? For the most extensive facilities meeting the latest legal specifications, **opt for newer accommodations.** If you reserve through a toll-free number, consider also calling the hotel's local number to confirm the information from the central reservations office. Get confirmation in writing when you can.

SIGHTS AND ATTRACTIONS

All of San Diego's top attractions require a good deal of walking. However, most attractions have parking spaces near the entrances reserved for people with disabilities, accessible rest rooms, and ramps. Travelers who use wheelchairs can see much of the **San Diego Zoo** via tram and get an overview of the **Wild Animal Park** from the monorail. **SeaWorld San Diego** has sign language interpreters, assistive listening devices, and wheelchairs for rent. **Cabrillo National Monument** waives admission fees for those with disabil-

ity placards and has text telephones. **Hornblower Cruises** has an accessible gangway ramp and rest room.

TRANSPORTATION

Most public buses and the San Diego Trolley are equipped with lifts. About one-third of the bus lines are served by buses with elevator ramps. The San Diego Trolley has wheelchair lifts. Call San Diego Transit (☞ Bus & Rail Travel around San Diego) for detailed information. MTS Access (☞ Disabilities & Accessibility) provides curb-to-curb transportation for those with restricted mobility; advance reservations are required.

➤ CAR RENTAL: **Avis Rental Cars at the Airport** (✉ 3180 N. Harbor Dr., ☎ 619/231–7171 or 800/852–4617 Ext. 5063) rents cars equipped for travelers with disabilities.

➤ COMPLAINTS: **Aviation Consumer Protection Division** (☞ Air Travel) for airline-related problems. **Departmental Office of Civil Rights** (for general inquiries, ✉ U.S. Department of Transportation, S-30, 400 7th St. SW, Room 10215, Washington, DC 20590, ☎ 202/366–4648, FAX 202/366–3571, WEB www.dot.gov/ost/docr/index.htm). **Disability Rights Section** (✉ NYAV, U.S. Department of Justice, Civil Rights Division, 950 Pennsylvania Ave. NW, Washington, DC 20530, ☎ ADA information line 202/514–0301, 800/514–0301, 202/514–0383 TTY, 800/514–0383 TTY, WEB www.usdoj.gov/crt/ada/adahom1.htm).

TRAVEL AGENCIES

In the United States, the Americans with Disabilities Act requires that travel firms serve the needs of all travelers. Some agencies specialize in working with people with disabilities.

➤ TRAVELERS WITH MOBILITY PROBLEMS: **Access Adventures** (✉ 206 Chestnut Ridge Rd., Scottsville, NY 14624, ☎ 716/889–9096, dltravel@prodigy.net), run by a former physical-rehabilitation counselor. **Accessible Vans of America** (✉ 9 Spielman Rd., Fairfield, NJ 07004, ☎ 877/282–8267; 888/282–8267 reservations, FAX 973/808–9713, WEB www.accessiblevans.com). **CareVacations** (✉ No. 5, 5110–50 Ave., Leduc, Alberta T9E 6V4, Canada, ☎ 780/

986–6404 or 877/478–7827, FAX 780/986–8332, WEB www.carevacations.com), for group tours and cruise vacations. **Flying Wheels Travel** (✉ 143 W. Bridge St., Box 382, Owatonna, MN 55060, ☎ 507/451–5005, FAX 507/451–1685, WEB www.flyingwheelstravel.com).

➤ TRAVELERS WITH DEVELOPMENTAL DISABILITIES: **New Directions** (✉ 5276 Hollister Ave., Suite 207, Santa Barbara, CA 93111, ☎ 805/967–2841 or 888/967–2841, FAX 805/964–7344, WEB www.newdirectionstravel.com).

DISCOUNTS AND DEALS

The International Visitor Information Center (☞ Visitor Information) has a free book, *Rediscover San Diego,* that contains discount coupons to attractions, hotels, and restaurants. Multiday passes to SeaWorld are available from some Mission Bay area hotels. **Times Arts Tix** sells half-price, same-day tickets for performances. You can get a combination pass good for the San Diego Zoo and Wild Animal Park at either attraction. **Passport to Balboa Park** provides unlimited admission to 13 park attractions for one week for $30.

Be a smart shopper and **compare all your options** before making decisions. A plane ticket bought with a promotional coupon from travel clubs, coupon books, and direct-mail offers or purchased on the Internet may not be cheaper than the least expensive fare from a discount ticket agency. And always keep in mind that what you get is just as important as what you save.

DISCOUNT RESERVATIONS

To save money, **look into discount reservations services** with Web sites and toll-free numbers, which use their buying power to get a better price on hotels, airline tickets, even car rentals. When booking a room, always **call the hotel's local toll-free number** (if one is available) rather than the central reservations number—you'll often get a better price. Always ask about special packages or corporate rates.

➤ AIRLINE TICKETS: ☎ 800/AIR–4LESS.

➤ HOTEL ROOMS: **Accommodations Express** (☎ 800/444–7666, WEB www.accommodationsexpress.com). **Hotel Reservations Network** (☎ 800/964–6835, WEB www.hoteldiscount.com). **Quikbook** (☎ 800/789–9887, WEB www.quikbook.com). **RMC Travel** (☎ 800/245–5738, WEB www.rmcwebtravel.com). **Turbotrip.com** (☎ 800/473–7829, WEB www.turbotrip.com).

PACKAGE DEALS

Don't confuse packages and guided tours. When you buy a package, you travel on your own, just as though you had planned the trip yourself. Fly/drive packages, which combine airfare and car rental, are often a good deal.

Packages combining lodging, dining, theater tickets, and museum admission within San Diego County are available through San Diego Art + Sol. Packages vary and change frequently; you can order a brochure, but allow four to six weeks for delivery.

➤ PACKAGERS: **San Diego Art + Sol** (☎ 800/270–9283, WEB www.sandiegoartandsol.com).

GAY AND LESBIAN TRAVEL

San Diego has a large and fairly visible gay community. Hillcrest is the main gay neighborhood and retail district, with many bars, cafés, and shops. The annual Lesbian and Gay Pride Parade, Rally, and Festival takes place during a weekend in July. For details about the gay and lesbian scene, consult *Fodor's Gay Guide to the USA* (available in bookstores everywhere).

➤ GAY- AND LESBIAN-FRIENDLY TRAVEL AGENCIES: **Different Roads Travel** (✉ 8383 Wilshire Blvd., Suite 902, Beverly Hills, CA 90211, ☎ 323/651–5557 or 800/429–8747, FAX 323/651–3678, lgernert@tzell.com). **Kennedy Travel** (✉ 314 Jericho Turnpike, Floral Park, NY 11001, ☎ 516/352–4888 or 800/237–7433, FAX 516/354–8849, WEB www.kennedytravel.com). **Now, Voyager** (✉ 4406 18th St., San Francisco, CA 94114, ☎ 415/626–1169 or 800/255–6951, FAX 415/626–8626, WEB www.nowvoyager.com). **Skylink Travel and Tour** (✉ 1006 Mendocino Ave., Santa Rosa, CA 95401, ☎ 707/546–9888 or 800/225–5759, FAX 707/

546–9891, WEB www.skylinktravel.
com), serving lesbian travelers.

➤ LOCAL RESOURCES: **Lesbian and Gay
Men's Community Center** (✉ 3909
Center St., San Diego 92103, ☎ 619/
692–2077, WEB www.thecentersd.org).
Update (☎ 619/299–0500), a weekly
gay paper, is available in Hillcrest and
at a few locations downtown. The
lesbian/gay bookstore, **Obelisk** (1029
University Ave., Hillcrest, ☎ 619/297–
4171), is another excellent resource
and hangout.

GUIDEBOOKS

Plan well and you won't be sorry.
Guidebooks are excellent tools—and
you can take them with you. You may
want to check out color-photo-illus-
trated *Fodor's Exploring California*
and *Compass American Guide:
Coastal California,* both thorough on
culture and history; *Fodor's Road
Guide USA: California,* for comprehensive restaurant, hotel, and attractions listings for driving vacations;
and *Fodor's upCLOSE California,*
which is loaded with budget options.

HEALTH

DIVERS' ALERT

**Do not fly within 24 hours of scuba
diving.**

HOLIDAYS

Major national holidays include New
Year's Day (Jan. 1); Martin Luther
King, Jr., Day (3rd Mon. in Jan.);
President's Day (3rd Mon. in Feb.);
Memorial Day (last Mon. in May);
Independence Day (July 4); Labor Day
(1st Mon. in Sept.); Thanksgiving Day
(4th Thurs. in Nov.); Christmas Eve
and Christmas Day (Dec. 24 and 25);
and New Year's Eve (Dec. 31).

INSURANCE

The most useful travel-insurance plan
is a comprehensive policy that includes coverage for trip cancellation
and interruption, default, trip delay,
and medical expenses (with a waiver
for preexisting conditions).

Without insurance you will lose all or
most of your money if you cancel
your trip, regardless of the reason.
Default insurance covers you if your
tour operator, airline, or cruise line
goes out of business. Trip-delay

covers expenses that arise because of
bad weather or mechanical delays.
Study the fine print when comparing
policies.

U.K. residents can buy a travel-
insurance policy valid for most vacations taken during the year in which
it's purchased (but check preexisting-
condition coverage).

Always **buy travel policies directly
from the insurance company**; if you
buy them from a cruise line, airline,
or tour operator that goes out of
business you probably will not be
covered for the agency or operator's
default, a major risk. Before making
any purchase, **review your existing
health and home-owner's policies** to
find what they cover away from
home.

➤ TRAVEL INSURERS: In the U.S.:
Access America (✉ 6600 W. Broad
St., Richmond, VA 23230, ☎ 800/
284–8300, FAX 804/673–1491 or 800/
346–9265, www.accessamerica.
com). **Travel Guard International**
(✉ 1145 Clark St., Stevens Point,
WI 54481, ☎ 715/345–0505 or
800/826–1300, FAX 800/955–8785,
WEB www.travelguard.com).

FOR INTERNATIONAL
TRAVELERS

For information on customs restrictions, *see* Customs & Duties.

CAR RENTAL

When picking up a rental car, non-U.S.
residents need a reservation voucher
for any prepaid reservations that were
made in the traveler's home country, a
passport, a driver's license, and a
travel policy that covers each driver.

CAR TRAVEL

Gas stations in San Diego are plentiful.
Most stay open late (24 hours along
large highways and in big cities),
except in rural areas, where Sunday
hours are limited and where you may
drive long stretches without a refueling
opportunity. Highways are well paved.
Interstate highways—limited-access,
multilane highways whose numbers
are prefixed by "I–"—are the fastest
routes. Interstates with three-digit
numbers encircle urban areas, which
may have other limited-access express-

ways, freeways, and parkways as well. Tolls may be levied on limited-access highways. So-called U.S. highways and state highways are not necessarily limited-access but may have several lanes.

Along larger highways, roadside stops with rest rooms, fast-food restaurants, and sundries stores are well spaced. State police and tow trucks patrol major highways and lend assistance. If your car breaks down on an inter-state, pull onto the shoulder and wait for help, or have your passengers wait while you walk to an emergency phone. If you carry a cell phone, dial *55, noting your location on the small green roadside mileage markers.

Driving in the United States is on the right. Do **obey speed limits** posted along roads and highways. Watch for lower limits in small towns and on back roads. On weekdays between 6 and 10 AM and again between 4 and 7 PM **expect heavy traffic.** To encourage carpooling, some freeways have special lanes for so-called high-occupancy vehicles (HOV)—cars carrying more than one passenger.

Book stores, gas stations, convenience stores, and rest stops sell maps (about $3) and multiregion road atlases (about $10).

CONSULATES AND EMBASSIES

➤ AUSTRALIA: **Australia** (✉ 2049 Century Park East, 19th Floor, Los Angeles, ☎ 310/229–4840).

➤ CANADA: **Canada** (✉ 300 S. Grand Ave., Los Angeles, ☎ 213/346–2700).

➤ NEW ZEALAND: **New Zealand** (✉ 4365 Executive Drive, No. 1600, San Diego, ☎ 619/699–2993).

➤ UNITED KINGDOM: **United King-dom,** (✉ 11766 Wilshire Blvd., No. 400, Los Angeles, ☎ 310/477–3322).

CURRENCY

The dollar is the basic unit of U.S. currency. It has 100 cents. Coins include the copper penny (1¢); the silvery nickel (5¢), dime (10¢), quarter (25¢), and half-dollar (50¢); and the golden $1 coin, replacing a now-rare silver dollar. Bills are denominated $1, $5, $10, $20, $50, and $100, all green and identical in size; designs vary. The exchange rate at

press time was US$1.42 per British pound, 63¢ per Canadian dollar, 53¢ per Australian dollar, and 44¢ per New Zealand dollar.

ELECTRICITY

The U.S. standard is AC, 110 volts/60 cycles. Plugs have two flat pins set parallel to each other.

EMERGENCIES

For police, fire, or ambulance, **dial 911** (0 in rural areas).

INSURANCE

Britons and Australians need extra medical coverage when traveling overseas.

➤ INSURANCE INFORMATION: In the U.K.: **Association of British Insurers** (✉ 51 Gresham St., London EC2V 7HQ, ☎ 020/7600–3333, FAX 020/7696–8999, WEB www.abi.org.uk). In Australia: **Insurance Council of Australia** (✉ Level 3, 56 Pitt St., Sydney, NSW 2000, ☎ 02/9253–5100, FAX 02/9253–5111, WEB www.ica.com.au). In Canada: **RBC Insurance** (✉ 6880 Financial Dr., Mississauga, Ontario L5N 7Y5, ☎ 905/816–2400 or 800/668–4342, FAX 905/813–4704, WEB www.rbcinsurance.com). In New Zealand: **Insurance Council of New Zealand** (✉ Level 7, 111–115 Customhouse Quay, Box 474, Wellington, ☎ 04/472–5230, FAX 04/473–3011, WEB www.icnz.org.nz).

MAIL AND SHIPPING

You can buy stamps and aerograms and send letters and parcels in post offices. Stamp-dispensing machines can occasionally be found in airports, bus and train stations, office buildings, drugstores, and the like. You can also deposit mail in the stout, dark blue, steel bins at strategic locations everywhere and in the mail chutes of large buildings; pickup schedules are posted.

For mail sent within the United States, you need a 37¢ stamp for first-class letters weighing up to 1 ounce (23¢ for each additional ounce) and 23¢ for domestic postcards. You pay 80¢ for 1-ounce airmail letters and 70¢ for airmail postcards. For Canada and Mexico you need a 60¢ stamp for a 1-ounce letter and 50¢ for a postcard. An aerogram—a single sheet of lightweight blue paper that folds into its own envelope, stamped for overseas airmail—costs 70¢.

To receive mail on the road, have it sent c/o General Delivery at your destination's main post office (use the correct five-digit ZIP code). You must pick up mail in person within 30 days and show a driver's license or passport.

PASSPORTS AND VISAS

When traveling internationally, **carry your passport** even if you don't need one (it's always the best form of I.D.) and **make two photocopies of the data page** (one for someone at home and another for you, carried separately from your passport). If you lose your passport, promptly call the nearest embassy or consulate and the local police.

Visitor visas are not necessary for Canadian citizens, or for citizens of Australia and the United Kingdom who are staying fewer than 90 days.

➤ AUSTRALIAN CITIZENS: **Australian State Passport Office** (☎ 131–232, WEB www.passports.gov.au). **United States Consulate General** (✉ MLC Centre, 19–29 Martin Pl., 59th floor, Sydney, NSW 2000, ☎ 02/9373–9200, 1902/941–641 fee-based visa-inquiry line, WEB www.usis-australia.gov/index.html).

➤ CANADIAN CITIZENS: **Passport Office** (to mail in applications: ✉ Department of Foreign Affairs and International Trade, Ottawa, Ontario K1A 0G3, ☎ 819/994–3500 or 800/567–6868, WEB www.dfait-maeci.gc.ca/passport).

➤ NEW ZEALAND CITIZENS: **New Zealand Passport Office** (☎ 04/474–8100 or 0800/22–5050, WEB www.passports.govt.nz). **Embassy of the United States** (✉ 29 Fitzherbert Terr., Thorndon, Wellington, ☎ 04/462–6000 WEB usembassy.org.nz). **U.S. Consulate General** (✉ Citibank Bldg., 3rd floor, 23 Customs St. E, Auckland, ☎ 09/303–2724, WEB usembassy.org.nz).

➤ U.K. CITIZENS: **London Passport Office** (☎ 0870/521–0410, WEB www.passport.gov.uk). **U.S. Consulate General** (✉ Queen's House, 14 Queen St., Belfast, Northern Ireland BT1 6EQ, ☎ 028/9032–8239, WEB www.embassy.org.uk). **U.S. Embassy** (enclose a SASE to ✉ Consular Information Unit, 24 Grosvenor Sq., London W1 1AE, for general information; ✉ Visa Branch, 5 Upper Grosvenor St., London W1A 2JB, to submit an application via mail; ☎ 09068/200–290 recorded visa information or 09055/444–546 operator service, both with per-minute charges; WEB www.usembassy.org.uk).

TELEPHONES

All U.S. telephone numbers consist of a three-digit area code and a seven-digit local number. Within most local calling areas, you dial only the seven-digit number. Within some area codes, you must dial "1" first. To call between area-code regions, dial "1" then all 10 digits; the same goes for calls to numbers prefixed by "800," "888," "866," and "877"—all toll-free. For calls to numbers preceded by "900" you must pay—usually dearly.

For international calls, dial "011" followed by the country code and the local number. For help, dial "0" and ask for an overseas operator. The country code is 61 for Australia, 64 for New Zealand, 44 for the United Kingdom. Calling Canada is the same as calling within the United States. Most local phone books list country codes and U.S. area codes. The country code for the United States is 1.

For operator assistance, dial "0". To obtain someone's phone number, call directory assistance, 555–1212 or occasionally 411 (free at public phones). To have the person you're calling foot the bill, phone collect; dial "0" instead of "1" before the 10-digit number.

At pay phones, instructions are usually posted. Usually you insert coins in a slot (10¢–50¢ for local calls) and wait for a steady tone before dialing. When you call long-distance, the operator tells you how much to insert; prepaid phone cards, widely available in various denominations, are easier. Call the number on the back, punch in the card's personal identification number when prompted, then dial your number.

LODGING

The lodgings we list are the cream of the crop in each price category. We always list the facilities that are available, but we don't specify whether they cost extra; when pricing accommodations, always ask what's included and what costs extra. Properties are assigned price categories based on the range from their least-expensive standard double room at high season (excluding holidays) to the most expensive. Assume that hotels operate on the **European Plan** (EP, with no meals) unless we specify otherwise.

APARTMENT RENTALS

If you want a home base that's roomy enough for a family and comes with cooking facilities, **consider a furnished rental.** These can save you money, especially if you're traveling with a group. Home-exchange directories sometimes list rentals as well as exchanges. Rental apartments and condominiums are available through realtors who specialize in Mission Beach, Pacific Beach, La Jolla's Golden Triangle/University City area, Carlsbad, and Escondido. In addition, there are five Residence Inns by Marriott (☞ Hotels) in San Diego; these sometimes offer good value for families traveling on weekends.

➤ INTERNATIONAL AGENTS: **Hideaways International** (✉ 767 Islington St., Portsmouth, NH 03801, ☎ 603/430–4433 or 800/843–4433, FAX 603/430–4444, WEB www.hideaways.com; membership $129).

➤ LOCAL AGENTS: **Penny Realty** (☎ 800/748–6704, WEB www.missionbeach.com) and **San Diego Vacation Rentals** (☎ 800/222–8281, WEB www.sdvr.com) handle rentals in the Mission Bay and La Jolla areas.

BED-AND-BREAKFASTS

San Diego is known more for its resorts and solid chain properties, but the city has several bed-and-breakfasts. Most of these are in private homes. Historic Julian, in the mountains east of San Diego, has many bed-and-breakfasts.

➤ RESERVATION SERVICES: **Bed and Breakfast Guild of San Diego** (☎ 619/523–1300, WEB www.bandbguildsandiego.org). **Julian Bed and Breakfast Guild** (☎ 888/765–4333, WEB www.julianbnbguild.com).

HOME EXCHANGES

If you would like to exchange your home for someone else's, **join a home-exchange organization,** which will send you its updated listings of available exchanges for a year and will include your own listing in at least one of them. It's up to you to make specific arrangements.

➤ EXCHANGE CLUBS: **HomeLink International** (✉ Box 47747, Tampa, FL 33647, ☎ 813/975–9825 or 800/638–3841, FAX 813/910–8144, WEB www.homelink.org; $106 per year). **Intervac U.S.** (✉ Box 590504, San Francisco, CA 94159, ☎ 800/756–4663, FAX 415/435–7440, WEB www.intervacus.com; $93 yearly fee includes one catalog and on-line access).

HOSTELS

No matter what your age, you can **save on lodging costs by staying at hostels.** In some 4,500 locations in more than 70 countries around the world, Hostelling International (HI), the umbrella group for a number of national youth-hostel associations, offers single-sex, dorm-style beds and, at many hostels, rooms for couples and family accommodations. Membership in any HI national hostel association, open to travelers of all ages, allows you to stay in HI-affiliated hostels at member rates; one-year membership is about $25 for adults (C$35 for a two-year minimum membership in Canada, £13 in the U.K., A$52 in Australia, and NZ$40 in New Zealand); hostels run about $10–$30 per night. Members have priority if the hostel is full; they're also eligible for discounts around the world, even on rail and bus travel in some countries.

➤ ORGANIZATIONS: **Hostelling International—American Youth Hostels** (✉ 733 15th St. NW, Suite 840, Washington, DC 20005, ☎ 202/783–6161, FAX 202/783–6171, WEB www.hiayh.org). **Hostelling International—Canada** (✉ 400–205 Catherine St., Ottawa, Ontario K2P 1C3, ☎ 613/237–7884 or 800/663–5777 in Canada, FAX 613/237–7868, WEB www.hihostels.ca).

Youth Hostel Association of England and Wales (✉ Trevelyan House, Dimple Rd., Matlock, Derbyshire DE4 3YH, U.K., ☎ 0870/870–8808, FAX 0169/592–702, WEB www.yha. org.uk). Youth Hostel Association Australia (✉ 10 Mallett St., Camperdown, NSW 2050, ☎ 02/9565–1699, FAX 02/9565–1325, WEB www.yha. com.au). Youth Hostels Association of New Zealand (✉ Level 3, 193 Cashel St., Box 436, Christchurch, ☎ 03/379–9970, FAX 03/365–4476, WEB www.yha.org.nz).

HOTELS

In San Diego and surrounding communities you can find a hotel that will meet your requirements, whatever they are. We always list the facilities that are available—but we don't specify whether they cost extra: when pricing accommodations, always ask what's included and what costs extra. Downtown hotels cater primarily to business travelers, while those at Mission Bay, in coastal locations such as Carlsbad and Encinitas, and at inland resorts offer luxury, golf, spa services, children's activities, and more. Summer is the busy season for most hotels, and spring and fall conventions can fill every downtown hotel room. Also, special sports events such as golf or tennis tournaments can fill rooms at the host resorts and nearby hotels. All hotels listed have private bath unless otherwise noted.

➤ TOLL-FREE NUMBERS: Best Western (☎ 800/528–1234, WEB www. bestwestern.com). Choice (☎ 800/ 424–6423, WEB www.choicehotels. com). Clarion (☎ 800/424–6423, WEB www.choicehotels.com). Comfort Inn (☎ 800/424–6423, WEB www. choicehotels.com). Days Inn (☎ 800/ 325–2525, WEB www.daysinn.com). Doubletree and Red Lion Hotels (☎ 800/222–8733, WEB www.hilton. com). Embassy Suites (☎ 800/362– 2779, WEB www.embassysuites.com). Fairfield Inn (☎ 800/228–2800, WEB www.marriott.com). Four Seasons (☎ 800/332–3442, WEB www. fourseasons.com). Hilton (☎ 800/ 445–8667, WEB www.hilton.com). Holiday Inn (☎ 800/465–4329, WEB www.sixcontinentshotels.com). Howard Johnson (☎ 800/654–4656, WEB www.hojo.com). Hyatt Hotels &

Resorts (☎ 800/233–1234, WEB www. hyatt.com). La Quinta (☎ 800/531– 5900, WEB www.laquinta.com). Marriott (☎ 800/228–9290, WEB www. marriott.com). Quality Inn (☎ 800/ 424–6423, WEB www.choicehotels. com). Radisson (☎ 800/333–3333, WEB www.radisson.com). Ramada (☎ 800/228–2828; 800/854–7854 international reservations, WEB www. ramada.com or www.ramadahotels. com). Sheraton (☎ 800/325–3535, WEB www.starwood.com/sheraton). Sleep Inn (☎ 800/424–6423, WEB www.choicehotels.com). Westin Hotels & Resorts (☎ 800/228–3000, WEB www.starwood.com/westin). Wyndham Hotels & Resorts (☎ 800/822–4200, WEB www. wyndham.com).

MAIL AND SHIPPING

Staff at most U.S. Post Offices are efficient and helpful. Letters headed overseas take 10 days to two weeks to reach their destination. Private mailing services such as Mail Boxes, Etc. will pack and ship items for you. Most are authorized shippers for United Parcel Service (UPS), Federal Express (FedEx), and the U.S. Post Office.

➤ POST OFFICES: San Diego Downtown (✉ 815 E St., ☎ 619/232– 8612, ☼ Weekdays 8:30–5); La Jolla Main (✉ 1140 Wall St., ☎ 858/459– 5476, ☼ Weekdays 7:30–5, Sat. 8:30– 1:30); Coronado Branch (✉ 1320 Ynez Pl., ☎ 619/437–2470, ☼ Weekdays 8:30–5, Sat. 8:30–noon)

OVERNIGHT SERVICES

Drop boxes for Federal Express and United Parcel Service can be found throughout the downtown area and at other locations in the county.

➤ MAJOR SERVICES: Federal Express (☎ 800/463–3339, WEB www.fedex. com). United Parcel Service (☎ 800/ 742–5877, WEB www.ups.com).

MEDIA

NEWSPAPERS AND MAGAZINES

San Diego's major daily newspaper is the *San Diego Union-Tribune,* and locals also read the *Los Angeles Times.* The leading weekly newspaper is the *San Diego Reader,* available free in sidewalk racks around town. *San*

Diego Magazine carries monthly entertainment listings.

RADIO AND TELEVISION

All the major television networks have local affiliates in San Diego including **KGTV** Channel 10, ABC; **KFMB** Channel 8, CBS; **KNSD** Channel 39, NBC; and **KPBS** Channel 15, PBS. There are also local affiliates of UPN, WB, Fox, PAX, and the Spanish-language network. Check the *San Diego Union-Tribune* for listings. Los Angeles television and radio stations can be received in many areas of the county.

Major radio stations include **KOGO-AM** 600, news/talk; **KFMB-AM** 760, CBS talk/sports; **KSON-AM** 1240, Radio Disney; **KPBS-FM** 89.5, National Public Radio; **XLTN-FM** 106.5, Spanish; and **KJOY-FM** 94.1, contemporary.

MEXICO

If you're planning a side trip to nearby Mexico, **note the travel requirements** detailed in Chapter 8 (☞ Tijuana, Playas de Rosarito, and Ensenada A to Z) and customs information under For International Travelers.

MONEY MATTERS

Average prices for accommodations, food, and in shops are comparable with those in Los Angeles. Expect to pay $1 to $2.50 for coffee, $6.95 for a sandwich, $4 for a beer, and $1.80 per mile for a taxi. Prices throughout this guide are given for adults. Substantially reduced fees are almost always available for children, students, and senior citizens. For information on taxes, *see* Taxes.

ATMS

Most ATMs in the San Diego area are linked to national networks that let you withdraw money from your checking account or take a cash advance from your credit card account for an additional fee. ATMs can be found at all banks and in many grocery and convenience stores. For more information on ATM locations that can be accessed with your particular account, call the phone number found on the back of your ATM or debit card.

CREDIT CARDS

Throughout this guide, the following abbreviations are used: **AE**, American Express; **D**, Discover; **DC**, Diners Club; **MC**, MasterCard; and **V**, Visa.

➤ REPORTING LOST CARDS: To report a stolen or lost credit card contact: **American Express**, ☏ 800/300–8765; **Diners Club**, ☏ 800/234–6377; **Discover**, ☏ 800/347–2683; **Master-Card**, ☏ 800/826–2181; and **Visa**, ☏ 800/336–8472.

NATIONAL PARKS

Look into discount passes to save money on park entrance fees. For $50, the National Parks Pass admits you (and any passengers in your private vehicle) to all national parks, monuments, and recreation areas, as well as other sites run by the National Park Service, for a year. (In parks that charge per person, the pass admits you, your spouse and children, and your parents, when you arrive together.) Camping and parking are extra. The $15 Golden Eagle Pass, a hologram you affix to your National Parks Pass, functions as an upgrade, granting entry to all sites run by the NPS, the U.S. Fish and Wildlife Service, the U.S. Forest Service, and the Bureau of Land Management (BLM). The upgrade, which expires with the parks pass, is sold by most national-park, Fish-and-Wildlife, and BLM fee stations. A percentage of the proceeds from pass sales funds National Parks projects.

Both the Golden Age Passport ($10), for U.S. citizens or permanent residents who are 62 and older, and the Golden Access Passport (free), for those with disabilities, entitle holders (and any passengers in their private vehicles) to lifetime free entry to all national parks, plus 50% off fees for the use of many park facilities and services. (The discount doesn't always apply to companions.) To obtain them, you must show proof of age and of U.S. citizenship or permanent residency—such as a U.S. passport, driver's license, or birth certificate—and, if requesting Golden Access, proof of disability. The Golden Age and Golden Access passes, as well as the National Parks Pass, are available at any NPS-run site that charges an entrance fee. The National Parks Pass is also available by mail and via the Internet.

➤ INFORMATION: **National Park Foundation** (⌷ 1101 17th St. NW, Suite 1102, Washington, DC 20036, ☎ 202/785–4500, WEB www. nationalparks.org). **National Park Service** (⌷ National Park Service/ Department of Interior, 1849 C St. NW, Washington, DC 20240, ☎ 202/208–4747, WEB www.nps.gov). **National Parks Conservation Association** (⌷ 1300 19th St. NW, Suite 300, Washington, DC 20036, ☎ 202/223–6722, WEB www.npca.org.)

➤ PASSES BY MAIL AND ON-LINE: **National Park Foundation** (WEB www.nationalparks.org). **National Parks Pass** (⌷ 27540 Ave. Mentry, Valencia, CA 91355, ☎ 888/GO–PARKS or 888/467–2757, WEB www. nationalparks.org); include a check or money order payable to the National Park Service for the pass, plus $3.95 for shipping and handling.

PACKING

San Diego's casual lifestyle and year-round mild climate set the parameters for what you'll want to pack. You can **leave formal clothes and cold-weather gear behind.**

Plan on warm weather at any time of the year. Cottons, walking shorts, jeans, and T-shirts are the norm. **Pack bathing suits and shorts regardless of the season.** Few restaurants require a jacket and tie for men. Women may want to bring something a little dressier than their sightseeing garb.

Evenings are cool, even in summer, so be sure to **bring a sweater or a light jacket.** Rainfall in San Diego is not usually heavy; you won't need a raincoat except during the winter months, and even then, an umbrella may be sufficient protection. Be sure you **take comfortable walking shoes** with you. Even if you don't walk much at home, you'll find yourself covering miles while sightseeing on your vacation.

Sunglasses are a must in San Diego. Binoculars can also come in handy, especially if you're in town during whale-watching season from December through March.

In your carry-on luggage, **pack an extra pair of eyeglasses or contact lenses and enough of any medication** you take to last a few days longer than the entire trip. You may also ask your doctor to write a spare prescription using the drug's generic name, since brand names may vary from country to country. In luggage to be checked, **never pack prescription drugs or valuables.** And don't forget to carry with you the addresses of offices that handle refunds of lost traveler's checks. Check *Fodor's How to Pack* (available in bookstores everywhere) for more tips.

To avoid customs and security delays, carry medications in their original packaging. Don't pack any sharp objects in your carry-on luggage, including knives of any size or material, scissors, manicure tools, and corkscrews, or anything else that might arouse suspicion.

CHECKING LUGGAGE

You are allowed one carry-on bag and one personal article, such as a purse or a laptop computer. Make sure that everything you carry aboard will fit under your seat or in the overhead bin. Get to the gate early, so you can board as soon as possible, before the overhead bins fill up.

If you are flying internationally, note that baggage allowances may be determined not by piece but by weight—generally 88 pounds (40 kilograms) in first class, 66 pounds (30 kilograms) in business class, and 44 pounds (20 kilograms) in economy.

Airline liability for baggage is limited to $2,500 per person on flights within the United States. On international flights it amounts to $9.07 per pound or $20 per kilogram for checked baggage (roughly $640 per 70-pound bag) and $400 per passenger for unchecked baggage. You can buy additional coverage at check-in for about $10 per $1,000 of coverage, but it excludes a rather extensive list of items, shown on your airline ticket.

Before departure, **itemize your bags' contents** and their worth, and label the bags with your name, address, and phone number. (If you use your home address, cover it so potential thieves can't see it readily.) Inside each bag, **pack a copy of your itinerary**. At check-in, **make sure that each bag is correctly tagged** with the destination airport's three-letter code. If your bags arrive damaged or fail to arrive at all, file a written report with the airline before leaving the airport.

PASSPORTS AND VISAS

When traveling internationally, **carry your passport** even if you don't need one (it's always the best form of I.D.) and **make two photocopies of the data page** (one for someone at home and another for you, carried separately from your passport). If you lose your passport, promptly call the nearest embassy or consulate and the local police.

U.S. passport applications for children under age 14 require consent from both parents or legal guardians; both parents must appear together to sign the application. If only one parent appears, he or she must submit a written statement from the other parent authorizing passport issuance for the child. A parent with sole authority must present evidence of it when applying; acceptable documentation includes the child's certified birth certificate listing only the applying parent, a court order specifically permitting this parent's travel with the child, or a death certificate for the nonapplying parent. Application forms and instructions are available on the Web site of the U.S. State Department's Bureau of Consular Affairs (www.travel.state.gov).

REST ROOMS

Major attractions and parks have public rest rooms. In the downtown San Diego area, you can usually use the rest rooms at major hotels and fast-food restaurants.

SAFETY

San Diego is generally a safe place for travelers who observe all normal precautions. Dress inconspicuously, remove badges when leaving convention areas, know the routes to your destination before you set out. At the beach check with lifeguards about any unsafe conditions such as dangerous rip tides or water pollution. San Diego Convention & Visitors Bureau pub-lishes a Visitor Safety Tips brochure listing normal precautions for many situations. It's available at the International Visitor Information Center in Horton Plaza and at racks in tourist areas throughout the county.

SENIOR-CITIZEN TRAVEL

To qualify for age-related discounts, **mention your senior-citizen status up front** when booking hotel reservations (not when checking out) and before you're seated in restaurants (not when paying the bill). Be sure to have identification on hand. When renting a car, ask about promotional car-rental discounts, which can be cheaper than senior-citizen rates.

➤ EDUCATIONAL PROGRAMS: Elderhostel (⊠ 11 Ave. de Lafayette, Boston, MA 02111-1746, ☎ 877/426–8056, FAX 877/426–2166, WEB www. elderhostel.org).

SIGHTSEEING TOURS

BALLOON TOURS

Weather permitting, hot-air balloons lift off from San Diego's North County and Temecula; the average cost is $140 per person. Most flights float at sunrise or sunset and are followed by a champagne toast.

➤ FEES AND SCHEDULES: **A Balloon Adventure by California Dreamin'** (⊠ 162 S. Rancho Santa Fe Rd., Suite F35, Encinitas, ☎ 800/373–3359, WEB www.caiforniadream.com). **A Skysurfer Balloon Company** (⊠ 1221 Camino del Mar, Del Mar, ☎ 858/481–6800; 800/660–6809, WEB www.skysurfer.systemtree.com).

BOAT TOURS

Three companies operate one- and two-hour harbor cruises. San Diego Harbor Excursion and Hornblower Invader Cruises boats depart from the Broadway Pier. No reservations are necessary for the $13–$18 voyages, and both vessels have snack bars. Classic Sailing Adventures has morning and afternoon tours of the harbor and San Diego Bay and evening cruises in summer for $60 per person. These companies also operate during whale-watching season from mid-December to mid-March. Others include H&M Landing and Seaforth Sportfishing.

➤ FEES AND SCHEDULES: **Classic Sailing Adventures** (✉ 1220 Rosecrans St. No. 137, ☎ 619/224–0800, WEB www.classicsailingadventures.com). **Hornblower Invader Cruises** (✉ 1066 N. Harbor Dr., ☎ 619/234–8687, WEB www.hornblower.com). **San Diego Harbor Excursion** (✉ 1050 N. Harbor Dr., ☎ 619/234–4111 or 800/442–7847, WEB www.harborexcursion.com). **H&M Landing** (✉ 2803 Emerson St., Point Loma, ☎ 619/222–1144, WEB www.hmlanding.com). **Seaforth Sportfishing** (✉ 1641 Quivera Rd., ☎ 619/223–1681, WEB www.seaforthboatrental.com).

BUS AND TROLLEY TOURS

Free two-hour bus tours of the downtown redevelopment area, including the Gaslamp Quarter, are conducted by Centre City Development Corporation Downtown Information Center. Groups leave on the first and third Saturday of the month at 10 AM and noon. Advance reservations are necessary. The tour may be canceled if there aren't enough passengers.

Coach USA in San Diego runs a fleet of open-top, double-decker buses. For $25, you get an unlimited day pass that lets you hop on and off the bus at any of the stops, which include Old Town, Balboa Park, the Gaslamp Quarter, SeaWorld, and the harbor. Purchase tickets at Old Town, Horton Plaza, Seaport Village, or from the bus driver.

Old Town Trolley Historic Tours take you to eight sites including Old Town, the Cruise Ship terminal, Seaport Village, Marriott Hotel near the Convention Center, Horton Plaza near the Gaslamp Quarter, Coronado, the San Diego Zoo, and El Prado in Balboa Park. The tour is narrated, and you can get on and off as you please at any stop. An all-day pass costs $24 for adults and $12 for children 4–12; under 4, free. The trolley, which leaves every 30 minutes, operates daily 9–4 in winter. It takes the trolley two hours to make a full loop. The company also offers several special-interest tours, like Ghosts & Gravestones and Seal Tour, aboard an amphibious vehicle which cruises Mission Bay and the San Diego Harbor. The San Diego

Passport is good for the trolley tour plus admission to the zoo, Maritime Museum, San Diego Museum of Art, one Hornblower cruise, and other goodies. The cost is $69.95 per person, and the passport is available at visitors centers and is good for one year.

Grey Line San Diego offers a number of half- and full-day city tours, which may include trips to the zoo, SeaWorld, Wild Animal Park, Legoland, or Mexico. Rates are $25–$52, admissions included. Contactours is another operator that offers guided excursions to area attractions, including Barona and Viejas casinos and Mexico. Prices start at $25.

➤ FEES AND SCHEDULES: **Centre City Development Corporation's Downtown Information Center** (✉ 225 Broadway, Suite 160, ☎ 619/235–2222, WEB www.ccdc.com). **Coach USA** (✉ 3500 Estudillo St., ☎ 619/527–4644, WEB www.sightseeingusa.com) **Contactours** (✉ 1726 Wilson Ave., National City, ☎ 619/477–8687, WEB www.contactours.com). **Gray Line Tours** (✉ 1775 Hancock St., No. 130, ☎ 619/491–0011; 800/331–5077 outside CA, WEB www.graylinesandiego.com). **Old Town Trolley** (✉ 2115 Kurtz St., ☎ 619/298–8687, WEB www.trolleytours.com).

WALKING TOURS

Several fine walking tours are available on weekdays or weekends; upcoming walks are usually listed in the Thursday Night and Day section of the *San Diego Union-Tribune*. Those by Walkabout are free; location and contact phone numbers vary week to week. The Gaslamp Quarter Historical Foundation leads two-hour historical walking tours of the downtown historic district on Saturday at 11 AM ($8).

➤ FEES AND SCHEDULES: **The Gaslamp Quarter Historical Foundation** (✉ 410 Island Ave., ☎ 619/233–4692).

STUDENTS IN SAN DIEGO

San Diego State University (SDSU) is located just east of Mission Bay, not to be confused with the University of California at San Diego (UCSD) in northern La Jolla. Most museums and other attractions have a discounted rate for students with identification.

➤ I.D.s AND SERVICES: **STA Travel** (☎ 212/627–3111 or 800/781–4040, FAX 212/627–3387, WEB www.sta.com). **Travel Cuts** (✉ 187 College St., Toronto, Ontario M5T 1P7, Canada, ☎ 416/979–2406 or 888/838–2887 in Canada, FAX 416/979–2406, WEB www.travelcuts.com).

TROLLEY TRAVEL

The San Diego Trolley light rail system connects with San Diego Transit buses. The bright-orange trolleys service downtown San Diego, Mission Valley, Old Town, South Bay, the U.S. Border, and East County. The trolleys operate seven days a week from about 5 AM to midnight, depending on the station, at intervals of about 15 minutes. Bus connections are posted at each station, and bicycle lockers are available at most. Trolleys can get crowded during morning and evening rush hours. On-time performance is excellent.

FARES AND SCHEDULES

San Diego Trolley tickets are priced according to the number of stations traveled. Quick Tripper tickets good for two hours are $1 to $2.25; Round Tripper tickets good for a return trip on the date purchased are $2 to $4.50. Tickets are dispensed from self-service ticket machines at each stop; exact fare in coins is recommended, although some machines accept bills in $1, $5, $10, and $20 denominations. Transfers between buses and/or the trolley are free or require an upgrade if the second fare is higher.

Day Tripper Passes are available for one, two, three, or four days ($5, $8, $10, and $12, respectively), which give unlimited rides on regional buses and the San Diego Trolley. They may be purchased from most trolley vending machines, at the Transit Store, and some hotels.

➤ TROLLEY INFORMATION: **San Diego Transit** (☎ 619/233–3004; 619/234–5005 TTY/TDD, WEB www.sdcommute.com) for city transit and San Diego Trolley.

TAXES

SALES TAX

In San Diego County a sales tax of 7.75% is added to the price of all goods and services, except food purchased at a grocery store. Hotel taxes are 9–13%.

TAXIS

Taxis departing from the airport are subject to regulated fares—all companies charge the same rate (generally $1.80 for the first mile, $1.20 for each additional mile). Fares vary among companies on other routes, however, including the ride back to the airport. If you call ahead and ask for the flat rate ($8) you'll get it, otherwise you'll be charged by the mile (which works out to $9 or so). Taxi stands are located at shopping centers and hotels, otherwise you must call and reserve one. The Transportation Network is comprised of companies that serve the greater San Diego area including the airport. The companies listed below do not serve all areas of San Diego County. If you're going someplace other than downtown, **ask if the company serves that area.**

➤ TAXI COMPANIES: **Silver Cabs** (☎ 619/280–5555). **Crown City Cab** (☎ 619/437–8885, WEB www.driveu.com). **Orange Cab** (☎ 619/291–3333, WEB www.home.pacbell.net/orangesd). **Transportation Network** (☎ 619/239–8061, WEB www.driveu.com). **Yellow Cab** (☎ 619/234–6161, WEB www.driveu.com).

TIME

San Diego is in the Pacific time zone. Pacific Daylight Time is in effect from early April through late October; Pacific Standard Time, the rest of the year. Clocks are set ahead one hour when Daylight Time begins, back one hour when it ends.

TIPPING

At restaurants, a 15%–20% tip is standard for waiters, depending on the level of service provided. The same goes for taxi drivers, bartenders, and hairdressers. Coat-check operators usually expect $1; bellhops and porters should get 50¢ to $1 per bag; hotel maids should get about $1 per day of your stay—$2 in upscale hotels. A concierge typically receives a tip of $5 to $10, with an additional gratuity for special services or favors. On package tours, conductors and drivers usually get $10 per day from the group as a whole; check whether this has already been figured into your cost. For local sightseeing tours, you may individually tip the driver-guide $1 if he or she has been helpful or informative. Ushers in theaters do not expect tips.

TOURS AND PACKAGES

Because everything is prearranged on a prepackaged tour or independent vacation, you spend less time planning—and often get it all at a good price.

BOOKING WITH AN AGENT

Travel agents are excellent resources. But it's a good idea to collect brochures from several agencies, as some agents' suggestions may be influenced by relationships with tour and package firms that reward them for volume sales. If you have a special interest, **find an agent with expertise in that area**; the American Society of Travel Agents (ASTA; ☞ Travel Agencies) has a database of specialists worldwide.

Make sure your travel agent knows the accommodations and other services of the place being recommended. Ask about the hotel's location, room size, beds, and whether it has a pool, room service, or programs for children, if you care about these. Has your agent been there in person or sent others whom you can contact?

Do some homework on your own, too: local tourism boards can provide information about lesser-known and small-niche operators, some of which may sell only direct.

BUYER BEWARE

Each year consumers are stranded or lose their money when tour operators—even large ones with excellent reputations—go out of business. So **check out the operator.** Ask several travel agents about its reputation, and try to **book with a company that has a consumer-protection program.** (Look for information in the company's brochure.) In the United States, members of the National Tour

Association and the United States Tour Operators Association are required to set aside funds to cover your payments and travel arrangements in the event that the company defaults. It's also a good idea to choose a company that participates in the American Society of Travel Agents' Tour Operator Program (TOP); ASTA will act as mediator in any disputes between you and your tour operator.

Remember that the more your package or tour includes the better you can predict the ultimate cost of your vacation. Make sure you know exactly what is covered, and **beware of hidden costs.** Are taxes, tips, and transfers included? Entertainment and excursions? These can add up.

➤ TOUR-OPERATOR RECOMMENDATIONS: **American Society of Travel Agents** (☞ Travel Agencies). **National Tour Association** (NTA; ✉ 546 E. Main St., Lexington, KY 40508, ☎ 859/226–4444 or 800/682–8886, WEB www.ntaonline.com). **United States Tour Operators Association** (USTOA; ✉ 275 Madison Ave., Suite 2014, New York, NY 10016, ☎ 212/599–6599 or 800/468–7862, FAX 212/599–6744, WEB www.ustoa.com).

TRAIN TRAVEL TO AND FROM SAN DIEGO

Amtrak serves downtown San Diego's Santa Fe Depot with daily trains to and from Los Angeles, Santa Barbara, and San Luis Obispo. Connecting service to Oakland, Seattle, Chicago, Texas, Florida, and points beyond is available in Los Angeles. Amtrak trains stop in San Diego North County at Solana Beach and Oceanside.

Coaster commuter trains, which run between Oceanside and San Diego Monday–Saturday, stop at the same stations as Amtrak plus others. The Oceanside, Carlsbad, and Solana Beach stations have beach access. You can pick up Coaster flyers or brochures with detailed itineraries for each stop, including walking directions and connections to local bus service. Trains are typically on time. No smoking is allowed.

Metrolink operates high-speed rail service between the Oceanside Transit Center and Union Station in Los Angeles.

CUTTING COSTS

Amtrak frequently offers discount passes that are good for travel within a specific geographic region of the United States, but you must book your schedule when buying the pass. If you want sleeping-car accommodations, in off-peak season you often can get a better price for a room by contacting the conductor after you board the train.

FARES AND SCHEDULES

You can obtain Amtrak timetables at any Amtrak station, or by visiting the Amtrak Web site, www.amtrak.com.

The Coaster runs between Oceanside and San Diego about every half hour during the rush hours on weekdays. There are four trains on Saturday, none on Sunday. One-way fares are $3.50 to $4.75, depending on the distance traveled.

➤ TRAIN INFORMATION: **Amtrak** (☎ 800/872–7245, WEB www.amtrak). **Coaster** (☎ 800/262–6883, WEB www. sdcommute.com). **Metrolink** (☎ 800/ 371–5465). **Oceanside train station** (☎ 760/722–4622). **Santa Fe Depot** (✉ 1050 Kettner Blvd., ☎ 619/239–9021). **Solana Beach Amtrak station** (☎ 858/259–2697).

PAYING

Amtrak and the Coaster vending machines accept all major credit cards. Metrolink requires cash.

RESERVATIONS

Many Amtrak trains require advance reservations, especially for long-distance transcontinental routes. Advance reservations are suggested for trains running on weekends between San Diego and Santa Barbara. For security reasons, Amtrak requires ticket purchasers to appear in person with photo ID.

TRANSPORTATION AROUND SAN DIEGO

Most of San Diego was laid out after the invention of the automobile; a car is a necessity for most visitors. Though public transportation serves most of the major attractions, getting from one place to another—from downtown to the beaches north of La Jolla, for instance—can take rather a long time. Two exceptions are the San Diego Trolley, which can save you time if you're heading from downtown to Old Town or Qualcomm Stadium, or to the Mexican border, and the Coronado Ferry, the scenic route from the harbor to Coronado. Public transportation agencies have integrated their services in an effort to provide convenient connections between rail and bus travel throughout San Diego County. You can obtain an itinerary that will get you from one place to another by accessing the Web site WEB www.sdcommute.com or calling ☎ 800/266–6883.

TRAVEL AGENCIES

A good travel agent puts your needs first. Look for an agency that has been in business at least five years, emphasizes customer service, and has someone on staff who specializes in your destination. In addition, **make sure the agency belongs to a professional trade organization.** The American Society of Travel Agents (ASTA)—the largest and most influential in the field with more than 24,000 members in some 140 countries—maintains and enforces a strict code of ethics and will step in to help mediate any agent-client disputes involving ASTA members if necessary. ASTA (whose motto is "Without a travel agent, you're on your own") also maintains a Web site that includes a directory of agents. (If a travel agency is also acting as your tour operator, see Buyer Beware in Tours and Packages.)

➤ LOCAL AGENT REFERRALS: **American Society of Travel Agents** (ASTA; ✉ 1101 King St., Suite 200, Alexandria, VA 22314, ☎ 800/965–2782 24-hr hot line, FAX 703/739–3268, WEB www.astanet.com). **Association of British Travel Agents** (✉ 68–71 Newman St., London W1T 3AH, ☎ 020/7637–2444, FAX 020/7637–0713, WEB www.abtanet.com). **Association of Canadian Travel Agents** (✉ 130 Albert St., Suite 1705, Ottawa, Ontario K1P 5G4, ☎ 613/237–3657, FAX 613/237–7052, WEB www.acta.ca). **Australian Federation of Travel**

Agents (⊠ Level 3, 309 Pitt St., Sydney, NSW 2000, ☎ 02/9264–3299, FAX 02/9264–1085, WEB www.afta.com.au). **Travel Agents' Association of New Zealand** (⊠ Level 5, Tourism and Travel House, 79 Boulcott St., Box 1888, Wellington 6001, ☎ 04/499–0104, FAX 04/499–0827, WEB www.taanz.org.nz).

VISITOR INFORMATION

For general information and brochures before you go, contact the San Diego Convention & Visitors Bureau, which publishes the helpful *San Diego Official Visitors Guide* and *San Diego Visitors Pocket Guide*. When you arrive, stop by one of the local visitors centers for general information.

➤ CITY-WIDE: **San Diego Convention & Visitors Bureau** (⊠ 401 B St., Suite 1400, San Diego, 92101, ⊠ Herschel Ave. at Prospect St., ☎ 619/236–1212, WEB www.sandiego.org).

➤ LOCAL INFORMATION: **Balboa Park Visitors Center** (⊠ 1549 El Prado, ☎ 619/239–0512, WEB www.balboapark.org), open daily 9–4. **International Visitor Information Center** (⊠ 11 Horton Plaza, at 1st Ave. and F St., ☎ 619/236–1212, WEB www.sandiego.org), open Monday–Saturday 8:30–5; June–Aug. and also Sun. 11–5. **San Diego Visitor Information Center** (⊠ 2688 E. Mission Bay Dr., off I–5 at the Clairemont Dr. exit, ☎ 619/275–8259, WEB www.infosandiego.com/visitor), open daily 9–dusk.

➤ SAN DIEGO COUNTY: **Borrego Springs Chamber of Commerce and Visitors Center** (⊠ 786 Palm Canyon Dr., 92004, ☎ 760/767–5555, WEB www.borregosprings.org). **Carlsbad Convention & Visitors Bureau** (⊠ 400 Carlsbad Village Dr., 92008, ☎ 800/721–1101, WEB www.carlsbadca.org). **Coronado Visitor Center** (⊠ 1100 Orange Ave., 92118, ☎ 619/437–8788, WEB www.coronadohistory.org/visitorcenter/). **Greater Del Mar Chamber of Commerce** (⊠ 1104 Camino del Mar, 92014, ☎ 858/793–5292, WEB www.delmarchamber.org). **Julian Chamber of Commerce** (⊠ 2129 Main St., 92036, ☎ 760/765–1857, WEB www.julianca.com). **La Jolla Town Council** (⊠ 7734 Herschel Ave., 92038, ☎ 858/454–1444). **California**

Welcome Center Oceanside (⊠ 928 N. Coast Hwy., 92054, ☎ 760/721–1011 or 800/350–7873, WEB www.oceansidechamber.com). **San Diego East Visitors Bureau** (⊠ 5005 Willows Rd., No. 208, Alpine 91901, ☎ 619/445–0180 or 800/463–0668, WEB www.visitsandiegoeast.com). **San Diego North Convention & Visitors Bureau** (⊠ 360 N. Escondido Blvd., Escondido 92025, ☎ 760/745–4741 or 800/848–3336, WEB www.sandiegonorth.com).

➤ STATE-WIDE: **California Division of Tourism** (⊠ 801 K St., Suite 1600, Sacramento, CA 95814, ☎ 916/322–2882 or 800/862–2543, WEB www.visitcalifornia.com).

➤ IN THE U.K.: **California Tourist Office** (⊠ ABC California, Box 35, Abingdon, Oxfordshire OX14 4TB, ☎ 0891/200–278). Calls cost 50p per minute peak rate or 45p per minute cheap rate; send check for £3 for brochures.

WEB SITES

Do check out the World Wide Web when planning your trip. You'll find everything from weather forecasts to virtual tours of famous cities. Be sure to **visit Fodors.com** (www.fodors.com), a complete travel-planning site. You can research prices and book plane tickets, hotel rooms, rental cars, vacation packages, and more. In addition, you can post your pressing questions in the Travel Talk section. Other planning tools include a currency converter and weather reports, and there are loads of links to travel resources.

The California Parks Department site, www.cal-parks.ca.gov, has information about state-run parks in the San Diego area. The National Park Service site, www.nps.gov, has listings about all San Diego–area parks and other lands administered by the park service. The Web site www.sandiegohistory.org is a wonderful site covering San Diego's history, buildings, and personalities with articles, archival photos, links, and more. The San Diego Zoo and Wild Animal Park maintain the Web site www.sandiegozoo.org, which has up-to-the-minute reports on new facilities and animal guests.

Homeport San Diego's web page, www.homeport-sd.com, carries regional weather and other information. *San Diego Magazine*'s www. sandiego-online.com carries feature stories about the city and capsule dining reviews. The site of the *San Diego Reader*, www.sdreader.com, isn't visually impressive, but it provides a thorough guide to dining, nightlife, and the arts. The *San Diego Union-Tribune* operates the site, www.signonsandiego.com, which does a good job covering local shopping and dining.

WHEN TO GO

For the most part, **any time of the year is the right time** for a trip to San Diego. The climate is generally close to perfect. Typical days are sunny and mild, with low humidity—ideal for sightseeing and for almost any sport that does not require snow and ice. From mid-December through mid-March gray whales can be seen migrating along the coast. In early spring wildflowers transform the mountainsides and desert into a rainbow of colors. In fall these same mountains present one of the most impressive displays of fall color to be found in southern California.

CLIMATE

The annual high temperature averages 70°F with a low of 55°F, and the annual rainfall is usually less than 10 inches. Most of the rain occurs in January and February, but precipitation usually lasts for only part of the day or for a day or two at most.

➤ FORECASTS: **Weather Channel Connection** (☎ 900/932–8437), 95¢ per minute from a Touch-Tone phone.

The following are average maximum and minimum temperatures for San Diego.

Jan.	62F	17C	May	66F	19C	Sept.	73F	23C
	46	8		55	13		62	17
Feb.	62F	17C	June	69F	21C	Oct.	71F	22C
	48	9		59	15		57	14
Mar.	64F	18C	July	73F	23C	Nov.	69F	21C
	50	10		62	17		51	11
Apr.	66F	19C	Aug.	73F	23C	Dec.	64F	18C
	53	12		64	18		48	9

FESTIVALS AND SEASONAL EVENTS

➤ FEB.: The **Buick Invitational Golf Tournament** (☎ 800/888–2842) attracts more than 100,000 people, including local and national celebrities, to the Torrey Pines Golf Course.

➤ FEB.–APR.: **Wildflowers in the desert** bloom during a two- to six-week period in these months. The span and extent of the bloom is determined by the winter rainfall. Phone the Anza-Borrego Desert State Park visitor center (☎ 760/767–4684) for information.

➤ MAR.: The **Kiwanis Ocean Beach Kite Festival** (☎ 619/531–1527) features a kite-making, decorating, and flying contest, plus a craft fair, food, and entertainment.

➤ MAR. OR APR.: The **La Jolla Easter Hat Parade** (☎ 858/454–2600) finds La Jollans and others parading in their Easter finest for prizes. Tiptoe through fields of brilliantly colored ranunculuses arranged rainbow-fashion on a hillside at **Flower Fields at Carlsbad Ranch** (☎ 760/431–0352) in Carlsbad.

➤ APR.: The **San Diego Crew Classic** (☎ 858/488–0700) brings together more than 2,600 high school, college, and masters athletes from across the United States for a rowing competition at Crown Point Shores in Mission Bay. The **ArtWalk Festival** (☎ 619/615–1090) showcases visual and performing artists in their studios and in staged areas; self-guided tours start downtown in Little Italy. The **Borrego Springs Grapefruit Festival** (☎ 760/767–5555) celebrates the ruby-red grapefruit, which is grown in the desert; you'll find music, food, arts, crafts, and games. The **Adams Avenue Roots Festival** (☎ 619/282–7329) is a free festival featuring vintage blues, folk, jazz, country, and international music on six outdoor stages.

➤ APR.–MAY: The **Del Mar National Horse Show** (☎ 858/792–4252) at the Del Mar Fairgrounds showcases international and national championship riders, draft horses, dressage, and western hunter/jumper competitions.

➤ MAY: **Fiesta Cinco de Mayo** (☎ 619/220–5427) brings entertainment and booths to Old Town San Diego State Historic Park and the Bazaar del Mundo. **Julian Wildflower Show** (☎ 760/765–1857) is an annual display of wildflowers gathered within a 15-mi radius of the mountain town, and usually includes desert blooms.

➤ JUNE: At the **Threshing Bee & Antique Engine Show** (☎ 760/941–1791), which takes place at the Antique Gas & Steam Engine Museum in Vista, you can see demonstrations on early American crafts, farming, log sawing, and blacksmithing, plus an antique tractor parade. **A Taste of the Gaslamp** (☎ 619/233–5227) features samples of the best dishes prepared by Gaslamp Quarter chefs. The **Annual Inter-Tribal Pow Pow** (☎ 760/724–8505), held at Mission San Luis Rey in Oceanside, draws participants from all over the United States, and features dancing, Native American arts and crafts, food booths, and games.

➤ JUNE–JULY: The **Del Mar Fair** (☎ 858/793–5555) is a classic county fair, with live entertainment, flower and garden shows, a carnival, livestock shows, and Fourth of July fireworks. In July the annual **Lesbian and Gay Pride Parade, Rally and Festival** ☎ (619/297–7683), a weekend of entertainment, takes place in Hillcrest and Balboa Park.

➤ JUNE–AUG.: During the **Summer Organ Festival** (☎ 619/702–8138), enjoy free Sunday-afternoon and Monday-evening concerts at Balboa Park's Spreckels Organ Pavilion. Free concerts are also offered here Tuesday, Wednesday, and Thursday evenings.

➤ JUNE–SEPT.: The **Nighttime Zoo** at the San Diego Zoo (☎ 619/234–

3153) and **The Park at Dark** at the San Diego Wild Animal Park (☎ 760/747–8702) are wild ways to spend the evening, with extended evening hours and additional entertainment through the beginning of September. **Carlsbad Jazz-in-the-Park Series** features free live performances at various parks in the Carlsbad area; call for schedule (☎ 760/434–2904).

➤ JULY: The **Over-the-Line Tournament** (☎ 619/688–0817) is a rowdy party, with more than 1,000 three-person teams competing in a sport that's a cross between softball and stickball; it takes place during two weekends on Fiesta Island in Mission Bay. Patriots observe **Coronado Independence Day Celebration** (☎ 619/437–8788) with a parade, U.S. Navy air/sea demonstrations, a concert in the park, and fireworks over Glorietta Bay. **Julian Independence Day Celebration** (☎ 760/765–1857) is an old-fashioned small-town celebration featuring a parade of animals, floozies, and bands; there's also a Confederate air-force fly-over, old-west shoot-out, barbecue, and quilt show. **U.S. Open Sandcastle Competition** (☎ 619/424–6663) at Imperial Beach Pier brings together sand sculptors of all ages for one of the largest castle-building events in the United States.

➤ JULY–SEPT.: The **Old Globe Theatre** (☎ 619/239–2255) features works of Shakespeare in repertory with other classic and contemporary plays at the Old Globe Theatre in Balboa Park. **San Diego Symphony Summer Pops Series** (☎ 888/848–7326) swings with occasional fireworks Friday and Saturday nights at Navy Pier.

➤ AUG.: **Body Surfing Contests** (☎ 760/435–4014) pit more than 200 of California's top competitors against one another; viewing from Oceanside Pier and Beach. The **Summerfest** (☎ 858/459–3728) chamber music festival at Sherwood Auditorium in La Jolla includes concerts, lectures, master classes, and open rehearsals.

➤ SEPT.: **Street Scene** (☎ 619/557–8490) transforms the historic Gaslamp Quarter into a rollicking three-day food and music festival, with 10 stages showcasing more than 100 bands from around the world.

Smart Travel Tips A to Z

The **San Diego Bayfair** (☎ 619/225–9160) draws thunderboat enthusiasts to Mission Bay for an exhilarating, deafening weekend of racing. The free outdoor **Adams Avenue Street Fair** (☎ 619/282–7329) annually attracts 50,000 jazz, blues, and rock fans to the Normal Heights neighborhood for concerts on five stages, the Fern Street Circus, food, games, and a carnival. The largest event of its type in southern California, it's popular with families.

➤ OCT.: **Octoberfest La Mesa** (☎ 619/462–3000) is a traditional German celebration featuring food, Bavarian bands, dancing, arts and crafts. Admission to the San Diego Zoo (☎ 619/234–3153) is free on **Founders Day,** the first Monday in October, and children get in free the entire month. Actors portray historical stories of life aboard the tallship **Star of India,** on the waterfront. (☎ 619/234–9153.).

➤ NOV.: The **Mum Festival** (☎ 619/234–6541), the largest display of its kind on the West Coast, features thousands of chrysanthemums trained into cascading bouquets and topiary throughout the Wild Animal Park. El Cajon's **Mother Goose Parade** (☎ 619/444–8712) is a two-hour nationally televised spectacular with 200 floats, bands, horses, and clowns. **Holiday of Lights** (☎ 858/793–5555) showcases more than 250 animated and lighted holiday displays in a drive-through setting at the Del Mar Fairgrounds.

➤ DEC.: **Christmas on the Prado** (☎ 619/239–0512), sponsored by the museums in Balboa Park, draws 100,000 guests on the first Friday and Saturday of December. Attractions include carolers, holiday food, music, dance, handmade crafts for sale, a visit from Saint Nick, a candlelight procession, and free admission to all the museums. **Old Town Holiday in the Park** (☎ 619/220–5422) includes candlelight tours of historic homes and other buildings in Old Town by costumed docents; reservations are required. The **Wild Animal Park Festival of Lights** (☎ 760/796–5615) includes free kid-oriented activities, Christmas caroling, live-animal presentations, and real snow. The **Port of San Diego Bay Parade of Lights** (☎ 619/296–3562) fills the harbor with lighted boats cruising in a procession starting at Shelter Island and ending at the Navy carrier turning basin. The **Ocean Beach Parade and Tree Festival** (☎ 619/226–8613) takes place on Newport Avenue, generally the second weekend in December. The Ocean Beach Geriatric Surf Club tops any entry in any parade, anywhere.

1 DESTINATION: SAN DIEGO

PARADISE FOUND

SUNSHINE YEAR-ROUND, miles of white-sand beaches, laid-back friendliness, history and Hispanic culture, and family-oriented outdoor entertainment at SeaWorld and the world-famous San Diego Zoo are enough to draw 14 million visitors annually to "America's finest city." But there's more than meets the eye here. If you look beyond the obvious, you'll discover why many longtime vacationers eventually become residents, and why residents have a hard time ever moving.

San Diego, occupying the southwest corner of California, boasts an almost perfect year-round climate. Most days are sunny, averaging 70°F and humidity is low. The cool coastal climate is ideal for the area's most colorful industry—flower growing. Summer temperatures frequently reach 100°F inland, particularly at the Wild Animal Park near Escondido; even so, nights are cool enough to make it a good idea to have a sweater or jacket handy.

San Diego is a big city, where locals take pride in its small-town feel. With more than 1 million people living within the city limits, San Diego is second only to Los Angeles in population among California cities and ranks as the seventh-largest municipality in the United States. It also covers a lot of territory, roughly 400 square mi of land and sea.

Central San Diego is delightfully urban and accessible. You can walk the entire downtown area—explore the exciting and trendy Gaslamp Quarter, stop and shop at whimsical Horton Plaza, dine Italian, hear a rock band, attend a play, take a sunset harbor stroll, picnic in the park, or visit a historic building. Downtown you can catch the trolley or take the bus to the Balboa Park museums and the zoo, Old Town historic sites, Mission Bay marine park, Qualcomm Stadium, diverse urban neighborhoods, and Tijuana.

To the north and south of the city are 70 mi of beaches. Hiking and camping territory lie inland, where a succession of long, low, chaparral-covered mesas are punctuated with deep-cut canyons that step up to savanna-like hills, separating the verdant coast from the arid Anza-Borrego Desert. Unusually clear skies make the inland countryside ideal for stargazing.

You'll find reminders of San Diego's Spanish and Mexican heritage throughout the region—in architecture and place-names, in distinctive Mexican cuisine, and in a handful of historic buildings in Old Town. The San Diego area, the birthplace of California, was claimed for Spain by Juan Rodríguez Cabrillo in 1542. The first European community, Mission Alta California, was established here in 1769, when a small group of settlers and soldiers set up camp on what is now called Presidio Hill. Franciscan Father Junípero Serra, leader of the settlers, celebrated the first Mass here in July of that year, establishing the Mission San Diego de Alcalá, the first of the 21 missions built by Spanish friars in California. San Diego, along with the rest of California, ultimately came under Mexican rule before entering the United States as the 31st state in 1850.

In 1867 developer Alonzo Horton, who called the town's bay-front "the prettiest place for a city I ever saw," began building a hotel, a plaza, and prefab homes on 960 downtown acres. The city's fate was sealed in 1908 when the U.S. Navy's battleship fleet sailed into San Diego Bay. The military continues to contribute to the local economy, operating many bases and installations throughout the county; San Diego is home to the largest military complex in the world.

San Diego has taken an orderly approach to inevitable development with the adoption of a general plan to run through the year 2020. More than 50 projects are under way or on the drawing board for downtown, including a new ballpark for the Padres, several hotels, and the creation of plazas, parks, and promenades along the waterfront.

Links between the south-of-the-border communities of Tijuana and Ensenada continue to strengthen. More than 50 million people cross the border at San

Ysidro annually, indicative of the two-nation nature of San Diego. In recent years Tijuana has grown into one of the biggest, most exciting cities in Mexico. You'll discover a sophisticated, pulsating city marked with excellent restaurants, trendy bars and discos, chic boutiques, discount malls, sports-betting parlors, broad boulevards congested with traffic, and new high-rise hotels.

Without question, San Diego is one of the warmest and most appealing destinations in the United States. As you explore, you'll make your own discoveries that will lead you to agree with most locals that this corner of California is just this side of paradise.

–Bobbi Zane

WHAT'S WHERE

Like a giant conch shell, San Diego spirals around the bay, with Balboa Park at its center. The following neighborhoods are organized geographically, just as they are in Chapter 2, *Exploring,* starting with Balboa Park, continuing with the San Diego Bay shoreline, and ending with the San Diego North County communities.

Balboa Park
Straddling two mesas overlooking downtown and the Pacific Ocean, Balboa Park is set on 1,200 beautifully landscaped acres. Home to the majority of San Diego's museums and the world-famous zoo, the park serves as the cultural center of the city, as well as a lush green space for animal lovers, picnickers, and strollers. Most of the downtown thoroughfares lead north to the park (it's hard to miss). From the west side of downtown take any east–west street until you hit Park Boulevard, and drive north into the park. From Old Town take Interstate 5 south and use any of the well-marked exits.

Hillcrest
Northwest of Balboa Park is eclectic Hillcrest, the heart of San Diego's gay and lesbian community, where you'll find excellent restaurants tucked between independent boutiques, movie theaters, juice bars, and unusual bookstores. North Park is an extension of Hillcrest, directly above (you

guessed it) Balboa Park. It's known for antiques, used-book stores, and vintage-clothing shops.

Downtown
San Diego's downtown and waterfront area is a bustling, colorful jumble of hotels, restaurants, shopping centers, gift shops, and seagoing vessels of every size and shape. The centerpiece is Horton Plaza, a shopping, dining, and entertainment complex that covers more than six city blocks. East of Horton Plaza is the Gaslamp Quarter, the city's hot dining and entertainment district with eateries, nightclubs, and boutiques housed in Victorian buildings and renovated warehouses. Downtown San Diego's main arteries are Harbor Drive, which runs along the Embarcadero; Broadway, which cuts through the center of downtown; and 6th Avenue as far as Balboa Park. South of the Embarcadero on Harbor Drive is Seaport Village, 14 acres of shopping plazas designed to reflect the architectural styles of early California.

Coronado
Coronado, on an islandlike peninsula across the bay from San Diego's waterfront, is a historic Victorian village that grew up around the ornate Hotel Del Coronado, a celebrity hangout from the late 19th century and now a national historic site. Accessible from the San Diego–Coronado Bridge and the San Diego–Coronado Ferry, Coronado has wide, graceful streets, well-manicured neighborhood parks, and grand Victorian homes. By ordinance, no two houses here share the same building plan. Wealthy suburbanites and the Coronado Naval Base, which includes the North Island air station and amphibious base, also make their home here. Boutiques and restaurants line Orange Avenue, and you catch some rays and splash in the surf at Silver Strand State Beach and Imperial Beach, which extend in a long arc to the south.

Harbor Island and Shelter Island
A man-made strip of land in the bay directly across from San Diego International Airport and a short drive from downtown, Harbor Island has several hotels and restaurants and makes a good base for a visit to San Diego. Shelter Island, known for its yacht-building and sport fish-

ing industries, is just west of Harbor Island, also a short drive from downtown.

Point Loma

Standing as a buffer against the temperamental Pacific Ocean, Point Loma curves along San Diego Bay and extends south into the sea. Beyond its main streets, which are cluttered with fast-food restaurants and motels, Point Loma is made up of well-to-do neighborhoods and bay-side estates (it's a favorite retirement spot for naval officers). From the bay side you can enjoy a terrific view of downtown San Diego, and for an incomparable view of the Pacific head to Sunset Cliffs, between Point Loma and Ocean Beach, among the most dramatic places in San Diego to watch the sunset.

La Jolla

Spanish for "the jewel," La Jolla lives up to its name in both beauty and expense with its dramatic beachfront, spectacular views, and huge designer homes. Boutiques and restaurants cater to the affluent local gentry, but the largely unspoiled scenery of its coast, coves, and verdant hillsides is still free. North of Mission Bay, La Jolla can be approached on the meandering coastal road (Mission and La Jolla boulevards) or via Interstate 5.

Mission Bay and SeaWorld

The coastal Mission Bay area, located west of Interstate 5 and north of Interstate 8, is San Diego's monument to sports and fitness, where locals and visitors interested in boating, running, sunning, or jet skiing spend their days. Portions of the amorphous 4,600-acre aquatic park, which has numerous coves and inlets, 27 mi of bay front, and 17 mi of beachfront, are specifically designated for swimming, waterskiing, and sailing. Terrestrial types can jog, bike, rollerblade, play basketball, or fly a kite on the bay's peninsulas and two main islands, Vacation Island and Fiesta Island. SeaWorld, easily the most popular attraction in Mission Bay (and for some, in all of San Diego), displays fish and captive marine mammals, including sea otters, dolphins, seals, and the trademark killer whales.

Old Town

A few miles north of downtown and east of Interstate 5, Old Town is essentially a collection of remnants from the original San Diego, the first European settlement in California. The former pueblo of San Diego is now preserved as a state historic park and contains several original and reconstructed buildings. The historic sites are clustered around Old Town Plaza, which is bounded by Wallace Street, Calhoun Street, Mason Street, and San Diego Avenue.

Mission Valley

The business and commercial center of San Diego, Mission Valley is home to hundreds of shops in Fashion Valley Shopping Center, Hazard Center, and Westfield Shoppingtown Mission Valley. Hotel Circle is where many business people and sports fans stay. The Chargers and Padres play at Qualcomm Stadium; the stadium is also the site of the 2003 Super Bowl. Mission Valley is north of downtown and Hillcrest, on the San Diego River.

San Diego North County and Beyond

The seaside towns north of La Jolla developed separately from San Diego, and from one another. Del Mar is a seaside preserve with expensive lodging, exclusive boutiques, and fancy restaurants. Small Solana Beach, long known for its mellow ambience, is evolving into a trendy art and design center. Encinitas is justly famous for its fabulous fields of flowers and gardens, which extend inland from excellent surfing waters. Carlsbad, once known for its healing waters, now lures families to Legoland California, and Oceanside shows off its harbor and Mission San Luis Rey. The coastal portion of North County is best accessed via Interstate 5, but traveling along Route S21 (old Highway 101) once you reach the area will give you a better feel for the differences among the communities.

Even though the coast is only a short drive away, the North County beach communities seem far removed from the resort/retirement town of Rancho Bernardo, the quiet lakes of Escondido, the avocado-growing country surrounding Fallbrook, the former gold-mining town of Julian, or the vineyards of Temecula. Home to old missions, San Diego Wild Animal Park, the Welk Resort Center, and innumerable three-generation California families, the inland area of North County is the quiet, rural sister to the rest of San Diego County. The Cleveland National Forest and Anza-Borrego Desert State Park mark the county's eastern boundaries; the busiest international border in the United States is its southern line.

Tijuana and Playas de Rosarito

Tijuana, just 23 mi south of San Diego, has grown during the past 20 years from a border town of 700,000 to a city of almost 2 million inhabitants; it continues to attract hordes of "yanquis" with its designer boutiques, souvenir shops, sports events, and great Mexican dining. Laid-back Playas de Rosarito (Rosarito Beach), 18 mi farther south, has become something of a weekend hangout for southern Californians.

PLEASURES AND PASTIMES

Beaches

The coastline in and around San Diego encompasses some of the best beaches on the West Coast. Some are wide and sandy, others narrow and rocky; some are almost always crowded with athletes and sun-worshipers, others seem created for solitary beachcombers and romantic pairs. Among the standouts are Imperial Beach, a classic southern California beach favored by surfers, swimmers, and Frisbee fliers; Silver Strand State Beach, relatively calm and family-friendly, and the underused north and central portions of Municipal Beach on the isthmus of Coronado; Ocean Beach, a.k.a. Dog Beach because of the number of canines found romping next to volleyball players and sunbathers; Mission Beach, which has a boardwalk popular with walkers, rollerbladers, and bicyclists; La Jolla Cove, where tidal pools and cliff coves provide exciting diversions for explorers; and Torrey Pines State Beach between La Jolla and Del Mar, one of the most accessible beaches in the area.

Outdoor Activities and Sports

As you would expect, the emphasis is on fun in the sun and surf—sailing, swimming, surfing, diving, and fishing head the list. Some favorite activities and the best places to enjoy them include scuba diving off La Jolla Cove, surfing at almost any of the beaches, golfing at Torrey Pines, La Costa, or Rancho Bernardo, in-line skating at Mission Bay, jogging along the Embarcadero, playing volleyball on Ocean Beach, windsurfing on Mission Bay, and jet skiing at the Snug Harbor Marina in Carlsbad. But the San Diego area also contains vast open spaces—mesas, plateaus, canyons, and oak-studded foothills, which appeal to nature lovers, hikers, and mountain bikers.

Shopping

Horton Plaza, in the heart of downtown, is the place to go for department stores, mall shops, and one-of-a-kind boutiques; the adjoining Gaslamp Quarter is chock full of art galleries, antiques shops, and specialty stores. Seaport Village on the waterfront is thick with theme shops and arts-and-crafts galleries. Coronado has a few blocks of fancy boutiques and galleries as well as Ferry Landing Marketplace, a waterfront shopping and dining center. Bazaar del Mundo in the historic Old Town district resembles a colorful Mexican marketplace, where you can browse in shops selling international goods, toys, souvenirs, and arts and crafts. Hillcrest is the place to go for vintage clothing, furnishings, and accessories. La Jolla has a collection of trendy designer boutiques and galleries along Prospect Street and Girard Avenue. Discounted designer fashions can also be found at the popular Carlsbad Company Stores.

FODOR'S CHOICE

Special Moments

Ferrying across San Diego Harbor. The ferry between San Diego and Coronado provides spectacular views of the harbor, downtown, and Coronado.

A morning stroll about La Jolla Cove. Palm-lined Ellen Browning Scripps Park on the cliffs overlooking the cove is one of the prettiest spots in the world. Try breakfast on the patio at Brockton Villa, which has a fantastic view of the cove.

Spotting a gray whale spouting during the winter migration. As many as 200 whales pass the San Diego coast each day on their way south to Mexico (starting in mid-December) or back north (until mid-March).

Hiking at Cabrillo National Monument on Point Loma. Perched at the end of the peninsula, this 144-acre preserve of rugged cliffs and shores and outstanding overlooks was set aside as a National Park Service site to commemorate Portuguese explorer Juan Rodríguez Cabrillo.

A Sunday picnic in Balboa Park. Forget about the park's museums (for one day, anyway) and settle down to your own custom-made meal on a grassy spot near one of the park's many gardens.

Winter stargazing in Anza-Borrego Desert State Park. The absence of city lights in the clear winter sky provides a backdrop for a veritable cascade of stars, planets, constellations, meteor showers, and passing comets.

Twilight Hot Air Ballooning over coastal North County. Several companies will fly you up to see incredible views of nearly the entire county from the ocean to the mountains.

Dining

Azzura Point. Coronado's best restaurant will enchant you with lovely contemporary creations and a gorgeous view of downtown and the bay. $$$–$$$$

El Bizcocho. In Rancho Bernardo, a Spanish-style dining room is the setting for modern twists on classic cuisine. $$$–$$$$

Star of the Sea. This spot on the Embarcadero is one of San Diego's top seafood restaurants. The terrace takes great advantage of its choice waterfront location. $$$–$$$$

Tapenade. This superb Provençal restaurant on a quiet La Jolla side street serves brisk, earthy flavors in an intimate, bistro-like dining room or a spacious terrace. $$$–$$$$

George's at the Cove. It's hard to say what's better here: the stunning view overlooking La Jolla Cove or the superb cooking. $$$

Roppongi. This La Jolla eatery's signature global cuisine includes imaginative Euro-Asian tapas. $$–$$$

Emerald Chinese Seafood Restaurant. Refined, Hong Kong–style cuisine based on seafood scooped live from tanks is the specialty at this spacious, well-decorated establishment on San Diego's "Asian Restaurant Row." $–$$$

El Agave. Crispy, spicy, and mouthwatering are what you can expect at this casual Mexican eatery in Old Town. Any of 800 types of tequila are available for you to sample. $–$$

Sushi Ota. San Diego's best sushi is found in this unlikely space on Mission Bay Drive. $–$$

Lodging

Four Seasons Resort Aviara. This sophisticated resort offers supreme luxury and service in the North County community of Carlsbad. Atop a serene hill it overlooks Batiquitos Lagoon. $$$$

La Valencia. An art deco landmark near the La Jolla village shops and restaurants, the venerable La Valencia is still in great shape and continues to attract repeat visitors enchanted by its setting. $$$$

Manchester Grand Hyatt San Diego. This high-rise is in an unbeatable location next to Seaport Village. You can watch the sunset from the 40th-floor bar and restaurant. $$$$

Rancho Valencia Resort. Tennis players, horse owners, and other affluent outdoorsy types favor this Rancho Santa Fe hideaway for its contemporary West Coast ambience, colorful gardens, discreet service, and fine restaurant. $$$$

Heritage Park Inn. A beautiful restored Victorian home with a wraparound porch, a French toast breakfast, and old movies in the evening—what more could you want? $$–$$$

Gaslamp Plaza Suites. This Gaslamp Quarter hotel has comfortable European-style accommodations and serves a complimentary Continental breakfast on the rooftop terrace. $–$$

GREAT ITINERARIES

Many folks spend their time in San Diego just lazing away on a beach—if you're thus inclined, you'll enjoy some of the best sand and surf in the country. But the more energetic will find sufficient outlets to satisfy their sightseeing urges. The following suggested itineraries will help you structure your visit efficiently. See the neighborhood tours in Chapter 2 for more information about individual sights.

San Diego in 5 Days

Day One. Start with the San Diego Zoo in Balboa Park in the morning. It would be easy to spend your entire visit to the park here—and if you're traveling with kids, you may have little choice in the matter—but at least walk down El Prado with its rows of architecturally interesting museums. It's an easy walk from the zoo, or a five-minute drive south of the zoo on Park Boulevard.

Day Two. Start downtown at Seaport Village; after browsing the shops catch a ferry from the Broadway Pier to Coronado. From Coronado's Ferry Landing Marketplace board a bus going down Orange Avenue to see the town's Victorian extravaganza, the Hotel Del Coronado. Back in San Diego after lunch, stroll north on the Embarcadero to Ash Street; if you've returned from Coronado early enough, you can view the Maritime Museum or the San Diego Aircraft Carrier Museum, if it's open. If it's whale-watching season, skip the trip to Coronado, tour the Embarcadero in the late morning, have lunch, and book an afternoon excursion boat from the Broadway Pier. Another option is to spend the entire day with Shamu and the gang at SeaWorld of California.

Day Three. If you set out early enough, you might get a parking spot near La Jolla Cove. Watch the sea lions lounging on the beach at the Children's Pool and then head inland one block to Prospect Street, where you'll see the pink La Valencia hotel and a clutch of tony shops and galleries; this is also a good spot for an ocean-view lunch. Walk east on Prospect for a spin through the Museum of Contemporary Art, and then retrieve your car and head back into town on Interstate 5 to the Gaslamp Quarter, where you can explore the historic streets and perhaps stop by the adjacent Horton Plaza shopping mall. Dine at one of the many restaurants in the area, and drop into a coffeehouse or a nightclub for some music.

Day Four. Begin with a morning visit to Cabrillo National Monument. Have lunch at one of the seafood restaurants on Scott Street, and then head over to Old Town (take Rosecrans Street north to San Diego Avenue) to see portions of San Diego's earliest history brought to life. If the daily schedule lists low tide for the afternoon, reverse the order to catch the tide pools at Cabrillo.

Day Five. If you're traveling with young children, make Legoland California in Carlsbad your main destination for Day Five. En route to North County stop off at Torrey Pines State Park. If you're not going to Legoland, take Interstate 5 north to Del Mar for lunch, shopping, and sea views. A visit to Mission San Luis Rey, slightly inland from Oceanside on Highway 76, will infuse some history and culture into the tour.

If You Have More Time

Get an early start on Day Six and tour the San Diego Wild Animal Park. Then head east to historic Julian, where you can explore a gold mine and overnight or continue on to the town of Borrego Springs. Spend Day Seven (except in summer) at Anza-Borrego Desert State Park.

Another option would be to return to San Diego on the evening of Day Six and head to Mexico on Day Seven. If you'll only be visiting for the day, take the San Diego Trolley to Tijuana. If you're going to extend your stay in Mexico, take a car instead. After you visit Tijuana, continue south to Rosarito Beach, which has overnight accommodations—and great places to sip margaritas by the beach.

If You Have 3 Days

Follow the itinerary above for the first three days.

2 EXPLORING SAN DIEGO

Exploring San Diego is an endless adventure. To newcomers the city and county may seem like a conglomeration of theme parks: Old Town and the Gaslamp Quarter, historically oriented; the wharf area, a maritime playground; La Jolla, a throwback to southern California elegance; Balboa Park, a convergence of the town's cerebral and action-oriented personae. There are, of course, real theme parks— SeaWorld and the San Diego Zoo—but the great outdoors, in the form of forests, landscaped urban areas, and sandy beaches, is the biggest of them all.

By Edie Jarolim

Updated by
Rob Aikins

EXPLORING SAN DIEGO may be an endless adventure, but there are limitations, especially if you don't have a car. San Diego is more a chain of separate communities than a cohesive city, and many of the major attractions are separated by some distance. Walking is good for getting an up-close look at how San Diegans live, but true southern Californians use the freeways that crisscross the county. I–5 runs a direct north–south route through the coastal communities from Orange County in the north to the Mexican border. Interstates 805 and 15 do much the same inland, with I–8 as the main east–west route. Routes 163, 52, and 94 serve as connectors.

If you are going to drive around San Diego, study your maps before you hit the road. The freeways are convenient and fast most of the time, but if you miss your turnoff or get caught in commuter traffic, you'll experience a none-too-pleasurable hallmark of southern California living—freeway madness. Drivers rush around on a complex freeway system with the same fervor they use for jogging scores of marathons each year. They particularly enjoy speeding up at interchanges and entrance and exit ramps. Be sure you know where you're going before you join the chase.

Public transportation has improved a great deal in the past decade: the San Diego Trolley has expanded from Old Town to beyond Mission Valley; a commuter line called the *Coaster* runs from Oceanside into downtown; and the bus system covers almost all of the county. However, it's time-consuming to make the connections necessary to see the various sights. Fashion Valley Shopping Center in Mission Valley is one of the three major bus transfer points—downtown and Old Town are the others—but because many of the city's major attractions are along the coast, and because the coast is in itself a major attraction, you'll be best off staying there if you're carless. The bike-path system is extensive and well marked, the weather is almost always bicycle-friendly, and lots of buses have bike racks, so two-wheeling is a good option for the athletic. The large distances between sights render taxis prohibitively expensive for general transportation, although cabs are useful for getting around once you're in a given area. Old Town Trolley Historic Tours has a hop-on, hop-off route of eight popular spots around the city, but it takes so long to cover the route that you're unlikely to see more than two areas before having to catch the last trolley.

San Diego County's warm climate nurtures some amazing flora. Golden stalks of pampas grass grow in wild patches near SeaWorld. Bougainvilleas cover roofs and hillsides in La Jolla, spreading magenta blankets over whitewashed adobe walls. Towering palms and twisted junipers are far more common than maples or oaks, and fields of wild daisies and chamomile cover dry, dusty lots. Red and white poinsettias proliferate at Christmas, and candy-color pink- and yellow-flower ice plants edge the roads year-round. Jasmine blooms on bushes and vines in front yards and parking lots; birds-of-paradise poke up straight and tall, tropical testimonials to San Diego's temperate ways. Citrus groves pop up in unlikely places, along the freeways and back roads. When the orange, lemon, and lime trees bloom in spring, the fragrance of their tiny white blossoms is nearly overpowering. Be sure to drive with your windows down—you'll be amazed at the sweet, hypnotic scent.

Unless you're on the freeway, it's hard *not* to find a scenic drive in San Diego, but an officially designated 52-mi Scenic Drive over much of central San Diego begins at the foot of Broadway. Road signs with a white sea gull on a yellow-and-blue background direct the way through

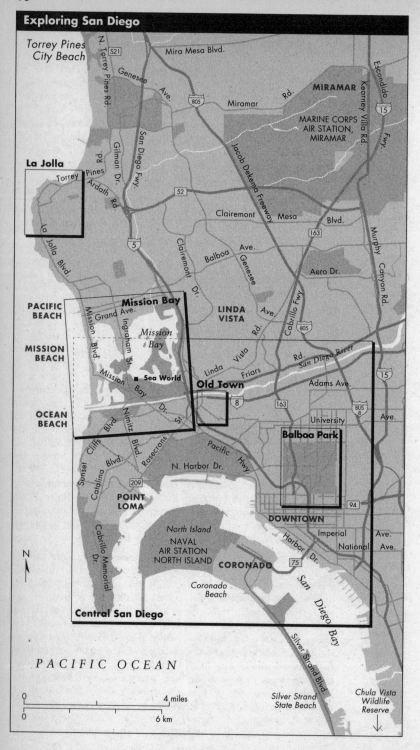

Exploring San Diego

Torrey Pines
City Beach

Mira Mesa Blvd.

MIRAMAR

MARINE CORPS
AIR STATION,
MIRAMAR

La Jolla

Torrey Pines

Clairemont Mesa Blvd.

Balboa Ave.

Aero Dr.

PACIFIC
BEACH

Mission Bay

LINDA
VISTA

MISSION
BEACH

Mission
Bay

Sea World

Old Town

Linda Vista

Friars Rd.
San Diego River

Adams Ave.

OCEAN
BEACH

University Ave.

Balboa Park

Pacific Hwy.

N. Harbor Dr.

POINT
LOMA

DOWNTOWN

Imperial

National Ave.

Coronado

North Island
NAVAL
AIR STATION
NORTH ISLAND

Harbor Dr.

San Diego Bay

N

Coronado
Beach

Central San Diego

PACIFIC OCEAN

0   4 miles
0   6 km

Silver Strand
State Beach

Chula Vista
Wildlife
Reserve

the Embarcadero to Harbor and Shelter islands, Point Loma and Cabrillo Monument, Mission Bay, Old Town, Balboa Park, Mount Soledad, and La Jolla. It's best to take this three-hour drive, outlined on some local maps, on the weekend, when the commuters are off the road.

BALBOA PARK

Overlooking downtown and the Pacific Ocean, 1,200-acre Balboa Park is the cultural heart of San Diego, where you'll find most of the city's museums and its world-famous zoo. Most first-time visitors just see the museums strung along El Prado and the animals, but Balboa Park is really a series of botanical gardens. Cultivated and wild gardens are an integral part of all of Balboa Park, thanks to the "Mother of Balboa Park," Kate Sessions, who first suggested that the park hire a landscape architect in 1889. She made sure both the park's developed and undeveloped acreage bloomed with the purple blossoms of the jacaranda tree and planted thousands of palms and other trees throughout. (A bronze statue of Sessions, unveiled in 1998, stands at Sefton Plaza at the west entrance to the park.) Left alone, Balboa Park would look like Florida Canyon—an arid landscape of sagebrush, cactus, and a few small trees—which lies between the main park and Morley Field, along Park Boulevard.

The parkland was set aside by the city's founders in 1868. (Only San Francisco's Golden Gate Park and New York's Central Park were established earlier.) In 1915 the park hosted the Panama–California International Exposition that celebrated the opening of the Panama Canal, and gained some Spanish colonial revival buildings meant to be temporary exhibit halls. City leaders realized the buildings' value and incorporated the structures into their plans for Balboa Park's acreage. The Spanish theme first instituted in the early 1900s was in part carried through in new buildings designed for the California Pacific International Exposition of 1935–36, but architectural details from the temples of the Maya and other indigenous peoples of the Americas were added.

The Laurel Street Bridge, also known as Cabrillo Bridge, is the park's official gateway; it leads over a vast canyon, filled with downtown commuter traffic on Route 163, to El Prado, which, beyond the art museum, becomes the park's central pedestrian mall. In recent years, many of the buildings on El Prado—the courtyard and walkway created for the 1915 exposition—have undergone major restoration or complete historic reconstruction. The 100-bell carillon in the California Tower, El Prado's highest structure, tolls the hour; figures of California's historic personages decorate the base of the 200-ft spire, and a magnificent blue-tile dome shines in the sun.

The parkland across the Cabrillo Bridge, at the west end of El Prado, has been set aside for picnics and athletics. Rollerbladers zip along Balboa Drive, which leads to the highest spot in the park, Marston Point, overlooking downtown. A throwback to an earlier era, ladies and gents in all-white outfits meet regularly on summer afternoons for lawn-bowling tournaments at the green beside the bridge. Dirt trails lead into pine groves with secluded picnic areas. Southwest of the museums along Park Boulevard, the park's main north–south thoroughfare, Pepper Grove has lots of picnic tables as well as ADA-accessible play equipment.

East of Plaza de Panama, El Prado becomes a pedestrian mall and ends at a footbridge that crosses over Park Boulevard to the perfectly tended Rose Garden, which has more than 2,000 rosebushes. In the adjacent

Cactus Garden, trails wind around prickly cacti and soft green succulents from around the world. Palm Canyon, north of the Spreckels Organ Pavilion, has more than 50 varieties of palms along a shady bridge.

Parking near Balboa Park's museums is no small accomplishment, especially on sunny summer days, when the lots, which are all free, fill up quickly. If you're driving in via the Laurel Street Bridge, the first parking area you'll come to is off El Prado to the right, going toward Pan American Plaza. Don't despair if there are no spaces here; you'll see more lots as you continue down along the same road. If you end up parking a bit far from your destination, consider the stroll back through the greenery part of the day's recreational activities. Alternatively, you can just park at Inspiration Point on the east side of the park, off Presidents Way. Free trams run from there to the museums every 8–10 minutes, 9:30–5:30 daily.

Numbers in the text correspond to numbers in the margin and on the Balboa Park map.

Two Good Walks

It's impossible to cover all the park's museums in one day, so choose your focus before you head out. If your interests run to the aesthetic, the Museum of Photographic Arts, the San Diego Museum of Art, the Mingei International Museum of Folk Art, and the Timken Museum of Art should be on your list; architecture buffs will want to add the Marston House. Those with a penchant for natural and cultural history shouldn't miss the San Diego Natural History Museum and the Museum of Man; folks oriented toward space and technology should see the Reuben H. Fleet Science Center, the San Diego Aerospace Museum, and the San Diego Automotive Museum. If you're traveling with kids, the Mingei and Reuben H. Fleet are musts.

On a nice day, you might just want to stroll outside and enjoy the architecture of the museum complex, with its wonderful Spanish and Mexican designs. A walk along El Prado is about 1 mi round-trip.

Enter via Cabrillo Bridge through the West Gate, which depicts the Panama Canal's linkage of the Atlantic and Pacific oceans. Park south of the **Alcazar Garden** ①. It's a short stretch north across El Prado to the landmark California Building, modeled on a cathedral in Mexico and now home to the **San Diego Museum of Man** ②. Look up to see busts and statues of heroes of the early days of the state. Next door are the **Globe Theatres** ③, which adjoin the sculpture garden of the **San Diego Museum of Art** ④, an ornate Plateresque-style structure built to resemble the 17th-century University of Salamanca in Spain.

Continuing east you'll come to the **Timken Museum of Art** ⑤, the **Botanical Building** ⑥, and the Spanish colonial revival–style Casa del Prado, where the San Diego Floral Association has its offices and a gift shop. At the end of the row is the **San Diego Natural History Museum** ⑦; you'll have to detour a block north to visit the **Spanish Village Art Center** ⑧. If you were to continue north, you would come to the **carousel** ⑨, the **miniature railroad** ⑩, and, finally, the entrance to the **San Diego Zoo** ⑪.

Return to the Natural History Museum and cross the Plaza de Balboa— its large central fountain is a popular meeting spot—to reach the **Reuben H. Fleet Science Center** ⑫. (Beyond the parking lot to the south lies the **Centro Cultural de la Raza** ⑬.) You're now on the opposite side of the Prado and heading west. You'll next pass **Casa de Balboa** ⑭; inside are the model-railroad and photography museums and the historical society. Next door in the newly reconstructed **House of Hospitality** ⑮ is the Balboa Park Visitors Center, where you can buy a reduced-price pass to the museums, and the Prado restaurant. Across the Plaza de Panama, the Franciscan mission–style **House of Charm** ⑯ houses a folk art museum and a gallery for San Diego artists. Your starting point, the Alcazar Garden, is west of the House of Charm.

A second walk leads south from the Plaza de Panama, which doubles as a parking lot. The majority of the buildings along this route date to the 1935 fair, when the architecture of the Maya and native peoples of the Southwest was highlighted. The first sight you'll pass is the **Japanese Friendship Garden** ⑰. Next comes the ornate, crownlike **Spreckels Organ Pavilion** ⑱. The round seating area forms the base, with the stage as its diadem. The road forks here; veer to the left to reach the **House of Pacific Relations** ⑲, a Spanish mission–style cluster of cottages and one of the few structures on this route built for the earlier exposition. Another is the Balboa Park Club, which you'll pass next. Now used for park receptions and banquets, the building resembles a mission church; you might want to step inside to see the huge mural. Continue on beyond the Palisades Building, which hosts the Marie Hitchcock Puppet Theater, to reach the **San Diego Automotive Museum** ⑳, appropriately housed in the building that served as the Palace of Transportation in the 1935–36 exposition.

The road loops back at the spaceshiplike **San Diego Aerospace Museum and International Aerospace Hall of Fame** ㉑. As you head north again you'll notice the Starlight Bowl, an amphitheater on your right. Next comes perhaps the most impressive structure on this tour, the Federal Building, the new home of the **San Diego Hall of Champions** ㉒. Its main entrance was modeled after the Palace of Governors in the ancient Mayan city of Uxmal, Mexico. You'll be back at the Spreckels Organ Pavilion after this, having walked a little less than a mile.

TIMING

Unless you're pressed for time, you'll want to devote an entire day to the perpetually expanding zoo; there are more than enough exhibits to keep you occupied for five or more hours, and you're likely to be too tired for museum-hopping when you're through. The zoo is free for kids the entire month of October.

Although some of the park's museums are open on Monday, most are open Tuesday–Sunday 10–4; in summer a number have extended hours—phone ahead to ask. On Tuesday the museums have free admission to their permanent exhibits on a rotating basis; call the Balboa Park Visitors Center for a schedule. Free architectural, historical, or nature tours depart from the visitor center every Saturday at 10, while park ranger–led tours start out from the visitor center at 1 PM every Wednesday and Sunday. Free concerts take place Sunday afternoons at 2 PM year-round and summer Monday evenings at the Spreckels Organ Pavilion, and the House of Pacific Relations hosts Sunday-afternoon folk-dance performances. Christmas on the Prado, celebrated the first Friday and Saturday in December, is not to be missed, while Buds 'n Blooms, throughout the month of May, dazzles with colorful extravaganzas like floral interpretations of 150 paintings housed at the San Diego Museum of Art.

Sights to See

❶ **Alcazar Garden.** The gardens surrounding the Alcazar Castle in Seville, Spain, inspired the landscaping here; you'll feel like royalty resting on the benches by the tiled fountains. The flower beds are ever-changing horticultural exhibits, with bright orange and yellow poppies blooming in spring and deep rust and crimson chrysanthemums appearing

Balboa Park

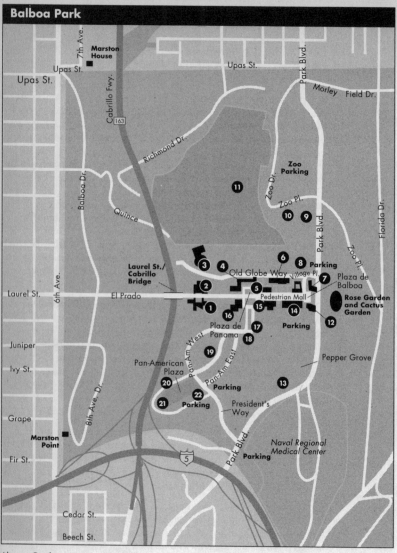

in fall. It's next to the House of Charm and across from the Museum of Man. *Off El Prado, Balboa Park.*

6 **Botanical Building.** The graceful redwood-lathed structure, built for the 1915 Panama-California International Exposition, now houses more than 2,000 types of tropical and subtropical plants plus changing seasonal displays. Ceiling-high tree ferns shade fragile orchids and feathery bamboo. There are benches beside miniature waterfalls for resting in the shade. The rectangular pond outside, filled with lotuses and water lilies, is popular with photographers. ⊠ *1550 El Prado, Balboa Park,* ☎ *619/239–0512.* ⊡ *Free.* ☉ *Fri.–Wed. 10–4.*

9 **Carousel.** Riders on this antique merry-go-round stretch from their seats to grab the brass rings suspended an arm's-length away to earn a free ride (it's one of the few carousels in the world where you can still grab yourself a bonus). Hand-carved in 1910, the bobbing animals include zebras, giraffes, and dragons; real horsehair was used for the tails. ⊠ *1889 Zoo Pl. (behind zoo parking lot), Balboa Park.* ⊡ *$1.25.* ☉ *Daily 11–6 during extended summer vacation; during school yr, only school holidays and weekends 11–5:30.*

14 **Casa de Balboa.** This building on El Prado's southeast corner houses three museums: the Museum of Photographic Arts, the San Diego Historical Society, and the San Diego Model Railroad Museum. ⊠ *1649 El Prado, Balboa Park.*

13 **Centro Cultural de la Raza.** An old water tower was converted into this center for Mexican, Native American, and Chicano arts. Attractions include a gallery with rotating exhibits and a theater, as well as a collection of mural art, a fine example of which may be seen on the tower's exterior. ⊠ *2004 Park Blvd., Balboa Park,* ☎ *619/235–6135,* WEB *www.centroraza.org.* ⊡ *Donation suggested.* ☉ *Thurs.–Sun. noon–5.*

OFF THE
BEATEN PATH

HILLCREST – Northwest of Balboa Park, Hillcrest is San Diego's center for the gay community and artists of all types. University, 4th, and 5th avenues are filled with cafés and interesting boutiques, including several indie new and used bookstores along 5th below University. Chain stores and eateries have been making strong inroads, however, and the self-contained residential-commercial Uptown District, on University Avenue at 8th Avenue, was built to resemble an inner-city neighborhood, with shops and restaurants within easy walking distance of high-price town houses. To the northeast, Adams Avenue, reached via Park Boulevard heading north off Washington Street, has many antiques stores. Adams Avenue leads east into Kensington, a handsome old neighborhood that overlooks Mission Valley.

3 **The Globe Theatres.** Even if you're not attending a play, this complex, comprising the Cassius Carter Centre Stage, the Lowell Davies Festival Theatre, and the Old Globe Theatre, is a pleasant place to relax between museum visits. The theaters, done in a California version of Tudor style, sit between the Sculpture Garden of the San Diego Museum of Art and the California Tower. A gift shop (open Tuesday–Sunday noon–9:30 when there are performances, noon–5 other days) sells theater-related wares, including posters, cards, and brightly colored puppets. ⊠ *1363 Old Globe Way, Balboa Park,* ☎ *619/239–2255,* WEB *www.theglobetheatres.org.*

16 **House of Charm.** This structure was rebuilt in the mid-1990s from the ground up to replicate the Franciscan Mission style of the original expo building. Inside are the main branch of the Mingei International

Museum of Folk Art and the San Diego Art Institute. ✉ *1439 El Prado, Balboa Park.*

⑮ House of Hospitality. In the Balboa Park Visitors Center's building, you can pick up schedules and route maps for the free trams that operate around the park. You can also purchase the Best of Balboa Park Combo, which affords entry to 13 museums and the zoo for $55; it's worthwhile if you want to visit more than a few museums and aren't entitled to the discounts that most give to children, senior citizens, and military personnel. In addition, you can pick up a flyer that details the excellent free park tours that depart from here (or phone for a schedule). Even if you don't want information or a discount pass, stop by to look at the beautiful new structure, which has won myriad awards for its painstaking attention to historical detail; 2,000 paint scrapes were taken, for example, to get the art deco colors exactly right. ✉ *1549 El Prado, Balboa Park,* ☎ *619/239–0512,* WEB *www.balboapark.org.* ☉ *Daily 9–4.*

⑲ House of Pacific Relations. This is not really a house but a cluster of red tile–roof, stucco cottages representing some 30 foreign countries. And the word "pacific" refers not to the ocean—most of the nations represented are European, not Asian—but to the goal of maintaining peace. The cottages, decorated with crafts and pictures, hold open houses each Sunday afternoon, during which you can chat with transplanted natives and try out different ethnic foods. From the first Sunday in March through the last Sunday in October folk song and dance performances take place on the outdoor stage around 2 PM—check the schedule at the park visitor center. Across the road from the cottages but not affiliated with them is the Spanish colonial–style **United Nations Building.** Inside, the United Nations Association's International Gift Shop, open daily, has reasonably priced crafts, cards, and books. ✉ *2160 Pan American Rd. W, Balboa Park,* ☎ *619/234–0739.* 🎟 *Free.* ☉ *Sun. noon–5; hrs may vary with season.*

⑰ Japanese Friendship Garden. A koi pond with a cascading water wall, a 60-ft-long wisteria arbor, a large activity center, and a sushi bar are highlights of the park's authentic Japanese garden, designed to inspire contemplation. You can wander the various peaceful paths, meditate in the traditional stone-and-sand garden, or, at times, learn such arts as origami and flower arranging at the exhibit hall. ✉ *2215 Pan American Rd., Balboa Park,* ☎ *619/232–2780,* WEB *www.niwa.org.* 🎟 *$3.* ☉ *Tues.–Sun. 10–4.*

Marston House. George W. Marston (1850–1946), a San Diego pioneer and philanthropist who financed the architectural landscaping of Balboa Park—among his myriad other San Diego civic projects—was visited by such prominent people as President Teddy Roosevelt and Booker T. Washington. His 16-room home at the northwest edge of the park, now maintained by the San Diego Historical Society, was designed in 1905 by San Diego architects Irving Gill and William Hebbard. It's a classic example of the American Arts and Crafts style, which emphasizes simplicity and functionality of form, as are the furnishings, which include pieces by Tiffany, Roycroft, and Gustav Stickley. On the 5-acre grounds is a lovely English Romantic garden, as interpreted in California. Hour-long docent tours—the only way to see the house—illuminate many aspects of San Diego history in which the Marstons played a part. ✉ *3525 7th Ave., Balboa Park,* ☎ *619/298–3142.* 🎟 *$5.* ☉ *Fri.–Sun. 10–4 (last tour at 3:15).*

★ ☺ **⑯ Mingei International Museum.** All ages will enjoy the colorful and creative exhibits of toys, pottery, textiles, costumes, and gadgets from around the globe at the Mingei. Traveling and permanent exhibits in the high-ceiling, light-filled museum include everything from antique American carousel horses to the latest in Japanese ceramics. The name Mingei comes from the Japanese words *min*, meaning "all people," and *gei*, meaning "art." Thus, the museum's name describes what you'll find under its roof: "art of all people." It's hard to predict what you'll see, but you can depend on it being delightful. ⊠ *House of Charm, 1439 El Prado, Balboa Park,* ☎ *619/239–0003,* WEB *www.mingei.org.* ⊡ *$5.* ☉ *Tues.–Sun. 10–4.*

☺ ⑩ **Miniature railroad.** Adjacent to the zoo parking lot, a pint-size, 48-passenger train runs a ½-mi loop through eucalyptus groves. The engine of this rare 1948 model train is a small-scale version of a General Motors F-3 locomotive. ⊠ *2885 Zoo Pl., Balboa Park,* ☎ *619/239–4748.* ⊡ *$1.25.* ☉ *Weekends and school holidays 11–5; during school summer break, daily 11–5.*

☺ **Morley Field Sports Complex.** The park's athletic center has a flying-disc golf course, with challenging "holes"—wire baskets hung from metal poles—where players toss their Frisbees over canyons and tree-tops to reach their goal. Morley Field also has a public pool, a velodrome, an archery range, playgrounds, and boccie, badminton, and tennis courts. The complex is at the northeast corner of Balboa Park, across Park Boulevard and Florida Canyon. ⊠ *2221 Morley Field Dr., Balboa Park,* ☎ *619/692–4919.*

★ ⑭ **Museum of Photographic Arts.** World-renowned photographers such as Ansel Adams, Imogen Cunningham, Henri Cartier-Bresson, and Edward Weston are represented in the permanent collection, which includes everything from 19th-century daguerreotypes to contemporary photojournalism prints and Russian Constructivist images (with many by Alexander Rodchenko). The 28,000-square-ft facility has a state-of-the-art theater for screening cinema classics as well as a learning center. On Thursday nights, the museum is open late for movie presentations and the occasional jazz recital. ⊠ *Casa de Balboa, 1649 El Prado, Balboa Park,* ☎ *619/238–7559,* WEB *www.mopa.org.* ⊡ *$6 for museum, $5 for theater.* ☉ *Daily 10–5, (til 9 on Thurs.).*

★ ☺ ⑫ **Reuben H. Fleet Science Center.** Children and adults alike enjoy the Fleet Center's clever interactive exhibits that are sneakily educational. You can reconfigure your face to have two left sides, or, by replaying an instant video clip, watch yourself coming and going at different speeds. The IMAX Dome Theater screens exhilarating nature and science films. The SciTours simulator is designed to take you on virtual voyages—stomach lurches and all. The Meteor Storm lets up to six players at a time have an interactive virtual-reality experience, this one sans motion sickness potential. ⊠ *1875 El Prado, Balboa Park,* ☎ *619/238–1233,* WEB *www.rhfleet.org.* ⊡ *Gallery exhibits $6.75; Gallery exhibits and one IMAX film $11.50; Gallery exhibits and two IMAX films $15.* ☉ *Mon.–Thurs. 9:30–5, Fri.–Sat. 9:30–8, Sun. 9:30–6 (hrs vary seasonally; call ahead).*

㉑ **San Diego Aerospace Museum and International Aerospace Hall of Fame.** The streamlined edifice commissioned by the Ford Motor Company for the 1935–36 exposition looks unlike any other structure in the park; at night, with a line of blue neon outlining it, the round building appears—appropriately enough—to be a landlocked UFO. Every available inch of space in the rotunda is filled with exhibits about aviation and aerospace pioneers, including examples of enemy planes during the world wars. A collection of real and replicated aircraft fills the central courtyard. ⊠ *2001 Pan American Plaza, Balboa Park,* ☎ *619/234–8291,* WEB *www.aerospacemuseum.org.* ⊡ *$8. Behind-the-scenes restorations are an extra $3.* ☉ *Daily 10–4:30 (5:30 in summer).*

⑯ **San Diego Art Institute.** Outside juries decide which works created by members of the Art Institute will be displayed in rotating shows, which change every six weeks. Painting, sculpture, watercolor—everything except crafts, reserved for the excellent small gift shop—are represented. The David Fleet Young Artists Gallery shows art executed by students at area schools. ✉ *House of Charm, 1439 El Prado, Balboa Park,* ☎ *619/236–0011,* WEB *www.sandiego-art.org.* ✑ *$3.* ☉ *Tues.–Sat. 10–4, Sun. noon–4.*

⑳ **San Diego Automotive Museum.** Even if you don't know a choke from a chassis, you're bound to admire the sleek designs of the autos in this impressive museum. The core collection comprises vintage motorcycles and cars, ranging from an 1886 Benz to a De Lorean, as well as a series of rotating exhibits from collections around the world. There's an ongoing automobile restoration program, and the museum sponsors many outdoor automotive events; call to find out about any rallies or concours d'elegance that might be scheduled. ✉ *2080 Pan American Plaza, Balboa ParK,* ☎ *619/231–2886,* WEB *www.sdautomuseum.org.* ✑ *$7.* ☉ *Daily 10–5 (last admission at 4:30).*

⊙ ㉒ **San Diego Hall of Champions.** In a 70,000-square-ft building, this museum celebrates local jock heroes via a vast collection of memorabilia, uniforms, paintings, photographs, and computer and video displays. An amusing bloopers film is screened at the Sports Theater. The Center Court activity area hosts changing programs—everything from a Chargers mini-training camp to interactive bobsled races. ✉ *Federal Bldg., 2131 Pan American Rd., Balboa Park,* ☎ *619/234–2544,* WEB *www.sandiegosports.org.* ✑ *$4.* ☉ *Daily 10–4.*

⑭ **San Diego Historical Society.** The San Diego Historical Society maintains its research library in the Casa de Balboa's basement and organizes shows on the first floor. Permanent and rotating exhibits, which are often more lively than you might expect, survey local urban history after 1850, when California entered the Union. A 100-seat theater hosts public lectures, workshops, and educational programs, and a gift shop carries a good selection of books on local history as well as reproductions of old posters and other historical collectibles. ✉ *Casa de Balboa, 1649 El Prado, Balboa Park,* ☎ *619/232–6203,* WEB *www. sandiegohistory.org.* ✑ *$5.* ☉ *Tues.–Sun. 10–4:30.*

⊙ ⑭ **San Diego Model Railroad Museum.** When the impressive, giant-scale exhibits of model trains of the Southwest are in operation, you'll hear the sounds of chugging engines, screeching brakes, and shrill whistles. And if you come in through the back door on Tuesday and Friday evenings, 7:30–11, there's no charge to watch the model-train layouts being created. Children under 15 get in free with an adult. ✉ *Casa de Balboa, 1649 El Prado, Balboa Park,* ☎ *619/696–0199,* WEB *www. sdmodelrailroadm.com.* ✑ *$4.* ☉ *Tues.–Fri. 11–4, weekends 11–5.*

★ ❹ **San Diego Museum of Art.** Known primarily for its Spanish Baroque and Renaissance paintings, including works by El Greco, Goya, Rubens, and van Ruisdael, San Diego's most comprehensive art museum also has strong holdings of South Asian art, Indian miniatures, and contemporary California paintings. The Baldwin M. Baldwin collection includes more than 100 pieces by Toulouse-Lautrec. If traveling shows from other cities come to San Diego, you can expect to see them here. An outdoor Sculpture Garden exhibits both traditional and modern pieces. The IMAGE (Interactive Multimedia Art Gallery Explorer) system allows you to call up the highlights of the museum's collection on a computer screen and custom-design a tour, call up historical information on the works and artists, and print color reproductions. Free docent tours are offered throughout the day. ⊠ *Casa de Balboa, 1450 El Prado, Balboa Park,* ☎ *619/232–7931,* WEB *www.sdmart.org.* ☑ *$8 ($10–$12 for special exhibits).* ⊘ *Tues.–Sun. 10–6 (till 9 on Thurs.).*

NEED A BREAK?	Take a respite from museum-hopping with a cup of coffee or a glass of California chardonnay in the San Diego Museum of Art's **Sculpture Garden Café** (☎ 619/696–1990), which also has a small selection of tasty sandwiches and salads Tuesday–Sunday 8:30–4 (it's often open for dinner, too, in the summer). You can also get coffee and various noshes from a food cart outside the café.

❷ San Diego Museum of Man. Exhibits at this highly respected anthropological museum focus on Southwestern, Mexican, and South American cultures. Carved monuments from the Mayan city of Quirigua in Guatemala, cast from the originals in 1914, are particularly impressive. Rotating shows might include examples of intricate beadwork from across the Americas, and demonstrations of such skills as weaving and tortilla-making are held regularly. Among the museum's more recent additions is the hands-on Children's Discovery Center. ⊠ *California Bldg., 1350 El Prado, Balboa Park,* ☎ *619/239–2001,* WEB *www. museumofman.org.* ☑ *$6.* ⊘ *Daily 10–4:30.*

☙ ❼ San Diego Natural History Museum. In 2001 the museum opened an annex with a grand atrium and a 300-seat theater that more than doubled the museum's size to 150,000 square ft. The new annex, part of a six-year renovation project that began in 1998, will house most of the permanent exhibits while the original building undergoes further restoration. Favorite exhibits include the Foucault pendulum, suspended on a 43-ft cable and designed to demonstrate the Earth's rotation; a full-size grey whale skeleton; and *Ocean Oasis,* the world's first large-format film about Baja California and the Sea of Cortés. Some exhibits may not be available during the renovation. The nature paintings of the California Impressionists and the wilderness photography of Robert Turner are scheduled to be on display in 2003. Call ahead for information on films, lectures, and free guided nature walks. ⊠ *1788 El Prado, Balboa Park,* ☎ *619/232–3821,* WEB *www.sdnhm.org.* ☑ *$5– $7, depending on exhibits.* ⊘ *Labor Day–Memorial Day, daily 9:30– 4:30; Memorial Day–Labor Day, daily 9:30–5:30.*

★ ☙ ⓫ San Diego Zoo. Balboa Park's—and perhaps the city's—most famous attraction is its 100-acre zoo, and it deserves all the press it gets. Nearly 4,000 animals of some 800 diverse species roam in hospitable, expertly crafted habitats that replicate natural environments as closely as possible. The flora in the zoo, including many rare species, is even more costly than the fauna. Walkways wind over bridges and past waterfalls ringed with tropical ferns; elephants in a sandy plateau roam so close you're tempted to pet them.

Exploring the zoo fully requires the stamina of a healthy hiker, but open-air trams that run throughout the day let you zip through 80% of the exhibits on a 35-minute, 3-mi tour. The Kangaroo bus tours include the same informed and amusing narrations as the others, but for a few dollars more you can get on and off as you like at eight stops. The Skyfari ride, which soars 170 ft above the ground, gives a good overview of the zoo's layout and, on clear days, a panorama of the park, downtown San Diego, the bay, and the ocean, far past the Coronado–San Diego Bay Bridge. Unless you come early, however, expect to wait to be moved around. The line for the regular tram, and especially for the top tier, can take more than 45 minutes; if you come at midday on a weekend or school holiday, you'll be doing the in-line shuffle for a while.

In any case, the zoo is at its best when you wander the paths, such as the one that climbs through the huge, enclosed **Scripps Aviary,** where brightly colored tropical birds swoop between branches just inches from your face, and into the neighboring **Gorilla Tropics,** among the zoo's latest ventures into bioclimatic zone exhibits. Here animals live in enclosed environments modeled on their native habitats. These zones may look natural, but they're helped a lot by modern technology: the sounds of the tropical rain forest emerge from a 144-speaker sound system that plays CDs recorded in Africa.

The zoo's simulated Asian rain forest, **Tiger River,** has 10 exhibits with more than 35 species of animals; tigers, Malayan tapirs, and Argus pheasants wander among the collection of exotic trees and plants. The mist-shrouded trails winding down a canyon into Tiger River pass by fragrant jasmine, ginger lilies, and orchids, giving you the feeling of descending into an Asian jungle. In **Sun Bear Forest** playful beasts constantly claw apart the trees and shrubs that serve as a natural playground for climbing, jumping, and general merrymaking. At the popular **Polar Bear Plunge,** where you can watch the featured animals take a chilly dive, Siberian reindeer, white foxes, and other Arctic creatures are separated from their predatory neighbors by a series of camouflaged moats. **Ituri Forest**—a 4-acre African rain forest at the base of Tiger River—lets you glimpse huge but surprisingly graceful hippos frolicking underwater, and buffalo cavorting with monkeys on dry land.

The San Diego Zoo houses the largest number of koalas outside Australia, and they remain major crowd pleasers, but these and other zoo locals are being overshadowed by the hoopla surrounding some overseas visitors and their offspring: Shi Shi and Bai Yun, a pair of giant pandas on loan for 12 years for conservation and behavior research from the People's Republic of China, are the parents to a female giant panda, Hua Mei. Born in August of 1999, she is the first cub born in the Western Hemisphere in a decade and the first born in the United States to survive past four days. Hua Mei, her mother (Bai Yun), and her father (Shi Shi) are on exhibit daily. Exact viewing times for each day vary but are posted at the zoo entrance. Another way to get a glimpse of these engaging bears is by watching them on the Panda Cam of the San Diego Zoo's Web site.

For a guaranteed hands-on experience there's the **Children's Zoo,** where goats, sheep, bunnies, and guinea pigs beg to be petted. There are two viewer-friendly nurseries where you may see various baby animals bottle feed and sleep peacefully in large-size baby cribs. Children can see entertaining creatures of all sorts at the Wegeforth National Park Sea Lion Show and the Wild Ones Show. Both are put on daily in a 3,000-outdoor seating amphitheater.

The zoo rents strollers, wheelchairs, and cameras; it also has a first-aid office, a lost and found, and an ATM. It's best to avert your eyes from the zoo's two main gift shops until the end of your visit; you can spend a half day just poking through the wonderful animal-related posters, crafts, dishes, clothing, and toys. One guilt-alleviating fact if you buy too much: some of the profits of your purchases go to zoo programs. Audio tours, behind-the-scenes tours, walking tours, tours in Spanish, and tours for people with hearing or vision impairments are available; inquire at the entrance. ⊠ *2920 Zoo Dr., Balboa Park,* ☎ *619/231–1515; 888/697–2632 Giant panda hot line,* WEB *www.sandiegozoo.org.* ⊡ *$19.50 includes zoo, Children's Zoo, and animal shows; $32 includes above, plus 40-min guided bus tour and round-trip Skyfari ride; Kangaroo bus tour $12 additional (only $3 additional for purchasers of $32 deluxe package); zoo free for children under 12* *in Oct. and for all on Founder's Day (1st Mon. in Oct.); $46.80 pass good for admission to zoo and San Diego Wild Animal Park within 5 days. AE, D, MC, V. ☉ May–Sept., daily 9–9; Sept.–May, daily 9–4; Children's Zoo and Skyfari ride close earlier.*

NEED A
BREAK?

Plenty of **food stands** sell popcorn, pizza, and enormous ice-cream cones at the zoo. If you want to eat among strolling peacocks—who will try to cadge your food—consider the **Flamingo Café,** inside the main entrance, serving sandwiches, salads, and light meals. Of the zoo's indoor restaurants, the best is **Albert's,** part of a three-tier dining complex near Gorilla Tropics. Grilled fish, homemade pizza, and fresh pasta are among the offerings, and this is the only place where wine and beer are sold.

⑧ Spanish Village Art Center. Glassblowers, enamel workers, wood-carvers, sculptors, painters, jewelers, photographers, and other artists rent space in the 35 red tile–roof studio-galleries that were set up for the 1935–36 exposition in the style of an ancient Spanish village. The artists give demonstrations of their work on a rotating basis, aware, no doubt, that it's fun to buy wares that you've watched being created. ⊠ *1770 Village Pl., Balboa Park,* ☎ *619/233–9050,* WEB *www.spanishvillageart.com.* 🎟 *Free.* ☉ *Daily 11–4.*

⑱ Spreckels Organ Pavilion. The 2,000-seat pavilion, dedicated in 1915 by sugar magnates John D. and Adolph B. Spreckels, holds the 4,445-pipe Spreckels Organ, the largest outdoor pipe organ in the world. You can hear this impressive instrument at one of the year-round, 2 PM Sunday concerts, regularly performed by civic organist Carol Williams. On Monday evenings in summer, military bands, gospel groups, and barbershop quartets also perform. At Christmastime the park's Christmas tree and life-size Nativity display turn the pavilion into a seasonal wonderland. ⊠ *2211 Pan American Rd., Balboa Park,* ☎ *619/702–8138.*

⑤ Timken Museum of Art. Somewhat out of place in the architectural scheme of the park, this modern structure is made of travertine marble imported from Italy. The small museum houses works by major European and American artists as well as a superb collection of Russian icons. ⊠ *1500 El Prado, Balboa Park,* ☎ *619/239–5548,* WEB *www.timkenmuseum.org.* 🎟 *Free.* ☉ *Tues.–Sat. 10–4:30, Sun. 1:30–4:30.*

DOWNTOWN

Downtown is San Diego's Lazarus. Written off as moribund by the 1970s, when few people willingly stayed in the area after dark, downtown is now one of the city's prime draws for tourists and real estate agents. Massive redevelopment started in the late 1970s, giving rise to the Gaslamp Quarter Historic District, Horton Plaza shopping center, and San Diego Convention Center, which have spurred an upsurge of elegant hotels, upscale condominium complexes, and swank, trendy cafés and restaurants that have people lingering downtown well into the night—if not also waking up there the next morning.

Downtown's natural attributes were easily evident to its original booster, Alonzo Horton (1813–1909), who arrived in San Diego in 1867. Horton looked at the bay and the acres of flatland surrounded by hills and canyons and knew he had found San Diego's heart. Although Old Town, under the Spanish fort at the Presidio, had been settled for years, Horton understood that it was too far away from the water to take hold as the commercial center of San Diego. He bought 960 acres along the bay at 27½¢ per acre and gave away the land to those who would develop it or build houses. Within months he had sold or given away 226 city blocks.

The transcontinental railroad arrived in 1885, and the land boom was on. Although the railroad's status as a cross-country route was short lived, the population soared from 5,000 to 35,000 in less than a decade—a foreshadowing of San Diego's future. In 1887 the Santa Fe Depot was constructed at the foot of Broadway, two blocks from the water. Freighters chugged in and out of the harbor, and by the early 1900s the U.S. Navy had moved in.

As downtown grew into San Diego's transportation and commercial hub, residential neighborhoods blossomed along the beaches and inland valleys. The business district gradually moved farther away from the original heart of downtown, at 5th Avenue and Market Street, past Broadway, up toward Balboa Park. Downtown's waterfront fell into bad times during World War I, when sailors, gamblers, and prostitutes were drawn to one another and the waterfront bars.

But Alonzo Horton's modern-day followers, city leaders intent on prospering while preserving San Diego's natural beauty, reclaimed the downtown area. The Centre City Development Corporation (CCDC), a public, nonprofit organization, spearheaded development of the Gaslamp District in 1975, which attracted a groundswell of investment after the adjacent Horton Plaza shopping complex opened to huge success in 1985. This in turn led the way for the hotels, restaurants, shopping centers, and housing developments that are now rising on every square inch of available space. Waterfront transformation also proceeded apace, as old shipyards and canneries were replaced by hotel towers and waterfront parks. The Martin Luther King Jr. Promenade project, which cost an estimated $25 million by the time it was completed in early 1999, put 14 acres of greenery, a pedestrian walkway, and lots of artwork along Harbor Drive from Seaport Village to the convention center, and landscaped the railroad right-of-way from the Santa Fe depot to 8th Avenue. The San Diego Convention Center, which hosted its first events in 1990, proved so successful with events like the 1996 Republican National Convention that it has doubled in size to about 1.7 million square ft.

Of the newest downtown projects—there are more than 100 in the works—the most ambitious is the 26-block Ballpark District, slated to occupy the East Village area that extends between the railroad tracks up to J Street, and from 6th Avenue east to around 10th Street. It will include a new 42,000-seat baseball stadium for the San Diego Padres; a distinctively San Diego–style, 8-acre "Park at the Park" from which fans can watch games while picnicking, containing gardens, an amphitheater, and a kids entertainment area; a sports-related retail complex; at least 850 hotel rooms; and several apartment and condominium complexes. The project was scheduled to be completed in 2003, and ground was broken for it in 1999, but a series of legal problems has held everything up—except the development fever that the delay has done nothing to dissipate. The ballpark is now slated to be ready for the Padres' season opener in April 2004.

Downtown's main thoroughfares are Harbor Drive, running along the waterfront; Broadway, through the center of downtown; and 6th Avenue, between Harbor Drive and Balboa Park. The numbered streets run roughly north–south; the lettered and named streets—Broadway, Market, Island, and Ash—run east–west. Only Broadway, Market Street, Harbor Drive, and Island Avenue have two-way traffic. The rest alternate one-way directions.

There are reasonably priced ($4–$7 per day) parking lots along Harbor Drive, Pacific Highway, and lower Broadway and Market Street. The price of many downtown parking meters is $1 per hour, with a maximum stay of two hours (meters are in effect Monday–Saturday [except holidays], 8–6); unless you know for sure that your stay in the area will be short, you're better off in a lot.

Numbers in the text correspond to numbers in the margin and on the Central San Diego map.

Two Good Walks

Most people do a lot of parking-lot hopping when visiting downtown, but for the energetic, two distinct areas may be explored on foot.

To stay near the water, start a walk of the **Embarcadero** ① at the foot of Ash Street on Harbor Drive, where the *Berkeley,* headquarters of the **Maritime Museum** ②, is moored. A cement pathway runs south from the *Star of India* along the waterfront to the pastel B Street Pier. If you're traveling with firehouse fans, detour inland six blocks and north two blocks to the **Firehouse Museum** ③, at the corner of Cedar and Columbia in Little Italy. Otherwise, another two blocks south on Harbor Drive brings you to the foot of Broadway and the Broadway Pier, where you can catch harbor excursion boats and the ferry to Coronado. Take Broadway inland two long blocks to Kettner Boulevard to reach the **Transit Center** ④—you'll see the mosaic-domed Santa Fe Depot and the tracks for the trolley to Tijuana out front—and, right next door, the downtown branch of the **Museum of Contemporary Art, San Diego** ⑤. (If you've detoured to the Firehouse Museum, take Kettner Boulevard south to the Transit Center.) Return to Harbor Drive and continue south past Tuna Harbor to **Seaport Village** ⑥.

A tour of the working heart of downtown can begin at the corner of 1st Avenue and Broadway, near Spreckels Theater, a grand old stage that presents pop concerts and touring plays. Two blocks east and across the street sits the historic **U. S. Grant Hotel** ⑦. If you cross Broadway, you'll be able to enter **Horton Plaza** ⑧, San Diego's favorite retail playland. Fourth Avenue, the eastern boundary of Horton Plaza, doubles as the western boundary of the 16-block **Gaslamp Quarter** ⑨. Head south to Island Avenue and Fourth Avenue to the **William Heath Davis House,** where you can get a touring map of the district. If you continue west on Island Avenue, you'll arrive at the **Children's Museum/Museo de los Niños** ⑩, which younger kids might prefer over a historical excursion.

TIMING

The above walks take about an hour each, although there's enough to do in downtown San Diego to keep you busy for at least two days. Weather is a determining factor in any Embarcadero stroll, which is pretty much an outdoors endeavor, but San Diego rarely presents any problems along that line. Most of downtown's attractions are open daily, but the Children's Museum and the Museum of Contemporary Art are closed on Monday, and the Firehouse Museum is only open from Thursday through Sunday. For a guided tour of the Gaslamp Quarter, plan to visit on Saturday. A boat trip on the harbor, or at least a hop over to Coronado on the ferry, is a must at any time of year, but from December through March, when the gray whales migrate between the Pacific Northwest and southern Baja, you should definitely consider booking a whale-watching excursion from the Broadway Pier.

Sights to See

⑩ **Children's Museum/Museo de los Niños.** With some 25,000 square ft of space devoted to interactive, experiential environments, this bilin-

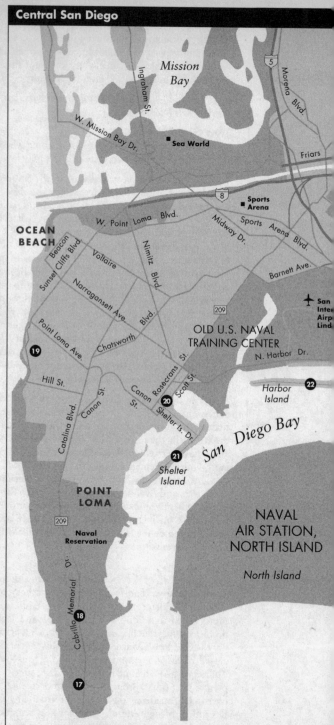

Central San Diego

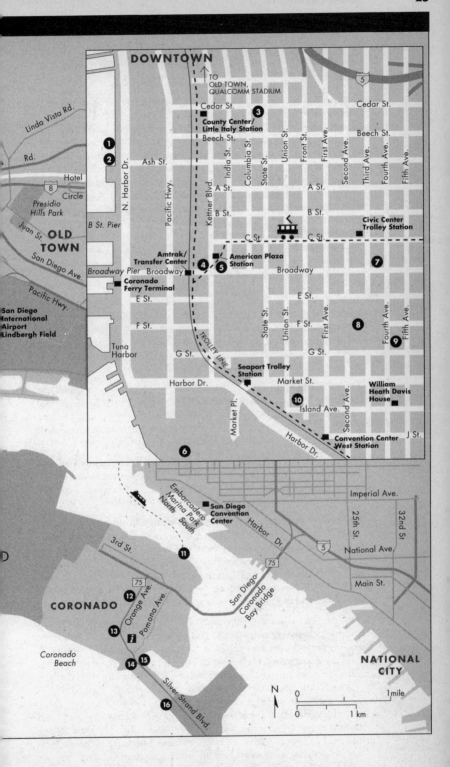

DOWNTOWN

TO
OLD TOWN,
QUALCOMM STADIUM

Cedar St.   Cedar St.

County Center/
Little Italy Station

Beech St.   Beech St.

Ash St.

Linda Vista Rd.

Rd.

Hotel
Circle

Presidio
Hills Park

Juan St.

OLD
TOWN

San Diego Ave.

Pacific Hwy.

San Diego
International
Airport
Lindbergh Field

B St. Pier

N. Harbor Dr.

Pacific Hwy.

Kettner Blvd.

India St.

Columbia St.

State St.

Union St.

Front St.

First Ave.

Second Ave.

Third Ave.

Fourth Ave.

Fifth Ave.

A St.   A St.

B St.   B St.

C St.   C St.

Civic Center
Trolley Station

Amtrak/
Transfer Center

American Plaza
Station

Broadway Pier Broadway

Coronado
Ferry Terminal

E St.

F St.

Tuna
Harbor

G St.

Broadway

E St.

State St.

Union St.

F St.

First Ave.

Fourth Ave.

Fifth Ave.

G St.   G St.

TROLLEY LINE

Seaport Trolley
Station

Market St.

Harbor Dr.

Market Pl.

Island Ave.

Second Ave.

William
Heath Davis
House

Harbor Dr.

Convention Center
West Station

J St.

Embarcadero
Marina Park
North   South

San Diego
Convention
Center

Imperial Ave.

Harbor   Dr.

25th St.

32nd St.

National Ave.

3rd St.

CORONADO

Orange Ave.

Pomona Ave.

San Diego-
Coronado
Bay Bridge

Main St.

Coronado
Beach

Silver Strand Blvd.

NATIONAL
CITY

N   0   1 mile

0   1 km

gual museum is a concentrated fun and learning zone for kids. Installations change annually. Art workshops may include bookmaking, T-shirt silk screening, and calligraphy. ✉ *200 W. Island Ave., Gaslamp Quarter,* ☎ *619/233–8792,* [WEB] *www.sdchildrensmuseum.org.* ⌲ *$6.* ☉ *Tues.–Sat. 10–4.*

OFF THE
BEATEN PATH
🐾 **CHULA VISTA NATURE INTERPRETIVE CENTER –** Kids can get up close and personal with bat rays, round rays, and small sharks at this low-key wet-land preserve about five minutes south of downtown via the freeway. Hands-on exhibits focus on marine life as well as other animal life typical of salt marshes; there's a walk-through shore bird aviary, as well as six aviaries of other native birds, including hawks, owls, and falcons. One and a half miles of trails lead to San Diego Bay. Free interpretive tours are given on Wednesday, Saturday, and Sunday at 2 PM. Take I–5 south to E Street, and park in the lot at E Street and Bay Boulevard, or take the trolley to the E Street Station. A shuttle will transport you from the parking lot or the trolley station (be sure to tell the stationmaster to call ahead) to the nature center. ✉ *1000 Gunpowder Point Dr., Chula Vista,* ☎ *619/ 409–5900,* [WEB] *www.chulavistanaturecenter.org.* ⌲ *$3.50; includes round-trip shuttle.* ☉ *Tues.–Sun. 10–5. Shuttle runs 10–4.*

❶ Embarcadero. The bustle along Harbor Drive's waterfront walkway comes less these days from the activities of fishing folk than from the throngs of tourists, but it remains the nautical soul of San Diego. People here still make a living from the sea. Seafood restaurants line the piers, as do sea vessels of every variety—cruise ships, ferries, tour boats, houseboats, and naval destroyers.

On the north end of the Embarcadero, at Ash Street, you'll find the Maritime Museum. South of it, the **B Street Pier** is used by ships from major cruise lines as both a port of call and a departure point. The cavernous pier building has a cruise-information center as well as a small bar—nice for cooling off on a hot day—and gift shop.

Day-trippers getting ready to set sail gather at the **Broadway Pier,** also known as the excursion pier. Tickets for the harbor tours and whale-watching trips are sold here. The terminal for the Coronado Ferry lies just beyond the Broadway pier.

The USS *Midway* is slated to dock on the south side of Navy Pier in early 2003. When the 1,000-ft-long USS *Midway* was commissioned in 1946, it would be the largest ship in the world for the next 10 years and the first too large to fit through the Panama Canal. Now retired, it will house the much-anticipated **San Diego Aircraft Carrier Museum,** (☎ 619/ 702–7700, [WEB] www.midway.org), which will include five aircraft, a flight simulator, and interactive exhibits focusing on naval aviation.

The U.S. Navy has control of the next few waterfront blocks to the south—**destroyers, submarines, and carriers** cruise in and out, some staying for weeks at a time. Unless the Navy is engaged in military maneuvers or activities, on weekends you can tour these floating cities. Check out the carrier USS *Constellation,* which docks across the harbor at North Island naval base when it's in port. (☎ Call 619/437–2735 for hours and types of ships; 619/545–1141 for aircraft carriers). **Tuna Harbor** is the former hub of one of San Diego's earliest and most successful industries, commercial tuna fishing. The tuna-fishing industry has gone south to Mexico, so these days there are more pleasure boats than tuna boats tied up at the adjoining G Street Pier, but the United States Tuna Foundation still has offices here. A pleasant park offers a great view across the bay of North Island, where aircraft carriers often dock.

The next bit of seafront greenery is a few blocks south along the paved promenade at **Embarcadero Marina Park North,** an 8-acre extension into the harbor from the center of Seaport Village. It's usually full of kite fliers, in-line skaters, and picnickers. Seasonal celebrations are held here and at the similar **Embarcadero Marina Park South.**

The **San Diego Convention Center,** on Harbor Drive between 1st and 5th avenues, was designed by Arthur Erickson. The backdrop of blue sky and sea complements the building's nautical lines. The center often holds trade shows that are open to the public, and tours of the building are available.

NEED A
BREAK?

Those waiting for their boats at the Broadway Pier can enjoy some New England–style clam chowder in an edible sourdough bowl at the **Bay Café** (✉ 1050 N. Harbor Dr., Embarcadero, ☎ 619/595–1083).

⑶ ❸ **Firehouse Museum.** Fire-fighting artifacts of all sorts fill this converted fire station, which at one time also served as the repair shop for all of San Diego's fire-fighting equipment. Three large rooms contain everything from 19th-century horse- and hand-drawn fire engines to 20th-century motorized trucks, the latest dating to 1942. Extinguishers, helmets, and other memorabilia are also on display. Ages 12 and under are free. ✉ *1572 Columbia St., Little Italy,* ☎ *619/232–3473.* 🎫 *$2.* ☉ *Thurs.–Fri. 10–2, weekends 10–4.*

❾ **Gaslamp Quarter.** The 16-block national historic district centered between 4th and 5th avenues from Broadway to Market Street contains most of San Diego's Victorian-style commercial buildings from the late 1800s, when Market Street was the center of early downtown. Businesses thrived in this area in the latter part of the 19th century, but at the turn of the century downtown's commercial district moved west toward Broadway, and many of San Diego's first buildings fell into disrepair. During the early 1900s the quarter became known as the Stingaree district. Prostitutes picked up sailors in lively area taverns and dance halls, and crime flourished; the blocks between Market Street and the waterfront were best avoided.

As the move for downtown redevelopment emerged, there was talk of bulldozing the buildings in the quarter and starting from scratch. History buffs, developers, architects, and artists formed the Gaslamp Quarter Council in 1974. Bent on preserving the district, they gathered funds from the government and private benefactors and began cleaning up the quarter, restoring the finest old buildings, and attracting businesses and the public back to the heart of New Town. Their efforts have paid off. Former flophouses have become choice office buildings, and the area is dotted with shops and restaurants.

The **William Heath Davis House** (✉ 410 Island Ave., at 4th Ave., Gaslamp Quarter, ☎ 619/233–4692), one of the first residences in town, now serves as the information center for the historic district. Davis was a San Franciscan whose ill-fated attempt to develop the waterfront area preceded the more successful one of Alonzo Horton. In 1850 Davis had this prefab saltbox-style house shipped around Cape Horn and assembled in San Diego (it was originally located at State and Market streets). Docents give tours ($3) of the rest of the house during museum hours, which are Tuesday–Sunday 11–3. The place is staffed solely by volunteers, however, so be sure to phone ahead. Regularly scheduled two-hour walking tours of the historic district leave from the house on Saturday at 11; the cost for these is $8. The museum also sells detailed self-guided tour maps of the district for $2; guided tours can be arranged by calling ahead.

The Victorian **Horton Grand Hotel** (✉ 311 Island Ave., Gaslamp Quarter, ☎ 619/544–1886) was created in the mid-1980s by joining together two historic hotels, the Kahle Saddlery and the Grand Hotel, built in the boom days of the 1880s; Wyatt Earp stayed at the Kahle Saddlery—then called the Brooklyn Hotel—while he was in town speculating on real estate ventures and opening gambling halls. The two hotels were dismantled and reconstructed about four blocks from their original locations. A small Chinese Museum serves as a tribute to the surrounding Chinatown district, a collection of modest structures that once housed Chinese laborers and their families.

The majority of the quarter's landmark buildings are on 4th and 5th avenues, between Island Avenue and Broadway. If you don't have much time, stroll down 5th Avenue, where highlights include the Backesto Building (No. 614), the Mercantile Building (No. 822), the Louis Bank of Commerce (No. 835), and the Watts-Robinson Building (No. 903). The Tudor-style **Keating Building** (✉ 432 F St., at 5th Ave., Gaslamp Quarter) was designed by the same firm that created the famous Hotel Del Coronado. Peer into the Hard Rock Cafe, at the corner of 4th Avenue and F Street, which occupies a restored turn-of-the-century tavern with a 12-ft mahogany bar and a spectacular stained-glass domed ceiling.

The section of G Street between 6th and 9th avenues has become a haven for galleries; stop in one of them to pick up a map of the downtown arts district. Just to the north, on E and F streets from 6th to 12th avenues, the evolving Urban Art Trail has added pizzazz to drab city thoroughfares by transforming such things as trash cans and traffic controller boxes into canvases. For additional information about the historic area, call the **Gaslamp Quarter Association** (☎ 619/233–5227) or log on to their Web site (WEB www.gaslamp.org).

NEED A
BREAK?
Fifth Avenue between F and G streets is lined with restaurants, many with outdoor patios. Hip coffeehouses have also sprung up in the Gaslamp Quarter. You can nurse a double espresso or imported beer at **Café LuLu** (✉ 419 F St., Gaslamp Quarter, ☎ 619/238–0114).

★ ❽ **Horton Plaza.** Downtown's centerpiece is the shopping, dining, and entertainment mall that fronts Broadway and G Street from 1st to 4th avenues and covers more than six city blocks. Designed by Jon Jerde and completed in 1985, Horton Plaza is far from what one would imagine a shopping center—or city center—to be. A collage of pastels with elaborate, colorful tile work on benches and stairways, banners waving in the air, and modern sculptures marking the entrances, Horton Plaza rises in uneven, staggered levels to six floors; great views of downtown from the harbor to Balboa Park and beyond can be had here. The complex's architecture has strongly affected the rest of downtown's development—new apartment and condominium complexes along G and Market streets mimic its brightly colored towers and cupolas.

Horton Plaza has a multilevel parking garage, although lines to find a space can be long. The first three hours of parking are free with validation; after that it's $1 for every 20 minutes. If you use this notoriously confusing fruit-and-vegetable–theme garage, be sure to remember at which produce level you've left your car. If you're staying downtown, inquire at your hotel about the complimentary Horton Plaza shopping shuttle, which stops at the cruise ship terminal and the convention center in addition to several downtown lodgings.

Macy's, Nordstrom, and Mervyn's department stores anchor the plaza, with an eclectic assortment of more than 140 clothing, sporting-goods, jewelry, book, and gift shops flanking them. Other attractions include the country's largest Sam Goody music store and a Planet Hollywood. A movie complex, restaurants, and a long row of take-out ethnic food shops and dining patios line the uppermost tier. The respected San Diego Repertory Theatre has two stages below ground level. Most stores are open 10–9 weekdays, 10–6 Saturday, and 11–7 Sunday, but during the winter holidays and the summer many places stay open longer (619/238–1596 for up-to-the-minute information).

The **International Visitors Information Center,** operated in the complex by the San Diego Convention and Visitors Bureau, is the best resource for information on the city. The staff members and volunteers who run the center speak many languages and are acquainted with myriad needs and requests of tourists. They dispense information (and discount coupons) on hotels, restaurants, and tourist attractions, including those in Tijuana. ⊠ *Visitors center: 11 Horton Plaza, street level at corner of 1st Ave. and F St., Gaslamp Quarter,* ☎ *619/236–1212,* WEB *www. sandiego.org.* ☉ *Mon.–Sat. 8:30–5; June–Aug. also Sun. 11–5.*

NEED A BREAK? Nice days see hungry shoppers seated at the counters and tables outside the informal eateries on Horton Plaza's top level, where you can get everything from fresh hot cinnamon rolls to pizza and sushi. Just want a caffeine recharge? Coffee carts include the **Expresso Bar,** outside Nordstrom on level 1. **Starbucks** fans can get their fix inside stores on level 1 and on the street level, off Broadway Circle.

★ ☺ ❷ **Maritime Museum.** A must for anyone with an interest in nautical history—or who has ever read a Patrick O'Brian novel—this collection of three restored ships affords a fascinating glimpse of San Diego during its heyday as a commercial seaport. The museum's headquarters are the *Berkeley,* an 1898 ferryboat moored at the foot of Ash Street. The steam-driven ship, which served the Southern Pacific Railroad at San Francisco Bay until 1958, played its most important role during the great earthquake of 1906, when it carried thousands of passengers across San Francisco Bay to Oakland. Its ornate carved-wood paneling, stained-glass windows, and plate-glass mirrors have been restored, and its main deck serves as a floating museum, with permanent exhibits on West Coast maritime history and complementary rotating exhibits; recent topics included the America's Cup Race and *The Titanic.* Anchored next to the *Berkeley,* the small Scottish steam yacht *Medea,* launched in 1904, may be boarded but has no interpretive displays.

The most interesting of the three ships is the *Star of India,* an iron windjammer built in 1863, when iron ships were still a novelty. The ship's high wooden masts and white sails flapping in the wind have been a harbor landmark since 1927. The *Star of India* made 21 trips around the world in the late 1800s, when it traveled the East Indian trade route, shuttled immigrants from England to New Zealand, and served the Alaskan salmon trade. The ship languished after being retired to San Diego Harbor, virtually ignored until 1959, when volunteers organized by the Maritime Museum began the laborious task of stripping the wooden decks, polishing the figurehead, and mending the sails. The oldest active iron sailing ship in the world, it makes rare short excursions but for the most part stays moored at the pier and open to visitors. ⊠ *1492 N. Harbor Dr., Embarcadero,* ☎ *619/234–9153,* WEB *www. sdmaritime.com.* ⌑ *$6 (includes entry to all 3 ships).* ☉ *Daily 9–8 (until 9 PM in summer).*

❺ **Museum of Contemporary Art, San Diego.** The downtown branch of the city's modern art museum, which first opened while the main building in La Jolla was undergoing renovation, has taken on its own personality. Its postmodern, cutting-edge exhibitions are perfectly complemented by the steel-and-glass transportation complex of which it's a part. Four small galleries in the two-story building host rotating shows, some from the permanent collection in the La Jolla branch, others loaned from far-flung international museums. Look for Wendy Jacob's "breathing" wall on the second floor's far gallery, an artful lesson in paying attention to your surroundings. ✉ *1001 Kettner Blvd., Downtown,* ☎ *619/234–1001.* 🎟 *Free.* 🕓 *Tues.–Sat. 10–5, Sun. noon–5.*

★ ☚ ❻ **Seaport Village.** On a prime stretch of waterfront that spreads out across 14 acres connecting the harbor with hotel towers and the convention center, the village's three bustling shopping plazas are designed to reflect the architectural styles of early California, especially New England clapboard and Spanish mission. A ¼-mi wooden boardwalk that runs along the bay and 4 mi of paths lead to specialty shops—everything from a kite store and rubber-stamp emporium to a shop devoted to left-handed people—as well as snack bars and restaurants, many with harbor views; there are about 75 in all. Seaport Village's shops are open daily 10 to 9 (10 to 10 in summer); a few eateries open early for breakfast, and many have extended nighttime hours, especially in summer.

I. D. Looff crafted the hand-carved, hand-painted steeds on the **Broadway Flying Horses Carousel** for the Coney Island amusement park in 1890. The ride was moved from its next home, Salisbury Beach in Massachusetts, and faithfully restored for Seaport Village's West Plaza; tickets are $1. Strolling clowns, balloon sculptors, mimes, musicians, and magicians are also on hand throughout the village to entertain kids; those not impressed by such pretechnological displays can duck into the Time Out entertainment center near the carousel and play video games. ✉ *Downtown,* ☎ *619/235–4014; 619/235–4013 for events hot line,* 🌐 *www.spvillage.com.*

NEED A
BREAK?

The food court near the carousel serves up fast Greek, Mexican, Italian, deli, and all-American fare—pretty much anything you can think of. You can sit at a table in a shaded courtyard, on a harborside patio, or perch on the nearby seawall. **Upstart Crow & Co.** (✉ Seaport Village, Central Plaza, Embarcadero, ☎ 619/232–4855), a combination bookstore and coffeehouse, serves good cappuccino and espresso with pastries and cakes.

❹ **Transit Center.** The Mission revival–style **Santa Fe Depot,** which replaced the original 1887 station on this site, serves Amtrak and Coaster passengers. A booth at the graceful, tile-domed depot has bus schedules, maps, and tourist brochures. Formerly an easily spotted area landmark, it's now overshadowed by **1 America Plaza** across the street. At the base of this 34-story office tower, designed by architect Helmut Jahn, is a center that links the train, trolley, and city bus systems. The building's signature crescent-shape, glass-and-steel canopy arches out over the trolley tracks. The Greyhound bus station (120 West Broadway) is a few blocks away. ✉ *Broadway and Kettner Blvd., Downtown.*

❼ **U. S. Grant Hotel.** Far more formal than most other hotels in San Diego, the doyenne of downtown lodgings has a marble lobby, gleaming chandeliers, attentive doormen, and other touches that hark back to the more gracious era when it was built (1910). Funded in part by the son of the president for whom it was named, the hotel was extremely opulent; 350 rooms of 437 had private baths, highly unusual for that time. Through the years it became noted for its famous guests—U.S. presidents from Woodrow Wilson to George Bush (the elder) have stayed

here. Taking up a city block—it's bounded by 3rd and 4th avenues, C
Street, and Broadway—the hotel occupies the site of San Diego's first
hotel, constructed by Alonzo Horton in 1870. ⊠ *326 Broadway,
Gaslamp Quarter,* ☎ *619/232–3121.*

OFF THE
BEATEN PATH

VILLA MONTEZUMA – The former residence of Jesse Shepard, a pianist,
spiritualist, and novelist, adapts the elements of high Queen Anne style
to Shepard's unique aesthetic interests. The 1887 house is filled with fascinating period and personal details: stained-glass windows depicting
Shakespeare, Beethoven, Mozart, Sappho, and Goethe; redwood pan-
els; tiled fireplaces; family portraits; and tributes from Shepard's famous
admirers. Villa Montezuma was restored by the San Diego Historical Society, whose docents give continuous tours. Architecture buffs will enjoy
combining a visit to this "Painted Lady," which is in a not-yet-gentrified
area east of I–5, with one to the Marston House in Balboa Park, 10 minutes to the north and also operated by the Historical Society. A dual admission ticket will save you $2.50. ⊠ *1925 K St., Downtown,* ☎ *619/
239–2211.* ⌨ *$5.* ☉ *Fri.–Sun. 10–4:30 (last tour at 3:45); Dec. also
open Thurs. 10–4:30.*

CORONADO

Although it's actually an isthmus, easily reached from the mainland if
you head north from Imperial Beach, Coronado has always seemed like
an island—and is often referred to as such. The Spaniards called it Los
Coronados, or "the Crowned Ones," in the late 1500s and the name
stuck. Today's residents, many of whom live in grand Victorian homes
handed down for generations, tend to consider their community to be
a sort of royal encampment, safe from the hassles and hustle of San
Diego proper.

North Island Naval Air Station was established in 1911 on Coronado's
north end, across from Point Loma, and was the site of Charles Lindbergh's departure on the transcontinental flight that preceded his famous
transatlantic voyage (a San Diego–area company manufactured the *Spirit
of St. Louis*). Today high-tech aircraft and seacraft arrive and depart from
North Island, providing a real-life education in military armament.
Coronado's long relationship with the U.S. Navy and its desirable real
estate have made it an enclave for wealthy military personnel; it's said
to have the most retired admirals per capita in the United States.

The streets of Coronado are wide, quiet, and friendly, with lots of neighborhood parks where young families mingle with the area's many senior citizens. Grand old homes face the waterfront and the Coronado
Municipal Golf Course, under the bridge at the north end of Glorietta
Bay; it's the site of the annual Fourth of July fireworks display. Community celebrations and concerts take place in Spreckels Park on
Orange Avenue.

Coronado is visible from downtown and Point Loma and accessible
via the arching blue 2³⁄₁₀-mi-long Coronado–San Diego Bay Bridge, a
landmark just beyond downtown's skyline. There is a $1 toll for cross-
ing the bridge into Coronado, but cars carrying two or more passengers may enter through the free carpool lane. The bridge handles more
than 67,000 cars each day, and rush hour tends to be slow, which is
fine, because the view of the harbor, downtown, and the island is
breathtaking, day and night.

Until the bridge was completed in 1969, visitors and residents relied
on the Coronado Ferry, which ran across the harbor from downtown.

When the bridge was opened, the ferry closed down, much to the dismay of those who were fond of traveling at a leisurely pace. In 1987 the ferry returned. Residents and commuting workers have quickly adapted to this traditional mode of transportation, and the ferry has become quite popular with bicyclists, who shuttle their bikes across the harbor and ride the wide, flat boulevards for hours.

San Diego's Metropolitan Transit System runs a shuttle bus, No. 904, around the island; you can pick it up where you disembark the ferry and ride it out as far as the Silver Strand State Beach. Buses start leaving from the ferry landing at 10:30 AM and run once an hour on the half hour until 6:30 PM.

You can board the ferry, operated by **San Diego Harbor Excursion** (☎ 619/234–4111; 800/442–7847 in CA), at downtown San Diego's Embarcadero from the excursion dock at Harbor Drive and Broadway; you'll arrive at the Ferry Landing Marketplace. Boats depart every hour on the hour from the Embarcadero and every hour on the half hour from Coronado, Sunday–Thursday 9–9, Friday and Saturday until 10; the fare is $2 each way, 50¢ extra for bicycles. San Diego Harbor Excursion also offers water taxi service from 10–10 between any two points in San Diego Bay. The fare is $5 per person for the North Bay, more for the South Bay. Call ☎ 619/235–8294 to book.

Numbers in the text correspond to numbers in the margin and on the Central San Diego map.

A Good Tour

Coronado is easy to navigate without a car. When you depart the ferry, you can explore the shops at the **Ferry Landing Marketplace** ⑪ and from there rent a bicycle or catch the shuttle bus that runs down **Orange Avenue** ⑫, Coronado's main tourist drag. You might disembark the bus near the tourist information office, just off Orange, and pick up a map, return to Orange to visit the nearby **Coronado Museum of History and Art** ⑬, and then keep strolling along the boutiques-filled promenade until you reach the **Hotel Del Coronado** ⑭ at the end of Orange Avenue. Right across the street from the Del is the **Glorietta Bay Inn** ⑮, another of the island's outstanding early structures. If you've brought your swimsuit, you might continue on to **Silver Strand State Beach** ⑯—just past the Hotel Del, Orange Avenue turns into Silver Strand Boulevard, which soon resumes its original across-the-bridge role as Route 75.

TIMING

A leisurely stroll through Coronado takes an hour or so, more if you shop or walk along the beach. If you're a history buff, you might want to visit on Tuesday, Thursday, or Saturday, when you can combine the tour of Coronado's historic homes that departs from the Glorietta Bay Inn at 11 AM with a visit to the Coronado Museum of History and Art, open Tuesday through Saturday. Whenever you come, if you're not staying overnight, remember to get back to the dock in time to catch the final ferry out. The last shuttle to the Ferry Landing Marketplace leaves from the Loews Coronado Bay Resort at 6:57.

Sights to See

⑬ **Coronado Museum of History and Art.** The neoclassical Historic First Bank building, constructed in 1910, was restored and reopened in summer 2000 as the headquarters and archives of the Coronado Historical Society and a museum. The collection celebrates Coronado's history with photographs and displays of its formative events and major sights. Three galleries house permanent displays while a fourth hosts traveling exhibits; all offer interactive activities for children and adults. To check out the town's historic houses, pick up a copy of the inexpensive *Coronado California Centennial History & Tour Guide* at the gift shop. There's also a café and lecture hall. ✉ *1100 Orange Ave., Coronado,* ☎ *619/435–7242.* ✉ *Donations accepted.* ⊙ *Weekdays 9–5, Sat 10–5, Sun. 11–4.*

⑪ Ferry Landing Marketplace. This collection of shops at the point of disembarkation for the ferry is on a smaller—and generally less interesting—scale than Seaport Village, but you do get a great view of downtown's skyline from here. The little shops and restaurants resemble the gingerbread domes of the Hotel Del Coronado. If you want to rent a bike or in-line skates, stop in at **Bikes and Beyond** (✉ No. 122, ☎ 619/435–7180). ✉ *1201 1st St., at B Ave., Coronado,* ☎ *619/435–8895.*

⑮ Glorietta Bay Inn. The former residence of John Spreckels, the original owner of North Island and the property on which the Hotel Del Coronado stands, is now a popular hotel. On Tuesday, Thursday, and Saturday mornings at 11 it's the departure point for a fun and informative 1½-hour walking tour of a few of the area's 86 officially designated historical homes. Sponsored by the Coronado Historical Association, the tour focuses on the Glorietta Bay Inn and the Hotel Del Coronado across the street. In addition, it includes—from the outside only—some spectacular mansions and the Meade House, where L. Frank Baum wrote additional stories of his most famous work, *The Wizard of Oz.* ✉ *1630 Glorietta Blvd., Coronado,* ☎ *619/435–3101; 619/435–5993 for tour information.* ✉ *$8 for historical tour.*

★ ⑭ Hotel Del Coronado. A recent $55 million face-lift has vastly improved the appearance of this hotel, selected as a national historic landmark in 1977. The hotel has a colorful history, integrally connected with that of Coronado itself. The Del, as natives call it, was the brainchild of financiers Elisha Spurr Babcock Jr. and H. L. Story, who saw the potential of Coronado's virgin beaches and its view of San Diego's emerging harbor. They purchased a 4,100-acre parcel of land in 1885 for $110,000 and threw a lavish Fourth of July bash for prospective investors in their hunting and fishing resort. By the end of the year they had roused public interest—and had an ample return on their investment. The hotel was opened in 1888, although it wasn't actually completed for another six years.

The Del's distinctive red-tile peaks and Victorian gingerbread architecture has served as a set for many movies, political meetings, and extravagant social happenings. It is said that the duke of Windsor first met Wallis Simpson here. Fourteen presidents have been guests of the Del, and the film *Some Like It Hot*—starring Marilyn Monroe, Jack Lemmon, and Tony Curtis—was filmed here.

Broad steps lead up to the main, balconied lobby, with grand oak pillars and ceiling, which in turn opens out onto a central courtyard and gazebo. To the right is the cavernous **Crown Room**, whose arched ceiling of notched sugar pine was constructed without nails. You can tell by looking at this space that the hotel's architect, James Reed, had previously designed railroad stations. A lavish Sunday brunch is served here from 9–2. To the left past the reception desk is the hotel's Signature Shop, as well as a stairwell descending to the 22-shop Galleria level. Also on this level is the History Gallery, which displays photos from the Del's early days.

The patio surrounding the swimming pool is a great place for sitting back and imagining what the bathers looked like during the 1920s, when the hotel rocked with the good times. To its right, the new Windsor Lawn provides a green oasis between the hotel and the beach. To the pool's left are the two, seven-story Ocean Tower accommodations. The gift shop sells books that elaborate on the hotel's history and resident ghost. Guided tours are available for registered hotel guests. ✉ *1500 Orange Ave., Coronado*, ☎ *619/435–6611*, WEB *www.hoteldel.com*.

⑫ **Orange Avenue.** It's easy to imagine you're on a street in Cape Cod when you stroll along this thoroughfare, Coronado's version of a downtown: the clapboard houses, small restaurants, and boutiques—selling everything from upscale clothing to surfboards—are in some ways more characteristic of New England than they are of California. But the East Coast illusion tends to dissipate as quickly as a winter fog when you catch sight of one of the avenue's many citrus trees—or realize it's February and the sun is warming your face. Just off Orange Avenue, the **Coronado Visitors Bureau** (✉ 1047 B Ave., Coronado, ☎ 619/437–8788, WEB www.coronadovisitors.com) is open weekdays 8–5, Saturday 10–5, and Sunday 11–4 year-round.

<table>
<tr><td>NEED A
BREAK?</td><td>There's an abundance of places to find a caffeine fix on Orange Avenue between 8th Street and the Hotel Del. At the hip **Cafe 1134** (✉ 1134 Orange Ave., Coronado, ☎ 619/437–1134) you can get a good curried tuna sandwich on French bread to accompany your espresso. Peruse the latest art magazine while sipping a latte at the sidewalk café of **Bay Books** (✉ 1029 Orange Ave., Coronado, ☎ 619/435–0070), San Diego's largest independent bookstore. For a deliciously sweet pick-me-up, check out the rich ice cream, frozen yogurt, and sorbet made fresh daily on the premises of **Mootime Creamery** (✉ 1025 Orange Ave., Coronado, ☎ 619/435–2422).</td></tr>
</table>

☝ ⑯ **Silver Strand State Beach.** The stretch of sand that runs along Silver Strand Boulevard from the Hotel Del Coronado to Imperial Beach dispels the illusion that Coronado is an island. The beach is a perfect family gathering spot, with rest rooms and lifeguards. Don't be surprised if you see groups exercising in military style along the beach; this is a training area for the U.S. Navy's SEAL teams. Across from the beach is the Coronado Cays, an exclusive community popular with yacht owners and celebrities, and the Loews Coronado Bay Resort.

En Route   San Diego's Mexican-American community is centered in Barrio Logan, under the Coronado–San Diego Bay Bridge on the downtown side. **Chicano Park,** spread along National Avenue from Dewey to Crosby streets, is the barrio's recreational hub. It's worth taking a short detour to see the huge murals of Mexican history painted on the bridge supports at National Avenue and Dewey Street; they're among the best examples of folk art in the city.

HARBOR ISLAND, POINT LOMA, AND SHELTER ISLAND

The populated outcroppings that jut into the bay just west of downtown and the airport demonstrate the potential of human collaboration with nature. Point Loma, Mother Nature's contribution to San Diego's attractions, has always afforded protection to the center city from the Pacific's tides and waves. It's shared by military installations, funky motels and fast-food shacks, stately family homes, huge estates, and private marinas packed with sailboats and yachts. Newer to the scene, Harbor and Shelter islands are poster children for landfill. Created out of sand dredged from the San Diego Bay in the second half of the past century, they've become tourist hubs, their high-rise hotels, seafood restaurants, and boat-rental centers looking as solid as those anywhere else in the city.

Numbers in the text correspond to numbers in the margin and on the Central San Diego map.

A Good Tour

Take Catalina Boulevard all the way south to the tip of Point Loma to reach **Cabrillo National Monument** ⑰; you'll be retracing the steps of the earliest European explorers if you use this as a jumping-off point for a tour. North of the monument, as you head back into the neighborhoods of Point Loma, you'll see the white headstones of **Fort Rosecrans National Cemetery** ⑱. Continue north on Catalina Boulevard to Hill Street and turn left to reach the dramatic **Sunset Cliffs** ⑲, at the western side of Point Loma near Ocean Beach. Return to Catalina Boulevard and backtrack south for a few blocks to find Canon Street, which leads toward the peninsula's eastern (bay) side. Almost at the shore you'll see **Scott Street** ⑳, Point Loma's main commercial drag. Scott Street is bisected by Shelter Island Drive, which leads to **Shelter Island** ㉑. For another example of what can be done with tons of material dredged from a bay, go back up Shelter Island Drive, turn right on Rosecrans Street, and make another right on North Harbor Drive to reach **Harbor Island** ㉒.

TIMING

If you're interested in seeing the tide pools at Cabrillo National Monument, call ahead or check the weather page of the *Union-Tribune* to find out when low tide will occur. Scott Street, with its Point Loma Seafoods, is a good place to find yourself at lunchtime, and Sunset Cliffs Park is where you might want to be when the daylight starts to wane. This drive takes about an hour if you stop briefly at each sight, but you'll want to devote at least an hour to Cabrillo National Monument.

Sights to See

★ ⑰ **Cabrillo National Monument.** This 144-acre preserve marks the site of the first European visit to San Diego, made by 16th-century explorer Juan Rodríguez Cabrillo (circa 1498–1543)—historians have never conclusively determined whether he was Spanish or Portuguese. Cabrillo, who had earlier gone on voyages with Hernán Cortés, came to this spot, which he called San Miguel, in 1542. Government grounds were set aside to commemorate his discovery in 1913, and today the site, with its rugged cliffs and shores and outstanding overlooks, is one of the most frequently visited of all the national monuments.

The **visitor center** presents films and lectures about Cabrillo's voyage, the sea-level tide pools, and migrating gray whales. The center has an excellent shop with books about nature, San Diego, and the sea. Maps of the region, whale posters, flowers, shells, and the requisite postcards, slides, and film are also on sale. Rest rooms and water fountains are plentiful along the paths that climb to the monument's various viewing points, but, except for a few vending machines at the visitor center, there is no food. Exploring the grounds consumes time and calories; bring a picnic and rest on a bench overlooking the sailboats.

Interpretive stations with recorded information in six languages—including, appropriately enough, Portuguese—have been installed along the walkways that edge the cliffs. Signs explain the views and wayside exhibits depict the various naval, fishing, and pleasure craft that sail into and fly over the bay. Directly south across the bay from the visitor center is the North Island Naval Air Station at the west end of Coronado. To the left on the shores of Point Loma is the Space and Naval

Warfare Systems Center; nuclear-powered submarines are now docked where Cabrillo's small ships anchored in 1542.

A **statue of Cabrillo** overlooks downtown from the next windy promontory, where people gather to admire the stunning panorama over the bay, from the snowcapped San Bernardino Mountains, 130 mi north, to the hills surrounding Tijuana to the south. The stone figure standing on the bluff looks rugged and dashing, but he is a creation of an artist's imagination—no portraits of Cabrillo are known to exist. The statue was donated by the Portuguese navy in 1957.

The moderately steep 2-mi **Bayside Trail** (☉ 9–4) winds through coastal sage scrub, curving under the cliff-top lookouts and bringing you ever closer to the bay-front scenery. You cannot reach the beach from this trail and must stick to the path to protect the cliffs from erosion and yourself from thorny plants and snakes—including rattlers. You'll see prickly pear cactus and yucca, black-eyed Susans, fragrant sage, and maybe a lizard or a hummingbird. The climb back is long but gradual, leading up to the old lighthouse.

The oil lamp of the **Old Point Loma Lighthouse** (☉ 9–5) was first lit in 1855. The light, sitting in a brass-and-iron housing above a white wooden house, shone through a state-of-the-art lens from France and was visible from the sea for 25 mi. Unfortunately, it was too high above the cliffs to guide navigators trapped in southern California's thick offshore fog and low clouds. In 1891 a new lighthouse was built 400 ft below. The old lighthouse, refitted with furnishings more accurate to the era when it was erected, is open to visitors. The U.S. Coast Guard still uses the newer lighthouse and a mighty foghorn to guide boaters through the narrow channel leading into the bay. On the edge of the hill near the lighthouse sits a refurbished radio room from World War I. It hosts displays of U.S. harbor defenses at Point Loma used during World War II.

The western and southern cliffs of Cabrillo National Monument are prime whale-watching territory. A sheltered **viewing station** has a tape-recorded lecture describing the great gray whales' migration from the Bering and Chukchi seas near Alaska to Baja California, and high-powered telescopes help you focus on the whales' water spouts. The whales are visible on clear days in January and February. Park rangers can help you spot whales during the annual Whale Watch Weekend, held the third weekend in January, which includes other interpretive programs and entertainment.

More accessible sea creatures can be seen in the **tide pools** (☉ 9–4:30) at the foot of the monument's western cliffs. Drive north from the visitor center to the first road on the left, which winds down to the coast guard station and the shore. When the tide is low you can walk on the rocks around saltwater pools filled with starfish, crabs, anemones, octopuses, and hundreds of other sea creatures and plants. ✉ *1800 Cabrillo Memorial Dr., Point Loma,* ☎ *619/557–5450,* WEB *www.nps. gov/cabr.* ✍ *$5 per car, $3 per person entering on foot or by bicycle (entrance pass allows unlimited admissions for one week from date of purchase); free for Golden Age, Golden Access, and Golden Eagle passport holders, and children under 17.* ☉ *Park daily 9–5:15 (call for later summer hrs, which vary).*

⑱ Fort Rosecrans National Cemetery. In 1934 eight acres of the 1,000 set aside for a military reserve in 1852 were designated as a burial site. About 79,000 people are now interred here; it's impressive to see the rows upon rows of white headstones that overlook both sides of Point Loma just north of the Cabrillo National Monument. Some of those laid to rest at this place were killed in battles that predate California's statehood; the graves of the 17 soldiers and one civilian who died in the 1874 Battle of San Pasqual between troops from Mexico and the United States are marked by a large bronze plaque. Perhaps the most impressive structure in the cemetery is the 75-ft granite obelisk called the Bennington Monument, which commemorates the 66 crew members who died in a boiler explosion and fire on board the USS *Bennington* in 1905. The cemetery, visited by many veterans, is still used for burials. ⊠ *Rte. 209, Point Loma,* ☎ *619/553–2084.* ◷ *Daily 9–5:30.*

㉒ Harbor Island. Following the success of nearby Shelter Island, the U.S. Navy decided to use the residue that resulted from digging berths deep enough to accommodate aircraft carriers to build another recreational island. In 1961 a 1½-mi-long peninsula was created adjacent to San Diego International Airport out of 12 million cubic yards of sand and mud dredged from San Diego Bay. Restaurants and high-rise hotels now line the inner shores of Harbor Island. The bay shore has pathways, gardens, and picnic spots for sightseeing or working off the calories from the various indoor or outdoor food fests. On the west point, Tom Ham's Lighthouse restaurant has a U.S. Coast Guard–approved beacon shining from its tower.

Across from the western end of Harbor Island, at the mainland's **Spanish Landing Park,** a bronze plaque marks the arrival in 1769 of a party from Spain that headed north from San Diego to conquer California. The group was a merger of the crew of two ships, the *San Carlos* and the *San Antonio,* and of a contingent that came overland from Baja California. No one knows exactly where the men landed and camped; we can only be certain it wasn't Harbor Island.

㉒ Scott Street. Running along Point Loma's waterfront from Shelter Island to the old Naval Training Center on Harbor Drive, this thoroughfare is lined with deep-sea fishing charters and whale-watching boats. It's a good spot from which to watch fishermen (and women) haul marlin, tuna, and puny mackerel off their boats.

NEED A BREAK?

The freshest and tastiest fish to be found along Point Loma's shores— some would say anywhere in San Diego—comes from **Point Loma Seafoods** (⊠ 2805 Emerson St., Point Loma, ☎ 619/223–1109), off Scott Street behind the Vagabond Inn. A fish market sells the catch of the day, and patrons crowd the adjacent take-out counter for seafood cocktails and salads, ceviche, and crab and shrimp sandwiches made with sourdough bread baked on the premises. There's outdoor and indoor seating, and you can expect crowds throughout the year. Park a few blocks away if you're coming on the weekend; the adjoining lot suffers from extreme gridlock.

㉑ Shelter Island. In 1950 San Diego's port director thought there should be some use for the sand and mud dredged by the Works Project Administration to deepen the ship channel in the 1930s and '40s. He decided it might be a good idea to raise the shoal that lay off the eastern shore of Point Loma above sea level, landscape it, and add a 2,000-ft causeway to make it accessible.

His hunch paid off. Shelter Island—actually a peninsula—now supports towering mature palms, a cluster of resorts, restaurants, and side-by-side marinas. It is the center of San Diego's yacht-building industry, and boats in every stage of construction are visible in the yacht yards. A long sidewalk runs from the landscaped lawns of the **San Diego Yacht Club** (tucked down Anchorage Street off Shelter Island Drive), past boat brokerages to the hotels and marinas, which line the inner shore, facing Point Loma. On the bay side, fishermen launch their boats or simply stand on shore and cast. Families relax at picnic tables along the grass, where there are fire rings and permanent barbecue grills. Within walking distance is the huge Friendship Bell, given to San Diegans by the people of Yokohama, Japan, in 1960.

⑲ Sunset Cliffs. As the name suggests, the 60-ft-high bluffs on the western side of Point Loma south of Ocean Beach are a perfect place to watch the sun descend over the sea. To view the tide pools along the shore, you can descend a staircase off Sunset Cliffs Boulevard at the foot of Ladera Street.

The dramatic coastline here seems to have been carved out of ancient rock. The impact of the waves is very clear: each year more sections of the cliffs sport caution signs. Don't ignore these warnings—it's easy to lose your footing and slip in the crumbling sandstone, and the surf can be extremely rough. Small coves and beaches dot the coastline and are popular with surfers drawn to the pounding waves and locals from the neighborhood who name and claim their special spots. Needle's Eye is considered especially challenging. The homes along the boulevard are fine examples of southern California luxury, with pink stucco mansions beside shingled Cape Cod–style cottages. ⊠ *Sunset Cliffs Blvd., Point Loma.*

LA JOLLA

La Jollans have long considered their village to be the Monte Carlo of California, and with good cause. Its coastline curves into natural coves backed by verdant hillsides covered with homes worth millions. Although La Jolla is considered part of San Diego, it has its own postal zone and a coveted sense of class; it's gotten far more plebeian these days, but old-monied residents still mingle here with visiting film stars and royalty who frequent established hotels and private clubs. Development and construction have radically altered the once serene and private character of the village, but it has gained a cosmopolitan air that makes it a popular vacation resort.

The Native Americans called the site La Hoya, meaning "the cave," referring to the grottoes that dot the shoreline. The Spaniards changed the name to La Jolla (same pronunciation as La Hoya), "the jewel," and its residents have cherished the name and its allusions ever since.

To reach La Jolla from I–5, if you're traveling north, take the Ardath Road exit, which veers into Torrey Pines Road, and turn right onto Prospect Street. If you're heading south, get off at the La Jolla Village Drive exit, which will also lead into Torrey Pines Road. Traffic is virtually always congested in this popular area, which is dotted with four-way stop signs and clogged with drivers dropping off passengers and/or trolling for a parking spot. Drive carefully and be prepared to stop frequently when you get into the village.

For those who enjoy meandering, the best way to approach La Jolla from the south is to drive through Mission and Pacific beaches on Mission Boulevard, past the crowds of rollerbladers, bicyclists, and sunbathers. The clutter and congestion ease up as the street becomes La Jolla Boulevard. Road signs along La Jolla Boulevard and Camino de la Costa direct drivers and bicyclists past homes designed by such respected architects as Frank Lloyd Wright and Irving Gill. As you approach the village, La Jolla Boulevard turns into Prospect Street.

Prospect Street and Girard Avenue, the village's main drags, are lined with expensive shops and office buildings. Girard holds the village's only movie house, which tends to show indie films. Through the years the shopping and dining district has spread to Pearl and other side streets. Wall Street, a quiet tree-lined boulevard off Girard Avenue, was once the financial heart of La Jolla, but banks and investment houses can now be found throughout the village. The La Jolla nightlife scene is an active one, with jazz clubs, piano bars, and watering holes for the well-heeled younger set.

Numbers in the text correspond to numbers in the margin and on the La Jolla map.

A Good Tour

At the intersection of La Jolla Boulevard and Nautilus Street, turn toward the sea to reach **Windansea Beach** ①, one of the best surfing spots in town. **Mount Soledad** ②, about 1½-mi east on Nautilus Street, is La Jolla's highest spot. In the village itself you'll find the town's cultural center, the **Museum of Contemporary Art, San Diego** ③, on the less trafficked southern end of Prospect. A bit farther north, at the intersection of Prospect Street and Girard Avenue, sits the pretty-in-pink **La Valencia hotel** ④. The hotel looks out onto the village's great natural attraction, **La Jolla Cove** ⑤, which can be accessed from Coast Boulevard, one block to the west. Past the far northern point of the cove, a trail leads down to **La Jolla Caves** ⑥.

The beaches along La Jolla Shores Drive north of the caves are some of the finest in the San Diego area, with long stretches allotted to surfers or swimmers. Nearby is the campus of the Scripps Institution of Oceanography. The institution's **Birch Aquarium at Scripps** ⑦ is inland a bit, off Torrey Pines Road, across from the campus of University of California at San Diego.

La Jolla Shores Drive eventually curves onto Torrey Pines Road, off which you'll soon glimpse the world-famous **Salk Institute** ⑧, designed by Louis I. Kahn. The same road that leads to the institute ends at the cliffs used as the **Torrey Pines Glider Port** ⑨. The hard-to-reach stretch of sand at the foot of the cliffs is officially named **Torrey Pines City Park Beach** ⑩, but locals call it Black's Beach. At the intersection of Torrey Pines Road and Genesee Avenue you'll come to the northern entrance of the huge campus of the **University of California at San Diego** ⑪ and, a bit farther north, to the stretch of wilderness that marks the end of what most locals consider San Diego proper, **Torrey Pines State Beach and Reserve** ⑫.

TIMING

This tour makes for a leisurely day, although it can be driven in a couple of hours, including stops to take in the views and explore the village of La Jolla (though not to hit any of the beaches—or even a fraction of all the pricey boutiques). The Museum of Contemporary Art is closed Monday, and guided tours of the Salk Institute are given on weekdays only.

Sights to See

⊘ ➐ **Birch Aquarium at Scripps.** The largest oceanographic exhibit in the United States, a program of the Scripps Institution of Oceanography, sits at the end of a signed drive leading off North Torrey Pines Road just north of La Jolla Village Drive. More than 30 tanks are filled with colorful saltwater fish, and a 70,000-gallon tank simulates a La Jolla kelp forest. Besides the fish themselves, attractions include a gallery with sea-theme exhibits, a simulated submarine ride, supermarket shelves stocked with products derived from the sea (including some surprisingly common ones), and other interactive educational exhibits. A concession sells food, and there are outdoor picnic tables. ✉ *2300*

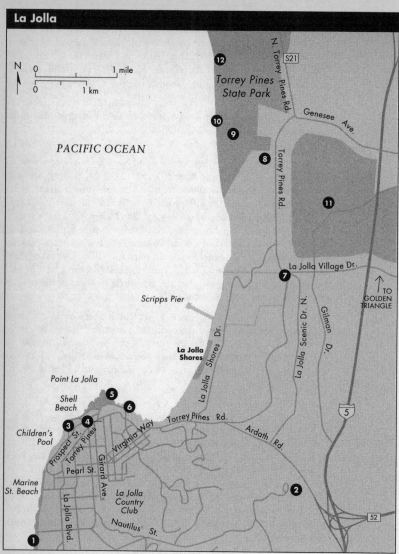

La Jolla

N

0   1 mile

0   1 km

PACIFIC OCEAN

12 Torrey Pines State Park

S21

N. Torrey Pines Rd.

Genesee Ave.

10

9

8

Torrey Pines Rd.

11

La Jolla Village Dr.

7

TO GOLDEN TRIANGLE

Scripps Pier

La Jolla Scenic Dr. N.

Gilman Dr.

La Jolla Shores Dr.

La Jolla Shores

Point La Jolla

Shell Beach

5

6

Children's Pool

3

4

Virginia Way

Torrey Pines Rd.

Ardath Rd.

Prospect St.

Torrey Pines

Girard Ave.

Pearl St.

Marine St. Beach

La Jolla Blvd.

La Jolla Country Club

2

Nautilus St.

52

5

1

Birch Aquarium
at Scripps **7**

La Jolla Caves **6**

La Jolla Cove **5**

La Valencia Hotel . . . **4**

Mount Soledad. **2**

Museum of
Contemporary
Art, San Diego **3**

Salk Institute **8**

Torrey Pines
City Park Beach . . . **10**

Torrey Pines
Glider Port **9**

Torrey Pines
State Beach and
Reserve **12**

University of
California at
San Diego **11**

Windansea Beach . . **1**

Expedition Way, La Jolla, ☎ *858/534–3474,* ⟨WEB⟩ *www.aquarium.ucsd. edu.* 🎫 *$8.50, parking $3.* 🕙 *Daily 9–5.*

Golden Triangle. The La Jolla area's newest enclave, spreading through the Sorrento Valley east of I–5, is a far cry from the beach communities with which the name La Jolla has long been associated. High-tech research-and-development companies, attracted to the Golden Triangle area in part by the facilities of the University of California at San Diego, the Scripps Institution of Oceanography, and the Salk Institute, have developed huge state-of-the-art compounds in areas that were populated solely by coyotes and jays not so long ago. The area along La Jolla Village Drive and Genesee Avenue has become an architectural proving ground for futuristic buildings. The most striking are those in the Michael Graves–designed Aventine complex, visible from I–5 at the La Jolla Village Drive exit. A bit south, near the Nobel exit, and eye-catching in another way, the huge, white Mormon Temple looks like a psychedelic medieval castle; completed in 1993, it still startles drivers heading up the freeway. ✉ *La Jolla*

⟨🌀⟩ **⑥ La Jolla Caves.** It's a walk down 145 sometimes slippery steps to Sunny Jim Cave, the largest of the grottoes in La Jolla Cove. For many years the caves were entered via the La Jolla Cave and Shell Shop, but in 1998 the shop moved to Seaport Village and the cave entrance came under the aegis of the Cave Store, a throwback to the 1902 shop that served as the underground portal. The Cave Store sells postcards and T-shirts as well as local landscapes and vintage watercolors; it also displays historic photos of La Jolla and collects cave admission fees. There's a coffee bar in the shop, and high tea is served in a lovely English-style garden in the back. ✉ *1325 Cave St., La Jolla,* ☎ *858/459–0746.* 🎫 *$2.* 🕙 *Daily 9 until dark.*

★ **⑤ La Jolla Cove.** The wooded spread that looks out over a shimmering blue inlet is what first attracted everyone to La Jolla, from Native Americans to the glitterati; it is the village's enduring cachet. You'll find the cove—as locals always refer to it, as though it were the only one in San Diego—beyond where Girard Avenue dead-ends into Coast Boulevard, marked by towering palms that line a promenade where people strolling in drop-dead designer clothes are as common as Frisbee throwers.

Smaller beaches appear and disappear with the tides, which carve small private coves in cliffs covered with ice plants. Pathways lead down to the beaches. Keep an eye on the tide to avoid getting trapped once the waves come in. A long layer of sandstone stretching out above the waves provides a perfect sunset-watching spot, with plenty of tiny tide pools formed in eroded pockets in the rocks; starfish, sea anemones, and hermit crabs cluster here when the tide is in. Be careful, because these rocks can get slippery.

An underwater preserve at the north end of La Jolla Cove makes the adjoining beach the most popular one in the area. On summer days, when the water visibility reaches 20 ft deep or so, the sea seems to disappear under the mass of bodies floating face down, snorkels poking up out of the water. The small beach is covered with blankets, towels, and umbrellas, and the lawns at the top of the stairs leading down to the cove are staked out by groups of scuba divers, complete with wet suits and tanks. The **Children's Pool,** at the south end of the park, has a curving beach protected by a seawall from strong currents and waves. Since the pool and its beach have become home to an ever-growing colony of Harbor seals, it's no longer open to swimmers, however it's the best place on the coast to view these engaging creatures.

If you're not here by noon, forget about finding a parking spot or a small square of sand for your towel. But no matter what time you arrive, walk through **Ellen Browning Scripps Park,** past the groves of twisted junipers to the cliff's edge. Perhaps one of the open-air shelters overlooking the sea will be free, and you can spread your picnic out on a table and enjoy the scenery.

4 **La Valencia.** The art deco–style La Valencia, which has operated as a luxury hotel since 1928, has long been a gathering spot for Hollywood celebrities; in the 1940s Gregory Peck would invite friends to La Valencia's Whaling Bar to try to persuade them to participate in one of his favorite projects, the La Jolla Theater. Today the hotel's grand lobby, with floor-to-ceiling windows overlooking La Jolla Cove, is a popular wedding spot, and the Whaling Bar is still a favorite meeting place for power brokers. ✉ *1132 Prospect St., La Jolla,* ☎ *858/454–0771.*

2 **Mount Soledad.** La Jolla's highest spot can be reached by taking Nautilus Street all the way east. The top of the mountain is an excellent vantage point from which to get a sense of San Diego's geography: looking down from here you can see the coast from the county's northern border to the south far beyond downtown—barring smog and haze. A half-acre on the summit is used to honor those killed in wars. The steel-and-concrete cross memorializes veterans, and services are held here on Memorial Day. ✉ *La Jolla*

★ **3** **Museum of Contemporary Art, San Diego.** The oldest section of San Diego's modern art museum was a residence designed by Irving Gill (1870–1936) for philanthropist Ellen Browning Scripps in 1916. Robert Venturi and his colleagues at Venturi, Scott Brown and Associates updated and expanded the compound in the mid-1990s. The architects respected Gill's original geometric structure and clean, mission-style lines while adding their own distinctive touches. The result is a striking contemporary building that looks as though it's always been here.

The light-filled Axline Court serves as the entrance to the museum; it does triple duty as reception area, exhibition hall, and forum for special events. A patterned terrazzo floor leads to galleries where the museum's permanent collection and rotating exhibits are on display. The artwork inside gets major competition from the setting: you can look out from the top of a grand stairway onto a landscaped garden that contains permanent and temporary sculpture exhibits as well as rare 100-year-old California plant specimens and, beyond that, to the Pacific Ocean. The bookstore and the refurbished Sherwood Auditorium have separate outside entrances, so you don't have to enter the museum to browse the modern-art volumes and stylish design gifts or attend the auditorium's programs.

The permanent collection of post-1950s art naturally has a strong representation of California artists but also includes examples of every major art movement of the past half-century—works by Andy Warhol, Robert Rauschenberg, Frank Stella, Joseph Cornell, and Jenny Holzer, to name a few. Important pieces by artists from San Diego and Tijuana were acquired in the 1990s. The museum also gets major visiting shows. The Museum Café serves soups, salads, and sandwiches as well as drinks. ✉ *700 Prospect St., La Jolla,* ☎ *858/454–3541,* WEB *www. mcasandiego.org.* ▢ *$4; free 1st Sun. and 3rd Tues. of month.* ☉ *Thurs. 11–8, Fri.–Tues 11–5.*

8 **Salk Institute.** The world-famous biological-research facility founded by polio vaccine inventor Jonas Salk sits on 26 cliff-top acres. For the original 1965 twin structures designed in consultation with Dr. Salk, modernist architect Louis I. Kahn used poured concrete and other low-maintenance materials to clever effect. The thrust of the laboratory–office complex is outward toward the Pacific Ocean, an orientation that is accentuated by a foot-wide "Stream of Life" that flows through the center of a travertine marble courtyard between the buildings. The courtyard and stream of water were inspired by architect Louis Barragán. Architects-to-be and building buffs enjoy the free tours of the property; call ahead to book, because the tours take place only when enough people express interest. ⊠ *10010 N. Torrey Pines Rd., La Jolla,* ☎ *858/453–4100 ext. 1200.* ⚏ *Free.* ⊙ *Grounds weekdays 9–5; guided architectural tours daily at 11 and noon.*

⑩ **Torrey Pines City Park Beach.** Black's Beach—as locals call it—is one of the most beautiful and secluded stretches of sand in San Diego, backed by cliffs whose colors change with the angle of the sun. There are no rest rooms, showers, or snack shops, although some hardy (and law-breaking) entrepreneurs lug ice chests filled with sodas and beer down the cliffs to sell to the unprepared. The paths leading down to the beach are steep, and the cliffs are unstable—pay attention to the safety signs and stick to the well-traveled trails. Black's Beach was clothing-optional for many years; although nudity is now prohibited by law, many people still shed their suits whenever the authorities are out of sight. ⊠ *La Jolla*

⑨ **Torrey Pines Glider Port.** On days when the winds are just right, gliders line the cliffs, waiting for the perfect gust to carry them into the sky. Seasoned hang gliders with a good command of the current can soar over the sea for hours, then ride the winds back to the cliffs. Less-experienced fliers sometimes land on the beach below, to the cheers and applause of the sunbathers who scoot out of the way. If you're coming via the freeway, take the Genesee Avenue exit west from I–5 and follow the signs when you approach the coast. ⊠ *La Jolla.*

⑫ **Torrey Pines State Beach and Reserve.** *Pinus torreyana,* the rarest native pine tree in the United States, enjoys a 1,750-acre sanctuary at the northern edge of La Jolla. About 6,000 of these unusual trees, some as tall as 60 ft, grow on the cliffs here. The park is one of only two places in the world (the other is Santa Rosa Island, off Santa Barbara) where the torrey pine grows naturally. The reserve has several hiking trails leading to the cliffs, 300 ft above the ocean; trail maps are available at the park station. Wildflowers grow profusely in the spring, and the ocean panoramas are always spectacular. When in this upper part of the park, respect the various restrictions. Not permitted: picnicking, smoking, leaving the trails, or collecting plant specimens.

You can unwrap your sandwiches, however, at Torrey Pines State Beach, just below the reserve. When the tide is out, it's possible to walk south all the way past the lifeguard towers to Black's Beach over rocky promontories carved by the waves (avoid the bluffs, however; they're unstable). **Los Peñasquitos Lagoon** at the north end of the reserve is one of the many natural estuaries that flow inland between Del Mar and Oceanside. It's a good place to watch shorebirds. Volunteers lead guided nature walks at 11:30 and 1:30 on most weekends. ⊠ *N. Torrey Pines Rd. (also known as Old Hwy. 101), La Jolla. Exit I–5 onto Carmel Valley Rd. going west, then turn left (south) on Old Hwy. 101,* ☎ *858/755–2063.* ⚏ *Parking $2 (2 large parking lots on both sides of Los Peñasquitos Lagoon; another up the hill by the park visitor center).* ⊙ *Daily 8–sunset.*

⑪ **University of California at San Diego.** The campus of San Diego's most prestigious research university spreads over 1,200 acres of coastal canyons and eucalyptus groves, where students and faculty jog, bike, and rollerblade to class. If you're interested in contemporary art, ask at one of the two information booths for a campus map that shows the location of the Stuart Collection, 14 thought-provoking sculptures arrayed around campus; Nam June Paik, William Wegman, Niki de St. Phalle, and Jenny Holzer are among the artists whose works are displayed. UCSD's Price Center has a well-stocked, two-level bookstore—the largest in San Diego—and a good coffeehouse, Espresso Roma. Look for the postmodern Geisel Library (named for longtime La Jolla residents "Dr. Seuss" and his wife), which resembles a large spaceship. ⊠ *Exit I–5 onto La Jolla Village Dr. going west; take the Gilman Dr. off-ramp to the right and continue on to the information kiosk at the campus entrance, La Jolla,* ☎ *858/534–4414 for campus tour information.* ☉ *90–min campus tours Sun. at 2 from the South Gilman Information Pavilion; reserve before 3 Fri.*

❶ Windansea Beach. Fans of pop satirist Tom Wolfe may recall *The Pump House Gang*, which pokes fun at the southern California surfing culture. Wolfe drew many of his barbs from observations he made at Windansea, the surfing beach west of La Jolla Boulevard near Nautilus Street. The wave action here is said to be as good as that in Hawai'i. ⊠ *La Jolla.*

NEED A BREAK?	A breakfast of the excellent buttery croissants or brioches at the **French Pastry Shop** (⊠ 5550 La Jolla Blvd., La Jolla, ☎ 858/454–9094) will prep you for some serious tanning at Windansea Beach.

MISSION BAY AND SEAWORLD

The 4,600-acre Mission Bay aquatic park is San Diego's monument to sports and fitness. Admission to its 27 mi of bay-shore beaches and 17 mi of ocean frontage is free. All you need for a perfect day is a bathing suit, shorts, and the right selection of playthings.

When explorer Juan Rodríguez Cabrillo first spotted the bay in 1542, he called it Bahía Falsa (False Bay) because the ocean-facing inlet led to acres of swampland that was inhospitable to boats and inhabitants. In the 1960s the city planners decided to dredge the swamp and build a bay with acres of beaches and lawns. Only 25% of the land was permitted to be commercially developed, and only a handful of resort hotels break up the striking natural landscape.

You don't have to go far from the freeway to experience the beach-party atmosphere of Mission Bay. A 5-mi-long pathway runs parallel to I–5 through the eastern section of the bay from a trailer park and miniature golf course, south past the high-rise Hilton Hotel to Sea World Drive. The sky above the lawns facing I–5 is flooded with the bright colors of huge, intricately made kites: the San Diego Kite Club meets on East Mission Bay Drive south of the Hilton, and on the weekends they set loose their amazing creations.

Playgrounds and picnic areas abound on the beach and low grassy hills of the park. Group gatherings, company picnics, and birthday parties are common sights; huge parking lots accommodate swelling crowds on sunny days. On weekday evenings, joggers, bikers, and skaters take over. In the daytime, swimmers, water-skiers, fishers, and boaters—some in single-person kayaks, others in crowded powerboats—vie for space in the water. The San Diego Crew Classic, which takes place in late March or April, fills this area of the bay with teams from all over the country. College reunions, complete with flying school colors and keg beer, are popular at the event.

North of Belmont Park to Pacific Beach, Mission Boulevard runs along a narrow strip embraced by the Pacific Ocean on the west, called Mission Beach, and the bay on the east. The pathways in this area are lined with vacation homes, many of which can be rented by the week or month. Those who are fortunate enough to live here year-round have the bay as their front yard, with wide sandy beaches, volleyball courts, and— less of an advantage—an endless stream of sightseers on the sidewalk.

One Mission Bay caveat: swimmers should note signs warning about water pollution; certain areas of the bay are chronically polluted, and bathing is strongly discouraged.

Numbers in the text correspond to numbers in the margin and on the Mission Bay map.

A Good Tour

If you're coming from I–5, the **San Diego Visitor Information Center** ① is just about at the end of the Clairemont Drive–East Mission Bay Drive exit (you'll see the prominent sign). At the point where East Mission Bay Drive turns into Sea WorldDrive you can detour left to **Fiesta Island** ②, popular with jet skiers and speedboat racers. Continue around the curve to the west to reach **SeaWorld of California** ③, the area's best-known attraction.

You'll next come to Ingraham Street, the central north–south drag through the bay. If you take it north, you'll shortly spot Vacation Road, which leads into the focal point of this part of the bay, the waterskiing hub of **Vacation Isle** ④. At Ingraham, Sea World Drive turns into Sunset Cliffs Boulevard and intersects with West Mission Bay Drive. Past this intersection, Quivira Way leads west toward **Hospitality Point** ⑤, where there are nice, quiet places to have a picnic.

If you continue west on West Mission Bay Drive, just before it meets Mission Boulevard, you'll come to the Bahia Resort Hotel, where you can catch the *Bahia Belle* ⑥ for a cruise around the bay. Ventura Cove, opposite the Bahia Hotel, is another good spot to unpack your cooler. Almost immediately south of where West Mission Bay Drive turns into Mission Boulevard is the resurrected **Belmont Park** ⑦.

TIMING

It would take less than an hour to drive this tour. You may not find a visit to SeaWorld fulfilling unless you spend at least a half day; a full day is recommended. The park is open daily, but not all its attractions are open year-round.

Sights to See

❻ *Bahia Belle.* At the dock of the Bahia Resort Hotel, on the eastern shores of West Mission Bay Drive, you can board a restored stern-wheeler for a sunset cruise of the bay and party on until the wee hours. There's always music, mostly jazz, rock, and blues, and on Friday and Saturday nights the bands are live. You can imbibe at the Belle's full bar, which opens at 9:30, but many revelers like to disembark at the Bahia's sister hotel, the Catamaran, and have a few rounds at the Cannibal Bar before reboarding (the boat cruises between the two hotels, which co-own it, stopping to pick up passengers every half hour). The first cruise on Sunday is devoted to kids, but most cruises get a mixed crowd of families, couples, and singles. ⊠ *998 W. Mission Bay Dr., Mission Bay,* ☎ *858/488–0551.* ☞ *$6 for unlimited cruising (9:30 PM or later, cruisers must be at least 21); free for guests of the Bahia and Catamaran hotels.* ☉ *Oct.–Nov. and Jan.–June, Fri.–Sat. 7:30 PM–1:30 AM, departures every hr on the ½ hr; July–Sept., Wed.–Sun. on same schedule.*

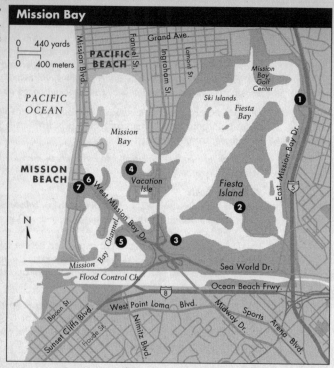

Mission Bay

👆 **7** **Belmont Park.** The once-abandoned amusement park between the bay
and Mission Beach boardwalk is now a shopping, dining, and recreation complex. Twinkling lights outline the **roller coaster** on which
screaming thrill-seekers ride more than 2,600 ft of track and 13 hills
(riders must be at least 4′2″). Created as the Giant Dipper in 1925 and
listed on the National Register of Historic Places, this is one of the few
old-time roller coasters left in the United States. **The Plunge,** an indoor
swimming pool, also opened in 1925 as the largest—60 ft by 125 ft—
saltwater pool in the world. It's had fresh water since 1951. Johnny
Weismuller and Esther Williams are among the stars who were cap-
tured on celluloid swimming across Belmont Park's favorite body of
water. Other attractions include **Pirate's Cove,** a fantastic maze of
brightly colored tunnels, slides, an obstacle course, and more, all with
a pirate theme; a video arcade; a submarine ride; bumper cars; a tilt-
a-whirl; an antique carousel; and a trampoline. Belmont Park is also
the place to pick up your neon surf suit or the latest volleyball equipment. ✉ *3146 Mission Blvd., Mission Bay,* ☎ *858/488–1549; 858/488–
3110 for pool,* 🌐 *www.belmontpark.com.* 🎟 *$4 for roller coaster,
$3 for bumper cars and tilt-a-whirl, all other rides $2; full-day unlimited
ride package $13.95 for 50″ and over, $8.95 for under 50″; all rides
75¢ June–Aug., Tues. 4 PM to closing; Pirate's Cove $6.50 ages 3–18
weekdays, $4.50 weekends; pool $2.75 for one-time entry.* 🕐 *Park opens
at 11 daily, ride hrs vary seasonally; pool open weekdays 5:30–8 AM,
noon–1 PM, and 2:30–8 PM and weekends 8–4.*

2 **Fiesta Island.** The most undeveloped area of Mission Bay Park is popular with bird-watchers (there's a large protected nesting site for the
California tern at the northern tip of the island) as well as with dog
owners—it's the only place in the park where their pets can run free.
Jet skiers and speedboat racers come here, too. At Christmas it provides an excellent vantage point for viewing the bay's Parade of Lights.
In July the annual Over-the-Line Tournament, a competition involv-

ing a local version of softball, attracts thousands of players and oglers, drawn by the teams' raunchy names and outrageous behavior. When you drive onto Fiesta Island you can't immediately turn back, as the road leads one way around the perimeter.

⑤ Hospitality Point. Enjoy lunch in this pretty, secluded spot, with a view of sailboats and yachts entering the open sea. At the entrance to Hospitality Point, the Mission Bay Park Headquarters supplies area maps and other recreational information. It's also the place to pick up a permit if you decide to throw a wedding in the park. ⊠ *2581 Quivira Ct., Mission Bay,* ☎ *619/221–8901.* ☼ *Weekdays 9–5; closed city holidays.*

NEED A
BREAK?

Sportsmen's Sea Foods (⊠ 1617 Quivira Rd., Mission Bay, ☎ 619/224–3551) serves good fish-and-chips to eat on the inelegant but scenic patio—by the marina, where sportfishing boats depart daily—or to take out to your chosen picnic spot.

❶ San Diego Visitor Information Center. In addition to being an excellent resource for San Diego tourists—it makes hotel and motel reservations, sells tickets to several attractions at a discount, offers various maps and guides, and has a small gift shop—the center is also a gathering spot for runners, walkers, and exercisers. For boaters it's the place to pick up a map detailing Mission Bay Park launch depths and speeds. ⊠ *2688 E. Mission Bay Dr., Mission Bay,* ☎ *619/276–8200.* ☼ *Mon.–Sat. 9–5 (until 6 in summer), Sun. 9:30–4:30 (until 5:30 in summer).*

☾ ❸ SeaWorld of California. One of the world's largest marine-life amusement parks, SeaWorld is spread over 100 tropically landscaped bayfront acres—and it seems to be expanding into every square inch of available space with new exhibits, shows, and activities.

The majority of the exhibits are walk-through marine environments. In a perpetual favorite, the **Penguin Encounter,** a moving sidewalk passes through a glass-enclosed Arctic area where hundreds of emperor penguins slide over glaciers into icy waters. (The penguins like it cold, so consider bringing a light sweater along for this one.) Kids get a particular kick out of the **Shark Encounter,** where they come face-to-face with sandtiger, nurse, bonnethead, black-tipped, and white-tipped reef sharks by walking through a 57-ft clear acrylic tube that passes through the 280,000-gallon shark habitat. The hands-on **California Tide Pool** exhibit gives you a chance to get to know San Diego's indigenous marine life. At **Forbidden Reef** you can feed bat rays and go nose-to-nose with creepy moray eels. At **Rocky Point Preserve** you can view bottlenose dolphins, as well as Alaskan sea otters. At **Wild Arctic,** which starts out with a simulated helicopter ride to a research post at the North Pole, beluga whales, walruses, and polar bears can be viewed in areas decked out like the wrecked hulls of two 19th-century sailing ships. **Manatee Rescue** lets you watch the gentle-giant marine mammals cavorting in a 215,000-gallon tank. Various **freshwater and saltwater aquariums** hold underwater creatures from around the world. And for younger kids who need to release lots of energy, **Shamu's Happy Harbor** is a hands-on fun zone that features, among other attractions, a two-story ship, where pretend pirates aim water cannons at one another (be prepared with a change of dry clothes).

SeaWorld's highlights are its four large-arena entertainments. You can arrive 10 or 15 minutes in advance to get front-row seats, and the stadiums are large enough for everyone to get a seat even at the busiest times. The traditional favorite is the **Shamu show,** with synchronized killer whales bringing down the house, but the less publicized **Fools With Tools** stars two California sea lions, Clyde and Seamore, as comic handymen whose best-laid plans are foiled by a supporting cast of Asian sea otters. Another favorite is the **Pirates 4-D** show, a hilarious tale of a hapless pirate crew and its wacky captain. More than a 3-D movie, Pirates 4-D introduces a "fourth dimension," namely special effects like sprays of water, blasts of air, and other wild surprises. The film stars Leslie Nielsen as Captain Lucky and *Monty Python's* Eric Idle, as Pierre, Captain Lucky's loyal first mate.

Trainer For A Day, allows you to get a first-hand look at how Sea World's trainers spend a work day. The $395 fee may seem hefty, but it buys a once-in-a-lifetime opportunity. **Shipwreck Rapids,** SeaWorld of California's first adventure ride, offers plenty of excitement—but you may end up getting soaked. For five minutes nine "shipwrecked" passengers careen down a river in a raftlike inner tube, encountering a series of obstacles, including several waterfalls. There's no extra charge, making this one of SeaWorld's great bargains—which means that you should expect long lines.

Not all the exhibits are water-oriented. **Pets Rule!** showcases the antics of more common animals like dogs, cats, birds, and even a pig, all set to prove the supremacy of our four-legged (or feathered) friends. One segment of the show actually has regular housecats climbing ladders and hanging upside down as they cross a high-wire. The majority of the animals used in the show were adopted from shelters. Those who want to head to higher ground might consider the **Southwest Airlines Skytower,** a glass elevator that ascends 320 ft; the views of San Diego County from the ocean to the mountains are especially spectacular in early morning and late evening. The **Bayside Sky Ride,** a five-minute aerial tram ride that leaves from the same spot, travels across Mission Bay. Admission for the Skytower and the tram is $2.75 apiece. The fact that Anheuser-Busch is the park's parent company is evident in the presence of the beer company's signature Clydesdales, huge horses that you can visit in their "hamlet" when they're not putting on shows.

SeaWorld is chockablock with souvenir shops and refreshment stands (the only picnic grounds are outside the park entrance), so it's hard to come away from here without spending a lot of money on top of the hefty entrance fee (the children's admission is $32.95) and $7 parking tab. It's smart to take advantage of the two-day entry option, only $4 more than a single-day admission: if you try to get your money's worth by fitting everything in on a single day, you're all likely to end up tired and cranky. Many hotels, especially those in the Mission Bay area, also offer SeaWorld specials that may include rate reductions or two days' entry for the price of one. It's also a good idea to take a change of clothes along, especially when the weather is on the cool side and you sit in the first 10 rows at one of the marine shows, or ride Shipwreck Rapids; you can rent a locker to stow belongings. ✉ *1720 South Shores Rd., near the west end of I–8, Mission Bay,* ☎ *619/226–3815; 619/226–3901 for recorded information,* 🕸 *www.seaworld.com.* 💰 *$42.95, 2-day package $46.95; parking $7 cars, $4 motorcycles, $9 RVs and campers; 90-min behind-the-scenes walking tours $10 additional. AE, D, MC, V.* ☉ *Daily 10–dusk; extended hrs in summer.*

NEED A BREAK?   One of the perks of visiting a theme park owned by a beer distributor is free samples of suds, a good way to wash down the corned-beef sandwiches and the like served at **The Deli,** in the Anheuser-Busch Hospitality Center near the park entrance. Healthier fare—grilled fish, vegetables, and salads, along with cheeseburgers and fries—are the order of the day at the huge **Shipwreck Reef Cafe,** where you're likely to be entertained by park animals and juggling castaways.

CALIFORNIA'S PADRE PRESIDENT

SAN DIEGO, the first European settlement in Southern California, was founded by Father Junípero Serra in July 1769. A member of the Franciscan order, Father Serra was part of a larger expedition that was headed by explorer Don Gaspar de Portola. King Charles III of Spain, responding to pressure from English and Russian explorers and traders moving down the West Coast, chartered the party to travel from outposts in Baja California north to explore and occupy the territory known then as Alta California.

When they arrived in San Diego, the Spaniards found about 20,000 Kumeyaay Indians living in a hundred or so villages along the coast and inland. To establish the foothold for the king, the missionaries attempted to convert the Kumeyaays to Christianity, and taught them agricultural and other skills so they could work what would become vast holdings of the missions.

Mission San Diego Alcalá, established on a hillside above what is now Mission Valley in San Diego, was the first of 21 that the Franciscans built along the coast of California. After establishing the mission and presidio in San Diego, Serra and Portola moved on, founding the Mission San Carlos Borromeo and presidio at Monterey. Mission San Carlos was later moved to Carmel, where Father Serra settled and maintained his headquarters until his death in 1784.

Father Serra, the padre president of California, established nine missions. These include: San Antonio de Padua, 1771; San Gabriel, 1771; San Luis Obispo, 1772; Mission Dolores, 1776;

San Juan Capistrano, 1776; Santa Clara, 1777; and San Buenaventura, 1777. He personally oversaw the planning, construction, and staffing of each mission. His work took him from Carmel to locations in northern and southern California, where he supervised the initial construction of the missions and conferred the sacraments. It's estimated that during this period he walked more than 24,000 mi in California to visit the other missions.

The missions, which became known as Serra's Beads, comprised millions of acres and were in fact small self-sufficient cities with the church as the centerpiece. In addition to converting the Indians to Christianity and teaching the Native Americans European ways, the padres managed farming, education, and industries such as candle making and tanning. San Diego is the southernmost mission, while the mission at Sonoma is the northernmost; each was established about 30 mi—or a day's walk between each—apart and linked by the El Camino Highway. The missions were also the earliest form of lodging in the Golden State, known far and wide for the hospitality afforded visitors.

Father Serra spent barely a year in San Diego before embarking on his journey to establish missions across California, but his presence left a lasting imprint on the city. You can see some of the history at the Serra Museum and at Mission San Diego Alcalá. And you can trace his footsteps along El Camino Real by driving U.S. 101, the historic route that traverses coastal California from south to north.

–Bobbi Zane

❹ Vacation Isle. Ingraham Street bisects the island, providing two distinct experiences for visitors. The west side is taken up by the San Diego Paradise Point Resort, but you don't have to be a guest to enjoy the hotel's lushly landscaped grounds and bay-front restaurants. The water-ski clubs congregate at **Ski Beach** on the east side of the island, where there's a parking lot as well as picnic areas and rest rooms. Ski Beach is the site of the Thunderboats Unlimited Hydroplane Championships, held in September. At a pond on the south side of the island children and young-at-heart adults take part year-round in motorized miniature boat races. ⊠ *Mission Bay.*

OLD TOWN

San Diego's Spanish and Mexican history and heritage are most evident in Old Town, north of downtown at Juan Street, near the intersection of Interstates 5 and 8. Old Town didn't become a state historic park until 1968, but private efforts kept the area's history alive until then, and a number of San Diego's oldest structures have been restored.

Old Town is the first European settlement in southern California, but the pueblo's true beginnings took place overlooking Old Town from atop Presidio Park, where Father Junípero Serra established the first of California's missions, San Diego de Alcalá, in 1769. Some of San Diego's original inhabitants, the Kumeyaay Indians—called the Diegueños by the Spaniards—were forced to abandon their seminomadic lifestyle and live at the mission. They were expected to follow Spanish customs and adopt Christianity as their religion, but they resisted fiercely; of all the California missions, San Diego de Alcalá was the least successful in carrying out conversions. For security reasons the mission was built on a hill, but it didn't have an adequate water supply, and food became scarce as the number of Kumeyaays and Spanish soldiers occupying the site increased.

In 1774 the hilltop was declared a Royal Presidio, or fortress, and the mission was moved 6 mi west to the San Diego River. The Kumeyaays, responding to the loss of their land as the mission expanded along the riverbed, attacked and burned it in 1775. A later assault on the presidio was less successful, and their revolt was short-lived. By 1800 about 1,500 Kumeyaays were living on the mission's grounds, receiving religious instruction and adapting to Spanish ways.

The pioneers living within the presidio's walls were mostly Spanish soldiers, poor Mexicans, and mestizos of Spanish and Native American ancestry, many of whom were unaccustomed to farming San Diego's arid land. When Mexico gained independence from Spain in 1821, it claimed its lands in California and flew the Mexican flag over the presidio. The Mexican government, centered some 2,000 mi away in Monterrey, stripped the missions of their landholdings, and an aristocracy of landholders began to emerge. At the same time, settlers were beginning to move down from the presidio to what is now Old Town.

A rectangular plaza was laid out along today's San Diego Avenue to serve as the settlement's center. In 1846, during the war between Mexico and the United States, a detachment of U.S. Marines raised the Stars and Stripes over the plaza. The flag was removed once or twice, but by early 1848 Mexico had surrendered California, and the U.S. flag remained. San Diego became an incorporated city in 1850, with Old Town as its center.

On San Diego Avenue, the district's main drag, art galleries and expensive gift shops are interspersed with tacky curios shops, restaurants, and open-air stands selling inexpensive Mexican pottery, jewelry, and blankets. The Old Town Esplanade on San Diego Avenue between Harney and Conde streets is the best of several mall-like affairs constructed in mock Mexican-plaza style. Shops and restaurants also line Juan and Congress streets.

Access to Old Town is easy thanks to the nearby Transit Center. Ten bus lines stop here, as do the San Diego Trolley and the Coaster commuter rail line. Two large parking lots linked to the park by an underground pedestrian walkway ease some of the parking congestion, and signage leading from I–8 to the Transit Center is easy to follow. If you're not familiar with the area, however, avoid the "Old Town" exit from I–5, which leaves you floundering near Mission Bay without further directions.

Numbers in the text correspond to numbers in the margin and on the Old Town San Diego map.

A Good Tour

It's possible to trek around Old Town and see all its sights in one day, but we recommend making this a walking-driving combination.

Visit the information center at Seeley Stable, just off Old Town Plaza, to orient yourself to the various sights in **Old Town San Diego State Historic Park** ①. When you've had enough history, cross north on the west side of the plaza to **Bazaar del Mundo** ②, where you can shop or enjoy some nachos on the terrace of a Mexican restaurant. Walk down San Diego Avenue, which flanks the south side of Old Town's historic plaza, east to Harney Street and the **Thomas Whaley Museum** ③. Then continue east 2½ blocks on San Diego Avenue beyond Arista Street to the **El Campo Santo** ④ cemetery. **Heritage Park** ⑤ is perched on a hill above Juan Street, north of the museum and cemetery. Drive west on Juan Street and north on Taylor Street to Presidio Drive, which will lead you up the hill on which **Presidio Park** ⑥ and the **Junípero Serra Museum** ⑦ sit.

TIMING

Try to time your visit to coincide with the free daily tours of Old Town given at 11 AM and 2 PM by costumed park service employees at Seeley Stable. It takes about two hours to walk through Old Town. If you drive to Presidio Park, allot another hour to explore the grounds and museum.

Sights to See

❷ **Bazaar del Mundo.** North of San Diego's Old Town Plaza lies the area's unofficial center, built to represent a colonial Mexican square. The central courtyard is always in blossom, with magenta bougainvillea, scarlet hibiscus, and irises, poppies, and petunias in season. Ballet Folklorico and flamenco dancers perform on weekend afternoons, and the bazaar frequently hosts arts-and-crafts exhibits and Mexican festivals. Colorful shops specializing in Latin American crafts and unusual gift items border the square. Although many of the shops here have high-quality wares, prices can be considerably higher than those at shops on the other side of Old Town Plaza; it's a good idea to do some comparative shopping before you make any purchases. ✉ *2754 Calhoun St., Old Town,* ☎ *619/296–3161,* WEB *www.bazaardelmundo.com.* ☉ *Shops daily 10–9.*

NEED A BREAK?   **La Panadería** bakery (✉ southeast corner of the Bazaar del Mundo, Old Town, ☎ 619/291–7662) sells hot *churros*—long sticks of fried dough coated with cinnamon and sugar. Get some to go and sit out on one of the benches and enjoy the live music at the bandstand (weekends only).

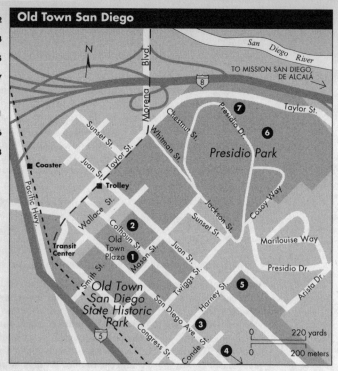

Old Town San Diego

4 El Campo Santo. The old adobe-walled cemetery established in 1849 was the burial place for many members of Old Town's founding families, as well as for some gamblers and bandits who passed through town until 1880. Antonio Garra, a chief who led an uprising of the San Luis Rey Indians, was executed at El Campo Santo in front of the open grave he was forced to dig for himself. These days the small cemetery is a peaceful stop for visitors to Old Town. Most of the markers give only approximations of where the people named on them are buried; some of the early settlers laid to rest at El Campo Santo really reside under San Diego Avenue. ⊠ *North side of San Diego Ave. S, between Arista and Ampudia Sts., Old Town.*

5 Heritage Park. A number of San Diego's important Victorian buildings are the focus of this 7%₁₀-acre park, up the Juan Street hill near Harney Street. The buildings were moved here and restored by Save Our Heritage Organization, and include southern California's first synagogue, a one-room classic revival–style structure built in 1889 for Congregation Beth Israel. The most interesting of the six former residences might be the Sherman Gilbert House, which has a widow's walk and intricate carving on its decorative trim. It was built for real estate dealer John Sherman in 1887 at the then-exorbitant cost of $20,000— indicating just how profitable the booming housing market could be. Bronze plaques detail the history of all the houses, some of which may seem surprisingly colorful; they are in fact accurate representations of the bright tones of the era. The homes are now used for offices, shops, and, in one case, a bed-and-breakfast inn. The climb up to the park is a little steep, but the view of the harbor is great. Only the synagogue is open to visitors. ⊠ *2455 Heritage Park Row (county parks office), Old Town,* ☎ *858/694–3049.*

7 Junípero Serra Museum. San Diego's original Spanish presidio (fortress) and California's first mission were perched atop the 160-ft hill overlooking Mission Valley. It's now the domain of a Spanish mission–style museum devoted to the history of the hill from the time it was occupied by the Kumeyaay Indians until 1929, when the museum was established, along with Presidio Park, by department store magnate and philanthropist George Marston. Artifacts include Kumeyaay baskets, Spanish riding gear, and a painting that Father Serra would have viewed in Mission San Diego de Alcalá. The education room has hands-on investigation stations where kids can grind acorns in metates, dig for buried artifacts with archaeology tools, or dress up in period costumes—one represents San Diego founding father Alonzo Horton. Ascend the tower to compare the view you'd have gotten before 1929 with the one you have today. The museum, now operated by the San Diego Historical Society, is at the north end of Presidio Park, near Taylor Street. ⊠ *2727 Presidio Dr., Old Town,* ☎ *619/297–3258.* ⌨ *$5.* ☉ *Fri.–Sun. 10–4:30.*

OFF THE
BEATEN PATH

MISSION SAN DIEGO DE ALCALÁ – It's hard to imagine how remote California's earliest mission once must have been; these days, it's accessible by a major freeway (I–15), and by the San Diego Trolley. Mission San Diego de Alcalá, the first of a chain of 21 missions stretching northward along the coast, was established by Father Junípero Serra in 1769 on Presidio Hill, and moved to its present location in 1774. There was no greater security from enemy attack here: Padre Luis Jayme, California's first Christian martyr, was clubbed to death by Kumeyaay Indians, whom he was trying to convert, in 1775. The present church is the fifth to be built on the site; it was reconstructed in 1931 following the outlines of the 1813 church. It's 150 ft long but only 35 ft wide because, without easy means of joining beams, the mission buildings were only as wide as the trees that served as their ceiling supports. Father Jayme is buried in the mission sanctuary, and a small museum named for him documents the history of the mission, exhibiting tools and artifacts from the early days. From the peaceful palm-bedecked gardens out back you can gaze at the 46-ft-high *campanario*, the mission's most distinctive feature; one of its five bells was cast in 1822. ⊠ *10818 San Diego Mission Rd., Mission Valley (from I–15, take Friars Rd. east and Rancho Mission Rd. south),* ☎ *619/281–8449.* ⌨ *$3.* ☉ *Daily 9–4:45.*

★ ❶ **Old Town San Diego State Historic Park.** The six square blocks on the site of San Diego's original pueblo are the heart of Old Town. Most of the 20 historic buildings preserved or re-created by the park cluster around **Old Town Plaza,** bounded by Wallace Street on the west, Calhoun Street on the north, Mason Street on the east, and San Diego Avenue on the south; you can see the presidio from behind the cannon by the flagpole. The plaza is a pleasant place for resting and regrouping as you plan your tour of the park and watch passers-by. San Diego Avenue is closed to vehicle traffic here.

Some of Old Town's buildings were destroyed in a fire in 1872, but after the site became a state historic park in 1968, efforts were begun to reconstruct or restore the structures that remained. Seven of the original adobes are still intact. The tour pamphlet available at Seeley Stable gives details about all of the historic houses on the plaza and in its vicinity; a few of the more interesting ones are noted below. Several reconstructed buildings serve as restaurants or as shops purveying wares reminiscent of those that might have been available in the original Old Town; Racine & Laramie, a painstakingly reproduced version of San Diego's first (1868) cigar store, is especially interesting. The noncommercial houses are open daily 10–5; none charge admission, though donations are appreciated.

The **Robinson-Rose House** (☎ 619/220–5422) was the original commercial center of old San Diego, housing railroad offices, law offices, and the first newspaper press. In addition to serving as the park's visitor center and administrative center, it now hosts a model of Old Town as it looked in 1872, as well as various historic exhibits. (An interpretive center, a replica of the Victorian-era McCoy house, was built behind the Robinson-Rose House in 2001.)

On Mason Street, at the corner of Calhoun Street, **La Casa de Bandini** is one of the prettiest haciendas in San Diego. Built in 1829 by a Peruvian, Juan Bandini, the house served as Old Town's social center during Mexican rule. Albert Seeley, a stagecoach entrepreneur, purchased the home in 1869, built a second story, and turned it into the Cosmopolitan Hotel, a comfortable way station for travelers on the daylong trip south from Los Angeles. Today the hacienda's colorful gardens and main-floor dining rooms house a popular Mexican restaurant.

Seeley Stable (✉ 2630 Calhoun St., Old Town, ☎ 619/220–5427), next door to La Casa de Bandini, became San Diego's stagecoach stop in 1867 and was the transportation hub of Old Town until near the turn of the century, when trains became the favored mode of travel. The stable houses a collection of horse-drawn vehicles, some so elaborate that you can see where the term "carriage trade" came from. Also inside are western memorabilia, including an exhibit on the California *vaquero*, the original American cowboy, and a collection of Native American artifacts. An excellent free walking tour of the park leaves from here daily at 11 and 2, weather permitting.

La Casa de Estudillo was built on Mason Street in 1827 by the commander of the San Diego Presidio, Jose Maria Estudillo. The largest and most elaborate of the original adobe homes, it was occupied by members of the Estudillo family until 1887. It was purchased and restored in 1910 by sugar magnate and developer John D. Spreckels, who advertised it in bold lettering on the side as "Ramona's Marriage Place." Despite the meticulous attention to historical detail of the restoration, Spreckel's claim that the small chapel in the house was the site of the wedding in Helen Hunt Jackson's popular novel *Ramona* had no basis in fact; that didn't stop people from coming to see it, however.

The **San Diego Union Newspaper Historical Museum** (✉ Twigg St. and San Diego Ave., Old Town, ☎ no phone) is in a New England–style, wood-frame house prefabricated in the eastern United States and shipped around Cape Horn in 1851. The building has been restored to replicate the newspaper's offices of 1868, when the first edition of the *San Diego Union* was printed.

Also worth exploring in the plaza area are the **Dental Museum, Mason Street School, Wells Fargo Museum, San Diego Courthouse, Commercial Kitchen Museum,** and the **Machade Stewart Adobe Museum.** Ask at the visitor center for locations.

❻ Presidio Park. The hillsides of the 40-acre green space overlooking Old Town from the north end of Taylor Street are popular with picnickers, and many couples have taken their wedding vows on the park's long stretches of lawn, some of the greenest in San Diego. You may encounter enthusiasts of a Californian sport, grass skiing, gliding over the grass and down the hills on wheels. It's a nice walk to the summit from Old Town if you're in good shape and wearing the right shoes—it should take about half an hour. You can also drive to the top of the park via Presidio Drive, off Taylor Street. Presidio Park has a private canyon surrounded by palms at the bottom of the hill, off Taylor Street before it intersects with I–8.

If you do decide to walk, look in at the Presidio Hills Golf Course on Mason Street, which has an unusual clubhouse: it incorporates the ruins of Casa de Carrillo, the town's oldest adobe, constructed in 1820. At the end of Mason Street, veer left on Jackson Street to reach the **Presidio Ruins,** where adobe walls and a bastion have been built above the foundations of the original fortress and chapel. Archaeology students from San Diego State University who excavated the area have marked off the early chapel outlines, although they reburied the artifacts they uncovered in order to protect them. Also on the site are the 28-ft-high Serra Cross, built in 1913 out of brick tiles found in the ruins, and a bronze statue of Father Serra. Before you do much poking around here, however, it's a good idea to get some historical perspective at the Junípero Serra Museum, just to the east. Take Presidio Drive southeast of the museum and you'll come to the site of Fort Stockton, built to protect Old Town and abandoned by the United States in 1848. Plaques and statues also commemorate the Mormon Battalion, which enlisted here to fight in the battle against Mexico. ✉ *1 block north of Old Town.*

③ Thomas Whaley Museum. Thomas Whaley was a New York entrepreneur who came to California during the gold rush. He wanted to provide his East Coast wife all the comforts of home, so in 1856 he had southern California's first two-story brick structure built. The house, which served as the county courthouse and government seat during the 1870s, stands in strong contrast to the Spanish-style adobe residences that surround the nearby historic plaza and marks an early stage of San Diego's "Americanization."

Period furnishings in the living quarters include a miniature dress dummy designed to look like Mary Todd Lincoln, a sofa from Andrew Jackson's White House, and a piano that belonged to singer Jenny Lind. Among the historical artifacts in the reconstructed courtroom is one of the six life masks that exist of Abraham Lincoln. A garden out back includes rosebushes from a pre-hybrid era. The place is perhaps most famed, however, for the ghosts that are said to inhabit it; this is one of the few houses authenticated by the U.S. Department of Commerce as being haunted. ✉ *2482 San Diego Ave., Old Town,* ☎ *619/297–7511.* ☞ *$5.* ⊙ *Oct.– May, Wed.–Mon. 10–4:30; June–Sept., daily 10–4:30.*

3　DINING

Striving to become one of the nation's premier "food cities" of the 21st century, sun-drenched San Diego has abandoned its former laid-back, laissez-faire attitude toward serious cooking and adopted the point of a view that a region this blessed with gorgeous vegetables, fruits, herbs, and seafood should make a culinary statement. The result is a new generation of chefs more eager to spend time in the kitchen than at the beach—a largely youthful group that likes to surprise, dazzle, and delight diners with inventive, up-to-the-millennium creations.

By David
Nelson

ONCE KNOWN BETTER AS A comfortable resort town than a dining destination, San Diego has retained its reputation as a vacationer's paradise even as it has grown to be both the seventh-largest city in the United States and a magnet for restaurateurs and chefs from around the globe. A good deal of the new talent also is homegrown, and it's not unusual for local youths to attend leading culinary academies and return home fired by the desire to remake San Diego cuisine.

The variety of dining possibilities offered by a city that once regarded a "surf 'n' turf" combination as the ultimate in classy chow is staggering, and while the town as yet fails to offer a Tibetan eatery, it now takes for granted exotic cuisines such as Cambodian, Ethiopian, Afghan, and Laotian. Many of these far-flung cuisines are served outside the center in the city's ever more diverse neighborhoods. Downtown, the dramatically restored, lively Gaslamp Quarter offers vigorous nightlife and some 90 restaurants. The eateries range from a few down-at-the-heels holdouts from the days when this historic area had declined to Skid Row status to stylish establishments priced for expense-account types doing business at the nearby San Diego Convention Center.

A stroll down the 5th Avenue restaurant row (which now extends both to 4th and 6th avenues) reveals San Diego's preference for Italian cuisine above all others, but the choice nonetheless is cosmopolitan and extends to casual and *haute* French fare, Spanish tapas and paellas, traditional and nuevo Mexican cuisine and all-American steaks cut thick enough to choke a horse. Really fine, expensive steak houses are still the hot San Diego trend, thanks partly to prosperity in the local high-tech industries, and perhaps partly to boredom with the warnings of health mavens. Seafood abounds, and there's a whole lot of "fusion" going on, which is to say that many menus now present their chef's own rendition of contemporary cuisine, which borrows idiosyncratically from a mixture of culinary traditions.

Near the waterfront on the upper western edge of downtown, the rapidly gentrifying Little Italy district has become a center for excellent, affordable Italian dining, both traditional and more contemporary. The area has a few surprises to offer, too, such as an authentic English pub that is the unofficial headquarters for Commonwealth loyalists from around the globe and a Southwestern-style grill that is the ultimate in trendiness.

In addition to downtown, other areas of San Diego share in the keen sense of energy, fueled by a collective caffeine high acquired in the coffeehouses (some of which are listed in Chapter 4) springing up everywhere from the Gaslamp Quarter to the gas station on the corner. The uptown neighborhoods centered by Hillcrest—a lively, urbane district with a hip San Francisco flavor—are marked by increasing culinary sophistication. Mission Valley, the city's commercial heart, abounds in big restaurants of varying quality, interspersed by smaller establishments devoted to superior fare. And rich, elegant La Jolla, with many of San Diego's most expensive restaurants, offers some of the best dining in the city. To be sure, great cooking blossoms beyond the city's official borders. In nearby Chula Vista, look for authentic, palate-pleasing Mexican fare, while Coronado—the peninsula city across San Diego Bay—has both casual, neighborhood-style eateries and grand hotel dining rooms with dramatic water views. And to the north in the plush suburbs of Del Mar, Solana Beach, and Rancho Santa Fe, elegant surroundings seem to encourage good fare.

The proximity of Mexico and the city's many ties to Japan, China, Vietnam, and other Asian countries account for the influences that San Diego's chefs add to a local cuisine well grounded in classical French technique. The Asian restaurants that abound along and near Convoy Street in the Kearny Mesa area are worth a visit, too.

San Diego is an informal city and few other American cities can offer so many outdoor dining options. The advised attire at most of the restaurants listed below is casual. Reservations are always a good idea, especially on weekends. Restaurants are grouped first by neighborhood, then by type of cuisine.

CATEGORY	COST*
$$$$	over $30
$$$	$20–$30
$$	$10–$20
$	under $10

*per person for a main course at dinner

Coronado

Contemporary

$–$$$ ✕ **Bistro d'Asia.** The name pretty well spells out the intent of this comfortable, sophisticated-looking restaurant within shouting distance of the Hotel Del Coronado. As at a French bistro, the mood is relaxed and the portions generous. The menu overall takes a Chinese point of view but spans the cuisines of East Asia, so that traditional Chinese offerings like the "Buddha's Delight" vegetables and crispy Cantonese panfried noodles are supplemented by spicy, Bangkok-style beef, a Vietnamese-influenced version of kung pao chicken, and even stir-fried tuna in red curry sauce. ⊠ 1301 Orange Ave., Coronado, ☎ 619/437–6677. MC, V.

$–$$ ✕ **Coronado Brewing Company.** The carefully crafted beers served by this casual establishment just two blocks from the bay are good by themselves, but they also make a good accompaniment to beer-steamed bratwurst and beer-battered onion rings, served in mountainous portions. There's indoor seating, a pair of sidewalk terraces and, best of all, a walled garden that provides a quiet haven from the bustle of Orange Avenue. Simple choices are the wisest, from the Philadelphia-style steak sandwich to wood-fired pizzas to baby back ribs basted with spicy, ginger-flavored barbecue sauce. ⊠ 170 Orange Ave., Coronado, ☎ 619/437–4452. MC, V.

Italian

$$–$$$ ✕ **Il Fornaio.** This handsome restaurant occupies an amazing waterfront location, framing stellar views of downtown San Diego with windows that stretch from floor to ceiling. The menu tends toward the creative side, and in deference to the restaurant's name, which means "The Oven," offers an abundance of baked specialties, including pizzas that arrive fragrant and bubbling from the wood-fired hearth. The house antipasto, served for two, is a nice way to start, no matter whether the main course will be lobster-stuffed ravioli or mesquite-grilled lamb chops flavored with thyme and garlic. The servers smile frequently, even when they're not entirely sure what they should be doing. ⊠ 1333 1st Ave., Coronado, ☎ 619/437–4911. AE, D, MC, V.

Seafood

$$$–$$$$ ✕ **Azzura Point.** Decorated in a romantic, 1930s style, Azzura Point ★ is ideal for a leisurely and memorable meal. The view up San Diego Bay to the Coronado Bridge and the downtown skyline is unbeatable. Expect thoroughly contemporary preparations of first-class seasonal

produce, such as quail egg and lobster crèpe, grilled swordfish dressed with foie gras and a tart huckleberry sauce, and herb-crusted rack of lamb with ratatouille. Dishes are often flavored with herbs from the restaurant's extensive garden. Several choice, artisan cheeses are offered as alternatives to the deftly executed desserts. ⊠ *Loews Coronado Bay Resort, 4000 Coronado Bay Rd., Coronado,* ☎ *619/424–4477. AE, DC, MC, V. Closed Mon. No lunch.*

$$$ ✕ **Prince of Wales.** The romance of the 1930s lives on in the Hotel Del Coronado's restored Prince of Wales, which affords sweeping ocean views from an elegant indoor room and a breezy terrace. The cooking has become quite inventive in recent years—consider such novelties as an "aerated" wild mushroom bisque; a parfait of layered warm potatoes, sour cream, and osetra caviar; and Hawaiian yellowfin tuna with sautéed foie gras and truffle sauce. Although seafood dominates the menu, you'll also find toothsome meat choices like roasted Sonoma County squab with Savoy cabbage and wild boar tenderloin in a peppery beet sauce. After all this, the red fruit consommé brings the evening to a tart conclusion. ⊠ *Hotel Del Coronado, 1500 Orange Ave., Coronado,* ☎ *619/435–6611. AE, D, DC, MC, V. No lunch.*

$$–$$$ ✕ **Peohe's.** If the view were less spectacular, the noise level might be a bit lower, but even if the towers of downtown were not on display across a few hundred yards of San Diego Bay, it seems likely that this Hawai'i-theme restaurant would remain a top draw. Besides the semitropical garden, with streams flowing past islands of greenery, the daily seafood offerings are usually first-rate, although the kitchen sometimes displays too much fondness for complicated sauces and garnishes. Many people arrive intent on dining on crunchy coconut shrimp or slowly-roasted prime rib. ⊠ *1201 1st St., Coronado,* ☎ *619/437–4474. AE, DC, MC, V.*

$–$$$ ✕ **Baja Lobster.** While not generally regarded as a tourist destination, Chula Vista harbors several fine Mexican restaurants and is just a 10-minute drive from downtown San Diego. To experience something akin to dining in Puerto Nuevo, Baja California—the famed lobstering village some 20 mi south of the border—head to Baja Lobster, which lies about 100 ft east of the H Street freeway exit. It's great for split, lightly fried local lobsters and family-style portions of fresh flour tortillas, creamy beans crammed with flavor, and well-seasoned rice. While lobsters are the big deal, steak and chicken options are on the menu, too. ⊠ *730 H St., Chula Vista,* ☎ *619/427–8690. MC, V.*

Downtown

American

$–$$ ✕ **Hard Rock Cafe.** If you've been to one Hard Rock, you've been to them all, but there's no denying that the mix of rock 'n' roll memorabilia, ear-splitting music, vivacious young servers, and generally satisfying, all-American fare can be fun on occasion. If you want to curb your appetite for a while, try a juicy, half-pound burger; the high-rising, bacon-rich "country club" sandwich; or—best of all—the "pig sandwich" of shredded smoked pork shoulder dressed with a sharp, vinegar-based barbecue sauce. As over-the-top as it may sound, a thick malted milk shake goes well with any of these gut-busters, or serves as a very good dessert. The bar hops at night. ⊠ *801 4th Ave., Gaslamp Quarter,* ☎ *619/615–7625. AE, DC, MC, V.*

$–$$ ✕ **Top of the Hyatt.** The Hyatt Regency San Diego is the tallest waterside building on North America's Pacific seaboard, a fact you can become intimately familiar with after riding the speedy elevators to the 40th floor. Here, the stylish Top of the Hyatt affords a 290° view encompassing most of San Diego and even a bit of Mexico. Primarily a

bar, it presents an excellent, carved-to-order sandwich list, plus soups
and salads, at lunch. Substantial appetizers are served from happy hour
'til late in the evening. Somehow, a turkey club sandwich tastes better
at 497 ft. ⊠ *1 Market Pl., Downtown,* ☎ *619/232–1234. AE, D, DC,
MC, V.*

$ ✕ **Ghirardelli Soda Fountain & Chocolate Shop.** Perfect for a midday
snack or after-dinner treat, this local outpost of San Francisco's famed
Ghirardelli chocolatier specializes in ice cream, served in every size and
form from a single scoop in a freshly baked waffle cone, to elaborate
sundaes and banana splits. Ambitious types can attempt the Earthquake,
a belly-busting construction of eight different ice creams, eight toppings,
bananas, nuts, embarrassing quantities of whipped cream, and heaps
of glistening red cherries. ⊠ *643 5th Ave., Gaslamp Quarter,* ☎ *619/
234–2449. AE, MC, V.*

Cajun and Creole

$$ ✕ **Bayou Bar and Grill.** Ceiling fans, dark-green wainscoting, and
light-pink walls help create a New Orleans mood appropriate for spicy
Cajun and Creole specialties. You might start with a bowl of yummy
seafood gumbo and then move on to the sausage, red beans and rice,
or any of the fresh Louisiana Gulf seafood dishes, such as stuffed soft-
shell crab or catfish *belle chasse* (stuffed with seafood). Rich Louisiana
desserts include a praline cheesecake and an unbeatable bread pudding.
The kitchen has been cooking this menu for years and has everything
down pat. ⊠ *329 Market St., Gaslamp Quarter,* ☎ *619/696–8747.
AE, D, DC, MC, V.*

Chinese

$$ ✕ **Panda Inn.** Reliable if unimaginative, and the only stylish Chinese
restaurant downtown, this dining room at the top of Horton Plaza serves
Mandarin and Szechuan dishes in an elegant room that feels far removed from the rush of commerce below. Try the honey walnut shrimp,
the Peking duck, the spicy bean curd, or the Panda beef. ⊠ *506 Horton Plaza, Downtown,* ☎ *619/233–7800. AE, D, DC, MC, V.*

Contemporary

$$–$$$ ✕ **Chive.** Chive aims to capture the urban and urbane moods of Lon-
don, New York, and San Francisco restaurants with an interior design
of flat surfaces and monochromatic colors that seems hard-edged at
first. On some evenings the crowd is determinedly under-30 and super
trendy, on other nights the restaurant may be occupied by large groups
of conventioneers. All sorts are drawn by a contemporary menu highlighted by clever treatments of Hudson Valley foie gras, lamb, and briny-
fresh seafood. For dessert, the fluffy, doughnut-like beignets with
pineapple custard sauce is recommended. ⊠ *558 4th Ave., Gaslamp
Quarter,* ☎ *619/232–4483. AE, D, MC, V. No lunch weekends.*

$$–$$$ ✕ **Grant Grill.** Wood-paneled walls, oil paintings of English hunting
scenes, and a thoroughly professional staff help this half-century old
dining room in the historic U. S. Grant hotel maintain its status as the
clubbiest eatery in town. The culinary direction is rooted in the 21st
century, however, and established favorites like mock turtle soup now
compete with such contemporary starters as sautéed veal sweetbreads
with a tartlet of Mission figs, and a smoked salmon Napoleon served
with cucumber relish. On the entrée list is grilled wild salmon dressed
with stone crab claws and roasted yellow peppers, and blackened beef
filet with Grand Marnier-spiked barbecue sauce. ⊠ *326 Broadway,
Downtown,* ☎ *619/232–3121. AE, D, DC, MC, V.*

French

$$$–$$$$ ✕ **Bertrand at Mister A's.** Operated by noted restaurateur Bertrand Hug,
★   the sumptuous dining room perches on the 12th floor of a midtown

Downtown Dining

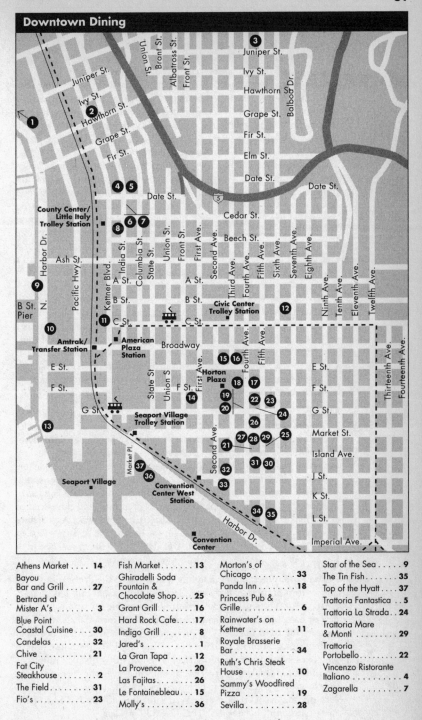

office building overlooking a view that stretches from the mountains in the east to Mexico, San Diego Bay, and a sliver of the blue Pacific. At both lunch and dinner you can watch the aerial ballet of jets descending upon nearby Lindbergh Field. Ideal for a special occasion, Bertrand at Mister A's serves luxurious seasonal dishes such as veal braised in white wine, pan-seared ocean perch with creamy celery root sauce, and Dover sole in lemon butter. The dessert list encompasses a galaxy of sweets, but the caramelized peach tart is so wonderful that those who have tasted it rarely experiment with anything else. ⊠ *2550 5th Ave., Middletown,* ☎ *619/239–1377. Reservations essential. Jacket required. AE, DC, MC, V. No lunch weekends.*

$$$ ✕ **Le Fontainebleau.** The Westgate Hotel looks like an ordinary, 1960s mid-rise from outside, but inside is a wealth of exquisite French antiques in breathtaking public rooms. Le Fontainebleau, on the second floor, is worthy of the famous chateau for which it is named. After decades of tired fare, the new millennium ushered in an era of expert French cuisine, characterized by such offerings as creamy artichoke soup with black truffles, a salad of asparagus spears in curry-scented pistachio oil, beef fillet poached in seasoned red wine, and pan-roasted grouper with lobster risotto. ⊠ *1055 Second Ave., Downtown,* ☎ *619/557–3655. Jacket required. AE, D, DC, MC, V.*

$$–$$$ ✕ **Royale Brasserie Bar.** San Diego's revivifying taste for French cook-
★ ing is well served by Royale. Culinary highlights include vast, iced platters of sparklingly fresh oysters and other shellfish; *rillettes,* a rich paste of shredded pork and duck; and steak or Belgian-style steamed mussels, with crisp, salty frites. You also can get classic sautés of veal or chicken served with rich, deeply flavorful brown sauces. The crêpes suzette dessert for two is good to the last droplet of sugary orange sauce. ⊠ *224 5th Ave., Gaslamp Quarter,* ☎ *619/237–4900. AE, DC, MC, V.*

Greek

$$–$$$ ✕ **Athens Market.** This cheerful eatery with an outdoor patio bustles with downtown office workers and members of San Diego's small but active Greek community. Appetizers such as *taramasalata* (fish roe dip), hummus, and stuffed grape leaves are particularly tasty. Entrées include *arni psito* (roast leg of lamb), a very convincing rendition of moussaka, and the house Greek pasta, with garlic, onion, and cheese. The *galtobouriko,* a layering of crisp phyllo pastry, eggy custard, and clove-scented syrup, makes an excellent dessert. San Diego Chargers owner Alex Spanos has been a fan of Athens Market for years. ⊠ *109 W. F St., Downtown,* ☎ *619/234–1955. AE, D, DC, MC, V. No lunch weekends.*

Irish

$–$$ ✕ **The Field.** Operated by a family that brought the decorations over intact from properties it owns in Ireland, this casual pub has character to spare. The small sidewalk terrace is suitable for sipping a Guinness or Bass, but diners prefer the bric-a-brac–adorned, dark-wood walls indoors for solid lunches and dinners of Irish stew, corned beef and cabbage, or, best of all, a *boxty.* Boxties are lacy but substantial potato pancakes, made to order and served crisp and hot with such fillings as sage-flavored chicken or Irish bacon and cheese. As the evening wears on, the crowd grows younger, livelier, louder, and sometimes rowdier. A traditional Irish breakfast is served Saturday and Sunday. ⊠ *544 5th Ave., Gaslamp Quarter,* ☎ *619/232–9840. MC, V.*

Italian

$$–$$$$ ✕ **Trattoria Mare & Monti.** The sea and mountains that contribute their special products to Italian cuisine are memorialized in the name of this comfortable Fifth Avenue restaurant, which serves on both a narrow sidewalk terrace and in a much more spacious dining room.

The menu attempts to differentiate itself from those of other restaurants in the neighborhood, and is notable for a refreshing tomato salad, fettuccine with shrimp in a creamy sauce, and grilled herbed rib-eye steak. On the simpler and more affordable side, the kitchen turns out excellent pizzas baked in a wood-fired oven. ⊠ *644 5th Ave., Gaslamp Quarter,* ☎ *619/235–8144.. AE, DC, MC, V.*

$$–$$$ ✗ **Trattoria La Strada.** Perhaps the busiest Italian restaurant in the Gaslamp Quarter, La Strada offers comfortable seating on both a spacious terrace and in an airy dining room whose broad windows assure good views of the bustle outside. Carpaccio appetizers are a house specialty. Moving on, try the polenta dressed with rich, melted Fontina cheese and wild mushrooms, or any one of the excellent pastas: fusilli with shrimp and fresh artichokes, and capellini with assorted shellfish in a white wine–enriched tomato sauce are two favorites. The second-course selection stars grilled lamb chops with herb sauce and filet mignon in a heady Chianti sauce. ⊠ *702 5th Ave., Gaslamp Quarter,* ☎ *619/239–3400. AE, DC, MC.*

$$–$$$ ✗ **Trattoria Portobello.** Gentle lighting and good service will help you enjoy a menu that includes such flavorful choices as *frito misto,* an appetizer of crisply fried baby squid, smelts, shrimp, and vegetables with a tangy, whole-grain mustard sauce. This is a good place to try risotti flavored with assorted wild mushrooms or hot and sweet Italian sausages. The pasta list offers numerous hard-to-find regional classics, such as Venice-style capellini with arugula, shrimp, and mushrooms, and Genoa-style *farafalline* ("small butterflies") pasta in a pungent basil cream sauce. Tarragon adds an extra and fascinating flavor to the tender, superbly savory osso bucco. ⊠ *715 4th Ave., Gaslamp Quarter,* ☎ *619/232–4440. AE, DC, MC, V.*

$–$$ ✗ **Sammy's Woodfired Pizza.** This small, homegrown chain was the first local outfit to serve imaginative gourmet pizzas like those invented by Los Angeles celebrity chef Wolfgang Puck. Pies may be topped with spicy, Jamaican-style shrimp; lamb sausage with wild mushrooms; and a surprisingly savory team of grilled zucchini and eggplant. The menu offers pastas, meats, and fish as well, among which the four-cheese ravioli with forest mushrooms and oak-roasted Idaho trout are favorites. The "messy" chocolate sundae feeds two and comes in a glass rolled in chocolate sauce and nuts. The Fifth Avenue location has deep, comfortable booths and a narrow sidewalk terrace. ⊠ *770 4th Ave., Gaslamp Quarter,* ☎ *619/230–8888;* ⊠ *702 Pearl St., La Jolla,* ☎ *858/456–5222;* ⊠ *12925 El Camino Real, Del Mar Heights,* ☎ *858/259–6600;* ⊠ *1620 Camino de la Reina, Mission Valley,* ☎ *619/298–8222. AE, MC, V.*

Mexican

$$–$$$ ✗ **Candelas.** The scents and flavors of nouvelle Mexican cuisine permeate this handsome, romantic little hideaway in the shadow of San Diego's tallest residential towers. Candles glow everywhere around the small, comfortable dining room and the bar. There isn't a burrito or taco in sight at this haven of stylish, imaginative cooking, where such fine openers as cream of black bean and beer soup, and salad of watercress with bacon and pistachios, set the stage for local lobster stuffed with mushrooms, jalapeño peppers and aged tequila; or tequila-flamed jumbo prawns over creamy, seasoned goat cheese. ⊠ *416 3rd Ave., Gaslamp Quarter,* ☎ *619/702–4455. MC, V. Closed Sun. No lunch.*

$$–$$$ ✗ **Las Fajitas.** Las Fajitas serves sizzling platters of highly seasoned steak and chicken, plus plump shrimp, local lobster, and swordfish. All fajitas are sided generously with rice, beans, guacamole, and tortillas. The rest of the menu largely devotes itself to seafood, notably shrimp in garlic sauce and sea bass Veracruz-style, but there are a few hard-

to-find Mexican classics as well, such as fried, stuffed chilies bathed in a creamy nut sauce, and panfried boneless quail basted with a garlic-chile glaze. Desserts include bananas flamed in rum and a smooth coconut flan. ⊠ *628 5th Ave., Gaslamp Quarter,* ☎ *619/232–4242.AE, D, MC, V.*

Seafood

$$$–$$$$ ✗ **Molly's.** Buried at the base of the original tower of the San Diego Marriott & Marina, Molly's exudes the confidence of an expense-account restaurant and has a contemporary, seafood-oriented menu with specialties like a jumbo shrimp Martini garnished with fried horseradish; cognac-splashed lobster bisque; and sea bass crusted with chanterelle mushrooms. The entrée list takes carnivores into account: try the stuffed pheasant breast with huckleberry chutney or grilled veal chop on a puree of truffled white beans. ⊠ *333 W. Harbor Dr., Downtown,* ☎ *619/234–1500. AE, D, DC, MC, V.*

$$$–$$$$ ✗ **Star of the Sea.** The flagship of the Anthony's chain of seafood restau-
   ★   rants ensconces its patrons in its most formal dining room, making it an all-around favorite for location, cuisine, and design (although dress is quite casual). The menu changes seasonally; you may find butter-poached lobster tail with wild mushrooms, a rich pairing of braised beef short ribs and tempura shrimp, or macadamia-crusted swordfish in a yellow curry sauce. The baked-to-order soufflés are puffy, fragrant, and lovely on the palate. The outdoor patio takes full advantage of the choice waterfront location. ⊠ *1360 N. Harbor Dr., Downtown,* ☎ *619/232–7408. AE, D, DC, MC, V. No lunch.*

$$–$$$$ ✗ **Fish Market.** Fresh mesquite-grilled fish is the specialty at this informal restaurant. There's also an excellent little sushi bar and good steamed clams and mussels. The view is stunning: enormous plate-glass windows look directly out onto the harbor. A more formal restaurant upstairs, the Top of the Market ($$$–$$$$), is expensive but worth the splurge, and is the place to find such rarities as true Dover sole, which the kitchen delicately browns in butter and finishes with a lemon-caper sauce. The Solana Beach branch, which does not include Top of the Market, is across the street from the Del Mar racetrack. ⊠ *750 N. Harbor Dr., Downtown,* ☎ *619/232–3474 for Fish Market; 619/234–4867 for Top of the Market. Reservations not accepted;* ⊠ *640 Via de la Valle, Solana Beach,* ☎ *858/755–2277. AE, D, DC, MC, V.*

$$–$$$ ✗ **Blue Point Coastal Cuisine.** High ceilings, gleaming woodwork, and expansive windows give this seafood establishment an urbane air. Blue Point adds Asian accents to an essentially Mediterranean menu. Among the starters, try the blue cheese and caramelized onion tart, or spicy Baja clam chowder, and follow these with a handsome tempura of shrimp and asparagus. The menu gives meat eaters a choice, too. The wine list is serious, and the service efficient and friendly. Allow room for desserts like the "harlequin" chocolate souffle. ⊠ *565 5th Ave., Gaslamp Quarter,* ☎ *619/233–6623. AE, D, DC, MC, V. No lunch.*

   $ ✗ **The Tin Fish.** On rare rainy days, the staff takes it easy at this eatery across the trolley tracks from the San Diego Convention Center, since all the seating is outdoors. The management arranges for live musical performances some evenings, making this a lively spot for dinners of grilled and fried fish and shellfish, as well as Mexican-style seafood burritos and tacos. The restaurant even bakes the bread used for sandwiches stuffed with fried oysters and the like. For kids (or unadventurous grown-ups) there is a $2.95 peanut butter and jelly sandwich. The quality here routinely surpasses that at grander establishments. ⊠ *170 6th Ave., Gaslamp Quarter,* ☎ *619/238–8100. Reservations not accepted. MC, V.*

Spanish

$$–$$$ ✕ **La Gran Tapa.** Spanish bullfight posters, marble-top tables, and a dark-wood bar all give this established restaurant the flavor of Madrid. You can make a meal out of the tapas: good bets are the *almejas romescu* (steamed clams in sweet red pepper sauce), the sautéed baby octopus, and the spicy black bean soup. Or turn to the entrées: try the *gambas* (shrimp) El Greco, the succulent grilled lamb chops, or the classic paella. Take advantage of the opportunity to try a good Spanish wine. ✉ *611 B St., Downtown,* ☎ *619/234–8272. AE, MC, V. Closed Sun. No lunch Sat.*

$$–$$$ ✕ **Sevilla.** Lines form on weekend nights, when youthful throngs wait to crowd the ground-floor bar for drinks, tapas, and professional flamenco dancing, and the downstairs club for classics from the Spanish kitchen and live music. There isn't a quiet corner to be found here. The kitchen does a respectable job with the paella; try the paella Valenciana with shellfish, sausage, and chicken. It also makes highly flavorful baked rabbit and roasted pork tenderloin. ✉ *555 4th Ave., Gaslamp Quarter,* ☎ *619/233–5979. AE, MC, V. No lunch.*

Steak Houses

$$$–$$$$ ✕ **Rainwater's on Kettner.** San Diego's premier home-grown steak
★ house also ranks as the longest running of the pack, not least because it has the luxurious look and mood of an old-fashioned Eastern men's club. Settle back into the exceptionally deep banquettes and start with Rainwater's signature black bean soup with Madeira. Continue with the tender, expertly roasted prime rib. The menu branches out to encompass superb calves' liver with onions and bacon, broiled free-range chicken, fresh seafood, and even pastas, all served in vast portions with plenty of hot-from-the-oven cornsticks on the side. The well-chosen wine list offers pricey but superior selections. ✉ *1202 Kettner Blvd., Downtown,* ☎ *619/233–5757. AE, D, MC, V. No lunch weekends.*

$$–$$$$ ✕ **Jared's.** On the lower deck of a Mississippi River–style stern-wheeler moored on San Diego Bay, this stylish, relaxed steak house is a fun destination for expensive, high-quality steak and seafood dinners. There's a display kitchen lined in burnished copper and a view of the downtown towers twinkling across the water. Massive meals can open classically with a cocktail of plump shrimp or with a delicate five-onion tart. Steaks and seafood cuts are all oversized. For dessert, try the peppermint-flavored chocolate tart. ✉ *880 E. Harbor Island Dr., Harbor Island,* ☎ *619/291–1028. AE, D, MC, V. No lunch.*

$$–$$$$ ✕ **Morton's of Chicago.** Housed in the soaring Harbor Club towers
★ near both the San Diego Convention Center and the Gaslamp Quarter, Morton's often teems with conventioneers out for a night on the town. Servers present the menu by wheeling up a cart laden with crimson prime steaks, behemoth veal and lamb chops, thick cuts of swordfish, and huge Maine lobsters that may wave their claws in alarm when they hear the prices (based on the market, but always astronomical) quoted. Expect a treat, since this restaurant knows how to put on a superb spread that takes the concept of self-indulgence to new heights. ✉ *The Harbor Club, 285 J St., Downtown,* ☎ *619/696–3369. AE, D, MC, V. No lunch.*

$$–$$$$ ✕ **Ruth's Chris Steak House.** This branch of the national chain occupies a second-story location that overlooks the Embarcadero and the bay, and often is so crowded that the din can be a challenge. Certainly, Ruth's Chris patrons seem bent on enjoying themselves. This restaurant recalls its New Orleans roots with Creole openers like seafood gumbo and chilled shrimp dressed with tangy mustard sauce, but the meats are what count, from rib eyes and New York strips served sizzling in butter on super-heated metal platters to oven-roasted chicken

66

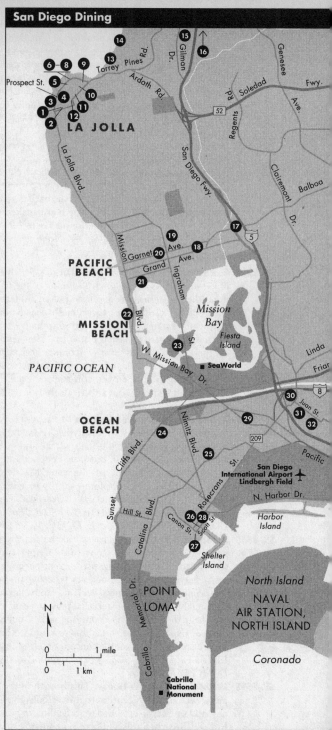

San Diego Dining

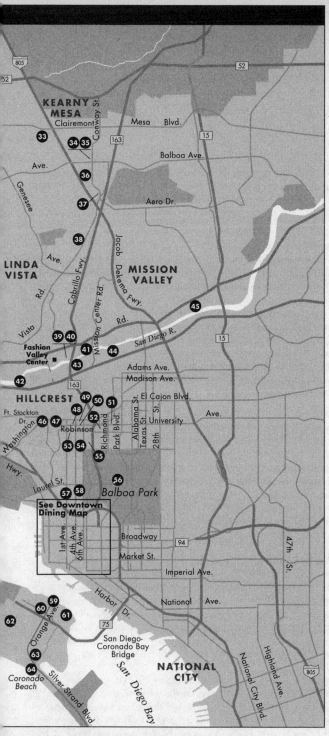

breast stuffed with garlic-and-herb-flavored cheese. ⊠ *1355 N. Harbor Dr., Downtown,* ☎ *619/233–1422.* ⊠ *11582 El Camino Real, Carmel Valley (near Del Mar),* ☎ *858/758–1454. AE, D, MC, V. No lunch.*

\$–\$\$\$\$ ✕ **Fat City Steakhouse.** The words "steakhouse" and "bargain" rarely are comfortable in each other's company, but the \$11.95, mesquite-grilled New York steak that is the featured house special here is without question one of the best deals in town. Served with a mound of crisp-from-the-fryer shoestring potatoes, this 12-ounce steak rivals much more expensive cuts found at other area restaurants. Not everything on the menu is such a bargain, but most items are reasonably priced and tasty, like the Asian-flavored "drunk steak" and the double breast of chicken in peppercorn sauce. Find excellent bargains, too, among the featured wines of the month. ⊠ *2137 Pacific Hwy., Downtown,* ☎ *619/232–9303. AE, MC, V. No lunch.*

Little Italy

British/Pub

\$ ✕ **Princess Pub & Grille.** Packed to the rafters during any televised British football (soccer) championship, this cheerful neighborhood place is unofficial headquarters for visiting Brits, Australians, and New Zealanders—but no matter where you're from, it's virtually always a lively place to hoist a mug. The selection of imported beers and ales, most of them from Merrie Olde, is quite impressive, and the menu complements them well with such offerings as sausage rolls, fish-and-chips, spicy chicken curry, and an elaborate Cheshire mixed grill of meats, sausage, egg, and mushrooms. The jeans-clad patrons seem equally fond of conversation and games of darts. ⊠ *1665 India St., Little Italy,* ☎ *619/702–3021. MC, V.*

Italian

\$\$–\$\$\$ ✕ **Vincenzo Ristorante Italiano.** Find excellent Italian cuisine at this small, attractive establishment, which places about half its tables outdoors on the sidewalk so that patrons can soak up the village-like neighborhood even as they regard the San Diego skyline. Dishes are cooked notably in the style of the Old Country, and pastas sometimes seem undersauced for that reason. Unusual and highly satisfying choices include an appetizer of seared ahi with chopped hazelnuts, mint, and a spicy sauce; a risotto with Italian sausage, saffron and shellfish; and grilled jumbo shrimp in a sauce of garlic, wine, and lemon. ⊠ *1702 India St., Little Italy,* ☎ *619/702–6180. MC, V. No lunch weekends.*

\$\$ ✕ **Trattoria Fantastica.** The shady, very private courtyard at the rear of this laid-back establishment is no secret, so reserve ahead if you want to score a table. Sicilian flavors abound on the menu, which is highlighted by such offerings as a salad of tomatoes, red onions, olive oil, and oregano; and the pasta Palermitana, rigatoni with spicy sausage, olives, capers, and marinara sauce. Many pastas come with cargoes of fresh seafood, and the pizzas baked in the wood-burning oven are robust and beautifully seasoned. ⊠ *1735 India St., Little Italy,* ☎ *619/ 234–1735. AE, DC, MC, V.*

\$\$ ✕ **Zagarella.** Take a seat in the small dining room or in the vast courtyard and relax to recorded opera music while studying a menu that suggests such appetizers as sautéed herbed shrimp on a bed of shoestring potatoes, or a plate of tender roasted peppers crowned with a whole school of anchovies. The Italian menu avoids clichés in favor of specialties like warm duck salad accented with pine nuts and golden raisins, baked eggplant timbale, ravioli tossed with radicchio braised in cream, and veal scallopini with artichokes and lemon sauce. ⊠ *1655 India St., Little Italy,* ☎ *619/236–8764. MC, V.*

Southwestern

$$–$$$ ✕ **Indigo Grill.** A showcase for chef/partner Deborah Scott's contemporary Southwestern cuisine, Indigo Grill has both a stone interior and a broad terrace whose cool breezes do nothing to moderate the chiles that heat such one-of-a-kind offerings as oven clams and jalapeño-maize pappardelle with prawns and smoked pineapple. Entrées like the wild blueberry–lacquered venison chop make a big impression, as do such desserts as a puff pastry confection dressed with pears, Stilton cheese, and balsamic vinegar. ✉ *1536 India St., Little Italy,* ☎ *619/234–6802. AE, D, DC, MC, V. No lunch weekends.*

Uptown

American

$–$$ ✕ **Hob Nob Hill.** This is the type of place where regulars arrive on the same day of the week at the same time and order the same meal they've been ordering for 20 years. With its dark-wood booths and patterned carpets, Hob Nob Hill seems suspended in the 1950s, but you don't need to be a nostalgia buff to appreciate the bargain-price American home cooking—dishes such as oat-raisin French toast, fried chicken, and corned beef like your mother never really made. The crowds line up morning, noon, and night. Reservations are suggested for Sunday breakfast. ✉ *2271 1st Ave., Middletown,* ☎ *619/239–8176. AE, D, MC, V.*

American/Casual

$$–$$$ ✕ **Hash House A Go Go.** Hillcrest cheered the arrival of this three-meals-a-day eatery, whose walls are covered with photos of farm machinery and other icons of middle America. At breakfast, huge platters carpeted with fluffy pancakes sail out of the kitchen and return empty in a matter of moments, while at noon, customers favor the overflowing chicken potpies crowned with flaky pastry. The parade of old-fashioned good eats continues at dinner with stuffed meat loaf, roasted butternut squash filled to bursting with cornmeal-crusted shrimp, and a grand combination of sage-flavored fried chicken, bacon-flavored waffle, and hot maple syrup. Hash House attracts a very trendy crowd. ✉ *3628 5th Ave., Hillcrest,* ☎ *619/298–4646. MC, V.*

$ ✕ **Corvette Diner Bar & Grill.** The absolute San Diego County favorite for children's parties and other family occasions, Corvette Diner features a real Corvette (changed every two or three months) in a kitschy, 1950s-style dining room dominated by vintage movie posters and singing servers. The menu has what you'd expect—macaroni and cheddar, plump burgers, piled-high deli sandwiches, spaghetti and meatballs, greasy chile-cheese fries, and thick milk shakes. ✉ *3946 5th Ave., Hillcrest,* ☎ *619/542–1001. AE, D, MC, V.*

Contemporary

$$–$$$$ ✕ **Laurel.** Laurel long has been regarded as a premier dinner address, especially among those attending a performance at the Old Globe Theatre in Balboa Park. Polished service and a smart, contemporary design set the stage for an imaginative, expertly prepared seasonal menu that takes its inspiration from Mediterranean cuisine. Look for appetizers such as pan-roasted sweetbreads with Sherry vinegar sauce, and warm tart of Roquefort cheese and caramelized onions. Among the main courses, reliable choices include the chicken roasted in a clay pot, grilled yellowfin tuna with Niçoise olive mashed potatoes, and pepper-crusted veal loin. ✉ *505 Laurel St., Middletown,* ☎ *619/239–2222. AE, D, DC, MC, V. No lunch.*

$$–$$$ ✕ **The Prado.** This beautiful restaurant in the House of Hospitality on Balboa Park's museum row brings an inventive, contemporary menu to an area that otherwise has to rely on picnic lunches for sustenance.

The striking interior has elegantly painted ceilings and elaborate glass sculptures, and the bar has become a fashionable pre- and post-theater destination for such light nibbles as crab cakes and steamed Manila clams. In the dining room, well-trained servers offer a menu that ranges from a dressy "farmer's salad" to truffled mushroom risotto, marinated pork prime rib, and Chilean sea bass steamed inside a banana leaf. ⊠ *1549 El Prado, Balboa Park,* ☎ *619/557–9441. AE, D, MC, V.*

Eclectic

$$–$$$ ✕ **Parallel 33.** True to its name, Parallel 33 traces this imaginary line around the globe, serving dishes based on American, Moroccan, Middle Eastern, Chinese, and Japanese cuisines. Chef/proprietor Amiko Gubbins has a sure handle on everything she cooks. Her Moroccan-style chicken-and-egg pie hides a deliciously savory filling inside a flaky, phyllo crust, and the Shanghai noodles with soft-shell crab and crab-coconut sauce caress the mouth with unexpected sharp and delicate flavors. Among other favorites are Asian-style cured duck salad and curry-braised lamb shank. The restaurant honors the lands of the 33rd parallel with fascinating artworks built especially for the restaurant. ⊠ *741 W. Washington St., Mission Hills,* ☎ *619/260–0033. AE, D, MC, V. Closed Sun. No lunch.*

Indian

$$ ✕ **Bombay Exotic Cuisine of India.** Notable for its elegant dining room,
★   Bombay employs a chef whose generous hand with raw and cooked vegetables gives each course a colorful freshness reminiscent of California cuisine, though the flavors definitely hail from India. Try the tandoori lettuce wrap appetizer and any of the stuffed *nan* (a delectably chewy tandoori bread). The unusually large selection of tasty curries may be ordered with meat, chicken, fish, or tofu. The curious should try the *dizzy noo shakk,* a sweet and spicy banana curry. Alone among local Indian eateries, Bombay offers a full, fixed-price option that includes an entrée, traditional sides, nan, dessert, and tea. ⊠ *Hillcrest Center, 3975 5th Ave., Suite 100, Hillcrest,* ☎ *619/298–3155. AE, D, DC, MC, V.*

Italian

$–$$$ ✕ **Busalacchi's Ristorante.** This long-running hit on the fringe of Hillcrest offers a romantic, low-key dining room and a stylish, sheltered patio that overlooks busy 5th Avenue. The lengthy menu zeroes in on elegant, fully flavored Sicilian specialties—it may be the only place in San Diego to sample a salad of chilled potatoes, green beans, onions, and cucumbers flavored with garlic and oregano. The pasta list mentions plenty of familiar favorites, but again turns classically Sicilian with macaroni in an aromatic sardine sauce; the stuffed, breaded veal *spiedini* (on skewers) also is superb. ⊠ *3683 5th Ave., Hillcrest,* ☎ *619/ 298–0119. AE, DC, MC, V. No lunch weekends.*

Mexican

$ ✕ **Chilango's Mexico City Grill.** Proof positive that good things come in small packages, this tiny but cheerful storefront restaurant serves burritos and *tortas* (sandwiches) like no other in the city. Daily specials might include enchiladas in *mole verde* (green chile sauce) and a fabulous chicken in *mole poblano* (a sauce made with chilies and bittersweet chocolate). This much-loved restaurant, which opens at 9 AM Friday–Sunday, quickly fills to overflowing in the evening, so consider coming in off-hours or ordering takeout. ⊠ *142 University Ave., Hillcrest,* ☎ *619/294–8646. No credit cards.*

Middle Eastern

$–$$ ✕ **Aladdin.** The star entrée at this low-key, comfortable café is a one-of-a-kind Middle Eastern dish of woven strips of marinated lamb and beef. Sprinkled with citric acid crystals, which give it a beguilingly tart flavor, the meat has an unusually pleasing texture. The tables on both the sidewalk terrace and in the dining room often are full of diners enjoying hearty portions of Tunisian sausage, chicken and lamb kebabs, and wood-fired pizzas. The impressive list of generously portioned salads makes Aladdin a favorite with vegetarians. ☒ *1220 Cleveland Ave., #101, Hillcrest,* ☎ *619/574–1111;* ☒ *5420 Clairemont Mesa Blvd., North Clairemont Mesa,* ☎ *858/573–0000. MC, V.*

Thai

$–$$ ✕ **Taste of Thai.** Usually packed with value-minded diners, this modest café seats you at close quarters but compensates by serving yummy Thai and vegetarian cuisine at reasonable prices. The menu includes spicy noodles with chicken, whole or filleted fish with garlic or ginger sauce, and red or yellow curries. Among enjoyable house specialties are freshwater prawns from the Mae Khong river, grilled and served with a choice of spicy sauces. ☒ *527 University Ave., Hillcrest,* ☎ *619/ 291–7525. AE, D, DC, MC, V.*

Kearny Mesa

Chinese

$$–$$$$ ✕ **Emerald Chinese Seafood Restaurant.** The first Hong Kong–style
★ restaurant to open in San Diego, Emerald holds pride of place among fanciers of elaborate, carefully prepared, and sometimes costly seafood dishes. The shrimp, prawns, lobsters, clams, and fish all reside in tanks until the moment of cooking. Simple preparations flavored with scallions, black beans, and ginger are among the best, although the kitchen gladly caters to those in the mood for fancy cooking. Other recommended dishes include beef with Singapore-style satay sauce, Peking duck served in two savory courses, and, at lunch, the dim sum. ☒ *3709 Convoy St., Kearny Mesa,* ☎ *858/565–6888. AE, MC, V.*

$$–$$$$ ✕ **Jasmine.** This cavernous, Hong Kong–style establishment seats no fewer than 800 people; even so, there frequently are lines outside during lunchtime on Saturday and Sunday, when groups arrive en masse to enjoy fragrant soups, steaming noodles, and dim sum pastries from carts that constantly circle the room. At dinner it's a hard choice between the seafood from the wall-mounted tanks and "Peking duck two ways"—the crisp skin sandwiched in tasty buns as a first course, the meat deliciously stir-fried for a savory follow-up. Boiled-in-the-shell fresh prawns are expensive and difficult to eat, but worth both the cost and the effort. ☒ *4609 Convoy St., Kearny Mesa,* ☎ *858/268–0888. AE, MC, V.*

$–$$ ✕ **Dumpling Inn.** Modest, family-style, and absolutely wonderful, this
★ tiny establishment loads its tables with bottles of aromatic and spicy condiments for the boiled, steamed, and fried dumplings that are the house specialty. These delicately flavored, hefty mouthfuls preface a meal that may continue simply, with hearty pork and pickled cabbage soup, or elaborately, with Shanghai-style braised pork shank. Ask about daily specials, which can be exotic and wonderful to palates raised on burgers and fries. You may bring your own wine or beer; the house serves only tea and soft drinks. ☒ *4619 Convoy St., #F, Kearny Mesa,* ☎ *858/ 268–9638. Reservations not accepted. No credit cards. Closed Mon.*

Vietnamese

$–$$ ✕ **Pho Pasteur.** Linda Vista Road is a continuation of Convoy Street, and Pho Pasteur continues the area's tradition as an exceptional option for authentic Vietnamese cuisine. Sparely decorated, Pho Pasteur retains regulars with meals built around *pho,* beef broth enriched with rice noodles and any of an astounding variety of garnishes. The 20 soups in this category make a steaming preface to the menu's other 179 dishes, which range from stuffed grape leaves to a Thai-style hot pot. In season, the kitchen prepares game specials. ✉ *7612 Linda Vista Rd., Linda Vista,* ☎ *858/569–7515. MC, V.*

$–$$ ✕ **Phuong Trang.** Widely considered the leading Vietnamese restaurant in San Diego, Phuong Trang offers speedy, sometimes curt service in a large, relatively spare dining room that gets packed to the rafters. The menu lists no fewer than 248 appetizers, soups, noodle dishes, and main courses, which can make choosing a meal a bewildering process for novices. Waiters tend to steer you toward tasty offerings like fried egg rolls, char-grilled shrimp paste wrapped around sugarcane, beef in grape leaves, and fresh spring rolls filled with pork and shrimp. Noodles topped with a grilled pork chop makes a satisfying meal. ✉ *4170 Convoy St., Kearny Mesa,* ☎ *858/565–6750. MC, V.*

Beaches

American/Casual

$ ✕ **Broken Yolk Cafe.** Since this ultracasual breakfast-and-lunch establishment lies a dozen blocks from the beach, it entertains a primarily local clientele. Regulars come in search of hearty, imaginative breakfasts and burger or sandwich lunches. The specialties without question are the hefty four-egg omelets stuffed with about everything but the kitchen sink. You're given the list of suggested fillings and invited to design your own creation. ✉ *1851 Garnet Ave., Pacific Beach,* ☎ *858/270–0045. MC, V. No dinner.*

$ ✕ **Mission Cafe and Coffeehouse.** This laid-back café opens early in the morning and remains open as a coffeehouse until the wee hours. The cuisine is dubbed "Chino-Latino." For breakfast try the French toast—homemade cinnamon bread over a drizzle of blackberry puree— or the tamales with eggs and green-chile salsa. For lunch or dinner sample the black beans and rice, the Asian pasta bowl, or one of the roll-ups (tortillas wrapped around creative fillings). All menu items can be made vegetarian. The café serves beer on tap, specialty coffees, and shakes and smoothies. The North Park branch has a more elaborate dinner menu. ✉ *3795 Mission Blvd., Mission Beach,* ☎ *858/488–9060;* ✉ *2801 University Ave., North Park,* ☎ *619/220–8992. AE, MC, V.*

Contemporary

$$$–$$$$ ✕ **Baleen.** This copy of the original Baleen in Miami does its best to
★ avoid the trappings of ordinary hotel dining, although it is Paradise Point Resort's main three-meals-daily dining room. In the heart of Mission Bay on Vacation Isle, you'll get striking water views from both the spacious terrace and the high-ceiling dining room. The menu is ambitious, intriguing, and pricey. If you order iced shellfish from the cart, confirm the prices in advance. The oysters, shrimp, and clams are superb, however, as are such dishes as the warm salad of roasted mushrooms and asparagus and the Asian-style bouillabaisse. ✉ *Paradise Point Resort, 1404 W. Vacation Rd., Vacation Isle, Mission Bay,* ☎ *858/490–6363. AE, D, DC, MC, V.*

German

$$–$$$ ✕ **Kaiserhof.** Without question the best German restaurant in San Diego County, Kaiserhof is so popular that reservations are a smart idea. The lively bar and sheltered beer garden work to inspire a sense of *Gemutlichkeit* (happy well-being), which is reinforced by a pleasing menu of many pages. Since the gigantic portions are accompanied by such side dishes as potato pancakes, bread dumplings, red cabbage, and spaetzle noodles, only the truly famished should attempt such starters as the snails in garlic butter and steak tartare. Entrées include sauerbraten, Wiener schnitzel, goulash, and smoked pork chops, plus excellent daily specials. ⊠ *2253 Sunset Cliffs Blvd., Ocean Beach,* ☎ *619/224–0606. MC, V. Closed Mon.*

Italian

$$ ✕ **The Venetian.** The spacious back room of this neighborhood eatery is actually a sheltered garden that you can enjoy in all weather. The menu takes a personal view of Italian cuisine with house specialties like seafood pasta in tangy marinara sauce, and bow-tie pasta tossed with prosciutto, peas, mushrooms, and a rose-tinted cream sauce. The well-priced selection of veal, chicken, and seafood dishes is excellent, but many regulars settle for the lavishly garnished antipasto salad and one of the tender-crusted pizzas. It seems to never change. ⊠ *3663 Voltaire St., Ocean Beach,* ☎ *619/223–8197. MC, V.*

$–$$ ✕ **Caffe Bella Italia.** Contemporary Italian cooking as prepared in Italy—an important point in fusion-mad San Diego—is the rule at this simple restaurant near one of the principle intersections in Pacific Beach. The menu presents Neapolitan-style macaroni with sausage and artichoke hearts in spicy tomato sauce, *pappardelle* (wide ribbons of pasta) with a creamy Gorgonzola and walnut sauce, plus formal entrées like chicken breast sautéed with balsamic vinegar, and slices of rare filet mignon tossed with herbs then topped with arugula and shavings of Parmesan cheese. ⊠ *1525 Garnet Ave., Pacific Beach,* ☎ *858/273–1224. MC, V. Closed Mon.*

$–$$ ✕ **Old Venice.** This long-running favorite near Shelter Island is treasured for its casual, welcoming atmosphere and for a menu that has both well-made pizzas and familiar Italian dishes like cannelloni baked in a rich meat sauce, generously stuffed lasagna, and eggplant parmigiana. A creamy pesto sauce adds glamour and a pungent flavor to the baked, spinach-stuffed chicken breast Florentine. ⊠ *2910 Canon St., Shelter Island,* ☎ *619/222–5888. MC, V. No lunch Sun.*

Japanese

$–$$ ✕ **Sushi Ota.** Wedged into a minimall between a convenience store and
★ a looming medical building, Sushi Ota initially seems less than prepossessing. But look closely at the expressions on customers' faces as they stream in and out of the doors, and you'll see eager anticipation and satisfied glows due to San Diego's best sushi. Besides the usual California roll and tuna and shrimp sushi, sample the sea urchin or surf clam sushi, and the soft-shell crab roll. Sushi Ota offers the cooked as well as the raw. There's additional parking behind the mall. ⊠ *4529 Mission Bay Dr., Pacific Beach,* ☎ *619/270–5670. Reservations essential. AE, D, MC, V. No lunch Sat.–Mon.*

Mexican

$–$$ ✕ **Miguel's Cocina.** On the arm that extends from the mainland to the island, this second-story, south-of-the-border restaurant has views of San Diego Bay, plus a tropical-decorated dining room ideal for kicking back and sipping margaritas. You can expect hearty fish tacos, shrimp sautéed with jalapeño peppers, and stuffed squid steak bathed in a creamy, chile-spiked sauce. The *carnitas* (slow-roasted pork garnished with several condiments) are served with tortillas. There is an endless selection of combo platters—of tacos, enchiladas, tamales, and burritos—that come with mounds of tasty rice and beans. ⊠ *2912 Shelter Island Dr., Shelter Island,* ☎ *619/224–2401. MC, V.*

Seafood

$ ✕ **Hudson Bay Seafood.** Part of the pleasure in this small, friendly, waterside fish house is watching the day-charter boats arrive at the adjacent dock and discharge their passengers, some seasoned fishermen and some first-timers who look grateful to be back on dry land. More than a few march up the wooden walkway to Hudson Bay, which bakes the sourdough rolls in which it sandwiches delicately fried fish fillets or shell-fish. The french fries are freshly cut, the fish tacos taste of Mexico, and even the tartar sauce is homemade. There are salads and excellent break-fasts, too. ⊠ *1403 Scott St., Shelter Island,* ☎ *619/222–8787. MC, V.*

Spanish

$–$$ ✕ **Costa Brava.** The paintings of bulls honor the traditions of the pro-prietor's hometown in northwestern Spain, and the long list of tapas, small plates of mild and highly seasoned hors d'oeurves, pay homage to the centuries-old traditions of the Spanish table. You can make a highly enjoyable meal out of several tapas, notably the clams in wine sauce, assorted cold-cuts plate, and fried potatoes served sizzling in *ali-oli* (garlic) mayonnaise. Entrées, while optional, can be good, especially the Porterhouse steak with roasted peppers, the assorted seafood in broth called "zarzuela," and the roast leg of lamb. ⊠ *1653 Garnet Ave., Pa-cific Beach,* ☎ *858/273–1218. MC, V.*

Thai

$ ✕ **Thai Time II.** An eye-pleasing interior and friendly service make this diminutive, casual spot not far from Ocean Beach a natural for fans of authentic, sometimes breathtakingly spicy Thai food. The kitchen generally balances flavors quite well, so that dishes like *tom yum* chicken soup present a symphony of sweet, tart, sour, and spicy tones. Not-to-be-missed items include the (hot!) *larb* salad of greens with sea-soned ground pork), the sweet *mee krob* noodles, and the creamy *panang* curry with beef or duck. Of the house specialties, try the peanut steak or the fried shrimp with spicy "Thai Time" sauce. ⊠ *3545 Midway Dr., Sports Arena,* ☎ *619/224–3245. MC, V. Closed Sun.*

La Jolla

Contemporary

$$$–$$$$ ✕ **Marine Room.** Diners can gaze at the ocean from this venerable La Jolla Shores mainstay and, if they're lucky, watch the grunion run or the waves race across the sand and beat against the glass. The Marine Room offers genteel beachfront dining-and-dancing and creative (although some will think *too* creative) contemporary cuisine. Appetizers include an *étude,* or "study," of foie gras served two ways, and a basket of skil-let-roasted forest mushrooms. A representative entrée would be New Zealand John Dory poached in almond broth. Sunday brunch is lav-ish; in winter call for information about the high-tide breakfasts. ⊠ *2000 Spindrift Dr., La Jolla,* ☎ *858/459–7222. AE, D, DC, MC, V.*

$$$–$$$$ ✕ **Top o' the Cove.** Although glitzier newcomers rival this once peer-less La Jolla institution, the elegant but comfortable Top o' the Cove still receives high marks from San Diego diners for the romantic ocean view from its cottage windows and its fine contemporary European-American cuisine. The menu provides plenty for the thoughtful diner to consider before ordering, such as tamarind-glazed Muscovy duck breast with five-spice–flavored pecans, and Chilean sea bass with baby artichokes and lemon. The service is attentive but not overbearing, and the wine list leaves nothing to be desired. ⊠ *1216 Prospect St., La Jolla,* ☎ *858/454–7779. AE, DC, MC, V.*

$$–$$$ ✕ **Azul La Jolla.** Blessed with what may be the most glamorous view of La Jolla Cove and the cliffs racing to the north, this sizable restau-rant has a broad, sheltered terrace. The interior, like the menu, takes its inspiration from the Mediterranean and is attractive but not dis-tracting. Good starters include the caramelized onion and goat cheese flatbread, Tuscan white bean soup, and a succulent salad of sliced heir-loom tomatoes and goat cheese. The entrée list pays attention to seafood with such plates as roasted white sea bass, but really shines

with olive-crusted rack of lamb and New York steak in musky Spanish blue cheese sauce. The chocolate "French toast" is one of the more clever desserts to surface in La Jolla. ⊠ *1250 Prospect St., La Jolla,* ☎ *858/454–9616. AE, D, MC, V. No lunch Mon.*

$$–$$$ ✕ **Cafe Japengo.** Framed by elegant marbled walls and accented with bamboo trees and unusual black-iron sculptures, this Pacific Rim restaurant serves Asian-inspired cuisine with many North and South American touches. The curry-fried calamari and the Japengo pot stickers appetizers are guaranteed to wake up your mouth. There's also a selection of grilled, wood-roasted, and wok-fried entrées; try the 10-ingredient fried rice, or the crispy whole striped bass. The sushi bar is always very fresh. The service can be slow, but the pace in the bar, crowded with young locals, is fast and lively. ⊠ *Aventine Center, 8960 University Center La., Golden Triangle, La Jolla,* ☎ *858/450–3355. AE, D, DC, MC, V. No lunch weekends.*

$$–$$$ ✕ **NINE-TEN.** A showcase for the "California Wine Country" cuisine of chef Michael Stebner, the dining room of the historic Grande Colonial Hotel is decorated sparely but richly with stone, wood, and contemporary artwork. The relatively brief dinner menu is written daily, and provides the option of ordering many entrées as either half-priced, small plates or pricier, full servings. In season, the salad of "market" tomatoes from specialty growers bursts with California goodness. Try the orange-glazed duck confit, sirloin steak with polenta fritters and red wine sauce, or veal ragout ladled over hand-rolled pasta. ⊠ *910 Prospect St., La Jolla,* ☎ *858/729–5395. AE, D, DC, MC, V.*

$$–$$$ ✕ **Roppongi.** A hit from the moment it opened, Roppongi serves global
★ cuisine with strong Asian notes. The contemporary dining room has a row of comfortable booths lining a wall, and is done in wood tones, accented with Asian statuary. It can get noisy when crowded; tables near the bar are generally quieter. Order the imaginative Euro-Asian tapas as appetizers or combine them for a full meal. Try the chicken and porcini mushroom dumplings, Vietnamese chicken salad, and the high-rising Polynesian crab stack. Good entrées are East-meets-West noodle preparations and fresh seafood. ⊠ *875 Prospect St., La Jolla,* ☎ *858/551–5252. AE, D, DC, MC, V.*

$–$$$ ✕ **Tamarindo.** Decorated in a kaleidoscope of bright colors, Tamarindo presents a nuevo Latino style of cooking that bridges the flavors of Mexico, the Caribbean, and other Latin American destinations known for spicy, distinctive foods. The extensive menu lists many, distinctive small plates (from smoked-trout quesadillas to barbecued-duck tacos) that, when combined, easily constitute a meal. Full entrées include a *sabana*-style steak with Argentina-inspired chimichurri sauce, and sautéed veal with corn salsa. This may be the only restaurant you'll ever find that serves cotton candy for dessert. ⊠ *1044 Wall St., La Jolla,* ☎ *858/551–7575. AE, DC, MC, V.*

Deli

$–$$ ✕ **Blumberg's.** This large, sometimes noisy eatery was once as close as coastal San Diego came to offering a real Jewish deli, and it continues to please with a vast menu and enormous portions. Good options include a lox plate for breakfast, and an overstuffed corned beef–and–slaw sandwich or one of the soup-and-sandwich specials (especially the whitefish when it's available) for lunch. These prodigious portions keep diners stuffed for the following 24 hours or so. ⊠ *8861 Villa La Jolla Dr., La Jolla,* ☎ *858/455–1462. AE, D, DC, MC, V.*

French

$$–$$$ ✕ **Tapenade.** French cuisine has made a comeback in San Diego, and
★ has shed some weight in the process. The celebrated restaurant Tapenade (named after the delicious Provençal black olive–and–anchovy

paste that accompanies the bread) takes its inspiration from the south of France. In an unpretentious, light, and airy room it serves cuisine to match. Very fresh ingredients, a delicate touch with sauces, and an emphasis on seafood characterize the menu. It changes frequently, but with good fortune may include old-fashioned cassoulet rich with sausage and other meats, porcini-stuffed rabbit, and roasted monkfish with eggplant. While the tables inside are a bit closely spaced, the terrace is pleasant and inviting. ⊠ *7612 Fay Ave., La Jolla,* ☎ *858/551–7500. AE, D, DC, MC, V.*

Italian

$$–$$$ ✕ **Piatti Ristorante.** On weekends this trattoria overflows with singles and families, and attempting to find a table without reservations can be futile. A wood-burning oven turns out flavorful pizzas; pastas include the *pappardelle fantasia* (wide saffron noodles with shrimp, fresh tomatoes, and arugula) and a garlicky spaghetti *con vongole verace* (with clams in the shell). Among the entrées are good rotisserie chicken and grilled rib eye steak. The weekday lunch menu includes elaborate salads and delicious *panini* (sandwiches); brunch is served weekends. The *sorbetti* are superior to the baked desserts. A fountain splashes softly on the tree-shaded patio, where heat lamps warm you on chilly evenings. ⊠ *2182 Avenida de la Playa, La Jolla,* ☎ *858/454–1589. AE, DC, MC, V.*

$$–$$$ ✕ **Trattoria Acqua.** Reservations are a good idea for this Mediterranean-inspired bistro above La Jolla Cove. On the lower level of Coast Walk center, this romantic eatery has dining rooms that are semi-open to the weather and the view, yet sufficiently sheltered for comfort. Trattoria Acqua is frequently packed with diners eager to sample the likes of stuffed, deep-fried zucchini blossoms, lobster-filled ravioli in a lobster-scented *beurre blanc* (white butter) sauce, and stuffed roasted quail flavored with bacon. The superb wine list earns kudos from aficionados. ⊠ *1298 Prospect St., La Jolla,* ☎ *858/454–0709. AE, DC, MC, V.*

Japanese

$$–$$$$ ✕ **Jin Sang.** Alone among San Diego County restaurants, Jin Sang specializes in *shabu shabu,* a Japanese concoction in which arrangements of seafood, chicken, or beef are cooked tableside in boiling broth, along with separate courses of vegetables and noodles. Because the cooking process is so simple, the restaurant emphasizes very high-quality ingredients, and the basic U.S. prime beef dinner is a treat. The server gets the party going, but guests learn to use chopsticks to drop items in the broth for quick cooking, and then retrieve them for dipping in the tangy sauces. ⊠ *7614 Fay Ave., La Jolla,* ☎ *858/456–4545. AE, D, MC, V. No lunch.*

$–$$ ✕ **Sushi on the Rock.** Young, hip, and noisy, this is very much the destination for inventive, sometimes off-the-wall sushi, including offerings with names like "baby conehead" (a spicy tempura eggplant roll) and the "911 Roll," filled with very spicy tuna. There is an excellent selection of salads and entrées, including a delightful dish of Hong Kong–style noodles topped with grilled shrimp, vegetables, and an unusual soy-sesame cream sauce. The rock music plays loudly, which pleases the college-age and Gen-X clientele. ⊠ *7734 Girard Ave., La Jolla,* ☎ *858/456–1138. AE, MC, V. No lunch weekends.*

Mexican

$–$$ ✕ **Alfonso's of La Jolla.** The sidewalk terrace is the place to grab a seat at this institution on busy Prospect Street, where you can review the passing parade while downing sizeable margaritas and plates laden with *carne asada.* This marinated, grilled steak is a house specialty and arrives both garnished *tampiquena*-style with a cheese enchilada, rice, and beans; or chopped as a filling for tacos and quesadillas. The menu extends to typical enchiladas and burritos, as well as to a couple of piquant shrimp preparations. That nothing ever changes seems to guarantee this landmark's popularity. ⊠ *1251 Prospect St., La Jolla,* ☎ *858/454–2232. AE, MC, V.*

Seafood

$$$–$$$$ ✕ **George's at the Cove.** Hollywood types and other visiting celebri-
★ ties can be spotted in the elegant main dining room, where a wall-length window overlooks La Jolla Cove. Renowned for fresh seafood specials and fine preparations of beef and lamb, this also is the place to taste seasonal produce from local specialty growers. When available, the sweet corn soup is a revelation of flavor. Next move on to the pancetta-wrapped salmon with garlic-lemon vinaigrette, or the rich, succulent free-range veal chop. Save room for the dark-chocolate soufflé cake served with fresh fruit compote. For more informal dining and a sweeping view of the coast try the rooftop Ocean Terrace ($–$$) or order from the terrace menu in the second-story bar. ⊠ *1250 Prospect St., La Jolla,* ☎ *858/454–4244. Reservations essential. AE, D, DC, MC, V.*

Mission Valley

American

$–$$ ✕ **Cheesecake Factory.** Out-of-town chains often don't fare well in San Diego, but the Cheesecake Factory opened with a bang in the city's hottest shopping mall, Fashion Valley, and has retained its immense popularity ever since. Part of the patronage is drawn by the huge, creamy cheesecakes, and more by the extremely friendly, eager-to-please servers. Everyone seems to like the multipage menu, which opens with such appetizers as barbecued duck–filled spring rolls and sweet-corn tamale cakes, and meanders leisurely through classic and innovative pizzas, gigantic salads, pastas, and such house specialties as chicken with biscuits, mashed potatoes, and country gravy. When the crowd is in full cry the noise can be deafening. ⊠ *Fashion Valley Center, 7067 Friars Rd., Mission Valley,* ☎ *619/683–2800. AE, D, MC, V.*

$–$$ ✕ **Mimi's Cafe.** The Mission Valley branch of this ultrapopular, New Orleans–theme chain hops from early morning breakfast through dinner, thanks to exceptionally welcoming service, an interior design that never fails to yield a wealth of conversation pieces, and a menu that takes self-indulgence to new heights with such creations as cream cheese–stuffed French toast, freshly baked chicken potpies, and old-fashioned pot roast that seems to melt at a glance. The creamy bread pudding sends the redolent odors of whiskey sauce wafting through the room. ⊠ *5180 Mission Center Rd., Mission Valley,* ☎ *619/491–0284. AE, DC, MC, V.*

$–$$ ✕ **Ricky's Family Restaurant.** Chain feederies haven't driven out San Diego's old-line family restaurants, and along with Hob Nob Hill, this unpretentious place on the quiet fringe of percolating Mission Valley remains dear to the city's heart. This three-meals-daily restaurant serves big portions of unassuming, well-prepared, all-American cooking, but is famed for its breakfasts, when savory corned-beef hash and fluffy, strawberry-crowned Belgian waffles are the rule. The most famed breakfast specialty is the spectacular apple pancake, a soufflé-like creation that takes 20 minutes to bake, arrives burning hot from the oven, and is irresistible to the last molecule of molten cinnamon sugar. ⊠ *2181 Hotel Circle S, Mission Valley,* ☎ *619/291–4498. MC, V.*

Chinese

$–$$ ✕ **P. F. Chang's China Bistro.** Given a menu that reads like a Top 40 Hits list of Chinese dishes, fans of authentic Chinese cuisine snicker at the suggestion that this huge Fashion Valley Center branch of a Phoenix-based chain serves the genuine article, but don't tell that to the crowds waiting patiently to be seated. The dramatic decor doubtless counts for some of the appeal. Meals often open with shrimp dumplings, marinated spare ribs, and stuffed wontons in chili-soy sauce. There are also good salads and standards like mu shu chicken, sweet-and-sour pork, Mongolian beef, and orange peel shrimp. ⊠ *7077 Friars Rd., Mission Valley*, ☎ *619/260–8484. AE, D, DC, MC, V.*

Seafood

$–$$$$ ✕ **King's Seafood Co.** This warehouse-size restaurant remains wildly popular with shoppers at Mission Valley's many malls, owing to extremely friendly and efficient service, tanks filled with lively lobsters and Dungeness crabs, and a daily-changing menu with a fine selection of fresh-shucked oysters. Specialties include New Orleans–style barbecued shrimp, and a full-size New England clambake complete with red potatoes and sweet corn on the cob. Fish and shellfish are char-grilled, deep-fried, sautéed, steamed, and skewered, and for the member of the party who can't stand anything with shells or scales, the menu obliges with skillet-roasted chicken and grilled sirloin. ⊠ *825 Camino de la Reina North, Mission Valley*, ☎ *619/574–1230. AE, DC, MC, V.*

Old Town

Latin American

$–$$ ✕ **Berta's Latin American Restaurant.** A San Diego rarity—and a surprise in a section of town where the food leans toward the safe and touristy—Berta's serves wonderful Latin American dishes. The wine list showcases good Chilean wines, and the food manages to be tasty and health-conscious at the same time. Try the Brazilian seafood *vatapa* (shrimp, scallops, and fish served in a sauce flavored with ginger, coconut, and chilies) or the Peruvian *pollo a la huancaina* (chicken with chilies and a feta-cheese sauce). The simple dining room is small, but there's also a little patio. ⊠ *3928 Twiggs St., Old Town*, ☎ *619/295–2343. AE, MC, V.*

Mexican

$–$$ ✕ **El Agave.** A charmer on the edge of historic Old Town, El Agave
★   promises caring service, a bar stocked with hundreds of tequilas (a collection that El Agave claims is unrivaled in the United States), and a delicious, truly unique Mexican menu. Make a meal of such appetizers as crisp chicken tacos covered with thick, tart cream and rolled taquitos stuffed with shredded pork. Or save room for entrées like chicken in spicy Don Julio mole sauce, and terrific, crisp-skinned roast leg of pork. ⊠ *2304 San Diego Ave., Old Town*, ☎ *619/220–0692. MC, V.*

Seafood

$$–$$$ ✕ **Cafe Pacifica.** The airy Cafe Pacifica serves eclectic contemporary cuisine with an emphasis on seafood. Fresh fish is grilled with your choice of savory sauces. Other good bets include the griddle-fried mustard catfish, the spicy garlic seafood fettuccine, and the grilled lamb chops. The crème brûlée is worth blowing any diet for. Cafe Pacifica's wine list has received kudos from *Wine Spectator* magazine, but also consider the pomegranate-flavored margarita. ⊠ *2414 San Diego Ave., Old Town*, ☎ *619/291–6666. AE, D, DC, MC, V. No lunch.*

4 · LODGING

San Diego has hotels in abundance, and
several on the drawing boards could add
more than 3,000 rooms in the next few
years. All this means lower prices for
those who shop around. When you make
reservations, ask about any specials. Several
properties in the Hotel Circle area of Mission
Valley offer special rates and free tickets to
local attractions, and many hotels promote
lower-priced weekend packages to fill rooms
after convention and business customers leave
town. Book well in advance, especially if you
plan to visit in the summer.

By Lenore
Greiner

S AN DIEGO IS SPREAD OUT, so the first thing to consider when
selecting lodging is location. If you choose a hotel with a waterfront location and extensive outdoor sports facilities, you
may never decide to leave. But if you plan to sightsee, take into account a hotel's proximity to attractions. In terms of price, even the most
expensive areas have some reasonably priced rooms. High season is
summer, and rates are lowest in the fall. If an ocean view is important,
request it when booking, but be aware the cost will be significantly
more than a non–ocean view room. You can assume that all rooms have
private baths, phones, TVs, and air-conditioning unless otherwise
noted. We always list a property's facilities but not whether you'll be
charged extra to use them, so when pricing accommodations, do ask
what's included.

San Diego has relatively few B&Bs, but most are very well maintained
and accommodating. If you are planning an extended stay or need lodgings for four or more people, consider an apartment rental. **Oakwood
Apartments** (☎ 800/888–0808, WEB www.oakwood.com) rents comfortable furnished apartments in the Mission Valley, La Jolla Colony,
and Coronado areas with maid service and linens; there's a one-week
to 30-day minimum stay depending on locations. Several hotels also
offer special weekly and monthly rates, especially in the beach communities.

The **Bed and Breakfast Guild of San Diego** (☎ 619/523–1300, WEB www.
bandbguildsandiego.org) lists a number of high-quality member inns.
The **Bed & Breakfast Directory for San Diego** (✉ Box 3292, 92163,
☎ 619/297–3130 or 800/619–7666, WEB www.sandiegobandb.com) covers San Diego County.

Several hostels (some with "HI"—Hostel International—in their name)
are located throughout San Diego. They cater to college students and
budget backpackers, and most require an international passport to check
in. Rooms are usually dorm style with four to six bunks; however, some
hostels have a few private or double rooms.

CATEGORY	COST*
$$$$	over $225
$$$	$160–$225
$$	$100–$160
$	under $100

*for a double room in high (summer) season, excluding 9–13% tax.

Children

Virtually all tourist-oriented areas of San Diego have hotels suited to
a family's pocketbook and/or recreational needs, and many allow kids
under 18 to stay free with their parents. You'll find the most choices
and diversity in and around Mission Bay, which is close to SeaWorld,
beaches, parks, and Old Town. Many Mission Bay hotels offer Sea-
World packages or discounts.

The resort Rancho Bernardo Inn has full- and half-day programs for
kids ages 5–17 that include swimming, arts and crafts, and, for kids
over 12, golf and tennis. The programs run during the major spring
and summer holidays and the month of August.

Within the italicized service information below each lodging review,
look for "children's programs" if these services are important to you.

Coronado

Quiet, out-of-the-way Coronado feels like something out of an earlier, more gracious era. With boutiques and restaurants lining Orange Avenue—the main street—and its fine beaches, Coronado is great for a getaway. But if you plan to see many of San Diego's attractions, you'll probably spend a lot of time commuting across the bridge or riding the ferry.

$$$$ 🏨 **Coronado Island Marriott Resort.** Near San Diego Bay, this snazzy hotel has many rooms with great views of downtown's skyline. Large rooms and suites in low-slung buildings are done in a cheerful California–country French fashion, with colorful Impressionist prints; all rooms have separate showers and tubs and come with plush robes. The spa facilities are top-notch, but the service can be somewhat uncouth. ✉ *2000 2nd St., Coronado 92118,* ☎ *619/435–3000 or 800/543–4300,* FAX *619/435–3032,* WEB *www.marriotthotels.com/sanci. 265 rooms, 35 suites. 4 restaurants, bar, room service, in-room data ports, cable TV with movies, 6 tennis courts, 3 pools, aerobics, health club, hair salon, 2 outdoor hot tubs, massage, sauna, spa, beach, snorkeling, windsurfing, boating, jet skiing, waterskiing, bicycles, shops, children's programs, laundry service, concierge, business services, convention center, meeting rooms, parking (fee); no smoking. AE, D, DC, MC, V.*

$$$$ 🏨 **Hotel Del Coronado.** Preserving the memory of seaside vacations long
★ gone by, "The Del" stands as a social and historic landmark, its whimsical red turrets, white siding, and balconied walkways taking you as far back as 1888, the year it was built. U.S. presidents, European royalty, and movie stars have stayed in the Victorian-decorated rooms and suites, which have been fully renovated to include all the necessities of modern-day life. The hotel's public areas are always bustling with activity; for quieter quarters, consider staying in the contemporary, seven-story Ocean Towers building or one of the eight beachfront cottages. Rates are defined largely by room views. ✉ *1500 Orange Ave., Coronado 92118,* ☎ *619/435–6611 or 800/468–3533,* FAX *619/522–8262,* WEB *www.hoteldel.com. 676 rooms. 2 restaurants, coffee shop, deli, room service, in-room data ports, cable TV with movies, 3 tennis courts, 2 pools, gym, hair salon, outdoor hot tub, massage, sauna, spa, steam room, beach, bicycles, 4 bars, piano bar, shops, children's programs, laundry service, concierge, business services, convention center, meeting rooms, parking (fee); no smoking. AE, D, DC, MC, V.*

$$$$ 🏨 **Loews Coronado Bay Resort.** You can park your boat at the 80-slip marina of this elegant resort set on a secluded 15-acre peninsula on the Silver Strand. Rooms are tastefully decorated, and all have furnished balconies with views of water—either bay, ocean, or marina. The hotel lounge has nightly entertainment. The Azzura Point restaurant specializes in seafood. ✉ *4000 Coronado Bay Rd., Coronado 92118,* ☎ *619/424–4000 or 800/815–6397,* FAX *619/424–4400,* WEB *www.loewshotels.com/coronado.html. 403 rooms, 37 suites. 3 restaurants, 3 bars, deli, room service, in-room data ports, minibars, cable TV with movies, 5 tennis courts, 3 pools, hair salon, health club, 3 hot tubs, beach, windsurfing, boating, jet skiing, waterskiing, bicycles, shop, children's programs, laundry service, concierge, business services, convention center, meeting rooms, parking (fee); no smoking. AE, D, DC, MC, V.*

$$–$$$$ 🏨 **Glorietta Bay Inn.** The main building of this property—adjacent to the Coronado harbor, and near many restaurants and shops—was built in 1908 for sugar baron John D. Spreckels, who once owned much of downtown San Diego. Rooms in this Edwardian-style mansion and in the newer motel-style buildings are attractively furnished. The inn is much smaller and quieter than the Hotel Del across the street. Tours ($8) of the island's historical buildings depart from the inn three morn-

LET YOUR HOST BE A GHOST

SAN DIEGO'S founding dates to 1769, and with its rich history comes a fair share of ghost stories. Two of these tales revolve around local hostelries.

One of the most infamous concerns a woman named Kate Morgan, who checked into the Hotel del Coronado in November 1892. She eventually checked out of the hotel, and soon after checked out for good. The story goes that Morgan, who was pregnant at the time, had been anticipating the arrival of her estranged husband, but he never showed. She was found dead along the hotel beachfront of a gunshot wound to the head. Investigators ruled her death a suicide, but rumors have long circulated to the contrary.

Kate's spirit is said to haunt room 3312 of the hotel, but there have been reports of ghostly occurrences in Room 3502 as well. Hotel guests and employees report having heard strange, unexplained noises and observed curtains billowing when windows are closed.

The Horton Grand Hotel is also said to have its phantoms in residence. Most famous of the hotel's spooks is a gambler from the 1880s named Roger Whitaker who is said to occupy Room 309. A number of peculiar occurrences here have ensured the hotel's reputation as being haunted by Whitaker, and maybe some other ghosts, too. According to legend,

Roger was caught cheating at cards one night at the hotel. He tried to hide in Room 309 but was found and shot and killed by an angry gunman.

Several staff members and guests have told of strange noises, beds shaking, lights going on and off by themselves, objects moved by unseen hands, and armoire doors opening in the middle of the night. It's been said that the temperature of Room 309 sometimes gets uncomfortably warm and neither air-conditioning nor opening the window helps. Sometimes the impression of someone having laid on the bed can be seen, even after the room has been freshly made up by the hotel maids. Also, occasionally while cards are being played by guests in the hotel bar, the sound of cards being shuffled reportedly can be heard from the otherwise unoccupied Room 309. The hotel is quick to point out that the ghosts are unintimidating and pose no threat to guests.

In fact, the managements of both properties provide information about the hauntings on their Web sites, and some of the hotel staff can expound further on the legends behind these spirits.

To find out more about San Diego's best haunts, take the **Ghosts and Gravestones Tour of San Diego** (☎ 619/298–8687 or 800/868–7482, WEB www.ghostsandgravestones.com).

ings a week. Some rooms have patios or balconies. Ginger snaps and lemonade are served daily from 3 to 5. ⊠ *1630 Glorietta Blvd., Coronado 92118,* ☎ *619/435–3101 or 800/283–9383,* FAX *619/435–6182,* WEB *www.gloriettabayinn.com. 100 rooms. Dining room, in-room data ports, some kitchenettes, refrigerators, cable TV with movies, pool, outdoor hot tub, bicycles, library, laundry service, concierge, business services, free parking; no smoking. AE, MC, V.*

$$–$$$ 🖼 **Crown City Inn & Bistro.** On Coronado's main drag, the Crown City Inn is close to shops, restaurants, and the beach. For the price, it's easily one of the best deals on the island. However, this two-story motor inn lacks the amenities and prestige of Coronado's bigger and better-known lodgings. A public park is across the street. ⊠ *520 Orange Ave., Coronado 92118,* ☎ *619/435–3116 or 800/422–1173,* FAX *619/435–6750,* WEB *www.crowncityinn.com. 33 rooms. Restaurant, room service, in-room data ports, minibars, microwaves, refrigerators, cable TV with movies, pool, bicycles, laundry facilities, parking (fee); no smoking. AE, D, DC, MC, V.*

Downtown

A lively, continuously revitalized downtown has helped make the city center the hotel hub of San Diego. Hotel types range from budget chains to boutique hotels to business accommodations and major high-rises. Much to see is within walking distance—Seaport Village, the Embarcadero, the Gaslamp Quarter, theaters and nightspots, galleries and coffeehouses, and the Horton Plaza shopping center. The zoo and Balboa Park are also nearby. And downtown has plenty of good restaurants, especially along 4th and 5th avenues south of Broadway in the Gaslamp Quarter.

$$$$ 🖼 **Manchester Grand Hyatt San Diego.** This high-rise adjacent to Sea-
★ port Village combines old-world opulence with California airiness. Palm trees pose next to ornate tapestry couches in the light-filled lobby, and all of the British Regency–style guest rooms have views of the water. The hotel's proximity to the convention center attracts a large business trade. The Business Plan includes access to an area with desks and office supplies; and business floor rooms have fax machines. A trolley station is one block away. Sally's serves inventive cuisine, and the 40th-floor lounge is one of the city's most romantic spots to watch the sun set. ⊠ *1 Market Pl., Embarcadero 92101,* ☎ *619/232–1234 or 800/233–1234,* FAX *619/233–6464,* WEB *www.hyatt.com. 820 rooms, 56 suites. 3 restaurants, 2 bars, room service, in-room data ports, minibars, pool, 4 tennis courts, outdoor hot tub, sauna, steam room, health club, boating, bicycles, shops, dry cleaning, laundry service, concierge, concierge floor, business services, meeting rooms, airport shuttle, car rental, parking (fee); no smoking. AE, D, DC, MC, V.*

$$$$ 🖼 **San Diego Marriott Hotel and Marina.** This 25-story twin tower next to the San Diego Convention Center has everything a businessperson—or leisure traveler—could want. Lagoon-style pools nestled between cascading waterfalls are among the appealing on-site features. Seaport Village and a trolley station are nearby. As a major site for conventions, the complex can be hectic and impersonal, and the hallways can be noisy. The standard rooms are smallish, but pay a bit extra for a room with a balcony overlooking the bay and you'll have a serene, sparkling world spread out before you. ⊠ *333 W. Harbor Dr., Embarcadero 92101,* ☎ *619/234–1500 or 800/228–9290,* FAX *619/234–8678,* WEB *www.marriotthotels.com/sandt. 1,300 rooms, 54 suites. 3 restaurants, 3 bars, in-room data ports, cable TV with movies, room service, 2 pools, hair salon, outdoor hot tub, massage, sauna, 6 tennis courts, aerobics, basketball, health club, boating, bicycles, recreation*

Downtown Lodging

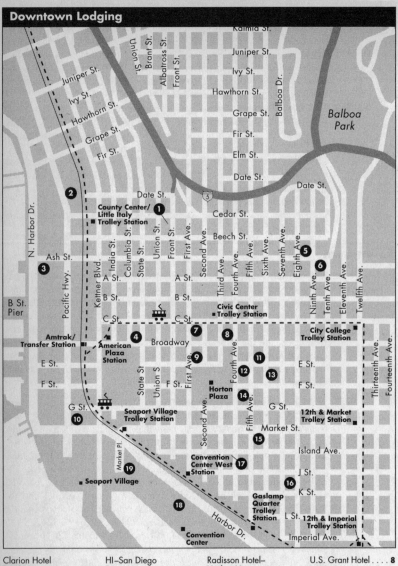

Kalmia St.

Juniper St.

Ivy St.

Hawthorn St.

Grape St.

Fir St.

Elm St.

Date St.

Date St.

Balboa Park

Juniper St.

Ivy St.

Hawthorn St.

Grape St.

Fir St.

Union St.
Brant St.
Albatross St.
Front St.

Balboa Dr.

N. Harbor Dr.

2

Date St.

County Center/
Little Italy
■ Trolley Station **1**

Cedar St.

Beech St.

5

Ash St.

3

Pacific Hwy.

Kettner Blvd.

India St.
Columbia St.
State St.
Union St.
Front St.
First Ave.
Second Ave.
Third Ave.
Fourth Ave.
Fifth Ave.
Sixth Ave.
Seventh Ave.
Eighth Ave.
Ninth Ave.
Tenth Ave.
Eleventh Ave.
Twelfth Ave.

6

A St.

A St.

B St.

B St.

C St.

C St.

Civic Center
■ Trolley Station

B St.
Pier

Amtrak/
Transfer Station

American
Plaza
Station

4

7

Broadway

8

9

E St.

F St.

State St.
Union S
F St.
First Ave.

Fourth Ave.

City College
Trolley Station

E St.

F St.

Thirteenth Ave.
Fourteenth Ave.

11

12

13

Horton
Plaza

14

G St.

10

Seaport Village
Trolley Station

Second Ave.

Fifth Ave.

G St.

15

12th & Market
Trolley Station

Market St.

Island Ave.

Market Pl.

19

■ Seaport Village

18

Convention
Center West
■ Station

17

16

J St.

K St.

Gaslamp
Quarter
Trolley
Station

L St.

12th & Imperial
Trolley Station

Harbor Dr.

Convention
Center

Imperial Ave.

Clarion Hotel Bay View **16**	HI–San Diego Downtown **15**	Radisson Hotel– Harbor View **1**	U.S. Grant Hotel **8**
Comfort Inn **6**	Holiday Inn San Diego– on the Bay **3**	Ramada Inn & Suites– Downtown **13**	USA Hostels **14**
Embassy Suites– San Diego Bay. **10**	Horton Grand Hotel. **17**	Residence Inn San Diego Downtown **2**	Westgate Hotel **7**
Gaslamp Plaza Suites. **11**	Manchester Grand Hyatt San Diego. **19**	Rodeway Inn **5**	Westin Hotel San Diego– Horton Plaza. **9**
Harbour Lights Resort **12**		San Diego Marriott Hotel and Marina . . . **18**	Wyndham San Diego at Emerald Plaza . . . **4**

room, *video game room, shops, laundry facilities, concierge, concierge floor, business services, convention center, meeting rooms, airport shuttle, car rental, parking (fee); no smoking. AE, D, DC, MC, V.*

$$$$ ⊡ **Westgate Hotel.** A nondescript, modern high-rise across from Hor-
★   ton Plaza hides what must be the most opulent hotel in San Diego. The lobby, modeled after the anteroom at Versailles, has hand-cut Baccarat chandeliers; rooms are individually furnished with antiques, Italian marble counters, and bath fixtures with 24-karat-gold overlays. From the ninth floor up the views of the harbor and city are breathtaking. Afternoon high tea is served in the lobby to the accompaniment of piano music. The San Diego Trolley stops right outside the door. ⊠ *1055 2nd Ave., Gaslamp Quarter 92101,* ☎ *619/238–1818 or 800/221–3802; 800/522–1564 in CA,* FAX *619/557–3737,* WEB *www.westgatehotel.com. 223 rooms. 2 restaurants, bar, deli, room service, in-room data ports, cable TV with movies, health club, hair salon, spa, bicycles, concierge, business services, meeting rooms, airport shuttle, parking (fee); no smoking. AE, D, DC, MC, V.*

$$$$ ⊡ **Westin Hotel San Diego–Horton Plaza.** You know you're there when you see the startling lighted blue obelisk fronting this high-rise hotel. Inside, it's all understated marble and brass. The spacious rooms are done blue and orange pastels. The lobby lounge is packed every night with business travelers and weary shoppers back from the adjacent Horton Plaza. ⊠ *910 Broadway Cir., Gaslamp Quarter 92101,* ☎ *619/ 239–2200 or 888/625–5144,* FAX *619/239–0509,* WEB *www.westin.com. 450 rooms, 14 suites. 2 restaurants,sports bar, room service, in-room data ports, cable TV with movies, pool, hot tub, 2 tennis courts, basketball, health club, lounge, shops, dry cleaning, laundry service, concierge, business services, meeting rooms, airport shuttle, car rental, parking (fee); no smoking. AE, D, DC, MC, V.*

$$$$ ⊡ **U. S. Grant Hotel.** Across the street from the Horton Plaza shopping center, this San Diego classic was built in 1910 by the grandson of President Ulysses S. Grant. Crystal chandeliers and polished marble floors in the lobby and Queen Anne–style mahogany furnishings in the stately rooms recall a more gracious era when such dignitaries as President Franklin D. Roosevelt and Charles Lindbergh stayed here. High-power business types still gather at the hotel's clubby Grant Grill, and English high tea is served in the lobby 2–6. ⊠ *326 Broadway, Gaslamp Quarter, 92101,* ☎ *619/232–3121 or 877/999–3223,* FAX *619/232–3626,* WEB *www.wyndham.com. 225 rooms, 60 suites. 2 restaurants, bar, café, room service, in-room data ports, cable TV with movies, gym, shops, Internet, concierge, business services, meeting rooms, airport shuttle, parking (fee); no smoking. AE, D, MC, V.*

$$$–$$$$ ⊡ **Clarion Hotel Bay View.** Close to the San Diego Convention Cen-
★   ter, this is a good hotel for conventioneers hoping to save a little money while still being close to the shopping, nightlife, and restaurants of the Gaslamp Quarter. Surrounded to the north and east by the warehouse district, the area around the hotel can seem a little seedy, but it's really safe. A trolley station is just two blocks away. The two-room suites rent wet bars, and you can request microwaves, mini-refrigerators, and video players. ⊠ *660 K St., Gaslamp Quarter 92101,* ☎ *619/696–0234 or 800/252–7466,* FAX *619/231–8199,* WEB *www.clarionbayview.com. 264 rooms, 48 suites. Restaurant, bar, room service, in-room data ports, minibars, cable TV with movies, pool, gym, hot tub, sauna, shops, Internet, baby-sitting, dry cleaning, laundry service, laundry facilities, concierge, meeting rooms, airport shuttle, car rental, parking (fee); no smoking. AE, D, DC, MC, V.*

$$$–$$$$ ⊡ **Holiday Inn San Diego–on the Bay.** On the Embarcadero and overlooking San Diego Bay, this twin high-rise hotel is perfect for vacationers and business travelers. Rooms are unsurprising but spacious, and

views from the balconies are hard to beat. While the hotel grounds are nice if fairly sterile, the bay is just across the street and offers boat rides, restaurants, and picturesque walking areas. The hotel is very close to the airport and Amtrak station. The English-style Elephant and Castle Pub is a great place for food, drink, and meeting people. ⊠ *1355 N. Harbor Dr., Embarcadero 92101,* ☎ *619/232–3861 or 800/877–8920,* FAX *619/232–4924,* WEB *www.basshotels.com. 600 rooms, 17 suites. 3 restaurants, bar, in-room data ports, 2 pools, outdoor hot tub, sauna, gym, shops, laundry facilities, concierge, business services, meeting rooms, airport shuttle, car rental, parking (fee); no smoking. AE, D, DC, MC, V.*

$$$–$$$$ 🏨 **Horton Grand Hotel.** A Victorian confection, the Horton Grand comprises two 1880s hotels moved brick by brick from nearby locations and fit together. The delightfully retro rooms are furnished with period antiques, ceiling fans, and gas-burning fireplaces. The choicest rooms overlook a garden courtyard that twinkles with miniature lights. The hotel is a charmer, but service can be erratic. ⊠ *311 Island Ave., Gaslamp Quarter 92101,* ☎ *619/544–1886 or 800/542–1886,* FAX *619/239–3823,* WEB *www.hortongrand.com. 132 rooms, 24 suites. Restaurant, piano bar, kitchenettes, microwaves, refrigerator, theater, business services, meeting rooms, airport shuttle, parking (fee); no smoking. AE, D, DC, MC, V.*

$$$–$$$$ 🏨 **Radisson Hotel–Harbor View.** This 22-story hotel dwarfs most buildings in the area (many are two-story Victorian homes), providing many rooms with great views of San Diego Bay and the downtown skyline. The art deco–inspired rooms are ordinary, but most have balconies. Although the hotel is practically adjacent to a freeway offramp, rooms are relatively free of noise. The airport and the eateries and coffeehouses of Little Italy are nearby. ⊠ *1646 Front St., Downtown 92101,* ☎ *619/239–6800 or 800/333–3333,* FAX *619/238–9561,* WEB *www.radisson.com. 313 rooms, 20 suites. 2 restaurants, bar. room service, cable TV with video games, pool, gym, hot tub, sauna, shops, laundry service, business services, meeting rooms, airport shuttle, parking (fee); no smoking. AE, D, DC, MC, V.*

$$$–$$$$ 🏨 **Wyndham San Diego at Emerald Plaza.** This property's office and conference facilities draw many business travelers. Still, the Wyndham is also fine for vacationers who want to be near downtown shopping and restaurants. The beige-dominated standard rooms are rather bland and not large, but many of the upper-floor accommodations have panoramic views. The health club is fully equipped and rarely crowded. ⊠ *400 W. Broadway, Gaslamp Quarter 92101,* ☎ *619/239–4500 or 800/996–3426,* FAX *619/239–4527,* WEB *www.wyndham.com. 416 rooms, 20 suites. Restaurant, bar, in-room data ports, minibar, cable TV with movies, pool, health club, outdoor hot tub, sauna, steam room, shops, laundry service, concierge, Internet, business services, meeting rooms, airport shuttle, parking (fee); no smoking. AE, D, DC, MC, V.*

$$–$$$$ 🏨 **Embassy Suites–San Diego Bay.** The front door of each spacious, contemporary suite opens out onto a 12-story atrium, and rooms facing the harbor have spectacular views. A cooked-to-order breakfast and afternoon cocktails are complimentary, as are airport transfers and a daily newspaper. Room rates vary greatly depending upon occupancy. The convention center, the Embarcadero, Seaport Village, and a trolley station are nearby. ⊠ *601 Pacific Hwy., Embarcadero 92101,* ☎ *619/239–2400 or 800/362–2779,* FAX *619/239–1520,* WEB *www.embassy-suites.com. 337 suites. Restaurant, bar, room service, in-room data ports, microwaves, refrigerators, cable TV with movies and video games, tennis court, pool, health club, hair salon, outdoor hot tub, sauna, bicycles, shops, laundry service, laundry facilities, concierge, business services, meeting* *rooms, airport shuttle, car rental, parking (fee); no smoking. AE, D, DC, MC, V.*

$$$ ⊞ **Harbour Lights Resort.** A good choice if you have children, this hotel furnishes each suite with a king-size bed and a queen-size pull-out. Plus all the suites have kitchens, including a dishwasher. You can rent videos from the hotel's library. It's a short walk to the stores and cinemas of Horton Plaza and the carousel at Seaport Village. ⊠ *911 Fifth St., Gaslamp Quarter 92101,* ☎ *619/236–8588,* FAX *619/233–0340. 56 suites. Kitchens, refrigerators, cable TV with movies, in-room VCRs, gym, massage, sauna, steam, laundry facilities, parking (fee); no smoking. AE, D, DC, MC, V.*

$$$ ⊞ **Ramada Inn & Suites–Downtown.** The historic, 12-story building was San Diego's tallest building when it opened in 1913. Now a boutique hotel at the north end of the Gaslamp Quarter, it's conveniently close to many restaurants, nightclubs, and shops, but away from the hustle and bustle on 4th and 5th avenues. Good value and location make up for small rooms. The suites come with robes, coffeemakers, and in some cases hot tubs, big-screen TVs, and breakfast nooks. ⊠ *830 6th Ave., Gaslamp Quarter 92101,* ☎ *619/431–8877 or 800/272–6232,* FAX *619/231–8307,* WEB *www.ramada.com. 87 rooms, 12 suites. Restaurant, room service, in-room data ports, minibars, cable TV with movies, meeting rooms, parking (fee); no smoking. AE, D, DC, MC, V.*

$$$ ⊞ **Residence Inn San Diego Downtown.** This all-suite hotel is near the harbor; it's a short, refreshing walk to the bayfront, where you can watch cruise ships set sail. The suites have full kitchens, but if you don't want to cook, the hotel serves a convenient, buffet-style, full breakfast accompanied by a morning paper. ⊠ *1747 Pacific Hwy., Little Italy 92101,* ☎ *619/388–8200 or 800/331–3131,* FAX *619/338–8219,* WEB *www. marriott.com. 121 suites. Dining room, in-room data ports, kitchens, refrigerator, cable TV with movies, pool, gym, outdoor hot tub, babysitting, laundry service, laundry facilities, concierge, Internet, business services, meeting room, car rental, travel services, parking (fee), some pets allowed (fee); no smoking. AE, D, DC, MC, V.*

$–$$$ ⊞ **Gaslamp Plaza Suites.** On the National Registry of Historic Places, ★ this 11-story structure a block from Horton Plaza was built in 1913 as one of San Diego's first "skyscrapers." Appealing public areas have old marble, brass, and mosaics. Although most rooms are rather small, they are well decorated with dark-wood furnishings that give the hotel an elegant flair. You can enjoy the view and a complimentary Continental breakfast on the rooftop terrace. Book ahead if you're visiting in summer. ⊠ *520 E St., Gaslamp Quarter 92101,* ☎ *619/232–9500 or 800/874–8770,* FAX *619/238–9945,* WEB *www.gaslampplaza.com. 52 suites. Restaurant, no a/c, microwaves, refrigerators, hot tub, bar, nightclub, parking (fee). AE, D, DC, MC, V.*

$–$$ ⊞ **Rodeway Inn.** On one of downtown's quieter streets, this chain property in Cortez Hill is clean, comfortable, and pleasantly decorated. Continental breakfast is complimentary. The hotel is near Balboa Park, the zoo, and freeways. ⊠ *833 Ash St., Downtown 92101,* ☎ *619/239–2285; 800/424–6423; 800/522–1528 in CA,* FAX *619/235–6951,* WEB *www. rodeway.com. 45 rooms. In-room data ports, refrigerators, cable TV with movies, hot tub, sauna, laundry facilities, business services, meeting rooms, free parking; no smoking. AE, D, DC, MC, V.*

$ ⊞ **Comfort Inn.** This three-story, stucco property surrounds a parking lot and courtyard. There's nothing fancy about the accommodations, but some rooms on the south side of the hotel have good views of the city skyline. It's close to downtown hot spots as well as the attractions of Balboa Park. ⊠ *719 Ash St., Downtown 92101,* ☎ *619/232–2525 or 800/404–6835,* FAX *619/687–3024,* WEB *www.comfortinn.com. 45 rooms. In-room data ports, microwave, cable TV with movies, hot tub,*

San Diego Lodging

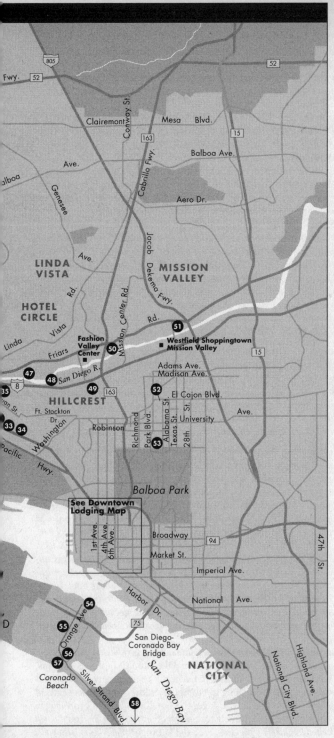

car rental, business services, airport shuttle, free parking; no smoking. AE, D, DC, MC, V.

$ 🏨 **HI–San Diego Downtown.** This two-story hostel has basic, modern furnishings and facilities. A special event—from pizza and movie parties to discussions on traveling in Mexico—is scheduled every evening. There are 150 beds, a large common kitchen, and a TV room. Most rooms are dorm style with four bunks each. There are a few doubles, coed dorms, and group rooms (with 10 beds). ⊠ *521 Market St., Gaslamp Quarter 92101,* ☏ *619/525–1531 or 800/909–4776 ext. 43,* FAX *619/338–0129. Bicycles, billiards, laundry facilities; no room phones, no room TVs, no smoking. MC, V.*

$ 🏨 **USA Hostels.** This bright, clean hostel is friendly and communal, but strictly for the independent backpacker (any nationality, any age) with a valid passport showing international travel. It makes its home in an 1887 Victorian hotel in the heart of the Gaslamp Quarter. There are 60 beds and five private rooms (two doubles and a triple). A variety of tours and parties are hosted weekly including beach and Tijuana trips. Continental breakfast is complimentary and there is a kitchen for guest use, but you are asked to clean up after yourself. ⊠ *726 5th Ave., Gaslamp Quarter 92101,* ☏ *619/232–3100 or 800/438–8622,* FAX *619/232–3106,* WEB *www.usahostels.com. Recreation room, laundry facilities, travel services, airport shuttle; no room phones, no room TVs, no smoking. MC, V.*

Harbor Island, Shelter Island, and Point Loma

Harbor Island and Shelter Island, two man-made peninsulas between downtown and the community of Point Loma, both have grassy parks, tree-lined paths, lavish hotels, and good restaurants. Harbor Island is closest to downtown and less than five minutes from the airport. Narrower Shelter Island is nearer to Point Loma. Both locations command views of the bay and the downtown skyline. Not all the lodgings listed here are on the islands themselves, but all are in the vicinity.

$$$$ 🏨 **Sheraton San Diego Hotel & Marina.** Of this property's two highrises, the smaller, more intimate West Tower has larger rooms with separate areas suitable for business entertaining. The East Tower has better sports facilities. Rooms throughout are decorated with plush, contemporary furnishings. Views from the upper floors of both sections are superb, but because the West Tower is closer to the water it has fine outlooks from the lower floors, too. ⊠ *1380 Harbor Island Dr., Harbor Island 92101,* ☏ *619/291–2900 or 888/625–5144,* FAX *619/ 692–2337,* WEB *www.sheraton.com. 1,045 rooms, 50 suites. 3 restaurants, 2 bars, deli, patisserie, room service, in-room data ports, minibars, cable TV with movies, 4 tennis courts, 3 pools, wading pool, health club, 2 outdoor hot tubs, massage, sauna, beach, boating, marina, bicycles, shop, dry cleaning, laundry service, concierge, business services, meeting rooms, airport shuttle, parking (fee); no smoking. AE, D, DC, MC, V.*

$$$–$$$$ 🏨 **Humphrey's Half Moon Inn & Suites.** This sprawling South Seas–style resort has grassy open areas with palms and tiki torches. Rooms, some with kitchens and some with harbor or marine views, have modern furnishings. Locals throng to Humphrey's, the on-premises seafood restaurant, and to the jazz lounge; the hotel also hosts outdoor jazz and pop concerts from June through October. ⊠ *2303 Shelter Island Dr., Shelter Island 92106,* ☏ *619/224–3411 or 800/542–7400,* FAX *619/ 224–3478,* WEB *www.halfmooninn.com. 128 rooms, 54 suites. Restaurant, bar, room service, in-room data ports, kitchenettes, minibars, refrigerators, cable TV with movies, putting green, pool, pond, health club, hot tub, boating, bicycles, croquet, Ping-Pong, concert hall, laun-*

When you pack your MCI Calling Card, it's like packing your loved ones along too.

Your MCI Calling Card is the easy way to stay in touch when you travel. Use it to call to and from over 125 countries. Plus, every time you call, you can earn frequent flier miles. So wherever your travels take you, call home with your MCI Calling Card. It's even easy to get one. Just visit **www.mci.com/worldphone** or **www.mci.com/partners**.

EASY TO CALL WORLDWIDE

1. Just enter the WorldPhone® access number of the country you're calling from.
2. Enter or give the operator your MCI Calling Card number.
3. Enter or give the number you're calling.

Aruba ✛	800-888-8
Bahamas ✛	1-800-888-8000

Barbados ✛	1-800-888-8000
Bermuda ✛	1-800-888-8000
British Virgin Islands ✛	1-800-888-8000
Canada	1-800-888-8000
Mexico	01-800-021-8000
Puerto Rico	1-800-888-8000
United States	1-800-888-8000
U.S. Virgin Islands	1-800-888-8000

✛ Limited availability.

EARN FREQUENT FLIER MILES

MCI.

Find America *with a Compass*

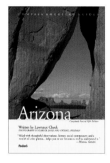

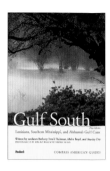

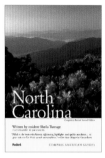

Written by local authors and illustrated throughout
with spectacular color images, Compass American
Guides reveal the character and culture of more than
40 of America's most fascinating destinations. Perfect
for residents who want to explore their own backyards
and for visitors who want an insider's perspective
on the history, heritage, and all there is to see and do.

dry facilities, business services, meeting rooms, airport shuttle, free parking; no smoking. AE, D, DC, MC, V.

$$–$$$ ⊞ **Bay Club Hotel & Marina.** Rooms in this appealing low-rise Shelter Island property are large, light, and furnished with rattan tables and chairs and Polynesian tapestries; all have views of either the bay or the marina from outside terraces. A buffet breakfast and limo service to and from the airport or Amtrak station are included. ⊠ *2131 Shelter Island Dr., Shelter Island 92106,* ☎ *619/224–8888 or 800/672–0800,* ℻ *619/225–1604,* WEB *www.bayclubhotel.com. 95 rooms, 10 suites. Restaurant, bar, room service, in-room data ports, refrigerators, cable TV with movies, pool, gym, outdoor hot tub, shop, concierge, business services, meeting rooms, airport shuttle, free parking; no smoking. AE, D, DC, MC, V.*

$$–$$$ ⊞ **Best Western Island Palms Hotel & Marina.** This waterfront inn, with an airy lobby brightened by skylights, is a good choice if you have a boat to dock; the adjacent marina has guest slips. Both harbor- and marina-view rooms are available. Standard accommodations are fairly small; if you're traveling with family or more than one friend, the two-bedroom suites with kitchens are a good deal. ⊠ *2051 Shelter Island Dr., Shelter Island 92106,* ☎ *619/222–0561 or 800/345–9995,* ℻ *619/ 222–9760,* WEB *www.islandpalms.com. 68 rooms, 29 suites. Restaurant, bar, fans, in-room data ports, kitchenettes, refrigerator, cable TV with movies and video games, pool, gym, outdoor hot tub, boating, laundry service, business services, meeting rooms, free parking; no smoking. AE, D, DC, MC, V.*

$$–$$$ ⊞ **Shelter Pointe Hotel & Marina.** This 11-acre property has been refurbished in a mixture of Mexican and Mediterranean styles. The spacious and light-filled lobby, with its Mayan sculptures and terra-cotta tiles, opens onto a lush esplanade that overlooks the hotel's marina. The rooms are well appointed, if a bit small, and most look out onto either the marina or San Diego Bay. The attractive hotel is a hot spot for business meetings. ⊠ *1551 Shelter Island Dr., Shelter Island 92106,* ☎ *619/ 221–8000 or 800/566–2524,* ℻ *619/221–5953,* WEB *www.shelterpointe. com. 206 rooms, 31 suites. Restaurant, bar, room service, kitchenettes, cable TV with movies with video games, 2 tennis courts, 2 pools, health club, 2 hot tubs, 2 saunas, beach, boating, marina, bicycles, volleyball, meeting rooms, airport shuttle, free parking; no smoking. AE, D, DC, MC, V.*

$$ ⊞ **Best Western Posada Inn at the Yacht Harbor.** Many of the rooms at this comfortable if plain inn have harbor views. Some rooms have microwaves, mini-refrigerators, and video players. Point Loma's seafood restaurants are within walking distance. Weekly rates, package plans, and senior discounts are available. Continental breakfast is included. ⊠ *5005 N. Harbor Dr., Point Loma 92106,* ☎ *619/224–3254 or 800/ 231–3811,* ℻ *619/224–2186,* WEB *www.bestwestern.com. 112 rooms. Restaurant, bar, in-room data ports, cable TV with movies, pool, gym, outdoor hot tub, laundry service, meeting rooms, airport shuttle, free parking; no smoking. AE, D, DC, MC, V.*

$$ ⊞ **Holiday Inn Express.** In Point Loma near the West Mission Bay exit ★ off I–8, this Holiday Inn Express is a surprisingly quiet lodging despite proximity to bustling traffic. The three-story building is only about a half mile from both SeaWorld and Mission Bay and offers free shuttles to the former. Continental breakfast is included. ⊠ *3950 Jupiter St., Sports Arena 92110,* ☎ *619/226–8000 or 800/320–0208,* ℻ *619/ 226–1409,* WEB *www.basshotels.com/holiday-inn. 70 rooms, 2 suites. In-room data ports, refrigerator, cable TV with movies, pool, hot tub, laundry service, concierge, business services, free parking; no smoking. AE, D, DC, MC, V.*

$–$$ ⊡ **Ramada Limited San Diego Airport.** The location is convenient, although on a busy street, and the rooms with bay views are quite a deal. Continental breakfast, daily newspaper, and local calls are complimentary. There is a heated pool and a bay-view bar with billiards, and there's a free shuttle to area attractions. ⊠ *1403 Rosecrans St., Point Loma 92106,* ☎ *619/225–9461 or 888/298–2054,* 𝔽𝔸𝕏 *619/225–1163,* 𝕎𝔼𝔹 *www.ramada.com. 83 rooms. Restaurant, bar, dining room, cable TV, pool, meeting rooms, airport shuttle, free parking, some pets allowed (fee); no smoking. AE, D, DC, MC, V.*

$ ⊡ **HI–San Diego Point Loma.** This hostel is in a large converted house, in a quiet area straddling the Ocean Beach and Point Loma neighborhoods. Though it's far from San Diego's attractions and nightlife, there's a bus stop nearby. Special events are scheduled weekly. The hostel has a large kitchen, a large patio, and a TV room. ⊠ *3790 Udall St., Ocean Beach 92107,* ☎ *619/223–4778 or 800/909–4779 Ext. 44,* 𝔽𝔸𝕏 *619/223–1883. 61 beds. Bicycles, laundry service, free parking; no room phones, no room TVs, no smoking. MC, V.*

$ ⊡ **Point Loma Travelodge.** You'll get the same view here as at the higher-price hotels—for far less money. Of course, there are fewer amenities and the neighborhood isn't as serene, but the rooms—all with coffeemakers—are adequate and clean. ⊠ *5102 N. Harbor Dr., Point Loma 92106,* ☎ *619/223–8171 or 800/578–7878,* 𝔽𝔸𝕏 *619/222–7330,* 𝕎𝔼𝔹 *www.travelodge.com. 45 rooms. In-room data ports, cable TV, pool, free parking; no smoking. AE, D, DC, MC, V.*

$ ⊡ **Vagabond Inn–Point Loma.** This two-story budget motel is safe, clean, and comfortable, close to the airport, yacht clubs, and Cabrillo National Monument—and the popular and excellent Point Loma Seafoods restaurant is next door. A daily newspaper and Continental breakfast are included. ⊠ *1325 Scott St., Point Loma 92106,* ☎ *619/224–3371,* 𝔽𝔸𝕏 *619/223–0646,* 𝕎𝔼𝔹 *www.vagabondinn.com. 40 rooms. Restaurant, bar, in-room safes, some kitchens, some refrigerators, cable TV with movies, pool, bar, airport shuttle, free parking; no smoking. AE, D, DC, MC, V.*

Old Town and Vicinity

Staying in Old Town affords easy access to SeaWorld and the beaches to the west, downtown and Mexico to the south, and Mission Valley and the zoo to the east. But most important, it puts you smack in the middle of the most popular park in the California state system. Old Town has a few picturesque lodgings and some modestly priced chain hotels near I–5; when you're making reservations, request a room that doesn't face the freeway. West of the freeway is the Midway District, with a few budget hotels near the San Diego Sports Arena.

$$–$$$ ⊡ **Heritage Park Inn.** The beautifully restored mansions in Heritage
★   Park include this romantic 1889 Queen Anne–style B&B. Rooms range from smallish to ample, and most are bright and cheery. A two-bedroom suite is decorated with period antiques, and there is also a mini-isuite. A full breakfast and afternoon tea are included. There is a two-night minimum stay on weekends, and weekly and monthly rates are available. Some rooms share a bath. Classic vintage films are shown nightly in the parlor on a small film screen. Transportation is available to area attractions, the airport, and the Amtrak station. ⊠ *2470 Heritage Park Row, Old Town 92110,* ☎ *619/299–6832 or 800/995–2470,* 𝔽𝔸𝕏 *619/299–9465,* 𝕎𝔼𝔹 *www.heritageparkinn.com. 10 rooms, 2 suites. Fans, in-room data ports, cable TV, in-room VCRs, library, meeting rooms, airport shuttle; no smoking. AE, MC, V.*

$$–$$$ ⊡ **Holiday Inn Hotel & Suites–Old Town.** This hacienda-style hotel has Spanish colonial–style fountains and courtyards, and painted tiles and

Southwestern decor in the rooms. Breakfast, cocktail reception, and transfers to the airport, bus, and Amtrak stations are complimentary. ✉ *2435 Jefferson St., Old Town 92110,* ☎ *619/260–8500 or 800/255–3544,* FAX *619/297–2078,* WEB *www.basshotels.com/holiday-inn. 174 rooms, 19 suites. Restaurant, bar, in-room data ports, cable TV with movies and video games, pool, outdoor hot tub, gym, bar, shop, laundry service, concierge, Internet, business services, meeting rooms, airport shuttle, free parking; no smoking. AE, D, DC, MC, V.*

$$ 🏨 **Best Western Hacienda Suites–Old Town.** Pretty and white, with balconies and Spanish-tile roofs, the Hacienda is in a quiet part of Old Town, away from the freeway and the main retail bustle. The layout is somewhat confusing, and accommodations are not large enough to earn the "suite" label the hotel gives them, but they're decorated in tasteful Southwestern style and are well-equipped. ✉ *4041 Harney St., Old Town 92110,* ☎ *619/298–4707 or 800/888–1991,* FAX *619/298–4771,* WEB *www.bestwestern.com. 169 rooms. Restaurant, bar, room service, microwaves, refrigerators, cable TV, in-room VCRs, pool, gym, outdoor hot tub, laundry service, concierge, car rental, business services, meeting rooms, travel services, airport shuttle, free parking; no smoking. AE, D, DC, MC, V.*

$$ 🏨 **Ramada Limited–Old Town.** Already an excellent value for Old
★ Town, this cheerful property throws in such perks as garage parking, Continental breakfast, and afternoon snacks. Rooms have a European look. If you've had enough of the heated pool off the shaded courtyard, the historic park's attractions and restaurants are nearby. ✉ *3900 Old Town Ave., Old Town 92110,* ☎ *619/299–7400 or 800/272–6232,* FAX *619/299–1619,* WEB *www.ramada.com. 125 rooms. Restaurant, room service, in-room data ports, microwaves, refrigerators, cable TV, pool, outdoor hot tub, shops, laundry service, concierge, business services, meeting rooms, airport shuttle, free parking; no smoking. AE, D, DC, MC, V.*

$–$$ 🏨 **Western Inn–Old Town.** The three-story Western Inn is decorated in
★ a Spanish motif and is close to shops and restaurants, but far enough away from the main tourist drag that you don't have to worry about noise and congestion. There is free Continental breakfast, and a barbecue area where you can cook for yourself. A bus, trolley, and Coaster station is a few blocks away. ✉ *3889 Arista St., Old Town 92110,* ☎ *619/298–6888 or 888/475–2353,* FAX *619/692–4497. 29 rooms, 6 suites. In-room data ports, refrigerator, airport shuttle, free parking; no smoking. AE, D, DC, MC, V.*

Mission Valley and Hotel Circle

Mission Valley once thrived as a dairy farm area, a history you'd never guess from its appearance today. Beginning in the late 1950s, hotels started popping up along what is now called Hotel Circle, in the western end of the valley. Today the area is paved over with shopping centers, car lots, Qualcomm Stadium, and hotels except for a narrow greenbelt lining the San Diego River. Most of the 20 hotels along Hotel Circle are reasonably priced, their quality ranging from a bit haggard and dated to brand new. A little farther east you'll find a selection of bigger and pricier properties, although this puts you farther from major attractions and the beaches.

$$ 🏨 **Doubletree Hotel San Diego Mission Valley.** Near Fashion Valley Center and adjacent to the Hazard Center—which has a seven-screen movie theater, four major restaurants, a food pavilion, and more than 20 shops—the Doubletree is also convenient to Route 163 and I–8. A San Diego Trolley station is within walking distance. Public areas are bright and comfortable, well suited to this hotel's large business clientele. Spacious rooms decorated in pastels have ample desk space; complimentary coffee, irons, and ironing boards are also provided. ⊠ *7450 Hazard Center Dr., Mission Valley 92108,* ☎ *619/297–5466 or 800/222–8733,* FAX *619/297–5499,* WEB *www.doubletree.com. 294 rooms, 6 suites. Restaurant, 2 bars, room service, in-room data ports, minibars, cable TV with movies, 2 tennis courts, 2 pools, gym, outdoor hot tub, sauna, shops, laundry facilities, laundry service, concierge, business services, meeting rooms, airport shuttle, free parking; no smoking. AE, D, DC, MC, V.*

$$ 🖫 **Red Lion Hanalei Hotel.** As the name suggests, the theme of this friendly property is Hawai'ian: palms, waterfalls, koi ponds, and tiki torches abound. Rooms are decorated in tropical prints. What used to be a golf course next door has been restored to a bird sanctuary. Free transportation is provided to local malls and Old Town. The hotel is virtually surrounded by heavy traffic, which can make for a noisy stay. ⊠ *2270 Hotel Circle N, Hotel Circle 92108,* ☎ *619/297–1101 or 800/ 882–0858,* FAX *619/297–6049,* WEB *www.hanaleihotel.com. 402 rooms, 14 suites. 2 restaurants, bar, room service, in-room data ports, pool, hot tub, gym, laundry service, business services, meeting rooms, travel services, car rental, parking (fee); no smoking. AE, D, DC, MC, V.*

$$ 🖫 **San Diego Marriott Mission Valley.** This 17-floor high-rise sits in the
★ middle of the San Diego River valley near Qualcomm Stadium and the Rio Vista Plaza shopping center, minutes from the Mission Valley and Fashion Valley malls. The San Diego Trolley stops across the street. The hotel is well equipped for business travelers—the front desk provides 24-hour fax and photocopy services, and rooms come with desks and private voice mail—but the Marriott also caters to vacationers by providing comfortable rooms (with individual balconies), a friendly staff, and free transportation to the malls. ⊠ *8757 Rio San Diego Dr., Mission Valley 92108,* ☎ *619/692–3800 or 800/228–9290,* FAX *619/692– 0769,* WEB *www.marriotthotels.com/sanmv. 350 rooms, 5 suites. Restaurant, sports bar, room service, in-room data ports, minibars, cable TV with movies, tennis court, pool, gym, health club, outdoor hot tub, sauna, nightclub, shops, laundry service, concierge, concierge floor, Internet, business services, meeting rooms, airport shuttle, parking (fee); no smoking. AE, D, DC, MC, V.*

La Jolla

Million-dollar homes line the beaches and hillsides of beautiful and prestigious La Jolla. Its exclusiveness and seclusion make it easy to forget that La Jolla is part of the city of San Diego and not a separate town. The village—the heart of La Jolla—is chockablock full with expensive boutiques, galleries, and restaurants. Don't despair, however, if you're not old money or nouveau riche; this popular vacation spot has sufficient lodging choices for every purse.

$$$$ 🖫 **Hilton La Jolla Torrey Pines.** The low-rise, high-class hotel blends
★ discreetly into the Torrey Pines cliff top, looking almost insignificant until you step inside the luxurious lobby and gaze through native and subtropical foliage at the Pacific Ocean and the 18th hole of the Torrey Pines Municipal Golf Course. Amenities include complimentary butler service and free town-car service to La Jolla and Del Mar. The oversize accommodations are simple but elegant; most have balconies or terraces. Torreyana Grille's menu changes with the seasons. Caesar salad and filet mignon are menu stalwarts, but you're likely to find lobster pot stickers and coffee-lacquered duck breast as well. ⊠ *10950 N. Torrey Pines Rd., La Jolla 92037,* ☎ *858/558–1500 or 800/774–1500,*

FAX *858/450–4584,* WEB *www.hilton.com. 377 rooms, 17 suites. 3 restaurants, 3 bars, room service, in-room data ports, in-room safes, minibars, putting green, 3 tennis courts, pool, gym, outdoor hot tub, sauna, bicycles, baby-sitting, children's programs, laundry service, concierge, business services, meeting rooms, airport shuttle, car rental, parking (fee); no smoking. AE, D, DC, MC, V.*

$$$$ ★ ▣ **The Grande Colonial.** This white wedding cake hotel has ocean views and is in central La Jolla village. Built in 1913 and expanded and redesigned in 1925–26, the Colonial is graced with charming European details: chandeliers, a marble hearth, mahogany railings, oak furnishings, and French doors. The hotel's restaurant, NINE-TEN, is run by chef Michael Stebner and is well liked by locals for its fresh, seasonal California cuisine. ✉ *910 Prospect St., La Jolla 92037,* ☎ *858/454–2181 or 800/826–1278,* FAX *858/454–5679,* WEB *www.thegrandecolonial. com. 58 rooms, 17 suites. Restaurant, bar, room service, in-room data ports, cable TV with movies and video games, pool, meeting rooms, parking (fee); no smoking. AE, D, DC, MC, V.*

$$$$ ▣ **Hotel Parisi.** A Zen-like peace welcomes you into the Hotel Parisi, beginning with the lobby, which has a skylit waterfall and Asian art. Your relaxation goes beyond the Feng Shui-decorated suites; besides room service, you can order up an in-room wellness treatment, a yoga session, or even the on-staff psychologist. The Parisi is Madonna's hotel of choice when she comes to San Diego. Each hushed, earth-tone suite has granite bathrooms, fluffy robes, and ergonomic tubs. The rooms are set back enough from the street noise, but in the ocean-view suites you have to look over buildings across the street to catch a glimpse of the Pacific. ✉ *1111 Prospect St., La Jolla 92037,* ☎ *858/454–1511,* FAX *858/454–1531,* WEB *www.hotelparisi.com. 20 suites. Room service, in-room data ports, in-room safes, minibar, cable TV with movies, in-room VCR, massage, business services, meeting rooms, free parking; no smoking. AE, D, MC, V.*

$$$$ ★ ▣ **La Valencia.** This pink Spanish-Mediterranean confection drew Hollywood film stars in the 1930s and '40s for its setting and views of La Jolla Cove. Many rooms have a genteel European look, with antique pieces and rich-color rugs. The personal attention provided by the staff, as well as the plush robes and grand bathrooms, make the stay even more pleasurable. All rooms have wet bars, coffeemakers, and video games. The hotel is near the shops and restaurants of La Jolla Village. Rates are lower if you're willing to look out on the village. Be sure to stroll around the tiered gardens in back. ✉ *1132 Prospect St., La Jolla 92037,* ☎ *858/454–0771 or 800/451–0772,* FAX *858/456–3921,* WEB *www.lavalencia.com. 117 rooms, 15 villas. 3 restaurants, bar, lounge, room service, in-room safes, minibars, cable TV with movies, in-room VCRs, pool, health club, outdoor hot tub, massage, sauna, beach, bicycles, Ping-Pong, shuffleboard, laundry facilities, concierge, business services, meeting rooms, airport shuttle, parking (fee); no smoking. AE, D, MC, V.*

$$$$ ★ ▣ **Lodge at Torrey Pines.** This beautiful Craftsman-style lodge sits on a bluff between La Jolla and Del Mar, and commands a view of miles of coastline. You know you're in for different sort of experience when you see the Scottish kilted doorman. Rooms, though dim, are very roomy and furnished with antiques and reproduction turn-of-the-20th-century pieces. The service is excellent and the restaurant, A. R. Valentin, serves fine California cuisine. Beyond the 6-acre grounds are the Torrey Pines Municipal Golf Course and scenic trails that lead to the Torrey Pines State Beach and Reserve. The village of La Jolla is a 10-minute drive away. ✉ *11480 N. Torrey Pines Rd., La Jolla 92037,* ☎ *858/453–4420 or 800/995–4507,* FAX *858/453–7464,* WEB *www.lodgetorreypines. com. 175 rooms. 2 restaurants, 2 bars, in-room data ports, in-room safes,* *kitchenettes, cable TV, 18-hole golf course, pool, gym, hot tub, massage, spa, Internet, meeting rooms, free parking; no smoking. AE, D, DC, MC, V.*

$$$$ 🏨 **Scripps Inn.** You'd be wise to make reservations well in advance for this small, quiet inn tucked away on Coast Boulevard; its popularity with repeat visitors ensures that it's booked year-round. Lower weekly and monthly rates (not available in summer) make it attractive to long-term guests. Rooms are done with Mexican and Spanish decor, with wood floors, and all have ocean views; some have fireplaces. Continental breakfast is served in the lobby each morning. ⊠ *555 S. Coast Blvd., La Jolla 92037,* ☎ *858/454–3391 or 800/439–7529,* ℻ *858/456–0389,* WEB *www.jcresorts.com. 14 rooms. In-room safes, some kitchens, free parking; no smoking. AE, D, MC, V.*

$$$$ 🏨 **Sea Lodge.** One of few hotels actually on the beach, the Sea Lodge is at the La Jolla Shores Beach and Tennis Club. Palms, fountains, red-tile roofs, and Mexican tile work lend character to the low-lying compound. Rooms have rattan furniture, floral-print bedspreads, and wood balconies overlooking the ocean. Hair dryers, coffeemakers, and irons are included. Tennis lessons are available. ⊠ *8110 Camino del Oro, La Jolla 92037,* ☎ *858/459–8271 or 800/237–5211,* ℻ *858/456–9346,* WEB *www.sealodge.com. 127 rooms, 1 suite. Restaurant, bar, room service, in-room data ports, some kitchenettes, refrigerators, cable TV, 2 tennis courts, pool, health club, outdoor hot tub, massage, sauna, beach, volleyball, laundry service, business services, meeting rooms, free parking; no smoking. AE, D, DC, MC, V.*

$$$–$$$$ 🏨 **Hyatt Regency La Jolla.** The Hyatt is in the Golden Triangle area,
   ★   about 10 minutes from the beach and the village of La Jolla. The post-modern design elements of architect Michael Graves' striking lobby continue in the spacious rooms, where warm cherry-wood furnishings contrast with austere gray closets. Fluffy down comforters and cushy chairs and couches make you feel right at home, though, and business travelers will appreciate the endless array of office and in-room services. The hotel's four trendy restaurants include Cafe Japengo. Rates are lowest on weekends. ⊠ *Aventine Center, 3777 La Jolla Village Dr., La Jolla 92122,* ☎ *858/552–1234 or 800/233–1234,* ℻ *858/552–6066,* WEB *www.hyatt.com. 419 rooms, 20 suites. 4 restaurants, bar, room service, minibar, cable TV with movies, 2 tennis courts, pool, health club, hair salon, outdoor hot tub, massage, basketball, dry cleaning, laundry service, concierge, business services, meeting rooms, parking (fee); no smoking. AE, D, DC, MC, V.*

$$$–$$$$ 🏨 **La Jolla Cove Suites.** It may lack the charm of some of the older properties of this exclusive area, but this motel with studios and suites (some with spacious oceanfront balconies) gives its guests the same first-class views of La Jolla Cove at lower rates. The beach is across the street and down a short cliff, and snorkelers and divers can take advantage of lockers and outdoor showers. Continental breakfast is served in the sunroom. The free underground lot is also a bonus in a section of town where a parking spot is a prime commodity. ⊠ *1155 S. Coast Blvd., La Jolla 92037,* ☎ *858/459–2621 or 800/248–2683,* ℻ *858/454–3522,* WEB *www.lajollacove.com. 96 rooms. In-room safes, kitchenettes, cable TV with movies, putting green, pool, hot tub, bicycles, laundry service, business services, meeting rooms, airport shuttle, free parking; no smoking. AE, D, DC, MC, V.*

$$–$$$ 🏨 **Holiday Inn Express–La Jolla.** Many rooms at this modest property in the southern section of La Jolla are remarkably large, with huge closets; some have kitchenettes. The decor is nothing to write home about, but this is a good value for families who want to stay in La Jolla and still have a few dollars left over for shopping and dining. Continental breakfast is included. ⊠ *6705 La Jolla Blvd., La Jolla 92037,* ☎ *858/ 454–7101 or 800/451–0358,* FAX *858/454–6957,* WEB *www.basshotels. com/holiday-inn. 61 rooms, 11 suites. In-room data ports, some kitchenettes, refrigerator, cable TV, pool, gym, outdoor hot tub, sauna, laundry service, business services, meeting rooms, airport shuttle, free parking; no smoking. AE, D, DC, MC, V.*

$$–$$$ 🏨 **La Jolla Inn.** One block from the beach and near some of the best shops and restaurants, this European-style inn with a delightful staff sits in a prime spot in La Jolla Village. Many rooms (some with kitchenettes) have sweeping ocean views from their balconies; one spectacular penthouse suite faces the ocean, another the village. An upstairs sundeck is a great spot to enjoy the delicious complimentary Continental breakfast. ⊠ *1110 Prospect St., La Jolla 92037,* ☎ *858/454–0133 or 800/433–1609,* FAX *858/454–2056,* WEB *www.lajollainn.com. 21 rooms, 2 suites. Room service, in-room data ports, some kitchenettes, some refrigerators, cable TV with movies, library, shop, dry cleaning, laundry facilities, concierge, business services, free parking; no smoking. AE, D, DC, MC, V.*

Mission Bay and the Beaches

Mission Bay Park, with its beaches, bike trails, boat-launching ramps, golf course, and grassy parks—not to mention SeaWorld—is a hotel haven. Mission Beach and Pacific Beach have many small hotels, motels, and hostels. The coastal areas have a casual atmosphere and busy thoroughfares that provide endless shopping, dining, and nightlife possibilities. You can't go wrong with any of these locations, as long as the frenzy of crowds at play doesn't bother you.

$$$$ 🏨 **Catamaran Resort Hotel.** Exotic birds often perch in the lush lobby
★ of this appealing hotel on Mission Bay. Tiki torches light the way through grounds thick with tropical foliage for guests staying at one of the six two-story buildings or the 14-story high-rise. The room design echoes the Hawaiian theme. The popular Cannibal Bar hosts rock bands; a classical or jazz pianist tickles the ivories nightly at the Moray Bar. The resort's many water-oriented activities include complimentary cruises on Mission Bay aboard a stern-wheeler. ⊠ *3999 Mission Blvd., Mission Beach 92109,* ☎ *858/488–1081 or 800/422–8386,* FAX *858/ 488–1387,* WEB *www.catamaranresort.com. 313 rooms. Restaurant, 2 bars, room service, in-room data ports, kitchenettes, refrigerators, cable TV with movies, pool, gym, outdoor hot tub, beach, boating, jet skiing, bicycles, volleyball, nightclub, shops, business services, meeting rooms, parking (fee); no smoking. AE, D, DC, MC, V.*

$$$$ 🏨 **Crystal Pier Hotel.** A landmark since 1927, the cottages of the Crystal Pier Hotel are rustic little oases with a charm all their own. True, they lack some of the amenities of comparably priced hotels, but you're paying for character and proximity to the ocean—the blue-and-white cottages here are literally on the pier. The units sleep four but cost the same no matter what the occupancy. Call four to six weeks in advance for reservations. The minimum stay permitted is three nights from mid-June through mid-September, two nights the rest of the year. The cottages are a bargain in off-season. ⊠ *4500 Ocean Blvd., Pacific Beach, 92109,* ☎ *858/483–6983 or 800/748–5894,* FAX *858/483–6811,* WEB *www. crystalpier.com. 29 cottages. Kitchenettes, cable TV, beach, fishing, free parking; no smoking. D, MC, V.*

$$$$ 🏨 **Hilton San Diego Resort.** Trees, Japanese bridges, and ponds surround the bungalow accommodations at this deluxe resort; rooms and suites in the high-rise building have views of Mission Bay. The well-appointed rooms have wet bars, coffeemakers, and spacious bathrooms; most have patios or terraces. Children stay free, and there's complimentary day care for children over 5 (daily in summer, on weekends the rest of the year). The sports facilities are excellent and aquatic sports equipment is available for rent at the nearby marina. ✉ *1775 E. Mission Bay Dr., Mission Bay 92109,* ☎ *619/276–4010 or 800/445–8667,* FAX *619/275–8944,* WEB *www.hilton.com. 337 rooms, 20 suites. 2 restaurants, 2 bars, room service, in-room data ports, minibars, refrigerator, cable TV with movies, 4 putting greens, 5 tennis courts, pool, wading pool, gym, hair salon, 2 outdoor hot tubs, massage, spa, beach, boating, waterskiing, bicycles, basketball, Ping-Pong, children's programs, playground, laundry service, concierge, business services, meeting rooms, travel services, car rental, free parking; no smoking. AE, D, DC, MC, V.*

$$$$ 🖼 **Pacific Terrace Hotel.** This terrific hotel, overlooking the beach, offers great ocean views from most rooms. It's the perfect place if you love to watch sunsets over the Pacific. Private balconies (or patios) and coffeemakers come with every room. Eight of the suites have indoor hot tubs. Continental breakfast is complimentary, as is the daily delivery of the *San Diego Union-Tribune.* Even the smallest room is fairly large. The friendly, casual staff makes for a comfortable stay. ✉ *610 Diamond St., Pacific Beach 92109,* ☎ *858/581–3500 or 800/344–3370,* FAX *858/274–3341,* WEB *www.pacificterrace.com. 73 rooms, 12 suites. In-room data ports, in-room safe, some kitchenettes, minibars, cable TV with movies with video games, pool, outdoor hot tub, laundry service, Internet, meeting rooms, parking (fee); no smoking. AE, D, DC, MC, V.*

$$$$ 🖼 **San Diego Paradise Point Resort.** The landscape at this 44-acre resort on Vacation Isle is so beautiful that it's been the setting for a number of movies, and it provides a wide range of recreational activities as well as access to a marina. Bright fabrics and plush carpets make for a cheery ambience; unfortunately, the walls here are motel-thin. Take a walk through the botanical gardens with their ponds, waterfalls, footbridges, waterfowl, and more than 600 varieties of tropical plants. ✉ *1404 W. Vacation Rd., Mission Bay 92109,* ☎ *858/274–4630 or 800/344–2626,* FAX *858/581–5929,* WEB *www.paradisepoint.com. 462 cottages. 3 restaurants, 2 bars, room service, in-room data ports, refrigerators, cable TV with movies, putting green, 6 tennis courts, 6 pools, pond, aerobics, gym, outdoor hot tub, massage, sauna, spa, beach, boating, jet skiing, bicycles, croquet, shuffleboard, volleyball, concierge, business services, meeting rooms, airport shuttle, free parking; no smoking. AE, D, DC, MC, V.*

$$$–$$$$ 🖼 **Bahia Resort Hotel.** This huge complex on a 14-acre peninsula in Mission Bay Park has furnished studios and suites with kitchens; many have wood-beam ceilings and a tropical theme. The hotel's *Bahia Belle* offers complimentary cruises on the bay at sunset and also has a Blues Cruise on Saturday night and live entertainment on Friday night. Rates are reasonable for a place so well located—within walking distance of the ocean—and with so many amenities, including use of the facilities at its sister hotel, the nearby Catamaran. ✉ *998 W. Mission Bay Dr., Mission Bay 92109,* ☎ *858/488–0551 or 800/576–4229,* FAX *858/488–1387,* WEB *www.bahiahotel.com. 321 rooms. Restaurant, 2 bars, room service, in-room data ports, kitchenettes, cable TV with movies, 2 tennis courts, pool, gym, outdoor hot tub, boating, bicycles, shops, children's program, business services, meeting rooms, free parking; no smoking. AE, D, DC, MC, V.*

$$$–$$$$ 🖼 **Hyatt Islandia.** This property has rooms in several low-level, lanai-style units, as well as marina suites and rooms in a high-rise building, all in Mission Bay Park. Many rooms overlook the hotel's gardens and koi fish pond; others have dramatic views of the bay area. This hotel is famous for its lavish Sunday champagne brunch. Whale-watching expeditions depart from the Islandia's marina in winter. ✉ *1441 Quivira Rd., Mission Bay 92109,* ☎ *858/224–1234 or 800/233–1234,* FAX *858/224–0348,* WEB *www.hyatt.com. 346 rooms, 76 suites. 2 restaurants, bar, room service, in-room data ports, some kitchenettes, cable TV with movies, pool, gym, outdoor hot tub, boating, fishing, shops, dry cleaning, laundry service, concierge, business services, meeting rooms, car rental, free parking; no smoking. AE, D, DC, MC, V.*

$$–$$$ ⊡ **Best Western Blue Sea Lodge.** All rooms in this low-rise have patios or balconies, and many have ocean views. Suites have kitchenettes, and many of them front the ocean. A shopping center with restaurants and boutiques is nearby. ✉ *707 Pacific Beach Dr., Pacific Beach 92109,* ☎ *858/488–4700 or 800/258–3732,* FAX *858/488–7276,* WEB *www. bestwestern-bluesea.com. 52 rooms, 48 suites. In-room safes, some kitchenettes, cable TV with movies, pool, outdoor hot tub, fishing, bicycles, laundry service, concierge, travel services, parking (fee); no smoking. AE, D, DC, MC, V.*

$$–$$$ ⊡ **Dana Inn & Marina.** This hotel with an adjoining marina is a bargain. Rooms are in bright pastels, and the lobby includes a fun aquarium. High ceilings in the second-floor rooms give a welcome sense of space, and some even have a view of the inn's marina. SeaWorld and the beach are within walking distance. The Marina Village Conference Center next door offers meeting and banquet rooms with bay views. ✉ *1710 W. Mission Bay Dr., Mission Bay 92109,* ☎ *619/222–6440 or 800/326–2466,* FAX *619/222–5916,* WEB *www.danainn.com. 196 rooms. Restaurant, bar, room service, cable TV with movies, 2 tennis courts, pool, outdoor hot tub, boating, waterskiing, fishing, bicycles, Ping-Pong, shuffleboard, laundry service, business services, meeting rooms, car rental, airport shuttle, free parking; no smoking. AE, D, DC, MC, V.*

$$–$$$ ⊡ **Diamond Head Hotel.** Many rooms of this hotel overlook the beach, but it's not a noisy place because it's far enough away from Pacific Beach's main drag—Garnet Avenue. Restaurants and nightspots are within walking distance. Continental breakfast is complimentary. ✉ *605 Diamond St., Pacific Beach 92109,* ☎ *858/273–1900,* FAX *858/274–3341. 21 rooms. Kitchenettes, cable TV with movies, beach, free parking, some pets allowed (fee); no smoking. AE, D, MC, V.*

$–$$ ⊡ **Beach Haven Inn.** This pleasant little hotel feels almost like an apartment building—rooms have exterior entrances and are situated around the pool and courtyard. It's on Mission Boulevard, the main beach drag, but on a fairly quiet stretch. Continental breakfast and a daily newspaper are included. Pacific Beach's sandy shoreline is about a block away, and the grassy Palisades Park, famous for its sunsets, is approximately three blocks away. ✉ *4740 Mission Blvd., Pacific Beach 92109,* ☎ *858/272–3812 or 800/831–6323,* FAX *858/272–3532,* WEB *www.beachhaveninn.com. 23 rooms. Kitchenettes, refrigerators, cable TV with movies, pool, outdoor hot tub, laundry service, free parking; no smoking. AE, D, DC, MC, V.*

$–$$ ⊡ **Pacific Shores Inn.** One of the better motels in the Mission Bay area, this property is less than a half block from the beach. Rooms, some of them spacious, are decorated in a simple contemporary style. Kitchen units with multiple beds are available at reasonable rates. Continental breakfast is included. ✉ *4802 Mission Blvd., Pacific Beach 92109,* ☎ *858/483–6300 or 800/826–0715,* FAX *858/483–9276,* WEB *www.psi. tierranet.com. 55 rooms. Kitchenettes, refrigerators, cable TV with movies, pool, laundry service, free parking, some pets allowed (fee); no smoking. AE, D, DC, MC, V.*

$-$$ 🏨 **Surfer Motor Lodge.** This four-story building is right on the beach and directly behind a shopping center with restaurants and boutiques. Rooms are plain, but those on the upper floors have good views. ⊠ *711 Pacific Beach Dr., Pacific Beach 92109,* ☎ *858/483–7070 or 800/ 787–3373,* ꜰᴀˣ *858/274–1670. 52 rooms. Restaurant, kitchenettes, pool, beach, bicycles, laundry service, free parking; no smoking. AE, DC, MC, V.*

$ 🏨 **Banana Bungalow San Diego.** Literally a few feet from the beach, this hostel's location is its greatest asset. However, dampness and sand take their toll, and some parts of the hostel are in need of repair. All dorm rooms are coed and there are a total of 70 beds. Keg and movie-night parties are held weekly, as are various organized events. Complimentary Continental breakfast is served on the sundeck. There are lockers and a small TV room. ⊠ *707 Reed Ave., Pacific Beach 92109,* ☎ *858/273–3060 or 800/546–7835,* ꜰᴀˣ *858/273–1440,* ᴡᴇʙ *www. bananabungalow.com. Beach, bicycles, volleyball, travel services, airport shuttle; no room phones, no room TVs, no smoking. MC, V.*

$ 🏨 **Ocean Beach International Backpackers Hostel.** This converted 1920s hotel is two blocks from the beach and offers free use of surfboards and boogie boards. There are 100 beds. Private rooms with private baths are available. Continental breakfast is complimentary, and dinner is free on Tuesday and Friday. The hostel, which is close to many Ocean Beach restaurants and nightspots, has kitchen facilities, a storage area, vending machines, a TV room, a recreation room, a patio, and Internet access. Weekly rates are available. ⊠ *4961 Newport Ave., Ocean Beach 92107,* ☎ *619/223–7873 or 800/339–7263,* ꜰᴀˣ *619/223– 7881,* ᴡᴇʙ *members.aol.com/obihostel/hostel. Bicycles, recreation room, laundry service, airport shuttle; no smoking. MC, V.*

$ 🏨 **Vagabond Inn Mission Bay.** This modest, three-story hotel is near freeways and Mission Bay, and the price is right for its simple but clean rooms. Continental breakfast is complimentary. There's no elevator. ⊠ *4540 Mission Bay Dr., Mission Bay 92109,* ☎ *858/274–7888 or 800/522–1555,* ᴡᴇʙ *www.vagabondinn.com. 116 rooms. In-room safes, pool, laundry service, airport shuttle, free parking, some pets allowed (fee); no smoking. AE, D, DC, MC, V.*

North Park

San Diego's North Park area melds into the neighborhoods of Hillcrest, Mission Hills, and University Heights. There are not a lot of hotels to choose from—quality or otherwise—but these neighborhoods offer pedestrian-friendly shopping districts and great restaurants. North Park is very close to the zoo and Balboa Park.

$–$$$ 🏨 **Balboa Park Inn.** This all-suites B&B is housed in four Spanish colonial–style 1915 residences connected by courtyards. Prices are reasonable for romantic one- and two-bedroom suites. Each has a different flavor, contemporary versions of Italian, French, Spanish, or early Californian; some have fireplaces, wet bars, whirlpool tubs, patios, and kitchens, and all have coffeemakers and mini-refrigerators. Complimentary continental breakfast is delivered to your door (on Monday–Saturday mornings, you also get a newspaper). The lack of off-street parking is inconvenient, but the location is great. The San Diego Zoo is a 10-minute stroll from here. ⊠ *3402 Park Blvd., North Park 92103,* ☎ *619/298–0823 or 800/938–8181,* ꜰᴀˣ *619/294–8070,* ᴡᴇʙ *www. balboaparkinn.com. 26 suites. Some kitchenettes, some microwaves, refrigerators, cable TV with movies; no smoking. AE, D, DC, MC, V.*

$–$$ ⊞ **Inn Suites Hotel San Diego.** Built in 1946, this four-story hotel is a bit off the beaten path. Hollywood stars stayed here in its early days and the pool was designed by Johnny Weismuller, Olympic swimmer and star of Tarzan movies. The rooms are quite large, but the furnishings are dated and some suffer from varying degrees of disrepair. The Red Fox Room Restaurant and its piano lounge are time capsules from the 1940s. Continental breakfast, daily newspaper, and local phone calls are included. ⊠ *2223 El Cajon Blvd., North Park, 92104,* ☎ *619/296–2101 or 877/343–4648,* FAX *619/296–0512. 147 rooms, 8 suites. 2 restaurants, piano bar, cable TV with movies, pool, gym, hot tub, recreation room, theater, business services, meeting rooms, airport shuttle, free parking; no smoking. AE, D, DC, MC, V.*

5 NIGHTLIFE AND THE ARTS

People come to San Diego for the sand and surf, but the fun in this coastal community doesn't end when the sun sets. Musical hot spots span the spectrum from jazz to disco to garage-band grunge to country-western. Downtown, especially in and around the Gaslamp Quarter, the city bustles with cultural events—symphony, theater, and opera.

NIGHTLIFE

Updated by
Rob Aikins

MUSIC AT LOCAL POP-MUSIC CLUBS ranges from easy-on-the-ears rock to edgy alternative fare from San Diego's finest up-and-coming bands. Dance clubs and bars in the Gaslamp Quarter, La Jolla, and at Pacific and Mission beaches tend to be the most crowded spots in the county on the weekends, but don't let that discourage you from visiting these quintessential San Diego hangouts. Authentic country-western music is also an option. Should your tastes run to softer music, there are plenty of piano bars in which to unfrazzle and unwind. Smooth jazz and classic jazz also fill the air at waterside venues and in crowded clubs. Trendy Hillcrest pulses with the majority of San Diego's lesbian and gay bars. And coffeehouse culture thrives in San Diego, especially downtown, in Hillcrest, and in the beach communities.

Check the *Reader* (it comes out every Thursday)—San Diego's free alternative newsweekly—for the 411 on nightlife, or *San Diego* magazine's "Restaurant & Nightlife Guide" for further ideas. Also, the *San Diego-Union Tribune* publishes a weekly (Thursdays) entertainment insert, *Night and Day.*

State law prohibits the sale of alcoholic beverages after 2 AM; last call is usually at about 1:40. You must be 21 to purchase and consume alcohol—be prepared to show ID. California also has some of the most stringent drunken-driving laws in the country; sobriety checkpoints are not an uncommon sight. Also, unless operated exclusively for private members, all bars, nightclubs, and restaurants are smoke-free—although many have patios or decks where smoking is permitted.

Bars and Nightclubs

Aero Club (⊠ 3365 India St., Middletown, ☎ 619/297–7211), named for its proximity to the airport, is practically a landmark in the Middletown neighborhood. The familiar crowd, friendly bartenders, and first-rate selection of beer have made this small, one-time dive thrive.

Bitter End (⊠ 770 5th Ave., Gaslamp Quarter, ☎ 619/338–9300) is a sophisticated martini bar and a hip dance club where you can kick up your feet. With its variety of beverages, music, and atmosphere, this dual-level hot spot in the heart of downtown should please the most finicky of cosmopolitans.

Blind Melons (⊠ 710 Garnet Ave., Pacific Beach, ☎ 858/483–7844), not named after the band, draws well-known local and national bands to play rock and blues tunes that will keep you groovin'. If you get bored, meander along the boardwalk or pier, just steps away.

Blue Tattoo (⊠ 835 5th Ave., Gaslamp Quarter, ☎ 619/238–7191) pulls in San Diego's young professionals, who often wait in long lines to get in. The club is open Thursday through Sunday with a strict dress code (no jeans, T-shirts, hats, sweatshirts, or tennis shoes) on Friday and Saturday nights. Entertainment varies nightly, and there is a nominal cover charge.

'Canes Bar and Grill (⊠ 3105 Ocean Front Walk, Mission Beach, ☎ 858/488–1780) is closer to the ocean than any other music venue in town. Step outside for a walk on the beach where the sounds of the national rock, reggae, and hip-hop acts onstage create a cacophony with the crashing waves.

Cannibal Bar (✉ 3999 Mission Blvd., Pacific Beach, ☎ 858/488–1081) offers an eclectic lineup of live music acts. Swing, jazz, rock, and reggae are possibilities, and some nights a DJ spins tunes. Because of its beach location, the tropical-theme nightclub in the Catamaran Resort Hotel attracts locals and visitors of all ages.

Dave & Buster's (✉ 2931 Camino Del Rio N, Mission Valley, ☎ 619/275–1515) comprises a restaurant, two bars, billiards, shuffleboard, and a midway packed with arcade games. It's a place to let your inner wild child show through—real kids must be accompanied by an adult and are banished from 10 PM on.

Hard Rock Café (✉ 801 4th Ave., Gaslamp Quarter, ☎ 619/615–7625; ✉ 909 Prospect St., La Jolla, ☎ 858/456–7625), the ubiquitous theme restaurant chain, has a pair of locales in greater San Diego, both filled with the usual house-blend of rock'n'roll memorabilia and costumes. Check out the restored stained-glass dome just above the Gaslamp location's bar. The La Jolla location is a great place to stop either before or after a stroll on the beach.

Jimmy Love's (✉ 672 5th Ave., Gaslamp Quarter, ☎ 619/595–0123) combines a dance club, a sports bar, and a restaurant. Rock, funk, reggae, and jazz bands alternate nightly. Expect lines, though—Jimmy's is loved by many.

Karl Strauss' Old Columbia Brewery & Grill (✉ 1157 Columbia St., Downtown, ☎ 619/234–2739; ✉ 1044 Wall St., La Jolla, ☎ 858/551–2739) was the first microbrewery in San Diego. The original locale draws an after-work downtown crowd and later fills with beer connoisseurs from all walks of life; the newer La Jolla version draws a mix of locals and tourists.

Live Wire (✉ 2103 El Cajon Blvd., North Park, ☎ 619/291–7450) is an underground twentysomething hole-in-the-wall with a dive bar feel. On Saturdays live indie rock brings out the pierced and tattooed set.

Maloney's on 5th (✉ 777 5th Ave., Gaslamp Quarter, ☎ 619/232–6000) is down a flight of stairs. Inside, big-screen TVs broadcast ballgames to this crowd of sports nuts, nine-to-fivers, and regular joes. Grab a seat in one of the comfy booths and make yourself at home.

Martini Ranch (✉ 528 F St., Gaslamp Quarter, ☎ 619/235–6100) mixes more than 30 varieties of its namesake. Actually two clubs in one, the original Martini Ranch space hosts jazz groups on weekdays and a DJ spining an eclectic mix on Friday and Saturday. Next door in the larger Shaker Room, local and traveling DJs spin all-star dance beats. In either room the bartenders might show you one of their tricks, like mixing a martini on their forehead or pouring five drinks at one time, if you ask nicely.

Moondoggies (✉ 832 Garnet Ave., Pacific Beach, ☎ 858/483–6550) is not just for Gidget anymore, but is home to a mixed, laid-back crowd who don't mind bumping into each other or minor beer spills. A large, heated outdoor patio draws smokers. Occasionally, there's live entertainment.

Moose McGillycuddy's (✉ 535 5th Ave., Gaslamp Quarter, ☎ 619/702–5595), a major pick-up palace, is also a great place to go with friends or hang out with the locals. A DJ spins house and Top 40 dance music that powers the dance floor while the staff serves up drinks and Mexican food.

O'Hungrys (✉ 2547 San Diego Ave., Old Town, ☎ 619/298–0133) is famous for its yard-long beers and sing-alongs. Be sure to drink up quickly, though—this landmark saloon closes at midnight.

Old Venice (✉ 2910 Canon St., Point Loma, ☎ 619/222–1404) draws a good crowd of locals on weekdays—they appreciate the casual, artsy atmosphere of this small restaurant-bar. On weekends, music aficionados pack in tightly to hear local blues and rock bands.

Onyx Room (✉ 852 5th Ave., Gaslamp Quarter, ☎ 619/235–6699) is one of San Diego's hippest hangs. It's actually two bars in one. In front there's a mood-lit cocktail lounge, and in the next room acid jazz bands and DJs keep the crowds dancing on the tiny dance floor.

Pacific Beach Bar & Grill (✉ 860 Garnet Ave., Pacific Beach, ☎ 858/272–4745) is a stumbling block away from the beach. The popular nightspot has a huge outdoor patio so you can enjoy star-filled skies as you party. The lines here on the weekends are generally the longest of any club in Pacific Beach. There is plenty to see and do, from billiards and satellite TV sports to an interactive trivia game.

The purple-neon-streaked **Tavern at the Beach** (✉ 1200 Garnet Ave., Pacific Beach, ☎ 858/272–6066) draws a fun-loving college-age crowd.

Coffeehouses

Like the rest of the country, San Diego has gotten into cafés and coffeehouses in a big way. If you're up for caffeine-hopping, the Hillcrest/North Park area on University Avenue is abuzz with options—all of them grinding a variety of elixirs and proffering everything from full meals to light pastries. Many offer live entertainment on weekends. Most open their doors by 7 AM and continue serving until midnight or later. The crowds are diverse, ranging from lesbian and gay fashion plates to bookish college students to yuppies.

Brockton Villa Restaurant (✉ 1235 Coast Blvd., La Jolla, ☎ 858/454–7393), a palatial café overlooking La Jolla Cove, has indoor and outdoor seating, as well as scrumptious desserts and coffee drinks. It closes at 9 most nights, earlier on Sunday and Monday.

Café Crema (✉ 1001 Garnet Ave., Pacific Beach, ☎ 858/273–3558) is a meeting spot for the pre- and post-bar crowd. It's easy to lose track of time here as you watch all the college-age singles come and go.

Claire de Lune (✉ 2906 University Ave., North Park, ☎ 619/688–9845), on a corner in artsy North Park, won an award for its redesign of the historic Oddfellows building. High ceilings and huge arched windows give it a funky charm. The wood-floor hangout has sofas and armchairs for lounging as well as tables for studying. Local musicians and poets take the stage on various nights, and San Diego's most popular, and longest running, open-mike poetry night takes place every Tuesday.

The name, **Extraordinary Desserts** (✉ 2929 5th Ave., Hillcrest, ☎ 619/294–7001), explains why there always seems to be a line here. Unique, award-winning desserts and a variety of coffee drinks bring the crowds. The Japanese-theme outside patio invites them to stay for awhile. The offerings change daily so it's worth going more than once.

Gelato Vero Caffe (✉ 3753 India St., Middletown, ☎ 619/295–9269) is where a mostly young crowd gathers for some fine desserts and a second-floor view of the downtown skyline. The place is usually occupied by regulars who stay for hours at a time.

Javanican (✉ 4338 Cass St., Pacific Beach, ☎ 858/483–8035; ✉ 3719 Mission Blvd., Mission Beach, ☎ 858/488–8065) has two locations serving the young beach-community set. Aside from a good cup of joe, live acoustic entertainment is a popular attraction. Adventurous musicians can sign up to play on the Pacific Beach location's stage on Tuesday night. The other location closes by 7 PM most evenings.

Living Room (✉ 1018 Rosecrans St., Point Loma, ☎ 619/222–6852) is near the end of a charming neighborhood community. It's a great place to catch a caffeine buzz before walking along Shelter Island.

Pannikin (✉ 7467 Girard Ave., La Jolla, ☎ 858/454–5453) is a bright coffeehouse, with indoor and outdoor seating, that draws a regular crowd but also serves folks who've been shopping and sightseeing in La Jolla's village. Several other locations are scattered throughout the county.

Upstart Crow (✉ 835 West Harbor Dr., Seaport Village, ☎ 619/232–4855) is a bookstore and coffeehouse in one. The secluded upstairs space contains the java joint and is ideal for chatting or perusing the book that you just bought. Funky gifts are sold, too.

Zanzibar Coffee Bar and Gallery (✉ 976 Garnet Ave., Pacific Beach, ☎ 858/272–4762), a cozy, dimly lit spot along Pacific Beach's main strip, is a great place to mellow out and watch the club-hopping singles make their way down the street.

Comedy and Cabaret

Comedy Store La Jolla (✉ 916 Pearl St., La Jolla, ☎ 858/454–9176), like its sister establishment in Hollywood, hosts some of the best national touring and local talent.

Lips (✉ 2770 5th Ave., Hillcrest, ☎ 619/295–7900) serves you dinner while female impersonators entertain. Their motto, "where the men are men and so are the girls," says it all.

At **Sing Sing** (✉ 655 4th Ave., Gaslamp Quarter, ☎ 619/231–6700), dueling pianos and rock 'n' roll sing-alongs make for a festive, even boisterous, ambience. Open Thursday, Friday, and Saturday only, it's recommended that you make reservations or come early to get a good seat.

Country-Western

In Cahoots (✉ 5373 Mission Center Rd., Mission Valley, ☎ 619/291–8635), with its great sound system, large dance floor, and DJ, is the destination of choice for cowgirls, cowboys, and city slickers alike. Free dance lessons are given every day except Wednesday, when seasoned two-steppers strut their stuff. Happy hour seven days a week is one of this bar's many lures.

Magnolia Mulvaney's (✉ 8861 N. Magnolia Ave., Santee, ☎ 619/448–8550) serves as country-music headquarters for East County residents.

Randy Jones' Big Stone Lodge (✉ 12237 Old Pomerado Rd., Poway, ☎ 858/748–1617), a former Pony Express station–turned–dance hall, showcases the two-steppin' tunes of the owners' band. If you don't know country-western dances, don't fret; free lessons are given some nights.

Tio Leo's (✉ 5302 Napa St., Bay Park, ☎ 619/542–1462) is a throwback to the days when lounges were dark and vinyl-filled. The crowd is retro-attired as well. The lounge is within a Mexican restaurant, and an incredible variety of country, rockabilly, and swing acts grace the small stage.

Dance Clubs

Buffalo Joe's (✉ 600 5th Ave., Gaslamp Quarter, ☎ 619/236–1616) may sound like a cowboy stop, but it's probably one of the best locales in the Gaslamp Quarter for a rocking dance floor. Retro disco and 1980s cover bands are the norm with an occasional dash of original rock and roll. Beware: it's also a guaranteed stop for bachelorette parties.

E Street Alley (✉ 919 4th Ave., Gaslamp Quarter, ☎ 619/231–9200) is a treat for the senses. One of the city's hotspots, "Club E" is a smartly designed, spacious dance club with a DJ spinning Top 40 and club tunes Thursday through Saturday. Chino's is an exquisite restaurant featuring American cuisine with a Southeast Asian flair and a sushi bar.

Olé Madrid (✉ 751 5th Ave., Gaslamp Quarter, ☎ 619/557–0146) is not for the meek or mild. Leave the squares at street level and head straight to the basement for deep house grooves and tribal rhythms spun by celebrated DJs from near and far. Between songs, sip a tangy sangria. Friday and Saturday the groove goes on 'til 4 AM in the Gaslamp Quarter's only after-hours club.

Plan B (✉ 945 Garnet Ave., Pacific Beach, ☎ 858/483–9920) has a stainless-steel dance floor and numerous places from which to view it, making the interior of this club a standout among the other beach clubs. DJs play a variety of high-energy dance music most nights. The crowd is more upscale than one usually finds at the beach. Plan B has the only permanent laser show in San Diego.

Rox (✉ 901 5th Ave., Gaslamp Quarter, ☎ 619/234–4166), underneath the Dakota Grill restaurant, spins house and Top 40 mix dance tunes Friday and Saturday only.

Sevilla (✉ 555 4th Ave., Gaslamp Quarter, ☎ 619/233–5979) brings a Latin flavor to the Gaslamp with its mix of contemporary and traditional music. Get fueled up at the tapas bar before venturing downstairs for dancing. This is the best place in San Diego to take lessons in salsa and lambada.

Gay and Lesbian Nightlife

Men's Bars

Bourbon Street (✉ 4612 Park Blvd., North Park, ☎ 619/291–0173) is a piano bar with live entertainment nightly. It resembles its New Orleans namesake with jazzy decor and a courtyard.

Brass Rail (✉ 3796 5th Ave., Hillcrest, ☎ 619/298–2233), a fixture since the early 1960s, is the oldest gay bar in San Diego. The club hosts dancing nightly, or you can just pass time playing pool on one of the three tables.

Club Montage (✉ 2028 Hancock St., Middletown, ☎ 619/294–9590) is one of the largest and best clubs in town. The three-level club was originally oriented to the gay crowd, but now all types come for the high-tech lighting system and world-class DJs. For a breath of fresh air, step out to view the skyline and enjoy a drink from the rooftop bar.

Flicks (✉ 1017 University Ave., Hillcrest, ☎ 619/297–2056), a hip video bar that's popular with the see-and-be-seen crowd, plays music and comedy videos on four big screens. Drink specials and videos vary each night.

Kickers (✉ 308 University Ave., Hillcrest, ☎ 619/491–0400) rounds up country-music cowboys to do the latest line dance on its wooden dance floor, Thursday through Saturday. It offers up disco, karaoke, and goth the rest of the time. Free lessons are given weeknights from 7 to 8:30. If you're hungry after all that dancing, Hamburger Mary's, on the premises, serves until 11 on weekends.

Numbers (✉ 3811 Park Blvd., North Park, ☎ 619/294–9005) has a giant-screen TV, six pool tables, darts, and daily drink specials.

Rich's (✉ 1051 University Ave., Hillcrest, ☎ 619/295–2195), a popular dance club, has frequent male revues. Thursday night's Club Hedonism spotlights groove house and tribal rhythms and is frequented by both gay and straight revelers.

Wolf's (✉ 3404 30th St., North Park, ☎ 619/291–3730) is a Levi's-leather bar. There's no actual sign for the club, but look for the wolf painted on the exterior, beside the front door.

Women's Bars
Club Bom Bay (✉ 3175 India St., Middletown, ☎ 619/296–6789) occasionally has live entertainment and always attracts a dancing crowd. It also hosts Sunday barbecues.

The Flame (✉ 3780 Park Blvd., Hillcrest, ☎ 619/295–4163) has a red neon sign resembling a torch with a flame on top. A San Diego institution, this friendly dance club caters to lesbians most of the week. On Tuesday the DJ spins for the popular and long-running Boys' Night.

Jazz

Crescent Shores Grill (✉ 7955 La Jolla Shores Dr., La Jolla, ☎ 858/459–0541), perched on the top floor of the Hotel La Jolla, delivers an ocean view and a lineup of locally acclaimed jazz musicians Tuesday through Saturday.

Croce's (✉ 802 5th Ave., Gaslamp Quarter, ☎ 619/233–4355), the intimate jazz cave of restaurateur Ingrid Croce (singer-songwriter Jim Croce's widow), books superb acoustic-jazz musicians.

Next door to Croce's, **Croce's Top Hat** (✉ 818 5th Ave., Gaslamp Quarter, ☎ 619/233–4355) puts on live R&B nightly from 9 to 2. Musician A. J. Croce, son of Jim and Ingrid, often headlines at both clubs.

Dizzy's (✉ 344 7th Ave., Gaslamp Quarter, ☎ 858/270–7467) is one of the few venues in town that's totally devoted to music and the arts. The late-night jazz jam is your best bet on Friday after midnight. During the week you can count on the best in jazz, art, and the occasional spoken-word event. Refreshments are sold, but no alcohol is served.

Humphrey's by the Bay (✉ 2241 Shelter Island Dr., Shelter Island, ☎ 619/523–1010 for concert information), surrounded by water, is the summer stomping grounds for musicians such as Harry Belafonte and Chris Isaak. From June through September this dining and drinking oasis hosts the city's best outdoor jazz, folk, and light-rock concert series. The rest of the year the music moves indoors for some first-rate jazz most Sunday, Monday, and Tuesday nights, with piano-bar music on other nights.

Juke Joint Café (✉ 327 4th Ave., Gaslamp Quarter, ☎ 619/232–7685) sports a bistro up front and a supper club in the back. It offers live music nightly. Choices range from jazz and R&B most nights to Gospel for Sunday brunch. Musicians play in the bistro most weeknights but move to the larger back room on Friday and Saturday nights. Enjoy some of the Southern-style cooking to complete the experience.

Night Bay Cruises

Bahia Belle (✉ 998 W. Mission Bay Dr., Mission Bay, ☏ 619/539–7779) is a paddlewheeler that offers relaxing evening cruises along Mission Bay that include cocktails, dancing, and live music. Board from the Bahia Hotel. Cruises run from Wednesday through Sunday in summer and Friday and Saturday in winter (but no cruises in December). The fare is less than most nightclub covers.

Hornblower Cruises (✉ 1066 N. Harbor Dr., Downtown, ☏ 619/686–8700) makes nightly dinner-dance cruises aboard the *Lord Hornblower*—passengers are treated to fabulous views of the San Diego skyline.

San Diego Harbor Excursion (✉ 1050 N. Harbor Dr., Downtown, ☏ 619/234–4111 or 800/442–7847) welcomes guests aboard with a glass of champagne as a prelude to nightly dinner-dance cruises.

Piano Bars/Mellow

Hotel Del Coronado (✉ 1500 Orange Ave., Coronado, ☏ 619/435–6611), the famous fairy-tale hostelry, has piano music in its Crown Room and Palm Court. The Ocean Terrace Lounge has live bands nightly 9–1.

Inn at the Park (✉ 525 Spruce St., Hillcrest, ☏ 619/296–0057) is tucked away in the hotel of the same name. It makes for a nice stop after a day in Balboa Park. There's live music most nights.

Palace Bar (✉ 311 Island Ave., Gaslamp Quarter, ☏ 619/544–1886), in the historical Horton Grand Hotel, is one of the most mellow lounges in the Gaslamp. Rest up in an overstuffed chair and cradle your drink while deciding what sights to see next.

Top of the Hyatt (✉ 1 Market Pl., Embarcadero, ☏ 619/232–1234) crowns the tallest waterfront building in California, affording great views of San Diego Bay, including Coronado to the west, the Coronado Bridge and Mexico to the south, and Point Loma and La Jolla to the North. The wood paneling and mood lighting affect one of the most romantic spots in town.

Top o' the Cove (✉ 1216 Prospect St., La Jolla, ☏ 858/454–7779), also a magnificent Continental restaurant, has pianists playing show tunes and standards from the 1940s to the '80s.

Westgate Hotel (✉ 1055 2nd Ave., Downtown, ☏ 619/238–1818), one of the most elegant settings in San Diego, has piano music in the Plaza Bar.

Rock, Pop, Folk, Reggae, and Blues

Belly Up Tavern (✉ 143 S. Cedros Ave., Solana Beach, ☏ 858/481–9022), a regular fixture on local papers' "best of" lists, has been drawing big crowds since it opened in the mid-'70s. Its longevity attests to the quality of the eclectic entertainment on its stage. Within converted Quonset huts, critically acclaimed artists play everything from reggae and folk to—well, you name it. The BUT attracts people of all ages.

Brick by Brick (✉ 1130 Buenos Ave., Bay Park, ☏ 619/275–5483) is always cranking out the music of San Diego's top alternative and experimental rock groups.

Casbah (✉ 2501 Kettner Blvd., Middletown,, ☎ 619/232–4355), near the airport, is a small club with a national reputation for showcasing up-and-coming acts. Nirvana, Smashing Pumpkins, and Alanis Morissette all played the Casbah on their way to stardom. You can hear every type of band here—except those that sound like Top 40.

Dream Street (✉ 2228 Bacon St., Ocean Beach, ☎ 619/222–8131) is the place to go to see up-and-coming local rock bands. The music is on the heavy side. This is not the place for a quiet evening out.

The Field (✉ 544 5th Ave., Gaslamp Quarter, ☎ 619/232–9840) is San Diego's resident Irish pub. True to its Celtic pride, the pub promotes local Irish folksingers.

4th & B (✉ 345 B St., Downtown, ☎ 619/231–4343) is a live-music venue housed in a former bank that is only open when a concert is booked. All styles of music and occasional comedy acts take the stage.

Patrick's II (✉ 428 F St., Gaslamp Quarter, ☎ 619/233–3077) serves up live New Orleans–style jazz, blues, and rock in an Irish setting.

Winston's Beach Club (✉ 1921 Bacon St., Ocean Beach, ☎ 619/222–6822) is a sure bet for quality music in Ocean Beach. In a bowling alley–turned–rock club, Winston's hosts local bands, reggae groups, and occasionally 1960s-style bands. The crowd, mostly locals, can get rowdy.

Singles Bars

Barefoot Bar and Grill (✉ San Diego Princess Resort, 1404 W. Vacation Rd., Mission Bay, ☎ 858/274–4630), a beachfront watering hole, attracts flocks of singles, especially on Sunday night in spring and summer. Live music and happy-hour specials fill the joint up early, making for long latecomer lines.

Dick's Last Resort (✉ 345 4th Ave., Gaslamp Quarter, ☎ 619/231–9100) is not for Emily Post adherents. The surly wait staff and abrasive service are part of the gimmick. The rudeness notwithstanding, fun-loving party people pile into this barnlike restaurant and bar. Dick's has live music nightly and one of the most extensive beer lists in San Diego.

Jose's (✉ 1037 Prospect St., La Jolla, ☎ 858/454–7655) is a hit with yuppies from La Jolla and other neighboring beach communities. This small but clean hole-in-the-wall's lack of space gives suave singles an excuse to get up close and personal.

Old Bonita Store & Bonita Beach Club (✉ 4014 Bonita Rd., Bonita, ☎ 619/479–3537), a South Bay hangout, has a DJ spinning retro house music every weekend.

RT's Longboard Grill (✉ 1466 Garnet Ave., Pacific Beach, ☎ 858/270–4030) appeals to the young, tanned beach crowd, who comes by to schmooze and booze under the indoor palapas that give this lively bar a south-of-the-border feel.

Typhoon Saloon (✉ 1165 Garnet Ave., Pacific Beach, ☎ 858/373–3444) is an obligatory stop for college age singles club-hopping on weekend nights. The small dance floor is the main attraction, with DJs spinning Top 40 dance mixes. After the dancing, replenish with a snack at Big Bertha's next door.

U. S. Grant Hotel (✉ 326 Broadway, Gaslamp Quarter, ☎ 619/232–3121), a favorite of the over-30 business set, is the classiest spot in town for meeting fellow travelers while relaxing with a Manhattan or a martini at the mahogany bar. The best local Latin, jazz, and blues bands alternate appearances.

THE ARTS

National touring companies perform regularly at the 3,000-seat Civic Theatre and Golden Hall, and in Escondido at the California Center for the Arts. Programs at San Diego State University, the University of California at San Diego, private universities, and community colleges host a range of artists, from well-known professionals to students. The *San Diego Union-Tribune* lists attractions and complete movie schedules. The *Reader* weekly devotes an entire section to upcoming cultural events. *San Diego* magazine publishes monthly listings and reviews. Those in the know rely on San Diego's many community micromags found in most coffeehouses.

Book tickets well in advance, preferably at the same time you make hotel reservations. Outlets exist for last-minute tickets, although you risk either paying top rates or getting less-than-choice seats—or both.

You can buy half-price tickets to most theater, music, and dance events on the day of performance at **Times Arts Tix** (⊠ Horton Plaza, Gaslamp Quarter, ☎ 619/497–5000). Only cash is accepted. Advance full-price tickets are also sold. **Ticketmaster** (☎ 619/220–8497) sells tickets to many performances. Service charges vary according to the event, and most tickets are nonrefundable.

Dance

California Ballet Company (☎ 858/560–6741) performs high-quality contemporary and traditional works, from story ballets to Balanchine, September–May. The *Nutcracker* is staged annually at the **Civic Theatre** (⊠ 202 C St., Downtown); other ballets are presented at the **Lyceum** (⊠ 79 Horton Plaza, Gaslamp Quarter) and the **Poway Center for the Performing Arts** (⊠ 15498 Espola Rd., Poway).

Film

Landmark Theatres, known for first-run foreign, art, American independent, and documentary offerings, operates four theaters in the San Diego area. The **Cove** (⊠ 7730 Girard Ave., La Jolla, ☎ 858/459–5404), in the village area of La Jolla, is an older one-screen theater with a distinctive 1950s ambience. **La Jolla Village Cinemas** (⊠ 8879 Villa La Jolla Dr., La Jolla, ☎ 858/453–7831) is a modern multiplex set in a shopping center. **Hillcrest Cinemas** (⊠ 3965 5th Ave., Hillcrest, ☎ 619/299–2100) is a posh multiplex right in the middle of uptown's action. **Ken Cinema** (⊠ 4061 Adams Ave., Kensington, ☎ 619/283–5909) plays a roster of art and revival films that changes almost every night (many programs are double bills), along with *The Rocky Horror Picture Show* every Saturday at midnight. It publishes its listings in the *Ken*, a small newspaper distributed in nearly every coffeehouse and music store in the county. The Ken Cinema is considered by many to be the last bastion of true avant-garde film in San Diego.

Part of the Museum of Contemporary Art, the **Sherwood Auditorium** (⊠ 700 Prospect St., La Jolla, ☎ 858/454–2594) hosts foreign and classic film series and special cinema events, including the wildly popular Festival of Animation, from January through March.

Science, space-documentary, observation-of-motion, and sometimes psychedelic films are shown on the IMAX screen at the **Reuben H. Fleet Science Center** (⊠ 1875 El Prado, Balboa Park, ☎ 619/238–1233).

Music

Coors Amphitheatre (✉ 2050 Otay Valley Rd., Chula Vista, ☎ 619/671–3500), the largest concert venue in town, can accommodate 20,000 concertgoers with reserved seats and lawn seating. It presents top-selling national and international acts during its late spring to late summer season.

Copley Symphony Hall (✉ 750 B St., Downtown, ☎ 619/235–0804) has great acoustics surpassed only by an incredible Spanish Baroque interior. Not just the home of the San Diego Symphony Orchestra, the renovated 2,200-seat 1920s-era theater has also presented such popular musicians such as Elvis Costello and Sting.

Cox Arena (✉ San Diego State University, 5500 Canyon Crest Dr., College Area, ☎ 619/594–6947) attracts top-name acts like Eric Clapton and Depeche Mode to its 12,500-person confines.

East County Performing Arts Center (✉ 210 E. Main St., El Cajon, ☎ 619/440–2277) hosts a variety of performing arts events, but mostly music. World-class jazz, classical, blues, and world-beat musicians have ensured its popularity among locals.

La Jolla Chamber Music Society (☎ 858/459–3728) presents internationally acclaimed chamber ensembles, orchestras, and soloists at Sherwood Auditorium and the Civic Theatre.

Open-Air Theatre (✉ San Diego State University, 5500 Campanile Dr., College Area, ☎ 619/594–6947) presents top-name rock, reggae, and popular artists in summer concerts under the stars.

San Diego Chamber Orchestra (☎ 760/753–6402), a 35-member ensemble, performs once a month, October–April, in a number of different venues, including St. Joseph's Cathedral downtown.

San Diego Opera (✉ Civic Theatre, 3rd Ave. and B St., Downtown, ☎ 619/232–7636) draws international artists. Its season runs January–May. Past performances have included *The Magic Flute, Faust, Idomeneo,* and *Aida,* plus concerts by such talents as Luciano Pavarotti.

San Diego Sports Arena (✉ 3500 Sports Arena Blvd., Sports Arena, ☎ 619/224–4176) holds 14,000-plus fans for big-name concerts.

San Diego State University School of Music and Dance (☎ 619/594–6884) presents concerts in many genres, including jazz, classical, and world music in different venues on campus.

San Diego Symphony Orchestra (✉ 750 B St., Downtown, ☎ 619/235–0804) presents year-round special events including classics, and summer and winter pops. Concerts are held at Copley Symphony Hall, except the Summer Pops series at the Navy Pier, on North Harbor Drive downtown.

Sherwood Auditorium (✉ 700 Prospect St., La Jolla, ☎ 858/454–2594), a 550-seat venue in the Museum of Contemporary Art, hosts classical and jazz events.

Spreckels Organ Pavilion (✉ Balboa Park, ☎ 619/702–8138) holds a giant outdoor pipe organ dedicated in 1915 by sugar magnates John and Adolph Spreckels. The beautiful Spanish Baroque pavilion hosts concerts by civic organist Carol Williams on most Sunday afternoons and on most Monday evenings in summer. Local military bands, gospel groups, and barbershop quartets also perform here. All shows are free.

Spreckels Theatre (✉ 121 Broadway, Downtown, ☎ 619/235–0494), a designated-landmark theater erected more than 80 years ago, hosts musical events—everything from mostly Mozart to small rock concerts. Ballets and theatrical productions are also held here. Its good acoustics and historical status make this a special venue.

Theater

California Center for the Arts, Escondido (✉ 340 N. Escondido Blvd., Escondido, ☎ 800/988–4253) presents mainstream theatrical productions such as *Grease* and *The Odd Couple.*

Coronado Playhouse (✉ 1775 Strand Way, Coronado, ☎ 619/435–4856), a cabaret-type theater near the Hotel Del Coronado, stages regular dramatic and musical performances. Friday and Saturday dinner packages are available.

Diversionary Theatre (✉ 4545 Park Blvd., North Park, ☎ 619/220–0097) is San Diego's premier gay and lesbian company.

Horton Grand Theatre (✉ Hahn Cosmopolitan Theatre, 444 4th Ave., Gaslamp Quarter, ☎ 619/234–9583) stages comedies, dramas, mysteries, and musicals at a 250-seat venue.

La Jolla Playhouse (✉ Mandell Weiss Center for the Performing Arts, University of California at San Diego, 2910 La Jolla Village Dr., La Jolla, ☎ 858/550–1010) crafts exciting and innovative productions under the artistic direction of Michael Greif, May–November. Many Broadway shows, such as *Tommy* and *How to Succeed in Business Without Really Trying,* have previewed here before heading for the East Coast.

La Jolla Stage Company (✉ Parker Auditorium, 750 Nautilus St., La Jolla, ☎ 858/459–7773) presents lavish productions of Broadway favorites and popular comedies year-round on the La Jolla High School campus.

Lamb's Players Theatre (✉ 1142 Orange Ave., Coronado, ☎ 619/437–0600) has a regular season of five productions from February through November and stages a musical, "Festival of Christmas," in December. "An American Christmas" is their dinner-theater event at the Hotel del Coronado.

Lyceum Theatre (✉ 79 Horton Plaza, Gaslamp Quarter, ☎ 619/544–1000) is home to the San Diego Repertory Theatre and also presents productions from visiting theater companies.

Marie Hitchcock Puppet Theatre (✉ 2130 Pan American Rd. W, Balboa Park, ☎ 619/685–5045) presents amateur and professional puppeteers and ventriloquists five days a week. The cost is just a few dollars for adults and children alike. If you feel cramped in the small theater, don't worry; the shows rarely run longer than a half hour.

Old Globe Theatre (✉ Simon Edison Centre for the Performing Arts, 1363 Old Globe Way, Balboa Park, ☎ 619/239–2255) is the oldest professional theater in California, performing classics, contemporary dramas, and experimental works. It produces the famous summer Shakespeare Festival at the Old Globe and its sister theaters, the Cassius Carter Centre Stage and the Lowell Davies Festival Theatre.

Poway Center for the Performing Arts (✉ 15498 Espola Rd., Poway, ☎ 858/748–0505), an ambitious theater in suburban San Diego, presents musical comedy and other lighthearted fare.

San Diego Comic Opera Company (⊠ Casa del Prado Theatre, Balboa Park, ☎ 619/239–8836) presents four different productions of Gilbert and Sullivan and similar works from October through July.

San Diego Junior Theater (⊠ Casa del Prado Theatre, Balboa Park, ☎ 619/239–8355) is a highly regarded school where children ages 6–18 perform and stage productions. Call for performance dates.

San Diego Repertory Theatre (⊠ Lyceum Theatre, 79 Horton Plaza, Gaslamp Quarter, ☎ 619/235–8025), San Diego's first resident acting company, performs contemporary works year-round.

San Diego State University Drama Department (⊠ Don Powell Theatre and elsewhere on campus, 5500 Campanile Dr., College Area, ☎ 619/594–6947) presents contemporary and classic dramas.

Sledgehammer Theatre (⊠ 1620 6th Ave., Uptown, ☎ 619/544–1484), one of San Diego's cutting-edge theaters, stages avant-garde pieces in St. Cecilia's church.

Starlight Musical Theatre (⊠ Starlight Bowl, 2005 Pan American Plaza, Balboa Park, ☎ 619/544–7827 during season), a summertime favorite, is a series of musicals performed in an outdoor amphitheater mid-June–early September. Because of the theater's proximity to the airport, actors often have to freeze mid-scene while a plane flies over.

Sushi Performance & Visual Art (⊠ 320 11th Ave., Downtown, ☎ 619/235–8469), a nationally acclaimed group, provides an opportunity for well-known performance artists to do their thing in the old Carnation Milk building, now dubbed the "rein-Carnation building." The white-walled interior provides an intimate setting for many an avant-garde performance.

Theatre in Old Town (⊠ 4040 Twiggs St., Old Town, ☎ 619/688–2494) presents punchy revues and occasional classics. Shows like *Forbidden Broadway, Ruthless, Gilligan's Island,* and *Forbidden Hollywood* have made this a popular place.

UCSD Theatre (⊠ Mandell Weiss Center for the Performing Arts, University of California at San Diego, 2910 La Jolla Village Dr. and Expedition Way, La Jolla, ☎ 858/534–4574) presents productions by students of the university's theater department, September–May.

Welk Resort Theatre (⊠ 8860 Lawrence Welk Dr., Escondido, ☎ 760/749–3448 or 800/932–9355), a famed dinner theater about a 45-minute drive northeast of downtown on I–15, puts on polished Broadway-style productions.

6 OUTDOOR ACTIVITIES AND SPORTS

At least one stereotype of San Diego is true—it is an active, outdoors-oriented community, thanks to the constant sunshine. People recreate more than spectate. It's hard not to, with the number of choices available, from boccie and ballooning to golf, surfing, sailing, and volleyball.

S AN DIEGO, WITH ITS MILD TEMPERATURES, is a great place to be
       outdoors. The northern coastal part of the county has lured many
       resident professional triathletes, surfers, and bicyclists, who all
Updated by   take advantage of the climate, both meteorological and social, which
Rob Aikins   looks favorably upon them. You can take in the abundant natural beauty
of the county by bicycling, horseback riding, hiking, or even on a balloon trip.

San Diego's beaches are among its greatest natural attractions. In some
places the shorefront is wide and sandy; in others it's narrow and rocky
or backed by impressive sandstone cliffs. You'll find beaches awhirl
with activity and deserted spots for romantic sunset walks.

BEACHES

Water temperatures are generally chilly, ranging from 55°F to 65°F from
October through June, and 65°F to 75°F from July through September. For a surf and weather report, call 619/221–8884. For a general
beach and weather report, call 619/289–1212. Pollution, which has
long been a problem near the Mexican border, is inching northward.
The weather page of the *San Diego Union-Tribune* includes pollution
reports along with listings of surfing and diving conditions.

Overnight camping is not allowed on any San Diego city beaches, but
there are campgrounds at some state beaches throughout the county
(☎ 800/444–7275 for reservations). Lifeguards are stationed at city
beaches from Sunset Cliffs up to Black's Beach in the summertime, but
coverage in winter is provided by roving patrols only. Leashed dogs
are permitted on most San Diego beaches and adjacent parks from 6
PM to 9 AM; they can run unleashed anytime at Dog Beach at the north
end of Ocean Beach and at Rivermouth in Del Mar. It is rarely a problem, however, to take your pet to isolated beaches during the winter.

Pay attention to signs listing illegal activities; undercover police often
patrol the beaches, carrying their ticket books in coolers. Glass is prohibited on all beaches, and fires are allowed only in fire rings or ele-
vated barbecue grills. Alcoholic beverages—including beer—are
completely banned on some city beaches; others allow you to partake
from 8 AM to 8 PM. Imbibing in beach parking lots, on boardwalks,
and in landscaped areas is always illegal. While it may be tempting to
take a starfish or some other sea creature as a souvenir from a tide pool,
it upsets the delicate ecological balance and is illegal to do, too.

Parking near the ocean can be hard to find in the summer but is un-
metered at all San Diego city beaches. Parking fees were eliminated or
cut in half at all state beaches in 2001. Del Mar has a pay lot and metered street parking around the 15th Street Beach. Oceanside has pay
lots and meters around the pier and also in the Oceanside harbor area.

The beaches below are listed from south to north, starting near the Mexican border. County Highway S21 runs along the coast between Torrey Pines State Beach/Reserve and Oceanside, although its local name,
Old Highway 101 or Coast Highway 101, for example, varies by community. Most of the beaches north of Del Mar are plagued by erosion
and bluff failure. It's always a wise idea to stay clear of the bluffs, whether
you're above or below them.

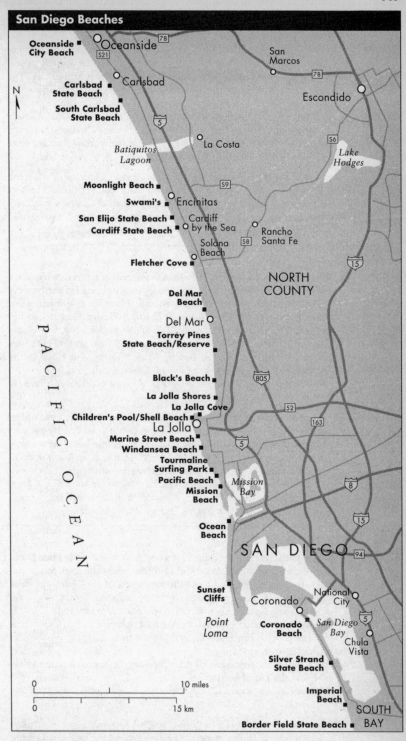

San Diego Beaches

Oceanside
City Beach
Oceanside
78
S21

San
Marcos

Carlsbad
State Beach
Carlsbad

South Carlsbad
State Beach

5

Escondido

La Costa

S6

Lake
Hodges

Batiquitos
Lagoon

S9

Moonlight Beach
Swami's
Encinitas

San Elijo State Beach
Cardiff State Beach
Cardiff
by the Sea
S8
Rancho
Santa Fe

Solana
Beach

Fletcher Cove

NORTH
COUNTY

15

Del Mar
Beach
Del Mar

Torrey Pines
State Beach/Reserve

805

Black's Beach

La Jolla Shores
La Jolla Cove
52

Children's Pool/Shell Beach
La Jolla
163

Marine Street Beach
Windansea Beach
5

Tourmaline
Surfing Park
Pacific Beach
Mission
Beach
Mission
Bay

8

Ocean
Beach

SAN DIEGO
94

15

P A C I F I C   O C E A N

Sunset
Cliffs

Coronado

National
City

Point
Loma

Coronado
Beach
San Diego
Bay

5

Chula
Vista

Silver Strand
State Beach

0   10 miles

0   15 km

Imperial
Beach
SOUTH
BAY

Border Field State Beach

South Bay

Border Field State Beach. This southernmost San Diego beach is different from most California beaches; for one, swimming is prohibited. Part of Border Field State Park, it is a marshy area with wide chaparral and wildflowers, a favorite among horseback riders and hikers. The park contains much of the Tijuana River Estuary, a haven for migrating birds. The beach is usually open 9–5. Beware that in winter the grounds are often posted with contamination signs because of sewer runoff from Tijuana. The beach has barbecue rings, parking is plentiful, and there are rest rooms. ⊠ *Exit I–5 at Dairy Mart Rd. and head west along Monument Rd.; South San Diego*

Imperial Beach. In August this classic southern California beach is the site of one of the nation's largest sand-castle competitions. The surf here is often excellent, but sewage contamination can be a problem. There are lifeguards in summer, rest rooms, parking, and nearby food vendors. ⊠ *Take Palm Ave. west from I–5 until it hits water.*

Coronado

Silver Strand State Beach. This quiet Coronado beach is ideal for families. The water is relatively calm, lifeguards and rangers are on duty year-round, and there are places to rollerblade or ride bikes. Four parking lots provide room for more than 1,500 cars. Sites at a campground ($12) for self-contained RVs are available on a first-come, first-serve basis; stays are limited to seven nights. Foot tunnels under Route 75 lead to a bay-side beach, which affords great views of the San Diego skyline. ⊠ *From San Diego–Coronado Bay Bridge, turn left onto Orange Ave., which becomes Rte. 75, and follow signs;* ☎ *619/ 435–5184.*

Coronado Beach. With the famous Hotel Del Coronado as a backdrop, this stretch of sandy beach is one of San Diego County's largest and most picturesque. It's perfect for sunbathing, people-watching, or Frisbee. Other exercisers include Navy SEAL teams, as well as the occasional Marine Recon unit, who have training runs on the beaches in and around Coronado. Parking can be difficult on the busiest days. There are plenty of rest rooms and service facilities, as well as fire rings. ⊠ *From the bridge, turn left on Orange Ave. and follow signs.*

Point Loma

Sunset Cliffs. Beneath the jagged cliffs on the west side of the Point Loma peninsula is one of the more secluded beaches in the area. It's popular with surfers and locals. At the south end of the peninsula, near Cabrillo Point, tide pools teeming with small sea creatures are revealed at low tide. Farther north the waves lure surfers and the lonely coves attract sunbathers. Stairs at the foot of Bermuda and Santa Cruz avenues provide beach access, as do some (treacherous at points) cliff trails. There are no facilities. A visit here is more enjoyable at low tide; check the local newspaper for tide schedules. ⊠ *Take I–8 west to Sunset Cliffs Blvd. and head west.*

San Diego

Ocean Beach. Much of this mile-long beach is a haven for volleyball players, sunbathers, and swimmers. The area around the municipal pier at the south end is a hangout for surfers and transients; the pier itself is open to the public for fishing and walking and has a restaurant at the middle. The beach is south of the channel entrance to Mission Bay. You'll find food vendors and fire rings; limited parking is available. Swimmers should beware of unusually vicious rip currents here. ⊠ *Take I–8 west to Sunset Cliffs Blvd. and head west. Turn right on Santa Monica Ave.*

Mission Beach. San Diego's most popular beach draws huge crowds on hot summer days. The 2-mi-long continuous stretch extends from the north entrance of Mission Bay to Pacific Beach. A recently widened boardwalk paralleling the beach is popular with walkers, runners, roller skaters, bladers, and bicyclists. Surfers, swimmers, and volleyball players congregate at the south end. In fact, thinly clad volleyball players practice on Cohasset Court year-round. Toward the north end, near the Belmont Park roller coaster, the beach narrows and the water becomes rougher. The crowds grow thicker and somewhat rougher as well. Parking can be a challenge, but there are plenty of rest rooms and restaurants in the area. ⊠ *Exit I–5 at Garnet Ave. and head west to Mission Blvd. Turn south and look for parking.*

Pacific Beach/North Pacific Beach. The boardwalk turns into a sidewalk here, but there are still bike paths and picnic tables along the beachfront. Pacific Beach runs from the north end of Mission Beach to Crystal Pier. North Pacific Beach extends from the pier north. The scene here is particularly lively on weekends. There are designated surfing areas, and fire rings are available. On-street parking is your best bet, or you can try the big lot at Belmont Park near the south end. ⊠ *Exit I–5 at Garnet Ave. and head west to Mission Blvd. Turn north and look for parking.*

La Jolla

The beaches of La Jolla combine unusual beauty with good fishing, scuba diving, and surfing. On the down side, they are crowded and have limited parking. Don't think about bringing your pet; dogs aren't even allowed on the sidewalks above some beaches here.

Tourmaline Surfing Park. This is one of the area's most popular beaches for surfing and sailboarding year-round. There is a 175-space parking lot at the foot of Tourmaline Street, but it's normally filled to capacity by midday. ⊠ *Take Mission Blvd. north (it turns into La Jolla Blvd.) and turn west on Tourmaline St.*

Windansea Beach. If the scenery here seems familiar, it's because Windansea and its habitués were the inspiration for Tom Wolfe's satirical novel *The Pump House Gang,* about a group of surfers who protect their surf-turf from outsiders. The beach's sometimes towering waves (caused by an underwater reef) are truly world class. With its incredible views and secluded sunbathing spots set among sandstone rocks, Windansea is also one of the most romantic of West Coast beaches, especially at sunset. ⊠ *Take Mission Blvd. north (it turns into La Jolla Blvd.) and turn west on Nautilus St.*

Marine Street Beach. Wide and sandy, this strand of beach often teems with sunbathers, swimmers, walkers, and joggers. The water is good for surfing and bodysurfing, although you'll need to watch out for riptides. ⊠ *Accessible from Marine St., off La Jolla Blvd.*

Children's Pool. In addition to panoramic views of ocean and coastline, this shallow lagoon, protected by a seawall, has small waves and no riptide. The area just outside the pool is popular with scuba divers who explore the offshore reef when the surf is calm. It's a good place to watch marine mammals—so many seals and sea lions frequent the cove that it is now closed to swimmers due to contamination. ⊠ *Follow La Jolla Blvd. north. When it forks, stay to the left, then turn right onto Coast Blvd.*

SURFING SAN DIEGO

SURFING MAY HAVE originated in Hawai'i, but modern surfing culture is inextricably linked to the southern California lifestyle. From the Malibu settings of *Beach Blanket Bingo* and *Gidget* to the surf-city sounds of Jan and Dean and the Beach Boys, the entertainment industry brought a California version of surfing to the landlocked, and in the process created an enduring mystique.

Today the billion-dollar surfing industry, centered around Orange and San Diego counties, sells the California surfing "dude" image worldwide. However, surfing is not just for dudes anymore. Women are entering the sport at a rate twice that of men, a trend that represents a return to surfing's Hawai'ian origins when surfing was enjoyed by people of both genders and all ages.

Surfing is a demanding sport that requires great reflexes, endurance, and balance. But besides being a strong athlete, a good surfer must be part oceanographer and part meteorologist in order to understand the subtle nuances of the ocean. Waves suitable for surfing are generated by the intense winds of offshore storms blowing across large expanses of water. When the waves reach the shallow water of the coast, they stand up and break. Because the quality and size of waves at any given spot is subject to many variables including ocean bottom contour, tides, and local winds, even the best spots may not be consistent. But with a little knowledge and luck, a surfer can fulfill his or her quest for the perfect wave.

Watching surfing from the shore can be a test of patience. Surfers spend a lot of time paddling into position and waiting to "take off" on the next wave. When someone takes off, look for one of two types of surfing: longboarding and short-boarding. Longboarders tend to ride boards more than 8 ft in length with rounded noses. Shortboarders ride the lightweight, high-performance boards from 5 to 7 ft in length that have pointed noses. A great longboarder will have a smooth, fluid style and will shuffle up and down the board, maybe even riding on the nose with the toes of both feet on the very edge ("hanging ten"). Shortboarders tend to surf faster and more aggressively. The best shortboarders surf vertical to the wave face and may even break free of the wave—known as "aerials" or "catching air." Non-surfers are often most impressed and amused by the mistakes. "Wipeouts," the sometimes spectacular falls, inevitably happen to all surfers.

In San Diego the biggest waves usually occur in the winter, although good-size swells can come any time of the year. Generally, in the winter, swells come from a northerly direction, while in the summer they tend to come from the south. Certain surf spots are better on different swells. In winter try beaches like Swami's in Encinitas or Black's Beach near La Jolla. Summer spots are Windansea in La Jolla and nearby Tourmaline Surfing Park.

Another good place for watching surfers is any municipal pier, which gives one a much closer vantage point on the action. To get a feel for the surfing culture at large, spend some time in the laid-back shops and restaurants of towns like Ocean Beach, Pacific Beach, and Encinitas. The truly adventurous can seek instruction from a qualified surf school and soon understand the stoke that one feels after shredding clean epic peaks during a dawn patrol (or, in plain English, feeling the elation of surfing good waves during an early morning surf session).

—Rob Aikins

Shell Beach. North of Children's Pool is a small cove, accessible by stairs, with a relatively secluded beach. The exposed rocks off the coast have been designated a protected habitat for sea lions; you can watch them sun themselves and frolic in the water. ⊠ *Continue along Coast Blvd. north from Children's Pool.*

La Jolla Cove. This is one of the prettiest spots in the world. A palm-lined park sits on top of cliffs formed by the incessant pounding of the waves. At low tide the tide pools and cliff caves provide a destination for explorers. Divers and snorkelers can explore the underwater delights of the San Diego–La Jolla Underwater Ecological Reserve. The cove is also a favorite of rough-water swimmers. ⊠ *Follow Coast Blvd. north to signs, or take the La Jolla Village Dr. exit from I–5, head west to Torrey Pines Rd., turn left, and drive downhill to Girard Ave. Turn right and follow signs.*

La Jolla Shores. On summer holidays all access routes are usually closed to one of San Diego's most popular beaches. The lures here are a wide sandy beach and the most gentle waves in San Diego. A concrete boardwalk parallels the beach. Arrive early to get a parking spot in the lot at the foot of Calle Frescota. ⊠ *From I–5 take La Jolla Village Dr. west and turn left onto La Jolla Shores Dr. Head west to Camino del Oro or Vallecitos St. Turn right.*

Black's Beach. The powerful waves at this beach, officially known as Torrey Pines City Park Beach, attract surfers, and its relative isolation appeals to nudist nature lovers (although by law nudity is prohibited). Access to parts of the shore coincides with low tide. There are no lifeguards on duty, and strong ebb tides are common—only experienced swimmers should take the plunge. Storms have weakened the cliffs in the past few years; they're dangerous to climb and should be avoided. ⊠ *Take Genesee Ave. west from I–5 and follow signs to Glider Port; easier access, via a paved path, available on La Jolla Farms Rd., but parking is limited to 2 hrs.*

Del Mar

Torrey Pines State Beach/Reserve. One of San Diego's best beaches contains 1,700 acres of bluffs, bird-filled marshes, and sandy shoreline. A network of trails leads through rare pine trees to the coast below. The large parking lot is rarely full. Lifeguards are on duty weekends (weather permitting) from Easter until Memorial Day, daily from then until Labor Day, and again on weekends through September. Torrey Pines tends to get crowded during the summer, but more isolated spots under the cliffs are a short walk in either direction. ⊠ *Take the Carmel Valley Rd. exit west from I–5, turn left on Rte. S21;* ☎ *858/755–2063.* 🅿 *Parking $2.*

Del Mar Beach. The numbered streets of Del Mar, from 15th north to 29th, end at a wide beach popular with volleyball players, surfers, and sunbathers. Parking can be a problem on nice summer days, but access is relatively easy. The portions of Del Mar south of 15th Street are lined with cliffs and are rarely crowded. Leashed dogs are permitted on most sections of the beach year-round; from October through May, dogs may run free at Rivermouth, Del Mar's northernmost beach. During the annual summer meeting of the Del Mar Thoroughbred Club, horse bettors can be seen sitting on the beach in the morning, working on the *Daily Racing Form* before heading across the street to the track. ⊠ *Take the Via de la Valle exit from I–5 west to Rte. S21 (also known as Camino del Mar in Del Mar) and turn left.*

Solana Beach

Most of the beaches in this little city are nestled under cliffs, and access is limited to private stairways. However, at the west end of Lomas Santa Fe Drive (at an area known as Pill Box because of the bunker-like structures on top of the cliffs), you'll find access to a small beach, known locally as **Fletcher Cove.** Also here are rest rooms and a large parking lot. During low tide it's an easy walk under the cliffs to nearby beaches. High tide can make some of the beach impassable. Tides and surf conditions are posted at a kiosk on top of the bluffs. ⊠ *From I–5 take Lomas Santa Fe Dr. west.*

Cardiff-by-the-Sea

Cardiff State Beach. This beach begins at the parking lot immediately north of the cliffs at Solana Beach. A reef break draws surfers, although this cobbly beach otherwise is not particularly appealing. ⊠ *From I–5 turn west on Lomas Santa Fe Dr. to Rte. S21 (Old Hwy. 101) and turn right;* ☎ *760/753–5091.* ⊞ *Parking $4.*

San Elijo State Beach. There are campsites (☎ 800/444–7275 for reservations) atop a scenic bluff at this park, which also has a store and shower facilities plus beach access for swimmers and surfers. Sites run $12–$18. ⊠ *From I–5 turn west on Lomas Santa Fe Dr. to Rte. S21 (Old Hwy. 101) and turn right;* ☎ *760/753–5091.* ⊞ *Parking $2 per car; or park for free nearby on U.S. 101.*

Encinitas

Swami's. Palms and the golden domes of the nearby Self-Realization Fellowship Retreat and Hermitage earned this picturesque beach its name. Extreme low tides expose tidepools that harbor anemones, starfish, and other sea life. Remember to look but don't touch; all sea life here is protected. The beach is also a top surfing spot; the only access is by a long stairway leading down from the cliff-top park. ⊠ *Follow Rte. S21 north from Cardiff, or exit I–5 at Encinitas Blvd., go west to Rte. S21, and turn left.*

Moonlight Beach. Large parking areas and lots of facilities make this beach, tucked into a break in the cliffs, a pleasant stop. To combat erosion sand is trucked in every year, making it a popular beach with sunbathers. The volleyball courts on the north end attract many competent players, including a few professionals who live in the area. ⊠ *Take the Encinitas Blvd. exit from I–5 and head west until you hit the Moonlight parking lot.*

Carlsbad

Carlsbad State Beach, South Carlsbad State Beach. Erosion from winter storms has made the southern Carlsbad beaches rockier than most beaches in southern California. This is particularly true of South Carlsbad, a stretch of which is named in honor of Robert C. Frazee, a local politician and civic booster. Still, it's a good swimming spot, there are fine street- and beach-level promenades outside of downtown Carlsbad, and there is **overnight camping** for self-contained RVs (☎ 800/444–7275). No overnight camping is allowed at Carlsbad State Beach, farther to the north, but there is a fishing area and a parking lot. ⊠ *Exit I–5 at La Costa Ave. and head west to Rte. S21. Turn north and follow coastline;* ☎ *760/438–3143.* ⊞ *Free at both beaches.*

Oceanside

Swimmers, surfers, and U.S. Marines (from nearby Camp Pendleton) often come to play on **Oceanside's beaches.** The surf is good around the Oceanside Pier near the foot of Mission Avenue and on either side of the two jetties. ⊠ *Take Vista Way west from I–5 to Rte. S21 (Coast Hwy.) and turn right. Best access points are from Cassidy St., the Oceanside Pier, and the Oceanside Harbor area.*

PARTICIPANT SPORTS AND FITNESS

Ballooning

Enjoy the views of the Pacific Ocean, the mountains, and the coastline south to Mexico and north to San Clemente from a hot-air balloon at sunrise or sunset. The conditions are perfect: necessary winds and wide-open spaces. **A Balloon Adventure by California Dreamin'** (⊠ 162 S. Rancho Santa Fe Rd., Suite F35, Encinitas, ☎ 800/373–3359) offers sunset and sunrise flights from several North County spots, as well as a sunrise flight from Otay Mesa for visitors to the South Bay. Temecula wine country flights are also available. **Skysurfer Balloon Company** (⊠ 1221 Camino del Mar, Del Mar, ☎ 858/481–6800 or 800/660–6809) takes off from several locations depending on wind and weather conditions and will take you on one-hour flights in North County or Temecula. Hors d'oeuvres and beverages are included.

Bicycling

On any given summer day **Route S21** from La Jolla to Oceanside looks like a freeway for cyclists. Never straying more than a quarter-mile from the beach, it is easily the most popular and scenic bike route around. Although the terrain is fairly easy, the long, steep Torrey Pines grade, heading south just past Del Mar, is world famous for weeding out the weak. Experienced cyclists follow **Lomas Santa Fe Drive** in Solana Beach east into Rancho Santa Fe, perhaps even continuing east on Del Dios Highway, past Lake Hodges, to Escondido. These roads can be narrow and winding in spots. For more leisurely rides, **Mission Bay, San Diego Harbor,** and the **Mission Beach boardwalk** are all flat and scenic. San Diego also has a **velodrome** in the Morley Field section of Balboa Park. Local bookstores and camping stores sell guides to some challenging mountain-bike trails in outer San Diego County. A free comprehensive map of all county bike paths is available from the local office of the **California Department of Transportation** (⊠ 2829 Juan St., Old Town 92110, ☎ 619/688–6699).

Bicycle Barn (⊠ 746 Emerald St., Pacific Beach, ☎ 858/581–3665) rents a variety of bikes—from mountain bikes to beach cruisers and tandems—to get you cruising the boardwalk in no time. Once you're off the boat at Coronado Ferry Landing, explore the charming community with a bike from **Bikes and Beyond** (⊠ 1201 1st Ave., Coronado, ☎ 619/435–7180). **Mission Beach Club** (⊠ 704 Ventura Pl. Mission Beach, ☎ 858/488–5050) is right on the boardwalk and rents bikes, skates, and boards of all types.

Boccie

The Italian version of lawn bowling is played on Monday, Wednesday, and Friday from 1 to 5 on courts in the Morley Field section of **Balboa Park** (☎ 619/692–4919). The games are open to the public, and there are usually boccie balls at the courts.

Bullfighting

California Academy of Tauromaquia (✉ Point Loma, ☎ 619/421–4289) is believed to be the only school of toreo in the United States. The academy promotes the art of bloodless bullfighting. They offer regular classes each week as well as four- to six-day intensive clinics that teach some fundamentals of bullfighting. Classes without animals are held in Ocean Beach or Point Loma, while instruction with live animals takes place on a bull ranch in northern Baja.

Diving

Enthusiasts the world over come to San Diego to snorkel and scuba-dive off La Jolla and Point Loma. At La Jolla Cove you'll find the **San Diego–La Jolla Underwater Ecological Park.** Because all sea life is protected here, it's the best place to see large lobster, sea bass, and sculpin, as well as numerous golden Garibaldi, the state marine fish. It's not uncommon to see hundreds of beautiful leopard sharks schooling on the north end of the cove, near La Jolla shores, especially during the summer. Farther north, off the south end of Black's Beach, the rim of **Scripps Canyon** lies in about 60 ft of water. The canyon plummets to more than 900 ft in some sections.

The HMCS *Yukon,* a decommissioned Canadian warship, was intentionally sunk off of **Mission Beach** in summer 2000. A mishap caused it to settle on its side, creating a surreal, M. C. Escher–esque diving environment. Beware and exercise caution: even experienced divers have become disoriented inside the wreck. Another popular diving spot is **Sunset Cliffs** in Point Loma, where the sea life and flora are relatively close to shore. Strong rip currents make it an area best enjoyed by experienced divers, who mostly prefer to make their dives from boats. It's illegal to take any wildlife from the ecological preserves in La Jolla or near Cabrillo Point. Spearfishing requires a license (available at most dive stores), and it is illegal to take out-of-season lobster and game fish. The *San Diego Union–Tribune* includes diving conditions on its weather page. For recorded diving information, contact the **San Diego City Lifeguard Service** (☎ 619/221–8824).

San Diego Divers Supply (✉ 4004 Sports Arena Blvd., Sports Arena, ☎ 619/224–3439) provides equipment and instruction, as well as boat trips and maps of local wrecks and attractions. **Ocean Enterprises Scuba Diving** (✉ 7710 Balboa Ave., Clairemont Mesa, ☎ 858/565–6054), a sister location of San Diego Divers Supply, provides the same full range of services. **Diving Locker** (✉ 1020 Grand Ave., Pacific Beach, ☎ 858/272–1120) has been a fixture in San Diego since 1959, making it the city's longest-running dive shop. Not for the faint of heart, **San Diego Shark Diving Expeditions** (✉ 6747 Friar's Rd. Mission Valley, ☎ 619/299–8560) will chum the water with blood and lower you in a cage to the frenzy below the surface. They do not offer instruction and cater to experienced divers only.

Fishing

The Pacific Ocean is full of corbina, croaker, and halibut. No license is required to fish from a public pier, such as the Ocean Beach and Oceanside piers. A fishing license from the state **Department of Fish and Game** (✉ 4949 Viewridge Ave., San Diego 92123, ☎ 858/467–4201), available at most bait-and-tackle and sporting-goods stores, is required for fishing from the shoreline. Children under 15 do not need a license.

County-operated **Lake Jennings** and **Lake Morena** are popular for fishing and camping. For information or to make reservations call

619/565–3600 weekdays between 8 AM and 5 PM. City-operated reservoirs, like **Sutherland** and **San Vicente,** are good spots for catching trout and bass, but have no campgrounds. Call 619/465–3474 for a 24-hour information line. Three freshwater lakes—**Dixon, Hodges, and Wohlford**—surround the North County city of Escondido. Both Wohlford and Dixon lakes are regularly stocked with trout, but have also become known for big bass, bluegill, and catfish. A state fishing license is required. Camping is allowed at Wohlford at the **Oakvale RV Park** (☎ 760/749–2895) on the south shore, which has a supply store and a boat ramp. On the north shore of Lake Wohlford, there's camping at **Wohlford Resort** ☎ 760/749–2755), complete with stores selling food, drinks, bait, tackle, and camping supplies. Boats can be rented at the boat ramp. **Lyle's at Dixon Lake** (☎ 760/741–3328; 760/839–4680 for ranger station) is a city-administered campground and offers similar amenities as the areas at Wohlford.

Fisherman's Landing (✉ 2838 Garrison St., Point Loma, ☎ 619/221–8500) has a fleet of luxury vessels from 57 ft to 124 ft long, offering long-range multiday trips in search of yellowfin tuna, yellowtail, and other deep-water fish. Whale-watching, and sometimes petting, trips are also available. **H&M Landing** (✉ 2803 Emerson St., Point Loma, ☎ 619/222–1144) schedules fishing trips, plus whale-watching excursions from December through March. **Seaforth Boat Rentals** (✉ 1641 Quivira Rd., Mission Bay, ☎ 619/223–1681) can take you out on Mission Bay in a rowboat or power skiff or can arrange a charter for an ocean adventure. **Helgren's Sportfishing** (✉ 315 Harbor Dr. S, Oceanside, ☎ 760/722–2133) is your best bet in North County, offering the full assortment of trips from Oceanside Harbor.

Fitness

Most major hotels have full health clubs, with weight machines, stationary bicycles, and spas. Several hotels have elaborate spas that offer one-day spa-and-fitness programs for nonguests.

The recently remodeled spa at **Hotel Del Coronado** (✉ 1500 Orange Ave., Coronado, ☎ 619/435–6611) offers body treatments and massages including the Del Aromatherapy Body Masque and the Del Massage. All services include full use of fitness facilities for the day. **L'Auberge Del Mar Resort and Spa** (✉ 1540 Camino Del Mar, Del Mar, ☎ 858/259–1515) has a full-service European spa with services that range from single treatments to full-day affairs. Facials are custom-blended to each client's needs, with no two being alike. A package at the **Rancho Bernardo Inn** (✉ 17550 Bernardo Oaks Dr., Rancho Bernardo, ☎ 858/675–8500) includes a massage, a facial, and use of the fitness center. Day-spa packages at the **Rancho Valencia Resort** (✉ 5921 Valencia Circle, Rancho Santa Fe, ☎ 858/756–1123) include massage, aromatherapy, and use of fitness facilities. **The Spa at the Coronado Island Marriott Resort** (✉ 2000 2nd St., Coronado, ☎ 619/435–3000) has pampering packages that include the use of fitness facilities and admission to exercise classes. **Chopra Center for Well Being** (✉ 7630 Fay Ave., La Jolla, ☎ 888/424–6772) was founded by New Age guru Dr. Deepak Chopra to teach and treat guests according to his holistic view of life. Day spa treatments and longer visits are offered, as well as free courses to the general public.

Frog's Athletic & Racquet Club (✉ 901 Hotel Circle S, Hotel Circle, ☎ 619/291–3500) has a weight room, saunas, and tennis and racquetball courts. Anyone can use the splendid facilities at the **Sporting Club at Aventine** (✉ 8930 University Center La., La Jolla, ☎ 858/552–8000).

The **24 Hour Fitness Centers** in the area (✉ 5885 Rancho Mission Rd., Mission Valley, ☎ 619/281–5543; ✉ 3675 Midway Dr., Sports Arena, ☎ 619/224–2902; ✉ 4405 La Jolla Village Dr., La Jolla, ☎ 858/457–3930) welcome nonmembers for a small fee. **Gold's Gym** (✉ 2949 Garnet Ave., Pacific Beach, ☎ 858/272–3400) allows drop-ins. **Bodyworks Health & Fitness** (✉ 1130 7th Ave., Downtown, ☎ 619/232–5500) allows nonmembers to use the facilities for a small fee. **Athletic Center** (✉ 1747 Hancock St., Middletown, ☎ 619/299–2639) has a low daily rate for visitors.

Frisbee Golf

This is like golf, except it's played with Frisbees. A course, laid out at Morley Field in Balboa Park, is open seven days a week from dawn to dusk. It costs $1 to play on weekdays and $1.50 on weekends. Equipment and playing times can be arranged with the Disc Golf Club on a first-come, first-serve basis. Rules are posted. Directions to the field are available from the **Balboa Park Disc Golf Club** (☎ 619/692–3607).

Golf

It would be difficult to find a better place to play golf year-round than San Diego. The climate—generally sunny, without a lot of wind—is perfect for the sport, and there are courses in the area to suit every level of expertise. Experienced golfers can play the same greens as PGA-tournament participants, and beginners or rusty players can book a week at a golf resort and benefit from expert instruction. You'd also be hard-pressed to find a locale that has more scenic courses—everything from sweeping views of the ocean to verdant hills inland.

As you might expect, these advantages make San Diego popular with golfers; during busy vacation seasons it can be difficult to get a good tee-off time. Call in advance to see if it's possible to make a reservation. You don't necessarily have to stay at a resort to play its course; check if the one you're interested in is open to nonguests. Most public courses in the area provide a list of fees for all San Diego courses. The **Southern California Golf Association** (☎ 818/980–3630) publishes an annual directory ($15) with detailed and valuable information on all clubs. Another good resource for golfers is the **Southern California Public Links Golf Association** (☎ 714/994–4747), which will answer questions over the phone or, for $5, will provide you with a roster of member courses.

The following is not intended to be a comprehensive list but provides suggestions for some of the best places to play in the area. The greens fee is included for each course; carts (in some cases mandatory), instruction, and other costs are additional.

Courses

The **Balboa Park Municipal Golf Course** (✉ 2600 Golf Course Dr., Balboa Park, ☎ 858/570–1234) is in the heart of Balboa Park, making it convenient for downtown visitors. Greens fee: $33–$38.

Carmel Mountain Ranch Country Club (✉ 14050 Carmel Ridge Rd., Poway, ☎ 858/487–9224) has 18 holes, a driving range, and equipment rentals. A challenging course with many difficult holes, Carmel Mountain Ranch is not particularly scenic: it's in a suburban area and runs through a housing development. Greens fee: $65–$85.

Coronado Municipal Golf Course (✉ 2000 Visalia Row, Coronado, ☎ 619/435–3121) has 18 holes, a driving range, equipment rentals, and a snack bar. Views of San Diego Bay and the Coronado Bridge from the back nine holes on this good walking course make it popular—but rather difficult to get on. Greens fee: $20–$34.

Cottonwood at Rancho San Diego Golf Club (✉ 3121 Willow Glen Rd., El Cajon, ☎ 619/442–9891) has a driving range, rentals, a restaurant, and two 18-hole courses. The Monte Vista course is the easier of the two. Ivanhoe often hosts tournaments. Both are good walking courses, and have nice practice putting greens. Greens fee: $36–$53.

Eastlake Country Club (✉ 2375 Clubhouse Dr., Chula Vista, ☎ 619/ 482–5757) has 18 holes, a driving range, equipment rentals, and a snack bar. A fun course for golfers of almost all levels of expertise, it's not overly difficult despite the water hazards. Greens fee: $50–$65.

Mission Bay Golf Resort (✉ 2702 N. Mission Bay Dr., Mission Bay, ☎ 858/490–3370) has 18 holes, a driving range, equipment rentals, and a restaurant. A not-very-challenging executive (par 3 and 4) course, Mission Bay is lighted for night play with final tee time at 8:15 PM. Greens fee: $18–$22.

Mount Woodson Country Club (✉ 16422 N. Woodson Dr., Ramona, ☎ 760/788–3555) has 18 holes, equipment rentals, a golf shop, and a snack bar. This heavily wooded course in the mountains outside San Diego has scenic views and wooden bridges. Greens fee: $56–$81.

Singing Hills Country Club (✉ 3007 Dehesa Rd., El Cajon, ☎ 619/442– 3425) has 54 holes, a driving range, equipment rentals, and a restaurant. The lush course, set in a canyon, has many water hazards. One of *Golf Digest*'s favorites, Singing Hills comes highly recommended by everyone who's played it. Hackers will love the executive par-3 course; seasoned golfers can play the championship courses. Greens fee: $50–$61.

Torrey Pines Municipal Golf Course (✉ 11480 N. Torrey Pines Rd., La Jolla, ☎ 800/985–4653) has 36 holes, a driving range, and equipment rentals. One of the best public golf courses in the United States, Torrey Pines has views of the Pacific from every hole and is sufficiently challenging to host the Buick Invitational in February. In 2001 the renovated par-72 South Course reopened to rave reviews from the touring pros. New greens, more length, and additional bunkers were added by acclaimed course designer Rees Jones. It's not easy to get a good tee time here as professional brokers buy up the best ones. Check the yellow pages for broker's numbers. Out-of-towners are better off booking the instructional Golf Playing Package, which includes cart, greens fee, and a golf-pro escort for the first three holes. Greens fee: $65–$105.

Resorts

Aviara Golf Club (✉ 7447 Batiquitos Dr., Carlsbad, ☎ 760/603–6900) has 18 holes (designed by Arnold Palmer), a driving range, equipment rentals, and views of the protected adjacent Batiquitos Lagoon and the Pacific Ocean. Greens fee: $175–$195.

Carlton Oaks Lodge and Country Club (✉ 9200 Inwood Dr., Santee, ☎ 619/448–4242) has 18 holes, a driving range, equipment rentals, a clubhouse, a restaurant, and a bar. Many local qualifying tournaments are held at this difficult Pete Dye–designed course with lots of trees and water hazards. Carts are included. Greens fee: $55–$80.

Carmel Highland Doubletree Golf and Tennis Resort (✉ 14455 Peñasquitos Dr., Rancho Peñasquitos, ☎ 858/672–9100), a fairly hilly, well-maintained course in inland North County, has 18 holes, a driving range, equipment rentals, and a clubhouse with restaurant. Greens fee: $55–$75.

La Costa Resort and Spa (⊠ 2100 Costa del Mar Rd., Carlsbad, ☎ 760/438–9111 or 800/854–5000) has two 18-hole PGA-rated courses, a driving range, a clubhouse, equipment rentals, an excellent golf school, and a pro shop. One of the premier golf resorts in southern California, it hosts the Accenture World Match Play Championships each February. The spa that it's part of was named "Best Spa in the World" by the *Robb Report*. All this doesn't come cheaply, but then again, how many courses will send a limo to pick you up at the airport? Greens fee: $195.

Morgan Run Resort and Club (⊠ 5690 Cancha de Golf, Rancho Santa Fe, ☎ 858/756–2471), a very popular walking course near polo grounds and stables, has 27 holes that can be played in three combinations of 18, a driving range, equipment rentals, and a pro shop. Greens fee: $80–$100.

Pala Mesa Resort (⊠ 2001 Old Hwy. 395, Fallbrook, ☎ 760/728–5881) has 18 holes, a driving range, and equipment rentals. Narrow fairways help make this a challenging course, but it's well maintained and has views of the inland mountains. Greens fee: $60–$80.

Rancho Bernardo Inn and Country Club (⊠ 17550 Bernardo Oaks Dr., Rancho Bernardo, ☎ 858/675–8470 Ext. 1) has 45 holes, a driving range, equipment rentals, and a restaurant. Guests can play three other golf courses at company-operated resorts: Mount Woodson, Temecula Creek, and Twin Oaks. Ken Blanchard's Golf University of San Diego, based here, is world famous. And Rancho Bernardo Inn lays out one of the best Sunday brunches in the county. Greens fee: $85–$110.

Redhawk (⊠ 45100 Redhawk Pkwy., Temecula, ☎ 909/310–3850 or 800/451–4295) has 18 holes in an arboretumlike setting, a driving range, a putting green, and a snack bar. The par-72 course offers enough challenges to have earned a 4-star rating from *Golf Digest* and a Top 10 ranking from *California Golf Magazine*. Greens fee: $50–$70.

Hang Gliding and Paragliding

The **Torrey Pines Glider Port** (⊠ 2800 Torrey Pines Scenic Dr., La Jolla), perched on the cliffs overlooking the ocean north of La Jolla, is one of the most spectacular—and easiest—spots to hang glide in the world. However, it is definitely for experienced pilots only. Hang gliding and paragliding lessons and tandem rides for inexperienced gliders are available from the **Hang Gliding/Paragliding Center** (☎ 858/452–9858) based here.

Hiking and Nature Trails

Guided hikes are conducted regularly through Los Penasquitos Canyon Preserve and the Torrey Pines State Beach and Reserve. The **San Dieguito River Valley Regional Open Space** (⊠ 21 mi north of San Diego on I–5 to Lomas Santa Fe Dr., east 1 mi to Sun Valley Rd., north into park; Solana Beach, ☎ 619/235–5440) is a 55-mi corridor that begins at the mouth of the San Dieguito River in Del Mar, heading from the riparian lagoon area through coastal sage scrub and mountain terrain to end in the desert just east of Volcan Mountain near Julian. The **Tijuana Estuary** (☎ 619/575–3613), mostly contained within Border Field State Park, is one of the last extant riparian environments in southern California. The freshwater and saltwater marshes give refuge to migrant and resident waterfowl. The visitor center has an amphitheater for interpretive talks. A list of scheduled walks appears in the Night and Day section of the Thursday *San Diego Union-Tribune* and in the *Reader* weekly.

Mission Trails Regional Parks (⊠ 1 Father Junípero Serra Tr., Mission Valley, ☎ 619/668–3275, WEB www.mtrp.org), which encompasses nearly 6,000 acres of mountains, wooded hillsides, lakes, and riparian streams, is only 8 mi northeast of downtown. Trails range from easy to difficult; they include one with a superb city view from Cowles Mountain and another along a historic missionary path.

Horseback Riding

Adventures on Horseback (☎ 619/445–3997), near the East County town of Descanso, leads 1½–9-hour rides, as well as 3–5-day rides with overnight stays in cabins or bed-and-breakfasts. All rides are in the Cuyamaca Mountains. They accommodate all skill levels and will provide lessons or rent easy-to-ride fox trotters. Children under 7 are not admitted. Bright Valley Farms (⊠ 12310 Campo Rd., Spring Valley, ☎ 619/670–1861) offers lessons and rentals to ride on the winding trails of the Sweetwater River Valley. Sandi's Rental Stable (⊠ 2060 Hollister St., Imperial Beach, ☎ 619/424–3124) leads rides through Border Field State Park. They offer lessons for beginners and will accommodate more advanced riders. Be sure to tell them your needs before you saddle up.

Ice-Skating

Ice Chalet (⊠ University Towne Centre, 4545 La Jolla Village Dr., La Jolla, ☎ 858/452–9110) offers open skating and hockey leagues. If you like to watch, you can get a meal from the mall's food court above the rink. Iceoplex Ice Center (⊠ 555 N. Tulip, Escondido, ☎ 760/489–5550) has two Olympic-size rinks, a fitness center, swimming pool, and restaurant. It offers lessons, hockey leagues, and public skate sessions. San Diego Ice Arena (⊠ 11048 Ice Skate Pl., Mira Mesa, ☎ 858/530–1825) is the place to learn hockey. It also has skate rentals, public sessions, and lessons.

Jet Skiing

Jet skis can be launched from most beaches, although they need to be ridden beyond surf lines, and some beaches have special regulations governing their use. Waveless Mission Bay and the small Snug Harbor Marina (☎ 760/434–3089), east of the intersection of Tamarack Avenue and I–5 in Carlsbad, are favorite spots. H2O Jet Ski Rentals (⊠ 1617 Quivira Rd., Mission Bay, ☎ 619/226–2754) rents jet skis for use on Mission Bay. Seaforth Boat Rentals (☎ 619/223–1681) rents jet skis for use in the South Bay Marina in Coronado, and they are also available at Snug Harbor in Carlsbad.

Jogging

The most popular run downtown is along the Embarcadero, which stretches around the bay. There are uncongested sidewalks all through the area. The alternative in the downtown area is to head east to Balboa Park, where trails snake through the canyons. Joggers can start out from any parking lot, but it's probably easiest to start anywhere along the 6th Avenue side. Entry to the numerous lots is best where Laurel Street connects with 6th Avenue. There is also a fitness circuit course in the park's Morley Field area. Mission Bay is renowned among joggers for its wide sidewalks and basically flat landscape. Trails head west around Fiesta Island, providing distance as well as a scenic route. Del Mar has the finest running trails along the bluff; park your car near 15th Street and run south along the cliffs for a gorgeous view of the ocean. Organized runs occur almost every weekend. They're listed in

Competitor magazine, which is available free at bike and running shops, or by calling the **San Diego Track Club** (☎ 800/450–7382), which organizes events and can give you maps to some of the more popular running trails in the area. **The Sports Authority** (✉ 8550 Rio San Diego Dr., Mission Valley, ☎ 619/295–1682) has all the supplies and information you'll need for running in San Diego. Don't run in bike lanes, and check the local newspaper's tide charts before heading to the beach.

Rock Climbing

San Diego offers a variety of indoor and outdoor climbing options for beginners through experts. **Mission Trails Regional Parks** (✉ 1 Father Junípero Serra Tr., Mission Valley, ☎ 619/668–3275) has a huge quantity of bouldering, top-roping, and single-pitch climbs. Call the park office for more information. **Solid Rock Gym** has two locations (✉ 2074 Hancock St., Old Town, ☎ 619/299–1124; ✉ 13025 Stowe Rd., Poway, ☎ 858/748–9011) with indoor routes for all skill levels. **Vertical Hold Sport Climbing Center** (✉ 9580 Distribution Ave., Mira Mesa, ☎ 858/586–7572) is the largest full-service indoor rock-climbing gym in southern California. It offers lessons, rentals, and party packages.

Rollerblading and Roller-Skating

The sidewalks at **Mission Bay** are perfect for rollerblading and skating; you can admire the sailboats and kites while you get some exercise. **Bicycle Barn** (✉ 746 Emerald St., Pacific Beach, ☎ 858/581–3665) rents blades for leisurely skates along the Pacific Beach boardwalk. **Bikes and Beyond** (✉ 1201 1st Ave., Coronado, ☎ 619/435–7180) is the place to go to rent skates, blades, and bikes with which to cruise the beachwalk of Coronado. **Mission Beach Club** (✉ 704 Ventura Pl., Mission Beach, ☎ 858/488–5050) took over the business for the long-running and popular Hamel's. Next to the Mission Beach boardwalk, their black, castlelike facade is easy to spot. They also rent lockers, skateboards, and almost everything else a beachgoer could need. **Skateworld** (✉ 6907 Linda Vista Rd., Linda Vista, ☎ 858/560–9349) has several public sessions daily, in addition to private group sessions for bladers and skaters.

Sailing and Boating

Winds in San Diego are consistent, especially in winter. If you're bringing your boat, there are several marinas that rent slips. Vessels of various sizes and shapes—from small paddleboats to sleek 12-meters and kayaks to Hobie Cats—can be rented from specialized vendors. Additionally, most bay-side resorts rent equipment for on-the-water adventures. Most are not intended for the open ocean, which is wise for the inexperienced. The **Bahia Resort Hotel** (✉ 998 W. Mission Bay Dr., Mission Bay, ☎ 858/539–7696) and its sister location, the **Catamaran Resort Hotel** (✉ 3999 Mission Blvd., Mission Beach, ☎ 858/488–2582) will rent paddleboats, kayaks, Waverunners, and sailboats from 14 ft to 22 ft. The Bahia also rents out a ski boat. The Bahia dock is closed winter, but Catamaran stays open year-round. **Harbor Sailboats** (✉ 2040 Harbor Island Dr., Suite 104, Harbor Island, ☎ 619/291–9568) rents sailboats from 22 ft to 46 ft long for open-ocean adventures. **Coronado Boat Rentals** (✉ 1715 Strand Way, Coronado, ☎ 619/437–1514) has kayaks, jet skis, fishing skiffs, and power boats from 15 ft to 19 ft in length as well as sailboats from 18 ft to 36 ft. They also can hook you up with a skipper. The **Mission Bay Sports Center**

(⌧ 1010 Santa Clara Pl., Mission Bay, ☎ 858/488–1004) rents kayaks, catamarans, single-hull sailboats, and power boats. **Seaforth Boat Rentals** (⌧ 1641 Quivira Rd., Mission Bay, ☎ 619/223–1681) not only rents jet skis, paddleboats, sailboats, and skiffs. **Carlsbad Paddle Sports** (⌧ 2780 Carlsbad Blvd., Carlsbad, ☎ 760/434–8686) handles kayak sales, rentals, and instruction for coastal North County.

Sailboat and powerboat charters and cruises can be arranged through the **Charter Connection** (⌧ 1715 Strand Way, Coronado, ☎ 619/437–8877). Contact **Fraser Charters** (⌧ 2353 Shelter Island Dr., Shelter Island, ☎ 800/228–6779) for yachting excursions. **Hornblower Dining Yachts** (⌧ 2825 5th Ave., Embarcadero, ☎ 619/686–8700) operates sunset cocktail and dining cruises. **San Diego Harbor Excursion** (⌧ 1050 N. Harbor Dr., Embarcadero, ☎ 619/234–4111) has one- and two-hour narrated harbor tours, as well as dinner cruises and a ferry to Coronado. **Classic Sailing Adventures** (⌧ 2051 Shelter Island Dr., Shelter Island, ☎ 619/224–0800) will take you on their 38-ft sailboat for champagne sunset cruises in summer, or daytime whale-watching in winter. For information, including tips on overnight anchoring, contact the **Port of San Diego Mooring Office** (☎ 619/686–6227). For additional information contact the **San Diego Harbor Police** at ☎ 619/686–6272.

Skateboard Parks

Skateboarding culture has always thrived in San Diego, and recent changes in liability laws have encouraged a jump in the number of skateparks. A good number of top pro skateboarders live in San Diego and often practice and perfect new moves at local skateparks. Pads and helmets (always a good idea anywhere) are required at all parks.

The **Carlsbad Skate Park** (⌧ 2560 Orion Way, Carlsbad, ☎ 760/434–2824) offers 15,000 square ft of concrete bowls and ledges and a pyramid and rails. It's also the only skating venue that doesn't charge a fee. **Escondido Sports Center** (⌧ 333 Bear Valley Pkwy., Escondido, ☎ 760/738–5425) has a miniramp, street course, and vertical ramp. **Magdalena Ecke YMCA** (⌧ 200 Saxony Rd., Encinitas, ☎ 760/942–9622) is very popular among the many pros in this beach town. It has a bowl, street course, miniramp, and a classic vertical ramp. **Ocean Beach Skatepark** (⌧ 2525 Bacon St., Ocean Beach, ☎ 619/525–8486) is the largest park in the city. It has a huge street plaza, bowls, ledges, grind rails, and quarterpipes.

Surfing

If you're a beginner, consider paddling in the waves off Mission Beach, Pacific Beach, Tourmaline, La Jolla Shores, Del Mar, or Oceanside. More experienced surfers usually head for Sunset Cliffs, the La Jolla reef breaks, Black's Beach, or Swami's in Encinitas. **Kahuna Bob's Surf School** (☎ 760/721–7700) conducts two-hour lessons in coastal North County seven days a week. **San Diego Surfing Academy** (☎ 858/565–6892) has surf camps and lessons in Cardiff-by-the-Sea. **Surf Diva Surf School** (⌧ 2160-A Avenida de la Playa, La Jolla, ☎ 858/454–8273) offers clinics, surf camps, surf trips, and private lessons especially formulated for women. Clinics and trips are for women only, but guys can book private lessons from the nationally recognized staff. All necessary equipment is included in the cost of all surfing schools.

Many local surf shops rent both surf and bodyboards. **Mission Beach Club** (⌧ 704 Ventura Pl., Mission Beach, ☎ 858/488–5050) is right on the boardwalk, just steps from the waves. **Star Surfing Company**

(⊠ 4652 Mission Beach, Pacific Beach, ☎ 858/273–7827) can get you out surfing around the Crystal Pier. **La Jolla Surf Systems** (⊠ 2132 Avenida de la Playa, La Jolla, ☎ 858/456–2777) takes care of your needs if you want to surf the reefs or beachbreaks of La Jolla. **Hansen's** (⊠ 1105 S. Coast Hwy. 101, Encinitas, ☎ 760/753–6595) is just a short walk from Swami's beach.

Swimming

The best pool in town is Belmont Park's 58-yard-long **Plunge** (⊠ 3115 Ocean Front Walk, Mission Beach, ☎ 858/488–3110) right next to the Belmont Park roller coaster. The **Copley Family YMCA** (⊠ 3901 Landis St., North Park, ☎ 619/283–2251) has a pool on the eastern edge of the city. The pools at the **Downtown YMCA** (⊠ 500 W. Broadway Ave., Suite B, ☎ 619/232–7451) are close to the Gaslamp Quarter and Balboa Park. The **Magdalena Ecke YMCA** (⊠ 200 Saxony Rd., Encinitas, ☎ 760/942–9622) is convenient for swimming in North County.

Tennis

Most of the more than 1,300 courts around the county are in private clubs, but a few are public. The **Balboa Tennis Club at Morley Field** (☎ 619/295–9278) has 25 courts, 19 of which are lighted. Courts are available on a first-come, first-serve basis for a $5-per-person fee. Heaviest usage is 9 AM–11 AM and after 5 PM; at other times you can usually arrive and begin playing. The **La Jolla Tennis Club** (⊠ 7632 Draper Ave., La Jolla, ☎ 858/454–4434) has nine free public courts near downtown La Jolla; five are lighted. The 12 lighted courts at the privately owned **Peninsula Tennis Club** (⊠ Robb Field, Ocean Beach, ☎ 619/226–3407) are available to the public for a $4 per person day-use fee.

Several San Diego resorts have top-notch tennis programs staffed by big-name professional instructors. **Rancho Bernardo Inn** (⊠ 17550 Bernardo Oaks Dr., Rancho Bernardo, ☎ 858/675–8500) has 12 tennis courts and packages that include instruction, accommodations, and meals. **Rancho Valencia Resort** (⊠ 5921 Valencia Circle, Rancho Santa Fe, ☎ 858/756–1123), which is among the top tennis resorts in the nation, has 18 hard courts and several instruction programs. **La Costa Resort and Spa** (⊠ Costa Del Mar Rd., Carlsbad, ☎ 760/438–9111), where the annual Acura Tennis Classic is held, has 21 courts including two Wimbledon-quality grass courts and two clay courts, professional instruction, clinics, and workouts.

Volleyball

Ocean Beach, South Mission Beach, Del Mar Beach, Moonlight Beach, and the western edge of Balboa Park are major congregating points for volleyball enthusiasts. Contact the **San Diego Volleyball Club** (☎ 858/486–6885) to find out about organized games and tournaments.

Waterskiing

Mission Bay is one of the most popular waterskiing areas in southern California. It's best to get out early, when the water is smooth and the crowds are thin. Boats and equipment can be rented from **Seaforth Boat Rentals** (⊠ 1641 Quivira Rd., Mission Bay, ☎ 619/223–1681). The private **San Diego and Mission Bay Boat and Ski Club** (⊠ 2606 N. Mission Bay Dr., ☎ 858/270–0840) operates a slalom course and ski jump in Mission Bay's Hidden Anchorage. Permission from the **Mission Bay Harbor Patrol** (☎ 619/221–8985) is required.

Windsurfing

Also known as sailboarding, windsurfing is a sport best practiced on smooth waters, such as Mission Bay or the Snug Harbor Marina at the intersection of I–5 and Tamarack Avenue in Carlsbad. Sailboarding rentals and instruction are available at the **Bahia Resort Hotel** (⊠ 998 W. Mission Bay Dr., Mission Bay, ☎ 858/488–0551). The **Catamaran Resort Hotel** (⊠ 3999 Mission Blvd., Mission Beach, ☎ 858/488–1081) is a sister location of the Bahia Resort Hotel and offers the same services. **Mission Bay Sports Center** (⊠ 1010 Santa Clara Pl., Mission Bay, ☎ 858/488–1004) is well equipped to handle your windsurfing equipment needs. Head to **Windsport** (⊠ 844 W. Mission Bay Dr., Mission Bay, ☎ 858/488–4642) if you're looking to see Mission Bay from a sailboard. The **Snug Harbor Marina** (⊠ 4215 Harrison St., Carlsbad, ☎ 760/434–3089) has rentals and instruction and can advise those looking to windsurf on Agua Hedionda lagoon. More experienced windsurfers will enjoy taking a board out on the ocean. Wave jumping is especially popular at the Tourmaline Surfing Park in La Jolla and in the Del Mar area.

SPECTATOR SPORTS

Cox Arena (⊠ College Ave. exit off I–8; San Diego State University, ☎ 619/594–6947) is home to the university's men's and women's basketball teams. The San Diego Padres and San Diego Chargers play at **Qualcomm Stadium** (⊠ 9449 Friars Rd., I–15 at I–8, Mission Valley, ☎ 619/525–8282), also known as the "Q." To get to the **San Diego Sports Arena** (⊠ 3500 Sports Arena Blvd., ☎ 619/224–4171), home of the San Diego Gulls hockey team, take the Rosecrans exit off I–5 and turn right onto Sports Arena Boulevard. The **ARCO Olympic Training Center** at Otay Lake (⊠ 1750 Wueste Rd., Chula Vista, ☎ 619/656–1500) has free tours of soccer, tennis, track and field, and other Olympic training facilities daily 9 to 5.

Baseball

The **San Diego Padres** (☎ 619/280–4636) has a strong fan base, which is largely why city voters passed a bill to build the team a new stadium, due to open April 2004. The team slugs it out for bragging rights in the National League West from April into October. Games with such rivals as the Los Angeles Dodgers and the San Francisco Giants are often the highlights of the home season at Qualcomm Stadium. Tickets are usually available on game day.

Basketball

The **San Diego State University Aztecs** (☎ 619/283–7378) compete in the Western Athletic Conference with such powers as the University of Utah and Brigham Young University. The Aztecs play December–March at Cox Arena on the San Diego State University campus.

The **University of San Diego Toreros** (☎ 619/260–4803 or 619/260–4600) take on West Coast Conference opponents Pepperdine University, the University of San Francisco, the University of California at Santa Barbara, and other teams. Games are played in the state-of-the-art **Jenny Craig Pavilion** (⊠ 5998 Alcalá Park, Linda Vista, ☎ 619/260–4803 or 619/260–4600).

Football

The **San Diego Chargers** (☎ 619/280–2121) of the National Football League fill Qualcomm Stadium from August through December. Games with AFC West rivals the Oakland Raiders and Denver Broncos are particularly intense.

The **San Diego State University Aztecs** compete in the Western Athletic Conference and attract the most loyal fans in town, with attendance rivaling and sometimes surpassing that of the NFL Chargers. The biggest game of the year is always a showdown with Brigham Young University. The WAC champion plays in the **Holiday Bowl** (☎ 619/283–5808), around the end of December in Qualcomm Stadium. The Aztecs also play their home games at Qualcomm.

Golf

The **Buick Invitational** brings the pros to the Torrey Pines Municipal Golf Course in mid-February (☎ 858/452–3226). The **Accenture World Match Play Championship** is held at the La Costa resort in February (☎ 760/438–9111).

Horse Racing

The annual summer meeting of the **Del Mar Thoroughbred Club** (☎ 858/755–1141) on the Del Mar Fairgrounds attracts the best horses and jockeys in the country. Racing begins in July and continues through early September, every day except Tuesday. You can also bet on races at tracks throughout California, shown on **TV via satellite** (☎ 858/755–1167). Take I–5 north to the Via de la Valle exit.

Ice Hockey

The three-time Taylor Cup champion **San Diego Gulls** (☎ 619/224–4625) of the minor-league West Coast Hockey League take to the ice from late October through March at the San Diego Sports Arena.

Over-the-Line

As much a giant beach party as a sport, this game is a form of beach softball played with three-person teams. Every July the world championships are held on Fiesta Island, with two weekends of wild beer drinking and partying. Some good athletes take part in the games, too. Admission is free, but parking is impossible and traffic around Mission Bay can become unbearable. Call the **Old Mission Beach Athletic Club** (☎ 619/688–0817) for more information.

7 SHOPPING

San Diego's shopping areas are a mélange of self-contained megamalls, historic districts, homey villages, funky neighborhoods, and chic suburbs. In addition to stores, restaurants, and amusements, Horton Plaza, for instance, has live theater. At Seaport Village you can ride in a horse-drawn carriage or on an 1890 carousel. In the beach towns, cruising the shops provides a break from the surf and sun.

Updated by
Lenore Greiner

S **HOPPING IN SAN DIEGO** ranges from the hip stores of Hillcrest to the world-class boutiques of La Jolla's Prospect Street and Girard Avenue to the trendy Gaslamp Quarter and the quaint village of Coronado. If you poke around some of the smaller neighborhoods—Del Mar, Solana Beach's Cedros Design District, Carlsbad's upscale outlet mall, and Julian—you may turn up some real finds.

Local malls and shopping areas are outdoors; they're pleasant places to stroll and enjoy the area's legendary sunny weather. Some, like Horton Plaza downtown, are visual feasts. Most major malls, however, offer merchandise you can find nearly anywhere. For San Diego–related memorabilia, browse the gift shops at major attractions like the zoo, Wild Animal Park, and Bazaar del Mundo in Old Town. You can also pick up a real-live San Diego keepsake at the flower nurseries around Carlsbad and Encinitas, and along inland farm trails.

Most establishments are open daily 10–6; department stores and shops within the larger malls stay open until 9 on weekdays. Sales are advertised in the *San Diego Union-Tribune* and in the *Reader*, a free weekly that comes out on Thursday. Also, check out the Web sites www.signonsandiego.com and www.sandiegoinsider.com for more details on local shops and sales.

Coronado

Shopping Center

With a staggering view of San Diego's downtown skyline across the bay, the **Ferry Landing Marketplace** (⊠ 1201 1st St., at B Ave., Coronado) is a delightful place to stroll and shop while waiting for a ferry. It has 30 boutiques and shops plus a Tuesday-afternoon **Farmers Market** where you can pick up fresh local fruits and vegetables.

Specialty Stores

Friendly shopkeepers make **Orange Avenue,** Coronado's main drag, a good place to browse. Both sides are lined with classy boutiques.

ANTIQUES

The Attic (⊠ 1011 Orange Ave., Coronado, ☎ 619/435–5432) specializes in Victoriana, quilts, linens, and white-painted furnishings.

BOOKS

Bay Books (⊠ 1029 Orange Ave., Coronado, ☎ 619/435–0070) feels like an old-fashioned bookstore. It has a large selection of foreign-language magazines and newspapers and a section in the back is devoted to children's books and games. There are plenty of secluded reading nooks and a sidewalk reading area with coffee bar.

GOURMET FOODS

In Good Taste (⊠ 1146 Orange Ave., Coronado, ☎ 619/435–8356) serves up smooth-as-silk chocolates and fudge, specialty cheeses, wine, truffles, and fresh bread.

HOME ACCESSORIES AND GIFTS

Forget-Me-Not (⊠ 1009-A Orange Ave., Coronado, ☎ 619/435–4331) is a relatively tacky gift shop where you might find a few surprises, including lots of reasonably priced glass baubles and miniature figures by Eickholt, Glass Eye Studio, and Goebel.

Hotel Del Coronado (⊠ 1500 Orange Ave., Coronado, ☎ 619/435–6611) is the peninsula's main historic attraction, and at its gift shop you can purchase everything from sweatshirts to Christmas ornaments.

Island Provenance (⊠ 1053 B Ave., Coronado, ☎ 619/435–8232) offers sophisticated bedding, crystal, porcelains, and home accessories.

La Provencale (⊠ 1122 Orange Ave., Coronado, ☎ 619/437–8881) carries a line of remarkable French-made acrylic trays and salad bowls filled with dried herbs and flowers by Amalgam. The shop has lots of imported linens, tableware, fashion accessories, and paintings, all in sunny colors.

WOMEN'S AND MEN'S APPAREL
Club Paris Boutique (⊠ 1154 Orange Ave., Coronado, ☎ 619/435–0514) carries trendy women's sportswear.

Dale's Swim Shop (⊠ 1150 Orange Ave., Coronado, ☎ 619/435–7301) is crammed with swim suits, hats, sunglasses, and sunscreen.

Kippys (⊠ 1114 Orange Ave., Coronado, ☎ 619/435–6218) is where the horse and rodeo sets find fine leather shirts, chaps, skirts, belts, and bags, most trimmed with gold and silver spangles and beads.

Pollack's Men's Shop (⊠ 1162 Orange Ave., Coronado, ☎ 619/435–3203) specializes in fine men's sportswear including a line of colorful Hawaiian shirts by Ryne Spooner and many sweaters.

Downtown

Shopping Centers
Westfield Shoppingtown Horton Plaza (Gaslamp Quarter, ☎ 619/238–1596), bordered by Broadway, 1st Avenue, G Street, and 4th Avenue, is within walking distance of most downtown hotels. An open-air visual delight, the multilevel shopping, dining, and entertainment complex has a lively terra-cotta color scheme and flag-draped facades. There are department stores, including Macy's, Nordstrom, and Mervyn's, fast-food counters, upscale restaurants, the Lyceum Theater, cinemas, and 140 other stores. Park in the plaza garage and any store where you make a purchase will validate your parking ticket, good for three free hours. The **San Diego City Store** (☎ 619/238–2489) sells city artifacts and memorabilia, such as street signs and parking meters, that make unusual souvenirs. Or pick up a yellow SURFING OK sign and other San Diego-inspired items.

Northwest of the San Diego Convention Center, **Seaport Village** (⊠ W. Harbor Dr. at Kettner Blvd., Embarcadero, ☎ 619/235–4014) is a waterfront complex of 75 shops and restaurants within walking distance of hotels (it also has a parking lot). Aside from the shops, there are horse and carriage rides, an 1890 Looff carousel, and usually some form of public entertainment.

Gaslamp Quarter

The historic heart of San Diego, the Gaslamp Quarter is alive with Victorian buildings and renovated warehouses along 4th and 5th avenues. Here you'll find art galleries, antiques, and specialty stores. Shops in this area tend to close early at various times, starting as early as 5.

Specialty Stores
ANTIQUES
Olde Cracker Factory (⊠ 448 W. Market, Gaslamp Quarter, ☎ 619/233–1669), historic home of the Bishop Cracker Factory, now houses a collection of antique shops. **Bobbie's Paper Dolls** (☎ 619/233–0055) displays Victorian paper goods. **Bert's Antiques** (☎ 619/239–5531) specializes in military memorabilia.

San Diego Hardware (✉ 840 5th Ave., Gaslamp Quarter, ☎ 619/232–7123) has been in the Gaslamp since the 1880s and may have that piece of reproduction Victorian hardware you've been seeking.

Unicorn Company Arts & Antiques Mall (✉ 704 J St., Gaslamp Quarter, ☎ 619/232–1696) is the largest antiques complex in San Diego, with 60 dealers purveying toys, jewelry, tools, and other items.

Four Winds Kiva Gallery (✉ 647 G St., Gaslamp Quarter, ☎ 619/702–3214) has quality Native American arts and crafts, textiles, basketry, jewelry, pottery, and fine art.

Opium Gallery (✉ 425 Market St., Gaslamp Quarter, ☎ 619/234–2070) sells furniture and accessories from the world over.

Many Hands Crafts Gallery (✉ 302 Island Ave., Gaslamp Quarter, ☎ 619/557–8303) is a cooperative crafts gallery showcasing the work of local artists in pottery, glass, wood, photography, fibers, and basketry.

Jacques Lelong (✉ 635 5th Ave., Gaslamp Quarter, ☎ 619/234–2583), housed in the 1882 Yuma Building, offers unique women's fashions.

Le Travel Store (✉ 745 4th Ave., Gaslamp Quarter, ☎ 619/544–0005) stocks luggage, totes, books, maps, and travel accessories.

Splash Wearable Art (✉ 376 5th Ave., Gaslamp Quarter, ☎ 619/233–5251) creates unique women's clothing from Balinese fabrics and has a fine collection of hand-beaded evening wear, all reasonably priced.

Western Hat Works (✉ 868 5th Ave., Gaslamp Quarter, ☎ 619/234–0457) has been selling every kind of hat from fedora to Stetson on this corner since 1922.

Hillcrest, North Park, Uptown

Although their boundaries blur, each of these three established neighborhoods north and northeast of downtown contains a distinct urban village with shops, many ethnic restaurants and cafés, and entertainment venues. Most of the activity is on University Avenue and Washington Street, and along the side streets connecting the two.

Gay-popular and funky **Hillcrest,** north of Balboa Park, has many gift, book, and music stores. Retro rules in **North Park.** Nostalgia shops along Park Boulevard and University Avenue at 30th Street carry clothing, accessories, furnishings, wigs, and bric-a-brac of the 1920s–1960s. The **Uptown District,** an open-air shopping center on University Avenue, includes several furniture, gift, and specialty stores.

Specialty Stores
Obelisk (✉ 1029 University Ave., Hillcrest, ☎ 619/297–4171) stocks a bounty of gay and lesbian literature, cards, and gifts.

Auntie Helen's (✉ 4028 30th St., North Park, ☎ 619/584–8438), a nonprofit thrift emporium, sells heirlooms, collectibles, seasonal items, furniture, and brand-name clothing. Proceeds provide medical equipment, clothing, and laundry service to people with AIDS.

Babette Schwartz (✉ 421 University Ave., Hillcrest, ☎ 619/220–7048) is not to be missed. This zany pop-culture store sells toys, books, T-shirts, and magnets.

Cathedral (✉ 435 University Ave., Hillcrest, ☎ 619/296–4046), voted the "Best Place to Smell" in a local poll, is worth a stop for a sniff. Specializing in candles and home and bath goods, here you'll find exotic gifts like cocoa-hazelnut spice candles, coriander-lavender bath foams, and Asian pear–and–ginger body scrubs.

Circa a.d. (✉ 3867 4th Ave., Hillcrest, ☎ 619/293–3328) carries an eclectic collection of gifts and home decor items from Asia and Europe such as kimono, Thai spirit houses, Russian icons, and Indonesian puppets.

Hillcrest Hardware (✉ 1007 University Ave., Hillcrest, ☎ 619/291–5988) offers a collection of hard-to-find, expensive holiday decorative accessories.

Metropolis (✉ 1003 University Ave., Hillcrest, ☎ 619/220–0632) specializes in reproduction Arts and Crafts items, antiques, and decorative accessories.

P. B. Home & Garden (✉ 3795 4th Ave., Hillcrest, ☎ 619/295–4851) is a good resource for Mexican pottery and folk art—perfect if you don't make it south of the border.

Pomegranate Home Collection (✉ 1037 University Ave., Hillcrest, ☎ 619/220–0225)—housed in one of Hillcrest's oldest buildings—has gifts, cards, and home accessories along with contemporary furnishings.

GOURMET FOOD

Henry's Marketplace (✉ 4175 Park Blvd., North Park, ☎ 619/291–8287) is a San Diego original for fresh produce, bulk grains, nuts, snacks, dried fruits, and health foods.

Original Paw Pleasers (✉ 1220 Cleveland Ave., Hillcrest, ☎ 619/670–7297) is a bakery for dogs and cats, where you'll find Oatmeal Dogolate Chip Cookies, carob brownies, and Itty Bitty Kitty Treats.

Trader Joe's (✉ 1090 University Ave., Hillcrest, ☎ 619/296–3122) stocks an affordable and eclectic selection of gourmet foods and wines from around the world.

La Jolla

This seaside village has chic boutiques, art galleries, and gift shops lining narrow twisty streets, often celebrity soaked. Parking is cramped in the village and store hours vary widely, so it's wise to call in advance. On the east side of I–5, office buildings surround Westfield Shoppingtown UTC, where you'll find department stores and familiar chain stores.

Shopping Center
Westfield Shoppingtown UTC (✉ La Jolla Village Dr., between I–5 and I–805, La Jolla, ☎ 858/546–8858), a handy outdoor mall east of La Jolla village, has 155 shops, a cinema, and 25 eateries, plus an ice-skating rink. Department stores include Nordstrom, Robinsons-May, Macy's, and Sears Roebuck.

Specialty Stores
A loose collection of buildings housing galleries and boutiques, the **Green Dragon Colony** (✉ Prospect St., near Ivanhoe St. La Jolla) is La Jolla's historic shopping area. It dates back to 1895, when the first structure was built by Anna Held, who was governess for Ulysses S. Grant Jr. The Coast Walk Plaza also has shops.

BOOKSTORE

Warwick's (✉ 7812 Girard Ave., La Jolla ☎ 858/454–0347) an upscale bookstore and La Jolla fixture since 1896, often hosts big-name author signings.

CHILDREN'S CLOTHING AND GIFTS

Gap Kids (✉ 7835 Girard Ave., La Jolla, ☎ 858/454–2052) is probably the best bet for children's togs.

The **White Rabbit** (✉ 7755 Girard Ave., La Jolla, ☎ 858/454–3518) carries children's books and dolls, and holds regular book signings.

FINE ART AND CRAFTS

Africa and Beyond (✉ 1250 Prospect St., La Jolla, ☎ 858/454–9983) carries Shona stone sculpture, textiles, crafts, masks, and jewelry.

Fingerhut Gallery (✉ 1205 Prospect St., La Jolla, ☎ 858/456–9900) displays an intriguing collection of contemporary paintings and sculpture by Jiang, Peter Max, and Dr. Seuss alongside etchings and lithographs by Picasso, Chagall, and Lautrec.

Mark Reuben Gallery (✉ 1298 Prospect St., La Jolla, ☎ 858/459–8914) hangs photos of celebrities and sports figures.

Prospect Place Fine Art (✉ 1268 Prospect St., La Jolla, ☎ 858/459–1978) displays etchings and lithographs by 19th- and 20th-century masters including Miró, Matisse, Rufino Tamayo, and Chagall.

Wyland Galleries (✉ 1025 Prospect St., Ste. 100, La Jolla, ☎ 858/459–8229) showcases bronzes, original paintings, and limited-edition work by California artist Wyland, famous for his murals depicting whales and other marine life. The mural on the ceiling is by the maestro himself.

HOME ACCESSORIES AND GIFTS

Bo Danica (✉ 7722 Girard Ave., La Jolla, ☎ 858/454–6107) stocks a tantalizing collection of contemporary tabletops, Lynn Chase jungle-motif china, Orrefors crystal, and handmade decorator items.

Everett Stunz (✉ 7624 Girard Ave., La Jolla, ☎ 800/883–3305) has the finest in luxury home linens, robes, and sleepwear in cashmere, silk, or Swiss cotton.

Lamano Gifts (✉ 1298 Prospect St., La Jolla, ☎ 858/454–7732) sells delightful papier-mâché and ceramic Carnival masks made in Venice.

JEWELRY

Fogel's Antique Beads (✉ 1128 Wall St., La Jolla, ☎ 858/456–2696) has European precious beads from the 1920s, including dazzling Austrian and Czech crystal beads; restringing is done here.

Philippe Charroil Boutique (✉ 1227 Prospect St., La Jolla, ☎ 858/551–4933), U.S. flagship store for this line of Swiss-made jewelry, glitters with Celtic jewels fashioned into necklaces and bracelets.

Pomegranate (✉ 1152 Prospect St., La Jolla, ☎ 858/459–0629) offers antique and estate jewelry plus fashions by Eileen Fisher and Harari.

ANTIQUES

Glorious Antiques (✉ 7643 Girard Ave., La Jolla, ☎ 858/459–2222) has a truly glorious selection of antiques, fine china, silver, crystal, and fine art. All profits benefit the San Diego Humane Society.

WOMEN'S AND MEN'S CLOTHING

Ascot Shop (✉ 7750 Girard Ave., La Jolla, ☎ 858/454–4222) has classy men's sportswear including fashions by Kenneth Gordon and Talbott, plus a colorful collection of Hawaiian shirts.

Carlisle & Co. (✉ 1237 Prospect St., La Jolla, ☎ 858/454–5466) shows appealing French and Italian lingerie by Lise Charmel, Valery, and Bolero.

Gentleman's Quarter (✉ 1200 Prospect St., La Jolla, ☎ 858/459–3351) specializes in European-designed suits and sportswear by Armani, Canali, and Zegna.

La Jolla Surf Systems (✉ 2132 Avenida de la Playa, La Jolla, ☎ 858/456–2777), near La Jolla Shores beach, sells swimsuits, beach and resort wear, surfboards, and boogie boards.

Rangoni of Florence (✉ 7646 Girard Ave., La Jolla, ☎ 858/459–4469) has a selection of fine Italian footwear for men and women.

Sigi Boutique (✉ 7888 Girard Ave., La Jolla, ☎ 858/454–7244) sells Italian sportswear and accessories for women.

Mission Valley/Hotel Circle Area

The Mission Valley/Hotel Circle area, northeast of downtown near I–8 and Route 163, has two major shopping centers, plus a number of smaller shopping centers that cater to residents in the surrounding areas.

Shopping Centers
Fashion Valley Center (✉ 7007 Friars Rd., Mission Valley), with lush landscaping, a contemporary Mission theme, and over 200 shops and restaurants, is San Diego's upscale shopping mall. There's a San Diego Trolley station in the parking lot, a shuttles that goes to and from major hotels, and Spanish-speaking sales associates in every store. The major department stores are Macy's, Nordstrom, Saks Fifth Avenue, Neiman Marcus, and Robinsons-May.

Park Valley Center (✉ 1750 Camino de la Reina, Mission Valley), across the street from Westfield Shoppingtown Mission Valley, is a U-shape strip mall, anchored by **OFF 5th** (☎ 619/296–4896), which offers last-season's fashions by Ralph Lauren, Armani, and Burberry once seen in Saks Fifth Avenue but at Costco prices.

Westfield Shoppingtown Mission Valley (✉ 1640 Camino del Rio N, Mission Valley), is San Diego's largest outdoor shopping mall. The colorful mall appeals to bargain hunters with discount stores carrying merchandise that might be found in the mall up the road at higher prices. Shops include Montgomery Ward; Macy's Home Store; Loehmann's; Bed, Bath and Beyond; Nordstrom Rack; Charlotte Russe; and Fredericks of Hollywood.

Ocean Beach, Mission Beach, Pacific Beach

Among the T-shirt shops, yogurt stands, and eateries that line the coast within San Diego proper are a few stores worthy of a browse. **Pilar's Beach Wear** (✉ 3745 Mission Blvd., Ocean Beach, ☎ 858/488–3056) has one of California's largest selections of major-label swimsuits. **Mallory's OB Attic** (✉ 4921 Newport Ave., Ocean Beach, ☎ 619/223–5048) sells collectibles and antique and used furniture. **Trader Joe's** (✉ 1211 Garnet Ave., Pacific Beach, ☎ 858/272–7235) proffers gourmet food, including wine, cheese, and dried fruits and nuts.

Great News (✉ 1789 Garnet Ave., Pacific Beach, ☎ 858/270–1582) stocks discount kitchen tools and gadgets to make a cook drool, even mandolines and chinois. There's a cooking school in the back, a very complete selection of cookbooks, and excellent customer service.

Old Town

North of downtown, off I–5, the colorful Old Town historic district recalls a Mexican marketplace. Adobe architecture, flower-filled plazas, fountains, and courtyards decorate the shopping areas of Bazaar del

Mundo and Old Town Esplanade, where you'll find international goods, toys, souvenirs, and arts and crafts.

Shopping Centers

Bazaar del Mundo (⊠ 2754 Calhoun St., Old Town, ☎ 619/296–3161) is a colorful shopping complex with boutiques selling designer items, crafts, fine arts, and fashions from around the world. The best time to visit is during the annual Santa Fe Market in March, when you can browse collections of jewelry, replica artifacts, wearable-art clothing and accessories, pottery, and blankets—all crafted by Southwestern artists. **Ariana** (☎ 619/296–4989) carries ethnic and artsy fashions. **The Guatemala Shop** (☎ 619/296–3161) specializes in clothing, fabrics, and decorator items from Central America. **Earth, Wind and Sea** (☎ 619/294–2028) sells decorative fountains, ceramics, wind chimes, and cacti.

Not far from Old Town is the home of San Diego's premier flea market. Bargain shoppers spend their weekend mornings at **Kobey's Swap Meet** (⊠ San Diego Sports Arena parking lot, 3500 Sports Arena Blvd., Sports Arena, ☎ 619/226–0650). The open-air event seems to expand every week, with sellers displaying everything from futons to fresh strawberries. The back section, with secondhand goods, is a bargain-hunter's delight. The swap meet is open Friday–Sunday 7–3; admission is 50¢ on Friday and $1 on weekends; parking is free.

Specialty Shops

GIFT SHOPS

Apache Indian Arts Center (⊠ 2425 San Diego Ave., Old Town, ☎ 619/296–9226) has a selection of Southwestern Indian jewelry, paintings, sculpture, and Pueblo baskets.

Maidhof Bros. (⊠ 1891 San Diego Ave., Old Town, ☎ 619/574–1891) is one of California's oldest and largest dealers in nautical and brass items.

Ye Olde Soap Shoppe (⊠ 2497 San Diego Ave., Old Town, ☎ 619/543–1300) carries a full line of soap-making supplies including kits, herbs, and vegetable bases.

FINE ARTS AND CRAFTS

Gallery Old Town (⊠ 2513 San Diego Ave., Old Town, ☎ 619/296–7877) showcases a rare collection of photojournalism by Alfred Eisenstaedt, Margaret Bourke-White, and Gordon Parks in an historic building on one of San Diego's oldest streets.

Studio Gallery of Old Town (⊠ 2501 San Diego Ave., Old Town, ☎ 619/294–9880) displays an extensive collection of Chuck Jones animation art.

8 SIDE TRIPS

San Diego County sprawls from the Pacific Ocean to suburban communities that seem to sprout overnight on canyons and cliffs. The Cleveland National Forest and Anza-Borrego Desert State Park mark the county's eastern boundaries; the busiest international border in the United States is its southern line. To the north, the U.S. Marines practice land, sea, and air maneuvers at Camp Pendleton, southern California's largest coastal greenbelt and the demarcation zone between congested Orange and Los Angeles counties and San Diego.

S AN DIEGO PROPER HAS MORE OPEN SPACE than most cities its
size, but even its residents like to retreat occasionally to the less-
congested (although rapidly growing) North County and Anza-
Borrego Desert. North County attractions continue to multiply: major
stops include the San Diego Wild Animal Park, the mountain town of
Julian, Legoland California, and miles of lovely shoreline.

By Lenore
Greiner

Pleasures and Pastimes

Beaches

San Diego North County's classic California coastline is popular with
locals, many of whom stake out their favorite sunning, surfing, body-
boarding, and walking territories at the easily accessible beaches of Del
Mar, Solana Beach, Encinitas, Carlsbad, or Oceanside.

Desert Adventures

Anza-Borrego Desert State Park encompasses more than 600,000 acres,
most of it wilderness. Springtime, when the wildflowers are in full bloom,
is a good season to visit. In sandstone canyons you can walk in the
footsteps of prehistoric camels, zebras, and giant ground sloths.

Dining

People in downtown San Diego don't think twice about driving north
for dinner, as prominent chefs oversee chic restaurants in wealthy
communities such as Del Mar, Carlsbad, Encinitas, Rancho Santa Fe,
and Rancho Bernardo. By contrast, casual dining is the rule in the beach
towns, inland mountain towns, and desert communities.

CATEGORY	COST*
$$$$	over $24
$$$	$17–$24
$$	$10–$17
$	under $10

per person for a main course at dinner, excluding 7.75% sales tax

Flowers

The North County is a prolific flower-growing region. Nurseries, some
open to the public, line the hillsides on both sides of I–5 in Encinitas,
Leucadia, and Carlsbad. In winter most of the poinsettias sold in the
United States get their start here. Quail Botanical Gardens in Encinitas displays native and exotic plants year-round. The gardens at the
San Diego Wild Animal Park attract nearly as many people as do the
animals.

Lodging

If you stay overnight in the North County, your choices are diverse,
from stylish hotels providing courtly, traditional service to basic motels catering to the beach crowd. Tennis and golf resorts and health-
oriented spas abound, and some fine bed-and-breakfast inns are tucked
into wooded hillsides around Julian.

CATEGORY	COST*
$$$$	over $200
$$$	$140–$200
$$	$80–$140
$	under $80

All prices are for a standard double room, excluding 9%–13% tax.

THE SAN DIEGO NORTH COAST
From Del Mar to Oceanside

To say the north coast of San Diego County is different from the city of San Diego is an understatement. From the northern tip of La Jolla to Oceanside a half dozen small communities developed separately from urban San Diego—and from one another. The rich and famous were drawn to Del Mar, for example, because of its wide beaches and Thoroughbred horse-racing complex. Up the road, agriculture, not glitterati, played a major role in the development of Solana Beach and Encinitas. Carlsbad, now reinventing itself as home of Legoland California and the Four Seasons Resort Aviara, still reveals its ties to the old Mexican rancheros and the entrepreneurial instinct of John Frazier, who promoted the area's water as a cure for common ailments. In the late 19th century, a few miles from the site of the posh La Costa Resort and Spa, Frazier attempted to turn the area into a massive replica of a German mineral-springs resort.

An explosion of development begun in the 1980s continues today, intensifying the north coast's suburbanization. Once-lovely hillsides have been bulldozed and leveled to make room for bedroom communities in Oceanside, Carlsbad, and even in such high-priced areas as Rancho Santa Fe and La Jolla.

Route S21 connects the beach towns going north: Del Mar, Solana Beach, Cardiff-by-the-Sea, Encinitas, Leucadia, Carlsbad, and Oceanside; though the road is known by a different name in each different town. (Signs say South or North Coast Highway 101 in Solana Beach and Oceanside. In Del Mar it's called Camino del Mar, and in Carlsbad, Carlsbad Blvd.) Whatever the alias, it's an awesome drive up the coast past fragile bluffs, rare Torrey pines, and ever-present surfers bobbing in the blue waters.

Numbers in the margin correspond to points of interest on the San Diego North County map.

Del Mar

23 mi north of downtown San Diego on I–5, 9 mi north of La Jolla on Rte. S21.

Del Mar is best known for its racetrack, chic shopping strip, celebrity visitors, and wide beaches. Along with its collection of shops, **Del Mar Plaza** also contains outstanding restaurants and landscaped plazas and gardens with Pacific views.

Access to Del Mar's beaches is from the streets that run east–west off Coast Boulevard. Summer evening concerts take place at the west end of **Seagrove Park** (⊠ 15th St., Del Mar), a small stretch of grass overlooking the ocean.

➊ The **Del Mar Fairgrounds** host the **Del Mar Thoroughbred Club** (⊠ 2260 Jimmy Durante Blvd., Del Mar, ☎ 858/755–1141, WEB www.dmtc. com). Crooner Bing Crosby and his Hollywood buddies—Pat O'Brien, Gary Cooper, and Oliver Hardy, among others—organized the club in the 1930s, primarily because Crosby wanted to have a track near his Rancho Santa Fe home. Del Mar soon developed into a regular train stop for the stars of stage and screen. Even now the racing season here (usually July–September, Wednesday–Monday, post time 2 PM) is one of the most fashionable in California. During the off-season, horse

146

San Diego North County

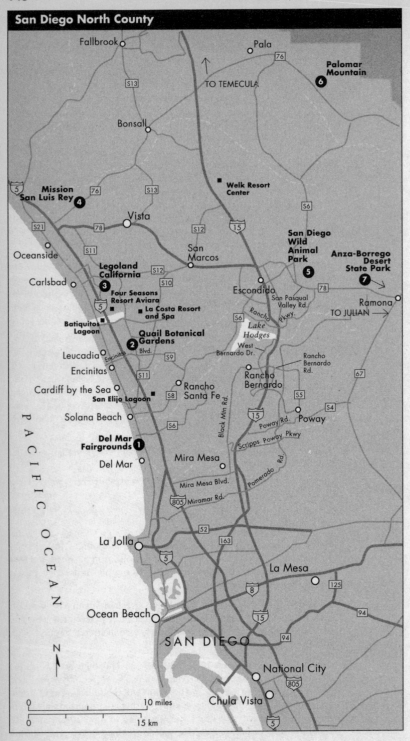

Fallbrook

Pala

76

Palomar
Mountain

S13

↑
TO TEMECULA

6

Bonsall

Mission
San Luis Rey

Welk Resort
Center

5

76

S13

S6

4

Vista

S21

78

S12

15

San Diego
Wild
Animal
Park

Anza-Borrego
Desert
State Park

Oceanside

S11

San
Marcos

Carlsbad

Legoland
California

S12

S10

5

7

Escondido

78

Ramona

3

Four Seasons
Resort Aviara

La Costa Resort
and Spa

San Pasqual
Valley Rd.

TO JULIAN →

Batiquitos
Lagoon

Quail Botanical
Gardens

Rancho

Lake
Hodges

Rancho
Bernardo
Rd.

Leucadia

2

Blvd.

S9

West
Bernardo Dr.

67

Encinitas

S11

Rancho
Santa Fe

Rancho
Bernardo

55

Cardiff by the Sea

S8

S4

San Elijo Lagoon

Poway Rd.

Poway

Solana Beach

S6

15

Del Mar
Fairgrounds

1

Scripps Poway Pkwy

Del Mar

Mira Mesa

Mira Mesa Blvd.

805

Miramar Rd.

52

163

La Jolla

5

La Mesa

125

8

Ocean Beach

15

SAN DIEGO

94

94

National City

805

Chula Vista

5

P A C I F I C   O C E A N

N

0   10 miles

0   15 km

players can bet on races at other California tracks televised via satellite at the Surfside Race Place. Times vary, depending on which tracks in the state are operating. Del Mar Fairgrounds hosts more than 100 different events each year, including the San Diego County Fair and a number of horse shows. ⊠ *Head west at I–5's Via de la Valle Rd. exit,* ☎ *858/793–5555.*

☺ **Freeflight,** a small exotic-bird training aviary adjacent to the Del Mar Fairgrounds, is open to the public. You are allowed to handle the birds—a guaranteed child pleaser. ⊠ *2132 Jimmy Durante Blvd., Del Mar,* ☎ *858/481–3148.* ☞ *$1.* ☉ *Daily 10–4.*

Dining and Lodging

$$$–$$$$ ✕ **Pacifica Del Mar.** This lovely restaurant overlooks the sea from the plush precincts of Del Mar Plaza. Highly innovative, the restaurant frequently rewrites the menu to show off such show-stoppers as a tower of layered ahi sashimi and Dungeness crab, a house-smoked salmon terrine flavored with a dash of caviar, and a dry-aged New York steak served with a Gorgonzola-potato tart. The crowd ranges from young hipsters at the bar to well-dressed businesspeople on the terrace, where glass screens block any hint of a chilly breeze. ⊠ *Del Mar Plaza, 1515 Camino del Mar, Del Mar,* ☎ *858/792–0476. AE, D, MC, V.*

$$$–$$$$ ✕ **Ruth's Chris Steak House.** In a spacious, handsomely decorated structure with a vast outdoor sculpture installation and a narrow view of the Pacific, this first North County outpost of the upscale chain serves over-size portions on red-hot metal plates. You might open with lobster bisque, a shrimp cocktail, or a fancy salad. Devotees come here for the steaks, however, which range in size from a petite fillet to a huge "cowboy" rib eye. Maine lobsters start at 2½ pounds. Although devouring dessert may seem improbable after consuming such mass quantities, keep in mind the chocolate-chunk bread pudding. ⊠ *11582 El Camino Real, Del Mar,* ☎ *858/755–1454. AE, D, DC, MC, V. No lunch.*

$$–$$$$ ✕ **Scalini.** A favorite of horse fans from the nearby Del Mar racetrack, Scalini overlooks the playing fields of the region's most exclusive polo club from the second floor of a small office building. The elegant eatery presents an oyster bar Thursday through Saturday evenings. There is pizza for those who must; otherwise, the menu concentrates on elegant pastas, such as the linguine frutti di mare, and on entrées like sautéed prawns in lobster cream sauce and pistachio-crusted lamb chops in port sauce. ⊠ *3790 Via de la Valle, Del Mar,* ☎ *858/259–9944. AE, DC, MC, V.*

$$$ ✕ **J. Taylor's.** Jacob Taylor built the first hotel in Del Mar early in the 20th century, and nearly a century later his legacy was immortalized in the form of this thoroughly revitalized dining room at posh L'Auberge Del Mar Resort and Spa. Elegant but relaxed, the room lacks the seaside view that some find de rigueur, but it does offer some of the best cooking in town. Breakfast and lunch are excellent, but the dinner menu truly takes off with such appetizers as a "steak" of fresh foie gras with blackberry sauce, followed by entrées like roasted Sonoma duck breast with sour-cherry glaze and herb-crusted pork tenderloin with toasted almond sauce. The old-fashioned butterscotch pudding is topped by a cloud of whipped cream flavored with Myer's rum. ⊠ *1540 Camino del Mar, Del Mar,* ☎ *858/720–6197. AE, D, DC, MC, V.*

$$–$$$ ✕ **Epazote.** The menu changes seasonally at this casual-chic eatery. Young but competent servers present the innovative, Southwestern-style dishes, which range from vegetable tamales with goat cheese to turkey–and–wild mushroom enchiladas or sesame-honey–seared ahi. Desserts, like the creamy, traditional caramel custard, help to cut the spice effects of the main dishes. The hand-shaken margaritas are on the expensive side but superb. There's an ocean view from the patio, which gets busy on weekend nights and during Sunday brunch. In winter, many sit outdoors where glass screens bar the breezes and heaters bring a semblance of summer. ⊠ *Del Mar Plaza, 1555 Camino del Mar, Suite 322, Del Mar,* ☎ *858/259–9966. AE, MC, V.*

$$–$$$ ✕ **Fish Market.** There's no ocean view at the North County branch of downtown's splashy restaurant, but this eatery remains popular with residents and tourists alike for its simple preparations of very fresh fish and shellfish. The scene is lively, crowded, and noisy. Singles flock here, but it's also a great place to bring the kids. ⊠ *640 Via De La Valle, Del Mar,* ☎ *858/755–2277. AE, D, DC, MC, V.*

$$–$$$ ✕ **Le Bambou.** Small, carefully decorated, and more elegant than any Vietnamese restaurant in San Diego proper, Le Bambou snuggles into the corner of a neighborhood shopping center and is easy to overlook. Those in the know, however, seek it out for authoritative versions of such classics as ground shrimp grilled on sugar cane; Imperial rolls generously stuffed with shrimp, noodles, and bamboo shoots; and cooked-at-the-table beef dishes. ⊠ *2634 Del Mar Heights Rd., Del Mar,* ☎ *858/259–8138. MC, V. Closed Mon.*

$–$$$ ✕ **Barone's Trattoria del Mare.** In sophisticated Del Mar, everyone knows that a *trattoria del mare* means an Italian seafood restaurant with an outdoor terrace, a fitting description for this small, lively establishment on the southern rim of town. Barone's specializes in good service and a sizable menu of sizable dishes; you are expected to be hungry, and you will be after reading the listings for crab-stuffed mushrooms, linguine with assorted shellfish, grilled swordfish, and grilled beef fillet. ⊠ *2234 Carmel Valley Rd., Unit A, Del Mar,* ☎ *858/259–9063. MC, V. No lunch Sun.*

$–$$$ ✕ **Blumberg's Delicatessen.** San Diegans are known to complain about the scarcity of decent, East Coast–type delicatessens. Well, this comfortable, no-frills establishment fits the bill. Blumberg's even cures its own corned beef on the premises. The vast menu extends to all the deli classics, including blintzes, chopped liver, smoked fish platters, skyscraping sandwiches, and baked beef brisket with potato pancakes. Some regulars cast their ballots repeatedly for the Miami-style baked short ribs. As a plus—this is Del Mar, after all—the restaurant offers dining on a pleasant outdoor terrace. ⊠ *2638 Del Mar Heights Rd., Del Mar,* ☎ *858/259–4880. MC, V.*

$–$$$ ✕ **Jake's Del Mar.** This enormously popular oceanfront restaurant has a close-up view of the water and a menu of simple but well-prepared fare that ranges from an appetizer of mussels steamed in aromatic saffron broth to a dressy halibut sandwich, crab-crowned swordfish Del Mar, and mustard-crusted lamb rack with port-flavored garlic sauce. A menu note reminds that the legendary, ice-cream stuffed hula pie is "what the sailors swam ashore for in Lahaina." If you arrive without a reservation, be prepared to wait. ⊠ *1660 Coast Blvd., Del Mar,* ☎ *858/755–2002. AE, DC, MC, V.*

$–$$$ ✕ **Villa Capri.** This suave, reasonably priced Italian bistro serves out-of-the-ordinary fare, with appetizers like sautéed prawns in a cognac-enriched grain-mustard sauce and thinly sliced smoked duck breast dressed with truffle oil and shavings of Parmesan cheese. The pasta list shines with such offerings as rigatoni with sausage ragu, artichoke hearts, and mozzarella. Among the entrées, consider the grilled chicken with rosemary-garlic sauce or the sea bass in a pungent tomato sauce flavored with capers and olives. ⊠ *3870 Valley Center Dr., Del Mar,* ☎ *858/720–8777. AE, D, MC, V. No lunch weekends.*

$–$$ ✕ **Milton's Delicatessen Grill Bakery.** There's a bunkerlike quality to this cavernous, semi-underground, Flower Hill Mall restaurant. It was built so that sunlight cascades down the walls, which are decorated with vintage magazine covers. Milton's offers belly-busting portions of traditional deli fare. The vast menu lists some 50 sandwiches, from a simple egg salad on rye to a pork chop sandwich with grilled onions. For breakfast, you might sample the *hoppel poppel,* an egg scramble of salami, peppers, onions, and potatoes. ✉ *2660 Via De La Valle, Del Mar,* ☎ *858/792–2225. AE, DC, MC, V.*

$–$$ ✕ **Taste of Thai.** Near the racetrack, this offshoot of the popular Hillcrest café is a crowd-pleaser. Flashing lights in the ceiling and other artistic tricks delight young and old as they await plates of crispy mee krob noodles, minced beef salad flavored with mint and chilies, and batter-fried calamari with sweet chili sauce. After these substantial snacks, diners get down to business with carefully prepared Thai curries, noodle dishes, and such house specialties as crisp-skinned duck in garlic sauce and grilled freshwater prawns in mild curry sauce. The mood is quite informal and the service low-key and pleasant. ✉ *15770 San Andreas Rd. (at the east end of the Flower Hill Mall), Del Mar,* ☎ *858/ 793–9695. AE, MC, V.*

$$$$ 🏨 **L'Auberge Del Mar Resort and Spa.** Although it looks rather like an upscale condominium complex, L'Auberge is modeled on the Tudor-style hotel that once stood here, a playground for the early Hollywood elite. Today's inn has a relaxed elegance, fitting for the repeat guests like Demi Moore, Jane Seymour, and Bruce Willis. The beach is a three-minute walk downhill, and the outdoor Pacific Terrace provides a glimpse of the ocean horizon between pine trees. Rooms are done in pink and green pastels and have marble bathrooms. Most rooms have balconies and gas fireplaces. Across the street are boutiques and restaurants at Del Mar Plaza. ✉ *1540 Camino del Mar, Del Mar 92014,* ☎ *858/259–1515 or 800/553–1336,* FAX *858/755–4940,* WEB *www.laubergedelmar.com. 112 rooms, 8 suites. Restaurant, bar, in-room data ports, cable TV with movies, 2 pools, outdoor hot tub, massage, spa, 2 tennis courts, gym, meeting room. AE, D, DC, MC, V.*

$$$–$$$$ 🏨 **Best Western Stratford Inn of Del Mar.** During racing season this equestrian-theme inn hosts horse owners and jockeys. Ample rooms, many with ocean views or kitchenettes, are surrounded by six lushly landscaped acres. There's a French day spa on the property, Spa Marisol de Menicucci. Room rates include Continental breakfast. ✉ *710 Camino del Mar, Del Mar 92014,* ☎ *858/755–1501 or 888/478– 7829,* FAX *858/755–4704,* WEB *www.bestwestern.com. 60 rooms, 33 suites. In-room data ports, some kitchenettes, cable TV with movies, 2 pools, outdoor hot tub, spa, concierge, laundry service, meeting room, business services. AE, D, DC, MC, V.*

Shopping

The tiered, Mediterranean-style **Del Mar Plaza** (✉ 15th St. and Camino Del Mar, Del Mar, ☎ 858/792–1555) has flower-filled courtyards, fountains, a spectacular view of the Pacific, and some fine restaurants. For women's fashions, **Black Market** (☎ 858/794–0355) stocks clothing mainly in basic black, and the **White House** (☎ 858/794–4038) sells stylish apparel mainly in white. **Silver Goose West Gifts** (☎ 858/755– 4810) specializes in jewelry, gifts, and collectibles.

Thinker Things (✉ 2670 Via de la Valle, Del Mar, ☎ 858/755–4488) carries children's dolls, puppets, crafts, and games.

Solana Beach

1 mi north of Del Mar on Rte. S21, 25 mi north of downtown San Diego on I–5 to Lomas Santa Fe Dr. west.

Once-quiet Solana Beach is quickly developing a reputation as *the* place to look for antiques, collectibles, and contemporary fashions and artwork. The Cedros Design District, occupying a long block near the Amtrak station, contains shops, galleries, designers' studios, and restaurants.

Dining

$$$–$$$$ ✕ **Red Tracton's.** Across the street from the Del Mar racetrack, this deluxe steak and seafood house is a high-roller's heaven. Everyone from the bar pianist to the exceptional waitresses is well aware that smiles and prompt service can result in tips as generously sized as the gigantic Australian lobster tails that the menu demurely lists at "market price." Tracton's serves simple but very good food, and the menu highlights roasted prime rib in addition to prime New York sirloin and filet mignon, top-grade pork back ribs, panfried scallops, and such starters as lobster bisque and a truly "jumbo" shrimp cocktail. ⊠ *550 Via de la Valle, Solana Beach,* ☎ *858/755–6600. AE, D, MC, V.*

$$$ ✕ **Pamplemousse Grille.** Justly celebrated as one of North County's
★ best restaurants, the "Grapefruit Grill," across the street from the racetrack, offers French country dining California style. Chef/proprietor Jeffrey Strauss brings a caterer's sensibilities to the details, like a mix-or-match selection of sauces to complement the simple but absolutely top-quality grilled meats and seafood. Appetizers can be very clever, like the huge, see-through wild mushroom ravioli. The comfortable rooms are painted with murals of bucolic country scenes, and the service is quiet and professional. ⊠ *514 Via de la Valle, Solana Beach,* ☎ *858/792–9090. AE, D, DC, MC, V. No lunch Sat.–Tues.*

$ ✕ **Don Chuy.** Small, family-run, unassuming, and utterly charming, Don Chuy offers authentic Mexican cuisine to a southern California audience that, before dining here, may have tasted only a pale version of the real thing. The flavors are savory and convincing, and the portions sufficient to banish hunger until the following day. For something straight from the soul of Mexican home cooking, try the *nopales con chorizo y huevos,* a scramble of tender cactus leaves, crumbled spicy sausage, and eggs; this is served with piles of rice and beans as well as a warm tortilla and the palate-warming house salsa. ⊠ *650 Valley Ave., Solana Beach,* ☎ *858/794–0535. Reservations not accepted. MC, V.*

Shopping

The **Cedros Design District** (WEB www.cedrosdesigndistrict.com) is a collection of 50 shops that specialize in interior design and gifts.

Antique Warehouse (⊠ 212 S. Cedros Ave., Solana Beach, ☎ 858/755–5156) offers American and European antiquities, art, books, glass, dolls, and jewelry. David Turner, owner of **Elements Furniture and Gifts** (⊠ 118 S. Cedros Ave., Solana Beach, ☎ 858/792–7773), who designed furnishings for TV's *Ellen* and *Seinfeld,* sells copies of the chairs, sofas, and accessories you see on those and other shows. **Trios Gallery** (⊠ 130 S. Cedros Ave., Solana Beach, ☎ 858/793–6040) showcases the work of local artists, glass art from the Pacific Northwest, and designer jewelry.

Rancho Santa Fe

4 mi east of Solana Beach on Rte. S8 (Lomas Santa Fe Dr.), 29 mi north of downtown San Diego on I–5 to Rte. S8 east.

Groves of huge, drooping eucalyptus trees cover the hills and valleys of exclusive Rancho Santa Fe. East of I–5 on Via de la Valle Road, Rancho Santa Fe is horse country. It's common to see entire families riding the many trails that crisscross the hillsides.

Lillian Rice, one of the first women to graduate with a degree in architecture from the University of California, designed the town, modeling it after villages in Spain. Her first structure, a 12-room house built in 1922, evolved into the Inn at Rancho Santa Fe, which became a gathering spot for celebrities such as Bette Davis, Errol Flynn, and Bing Crosby. The challenging Rancho Santa Fe Golf Course, the original site of the Bing Crosby Pro-Am and considered one of the best courses in southern California, is open only to members of the Rancho Santa Fe community and guests of the inn.

Dining and Lodging

$$$$ ✕ **Mille Fleurs.** Mille Fleurs has a winning combination, from its lo-
★ cation in the heart of wealthy, horsey Rancho Santa Fe to the warm Gallic welcome extended by proprietor Bertrand Hug, and the talents of chef Martin Woesle. The quiet dining rooms are decorated like a French-Moroccan villa. Menus are written daily to reflect the market and Woesle's mood, but sometimes feature a soup of *musque de Provence* (pumpkin with cinnamon croutons), sautéed *lotte* (monkfish) with okra and curry sauce, stuffed quail with peaches, and oven-roasted baby lamb with summer vegetable ratatouille. Jacket and tie are suggested, but not required. ⊠ *Country Squire Courtyard, 6009 Paseo Delicias, Rancho Santa Fe,* ☎ *858/756–3085. Reservations essential. AE, D, MC, V. No lunch weekends.*

$$$$ ✕🏠 **Rancho Valencia Resort.** One of southern California's hidden trea-
★ sures has luxurious accommodations in Spanish-style casitas scattered on 40 acres of landscaped grounds. Suites have corner fireplaces, luxurious Berber carpeting, and shuttered French doors leading to private patios. Rancho Valencia is one of the top tennis resorts in the nation and is adjacent to three well-designed golf courses. The inn's first-rate restaurant has a seasonal menu that might include a foie gras Napoleon; pasilla-chile crab cakes; farm-raised abalone steaks with a miso shiro butter sauce; and prime rib-eye steak in a Calvados-scented brown sauce. ⊠ *5921 Valencia Cir., Rancho Santa Fe 92067,* ☎ *858/756–1123 or 800/548–3664,* 𝖥𝖠𝖷 *858/756–0165,* 𝖶𝖤𝖡 *www.ranchovalencia.com. 43 suites. Restaurant, room service, bar, minibars, cable TV with movies, 2 pools, health club, 3 outdoor hot tubs, spa, 18 tennis courts, croquet, hiking, bicycles. AE, DC, MC, V.*

$$$–$$$$ 🏠 **Morgan Run Resort & Club.** This business-oriented golf resort resembles a Kentucky horse ranch with its clapboard exterior and nicely appointed rooms, and it attracts many conferences and meetings. Fairly large rooms have fireplaces, wet bars, and patios or balconies with lovely views of the golf course or garden. The golf course is private, open only to hotel guests and members of the country club. ⊠ *5690 Cancha de Golf, Rancho Santa Fe 92091,* ☎ *858/756–2471 or 800/378–4653,* 𝖥𝖠𝖷 *858/756–3013,* 𝖶𝖤𝖡 *www.morganrun.com. 82 rooms, 7 suites. Restaurant, bar, refrigerators, cable TV with movies, pool, outdoor hot tub, 27-hole golf course, 11 tennis courts, health club, pro shop, business services, meeting room. AE, MC, V.*

$$–$$$ 🏠 **Inn at Rancho Santa Fe.** Understated elegance is the theme of this genteel old resort in the heart of the village. This is the sort of place where people don their "whites" and play croquet on the lawn Sunday afternoons. Most accommodations are in red-tile-roof cottages scattered about the property's 20 acres. Some cottages have two bedrooms, private patios, fireplaces, and hot tubs. The inn also maintains a beach house at Del Mar for guest use and has membership at the exclusive Rancho Santa Fe Golf Club. You also can have access to five other nearby, and very exclusive, courses. ⊠ *5951 Linea del Cielo, Rancho Santa Fe 92067,* ☎ *858/756–1131 or 800/843–4661,* 𝖥𝖠𝖷 *858/759–1604,* 𝖶𝖤𝖡 *www.theinnatranchosantafe.com. 73 rooms, 19 suites. Bar, dining room, room service, cable TV with movies, pool, 18-hole golf course, 3 tennis courts, croquet, gym, library, meeting room. AE, DC, MC, V.*

BOUNTIFUL BEAUTY

SOUTHERN CALIFORNIA'S famous warm, sunny climate has blessed this corner of the continent with an ever-changing, year-round palette of natural color. It's hard to find a spot anywhere around the globe that produces as spectacular a scene as spring in San Diego—from the native plant gardens found tucked away in mountain canyons and streambeds to the carpets of wildflowers on the desert floor. You'll have to see it yourself to believe just how alive the deceptively barren desert really is.

Spring debuts in late February or early March. Heavy winter rains always precede the best bloom seasons. And good blooms also bring even more beauty—a bounty of butterflies. But here in this generally temperate climate, the bloom season lasts nearly all year.

Visit the Cuyamaca and Laguna mountains for a brilliant display of rare western redbud trees erupting into a profusion of crimson flowers, sometimes starting as early as February. Native California lilacs (ceanothus) blanket the hillsides with fragrant blue and white blossoms starting in May and showing until August.

Native varieties of familiar names show up in the mountain canyons and streambeds. A beautiful white western azalea would star in anyone's garden. A pink California rose blooms along streambeds in spring and summer. Throughout the year three varieties of native dogwood show off white blooms and beautiful crimson fall foliage. The Cuyamaca Mountains usually put on a display of fall color as the native oaks, aspen, cottonwood, and dogwood turn gold and red. By winter the rare toyon, known as the California Christmas tree, shows off its red berries alongside the roads and trails. Rewarding walks in Cuyamaca include the Azalea Glen trail and the Harvey Moore Trail.

You can get a good introduction to mountain wildflowers by visiting Julian in early May, when the Women's Club puts on its annual Wildflower Show. For more than seven decades members have collected and displayed native plants and flowers from hillsides, meadows, and streambeds surrounding the mountain town. For information on exact dates call the Julian Chamber of Commerce (☎ 760/765–1857).

Farther east in the Anza-Borrego Desert State Park, the spring wildflower display can be spectacular: carpets of pink, purple, white, and yellow verbena and desert primrose as far as the eye can see. Rocky slopes yield clumps of beavertail cactus topped with showy pink blossoms, clumps of yellow brittlebush tucked among the rocks, and crimson-tip ocotillo trees. For a good introduction to desert vegetation, explore the visitor center garden, adjacent to the park's underground headquarters.

San Diego County is a leading flower supplier to the nation, with dozens of nurseries turning out poinsettias, ranunculuses, bromeliads, orchids, begonias, and other subtropical plants. Many can be seen and visited in the western part of the county. In the spring, tour the brilliant acres of ranunculus blooms at the Flower Fields at Carlsbad Ranch (✉ Palomar Airport Rd., east of I–5, ☎ 760/431–0352, www.theflowerfields.com).

For a vivid view of both the mountain and desert spring flora, take Interstate 8 east to Route 79, go north to Julian, and then east on Route 78 into Anza-Borrego park.

For more information about desert wildflowers, send a self-addressed, stamped envelope to: Wildflowers, Anza-Borrego Desert State Park, Box 299, Borrego Springs, CA 92004-0299. You can also call the Wildflower Hotline (☎ 760/767–4684) and the Thomas Payne Foundation (☎ 818/768–3533) for details about what to expect in a particular year.

Shopping

Tony boutiques here cater to the ultrawealthy. However, a couple of shops are worthy of note, even if you don't have a fat wallet. **Country Friends** (✉ 6030 El Tordo, Rancho Santa Fe, ☎ 858/756–1192) is a great place for unusual gifts. Operated by a nonprofit foundation, it carries collectibles, silver, and antiques donated or consigned by the community's residents. **Chino's Vegetable Shop** (✉ 6123 Calzada del Bosque, Rancho Santa Fe, ☎ 858/756–3184) at Chino's farm grows premium (and very expensive) fruits and rare baby vegetables for many of San Diego's upscale restaurants, as well as for famed California eateries such as Chez Panisse in Berkeley and Spago in Los Angeles.

Encinitas

6 mi north of Solana Beach on Rte. S21, 7 mi west of Rancho Santa Fe on Rte. S9, 28 mi north of downtown San Diego on I–5.

Flower breeding and growing has been the major industry in Encinitas since 1922; the town now calls itself the Flower Capital of the World due to the large number of nurseries operating here. The city, which encompasses the coastal towns of Cardiff-by-the-Sea and Leucadia as well as inland Olivenhain, is home to Paul Ecke Poinsettias, the largest producer and breeder (open only to the trade) of the Christmas blossom. During the spring blooming season some commercial nurseries east of I–5 are open to the public. The palms and the golden domes of the Self-Realization Fellowship Retreat and Hermitage mark the southern entrance to downtown Encinitas.

U.S. 101 (now Route S21) was the main route connecting all the beach towns between southern Orange County and San Diego before the I–5 freeway, to the east of Encinitas, was constructed. Local civic efforts are bringing back the California–U.S. 101 signs on Route S21 and restoring the boulevard's historic character.

The **San Elijo Lagoon Ecological Reserve,** between Solana Beach and Encinitas, is the most complex of the estuary systems in San Diego North County. A network of trails surrounds the area, where more than 300 species of plants and many fish and migrating birds live. Docents offer free public walks here; call for dates and times. ✉ *From Rte. S21, head east at Chesterfield Dr., cross the train tracks, and head south at San Elijo Ave., which becomes Manchester Ave. Lagoon entrance is ⁹⁄₁₀ mi from Rte. S21 and Chesterfield; Box 230634, Encinitas 92023,* ☎ *760/436–3944,* WEB *www.sanelijo.org.* ☞ *Free.* ☉ *Daily sunrise–sunset.*

The **Self-Realization Fellowship Retreat and Hermitage** was founded in 1936 as a retreat and place of worship by Paramahansa Yogananda. There are two beautiful meditation gardens that have sweeping views of the Pacific and are open to the public. The gardens are planted with flowering plants and trees, and contain a series of ponds connected by miniature waterfalls populated by tropical fish. Wandering through this peaceful place, you may come across a wedding taking place over the Pacific. ✉ *215 K St., Encinitas,* ☎ *760/753–2888,* WEB *www. yogananda-srf.org.* ☞ *Free.* ☉ *Tues.–Sun. 9–5.*

❷ **Quail Botanical Gardens** displays more than 3,000 rare and exotic plants on 30 landscaped acres. There are 15 collections. Individual displays include Central American, Himalayan, Australian, and African tropical gardens; the largest collection of bamboo in North America; California native plants; an old-fashioned demonstration garden; and subtropical fruit. ✉ *230 Quail Gardens Dr., Encinitas,* ☎ *760/436–3036,* WEB *www.qbgardens.com.* ☞ *$5.* ☉ *Daily 9–5.*

Dining and Lodging

$$$-$$$$ ✕ **La Bonne Bouffe.** A longtime North County favorite, this restaurant offers expertly prepared classic French fare, including a delicious beef bourguignonne, roast duckling in green peppercorn sauce, Dover sole, and frogs' legs. With lace curtains, white tablecloths, and bistro chairs, you can pretend you're dining in France. ✉ *471 Encinitas Blvd., Encinitas,* ☎ *760/436–3081. Reservations essential. AE, D, DC, MC, V. Closed Sun.–Mon. No lunch.*

$$-$$$ ✕ **Vigilucci's Pizzeria.** Combining the breezy openness of a beach café with the interior of a traditional Italian trattoria-pizzeria, this casual restaurant has a wood-burning oven that turns out thin-crust pizzas, light on the toppings. The menu offers main-course salads, grilled meats, and tasty pastas, too. Try the pasta baked with eggplant. This is a sister restaurant to Vigilucci's Trattoria downtown, but the food here is better and the heated deck has an ocean view. ✉ *1933 San Elijo Ave., Cardiff-by-the-Sea,* ☎ *760/634–2335. AE, D, DC, MC, V.*

$-$$ ✕ **La Especial Norte.** Casual to the point of funkiness, this Mexican café is a great hit with locals who flock here to slurp up large bowls of delicious homemade soups. Try the chicken, beans, and rice, or the Seven Seas fish soup accompanied by tortillas and a dish of cabbage salad. They also make good renditions of the standard burrito, enchilada, and taco, and premium margaritas. ✉ *644 N. U.S. 101, Encinitas,* ☎ *760/942–1040. AE, MC, V.*

$ ✕ **Italian Market.** A gregarious Franco-Italian couple, Jean and Rosanna, run this small, well-stocked Italian market and deli in old Encinitas. Arrive here early for a breakfast of Jean's own pastries and serious cappuccino. At lunch, there are great deli sandwiches on homemade bread (try the prosciutto and provolone on focaccia) and excellent pizzas. There are a few tables inside and several more on the front and back patios. You can buy sandwiches, pizza, bread, and lasagna to go, too, but be sure to arrive before the market closes at 5. ✉ *806 1st St. (U.S. 101), Encinitas,* ☎ *760/942–0738. AE, MC, V. Closed Sun. No dinner.*

$$-$$$ 🏨 **Best Western Encinitas Inn and Suites at Moonlight Beach.** This hotel, tucked into a hillside west of I–5 with ocean or city views from all rooms, offers a great deal. Unusually spacious rooms are well equipped for business travelers. There's an attractive swimming pool area and a popular Japanese restaurant, Tomiko, on site. Continental breakfast is complimentary. ✉ *85 Encinitas Blvd., Encinitas 92024,* ☎ *760/942–7455, FAX 760/632–9481, WEB www.bestwestern.com. 60 rooms, 34 suites. In-room data ports, refrigerators, cable TV with movies, concierge, laundry service, restaurant, bar, pool, outdoor hot tub, meeting room, business services, airport shuttle. AE, D, DC, MC, V.*

$$ 🏨 **Moonlight Beach Motel.** This folksy, laid-back motel is a short walk from the beach. Rooms are basic but spacious and clean. Most have balconies and ocean views. ✉ *233 2nd St., Encinitas 92024,* ☎ *760/753–0623, FAX 760/944–9827. 24 rooms. Kitchenettes, cable TV. AE, D, MC, V.*

$-$$ 🏨 **Ocean Inn.** Across from the train tracks on the main drag through town, this lodging is apt to be somewhat noisy. However, it's just steps from the beach, and a Continental breakfast is included in the price. The simple guest rooms are done in pleasant shades of nautical blue and white. ✉ *1444 N. Coast Hwy. 101, Encinitas 92024,* ☎ *760/436–1988 or 800/546–1598, FAX 760/436–3921, WEB www.oceaninnhotel.com. 50 rooms. Kitchenettes, microwave, cable TV, refrigerator, laundry facilities. AE, D, DC, MC, V.*

Shopping

Souvenir items are sold at shops along U.S. 101 and in the Lumber-yard shopping center. Encinitas also abounds in commercial plant nurseries where you can pick up a bit of San Diego to take home. Look for bulbs, cut flowers, seeds, starter cuttings, unusual small plants, and cactus in nursery gift shops.

Anderson's La Costa Nursery (✉ 400 La Costa Ave., Encinitas, ☎ 760/753–3153) offers rare and hard-to-find orchids, bromeliads, cactus, and succulents. **Bailey's–That Cat Place** (✉ 162 S. Rancho Santa Fe Rd., Encinitas, ☎ 760/944–5783), caters to cat-lovers with feline toys and supplies, and cat-theme human apparel, jewelry, and gifts. **Hansen's** (✉ 1105 S. Coast Hwy. 101, Encinitas, ☎ 760/753–6595, WEB www.hansensurf.com), one of San Diego's oldest surfboard manufacturers, is owned by Don Hansen, surfboard shaper extraordinaire, who came here from Hawai'i in 1962. The store, about a block south of the Lumberyard strip mall, also stocks a full line of recreational clothing and casual wear.

The **Lumberyard Shopping Center** (✉ S. Coast Hwy. 101, Encinitas, ☎ 760/558–5678) contains several specialty shops. **The Third Bird** (✉ 937 S. Coast Hwy. 101, #110, Encinitas, ☎ 760/753–3383) sells jewelry and gift items made of shells. **Heaven on Earth** (✉ 765 S. Coast Hwy. 101, Encinitas, ☎ 760/753–2345) offers a selection of New Age books, tapes, gifts, and candles.

Weideners' Gardens (✉ 695 Normandy Rd., Encinitas, ☎ 760/436–2194) carries begonias, fuchsias, and other flowers. It's closed sporadically in the fall and winter; call for hours.

Carlsbad

6 mi from Encinitas on Rte. S21, 36 mi north of downtown San Diego on I–5.

The millennium marked a turning point for once laid-back Carlsbad, a Bavarian-inspired coastal community that is popular with beachgoers and sun seekers. The 1999 opening of the Legoland California theme park moved much of the visitor appeal inland east of I–5. The park is at the center of a tourist complex that includes resort hotels, a discount shopping mall with a winery, colorful spring-blooming flower fields, and golf courses. During the mid-20th century, farming was the main industry in Carlsbad, with truckloads of avocados, potatoes, and other vegetables shipped out year-round. Today's farmers develop and grow new varieties of flowers including the ranunculus that transform a hillside into a rainbow each spring.

Carlsbad owes its name and Bavarian look to John Frazier, who lured people to the area a century ago with talk of the healing powers of mineral water bubbling from a coastal well. The water was found to have the same properties as water from the German mineral wells of Karlsbad—hence the name of the new community. Remnants from this era, including the original well and a monument to Frazier, are found at the **Alt Karlsbad Haus** (✉ 2802 Carlsbad Blvd., Carlsbad, ☎ 760/434–1887), a stone building that houses a small day spa and the Carlsbad Famous Water Co., a 21st-century version of Frazier's waterworks.

Development has destroyed many of the lagoons and saltwater marsh wildlife habitats that punctuated the North County coastline, but **Batiquitos Lagoon** has been restored to support fish and bird populations. A local group is developing trails to the best viewing spots around the lagoon. This is a quiet spot for contemplation or a picnic. ✉ *Batiquitos Dr. south (east of I–5's Poinsettia La. exit), Carlsbad,* ☎ *760/943–7583,* WEB *www.batiquitosfoundation.org.* ☉ *Tours on weekends and Fridays; call ahead.*

★ ❸ **Legoland California,** the centerpiece of a development that includes resort hotels and a designer discount shopping mall, offers a full day of entertainment for pint-size fun-seekers and their parents. The experience is best appreciated by kids ages 2 to 10, who often beg to ride the mechanical horses around the Royal Joust again and again, or take just one more turn through the popular Driving School. Miniland, an animated collection of cities constructed entirely of Lego blocks, captures the imaginations of both kids and their adult companions. Other attractions include a castle; pint-size Dragon and Spellbound roller coasters; and Aquazone Wave Racers, the first power-ski water ride in North America. Kids can climb on and over, operate, manipulate, and explore displays and attractions constructed out of plastic blocks. Included are a nature maze and power tower with an ocean view; a driving school with miniature cars and boats; a waterworks operated by joysticks; and a junior roller coaster. Stage shows and restaurants with kid-friendly buffets are also part of the mix. ⊠ *1 Lego Dr. (exit I–5 at Cannon Rd. and follow signs east ¼ mi), Carlsbad,* ☎ *760/918–5346,* WEB *www.legolandca.com.* ⊠ *$39; children $33.* ☉ *Mid-Sept.–mid-June, daily 10–5; mid-June–Labor Day, daily 9–9.*

In spring the hillsides are abloom at **Flower Fields at Carlsbad Ranch,** the largest bulb production farm in southern California, where you can walk through fields planted with thousands of ranunculus displayed against a backdrop of the blue Pacific Ocean. In 2001 a rose walk of fame was added, lined with examples of award-winning roses selected during the last half century, and a pair of demonstration gardens created by artists who normally work with paint and easels. The unusually large and well-stocked Armstrong Garden Center at the exit carries plants, garden accessories, and ranunculas bulbs. ⊠ *5704 Paseo del Norte, east of I–5, Carlsbad,* ☎ *760/431–0352,* WEB *www.theflowerfields.com.* ⊠ *$5.* ☉ *Mar.–May, daily 10–6.*

Take an interactive journey through 100 years of popular music at the **Museum of Making Music,** which displays more than 450 vintage instruments and samples of memorable tunes from the past century. Hands-on activities include playing a digital piano, drums, guitar, and electric violin. ⊠ *5790 Armada Dr., east of I–5, Carlsbad,* ☎ *760/438–5996,* WEB *www.museumofmakingmusic.org.* ⊠ *$5.* ☉ *Tues.–Sun. 10–5.*

The **Children's Discovery Museum of North County** provides playful, hands-on experiences that teaches kids about science and the environment. ⊠ *Village Faire Shopping Centre, 300 Carlsbad Village Dr. #103, Carlsbad,* ☎ *760/720–0737,* WEB *www.museumforchildren.org.* ⊠ *$4.* ☉ *May–Sept., daily 10–5; Sept.–May, Tues.–Thurs. and Sun. noon–5, Fri.–Sat. 10–5.*

Dining and Lodging

$$$ ✕ **Bellefleur Restaurant.** At the north end of Carlsbad Company Stores, this restaurant is a popular local gathering spot. Favorite dishes include mussels in broth with herbed rice, spinach ravioli with leek cream and scallops, and veal chops. Also available are single-portion pizzas. The dining room is open for lunch and dinner, but appetizers and small plates are available from mid-afternoon in the Vintner's Bar. ⊠ *5610 Paseo del Norte, Carlsbad,* ☎ *760/603–1919. AE, D, DC, MC, V.*

$$–$$$ ✕ **Vivace.** This stylish dining room in the Four Seasons Aviara Resort serves innovative Italian cuisine. Start with the creamy Maine lobster risotto or smoked tuna and lobster carpaccio. Follow with a pasta selection such as ricotta gnocchi or rigatoni with beef Bolognese, a roasted fish, or meat entrée. The wine list includes selections from Italy and California, some quite reasonably priced. Original paintings mark

the salmon-colored walls. ⊠ *7100 Four Seasons Point, Carlsbad,* ☎ *760/603–3773. AE, D, DC, MC, V. No lunch.*

$–$$$ ✕ **Armenian Cafe.** In a small cottage with an ocean-view deck, this casual family café serves breakfast, lunch, and dinner. The food is Middle Eastern and American, featuring fresh Belgian waffles and egg dishes in the mornings; kebab pita sandwiches, burgers, and salads at lunch; and kebabs, gyros, an acclaimed rack of lamb, and Armenian versions of moussaka and spanakopita at dinner. Garlic lovers should not miss the aromatic house dip. ⊠ *3126 Carlsbad Blvd., Carlsbad,* ☎ *760/720–2233. AE, D, DC, MC, V.*

$$$$ ✕▥ **Four Seasons Resort Aviara.** This hilltop resort sitting on 30 acres
★ overlooking Batiquitos Lagoon is one of the most luxurious in the San Diego area, with gleaming marble corridors, original artwork, crystal chandeliers, and enormous flower arrangements. Rooms, somewhat smaller than those in nearby resorts, have every possible amenity: oversize closets, private balconies or garden patios, and marble bathrooms with double vanities and deep soaking tubs. The spa has private outdoor treatment rooms and a couples treatment room. The Arnold Palmer–designed Aviara Golf Club on the premises is ranked among the top resort golf courses. ⊠ *7100 Four Seasons Point, Carlsbad 92009,* ☎ *760/603–6800 or 800/332–3442,* FAX *760/603–6878,* WEB *www. fourseasons.com/aviara. 287 rooms, 44 suites. 4 restaurants, room service, in-room data ports, in-room safes, minibar, cable TV with movies, 18-hole golf course, 6 tennis courts, 3 pools, health club, hair salon, massage, sauna, spa, steam room, bicycles, hiking, shops, baby-sitting, children's programs, laundry service, concierge, business services, meeting room, airport shuttle, car rental, some pets allowed (fee). AE, D, DC, MC, V.*

$$$$ ✕▥ **La Costa Resort and Spa.** Don't expect glitz and glamour at this famous resort; it's surprisingly low-key, with low-slung buildings and vaguely Southwestern contemporary–style rooms. Rooms are unusually large with opulent marble bathrooms; many have garden patios. The resort also has one of the most comprehensive sports programs in the area. There are two PGA championship golf courses and a golf school, plus a large tennis center. The spa provides nutritional counseling in separate men's and women's facilities; healthy cuisine is available in three restaurants. ⊠ *2100 Costa del Mar Rd., Carlsbad 92009,* ☎ *760/ 438–9111 or 800/854–5000,* FAX *760/931–7569,* WEB *www.lacosta.com. 397 rooms, 82 suites. 2 restaurants, bar, room service, in-room data ports, driving range, 2 18-hole golf courses, 21 tennis courts, pro shop, 5 pools, health club, hair salon, hot tub, massage, sauna, steam room, spa, bicycles, croquet, hiking, shops, babysitting, children's programs (ages 5–12), laundry service, concierge, business services, meeting rooms, airport shuttle, car rental. AE, D, DC, MC, V.*

$$$–$$$$ ▥ **Carlsbad Inn Beach Resort.** Gabled roofs, half-timber walls, and stone supports are among the architectural elements of note at this sprawling inn and time-share condominium complex, steps from the beach. Rooms, which range from large to cramped, are furnished European fashion, with pencil-post beds and wall sconces. Many have ocean views and kitchenettes; some also have fireplaces and hot tubs. With sprawling, landscaped grounds the inn is well-equipped to accommodate families. Kids are included in a number of the resort's scheduled activities. ⊠ *3075 Carlsbad Blvd., Carlsbad 92008,* ☎ *760/434–7020 or 800/235–3939,* FAX *760/729–4853,* WEB *www.carlsbadinn.com. 61 rooms, 1 suite. Some in-room hot tubs, some kitchenettes, cable TV, pool, outdoor hot tub, gym, hair salon, sauna, bicycles, shops, children's programs, playground, laundry facilities, meeting rooms. AE, D, DC, MC, V.*

$$–$$$ 🖵 **Inns of America Suites.** An excellent choice to stay with your family on a trip to Legoland, this all-suite hotel is less than a mile from the park. You can buy tickets at the hotel and catch a free shuttle to the entrance. Despite proximity to I–5, the suites are very quiet; and all are equipped with kitchenettes or full kitchens. A Mexican fountain in the marble lobby and details like granite counters and hand-painted ceramic sinks complete the picture. Breakfast is served in a pleasant, south-of-the-border-style breakfast room. ⊠ *5010 Avenida Encinas, Carlsbad 92008,* ☎ *760/929–8200,* FAX *760/929–8219,* WEB *www.innsofamerica.com. 98 suites. In-room data ports, kitchens or kitchenettes, cable TV with movies and video games, pool, outdoor hot tub, gym, laundry facilities, business services, meeting rooms. AE, D, DC, MC, V.*

Shopping

Carlsbad Company Stores (⊠ 5620 Paseo Del Norte, Carlsbad, ☎ 760/804–9000 or 888/790–7467, WEB www.carlsbadcompanystores.com) is the only upscale designer factory outlet in the San Diego area. Inside are Barneys New York, Donna Karan Company Store, and Polo Ralph Lauren. **Thousand Mile Outdoor Wear** (☎ 760/804–1764) makes the bathing suits used by most lifeguards in southern California and also has a line of outerwear manufactured from recycled soft-drink bottles. **California Luggage Outlet** (☎ 760/931–0600) carries a large selection of discount upscale luggage and travel accessories by Delsey, Samsonite, Hartman, Tumi and Kipling.

Oceanside

8 mi north of Carlsbad on Rte. S21, 37 mi north of downtown San Diego on I–5.

California Welcome Center Oceanside offers complete state travel information, foreign language assistance, and a concierge service inside a mission-style, white-arched building. You can buy discount tickets to many Southern California attractions. ⊠ *928 Coast Hwy., Oceanside 92054,* ☎ *760/721–1101,* WEB *www.gocalif.com.* ☉ *Daily 9–5.*

With 900 slips, **Oceanside Harbor** (☎ 760/435–4000) is North County's center for fishing, sailing, and watersports. **Helgren's Sportfishing** (⊠ 315 Harbor Dr. S, Oceanside, ☎ 760/722–2133) schedules daily ocean fishing trips and whale-watching coastal excursions. South of the Harbor, **Oceanside Pier,** at 1,942 ft, is one of the longest on the West Coast. A restaurant, Ruby's Diner, stands at the end of the wooden pier's long promenade.

California Surf Museum displays a large collection of surfing memorabilia, photos, vintage boards, apparel, and accessories. ⊠ *223 N. Coast Hwy., Oceanside,* ☎ *760/721–6876,* WEB *www.surfmuseum.org.* 🆓 *Free.* ☉ *Daily 10–4.*

Camp Pendleton, encompasses 17 mi of Pacific shoreline as the nation's largest amphibious military training complex. It's not unusual to see herds of tanks and flocks of helicopters maneuvering through the dunes and brush alongside I–5. You may also see herds of sheep keeping the bushland down and fertile fields growing next to the Pacific coastline.

★ ➍ **Mission San Luis Rey** was built by Franciscan friars in 1798 under the direction of Father Fermin Lasuen to help educate and convert local Native Americans. Once a location for filming Disney's *Zorro* TV series, the well-preserved mission is still owned by Franciscan friars. The San Luis Rey was the 18th and largest of California's missions. The *sala* (parlor), a friar's bedroom, a weaving room, the kitchen, and a collection of religious art convey much about early mission life. Retreats are still held here, but a picnic area, a gift shop, and a museum (which has the most extensive collection of old Spanish vestments in the United States) are also on the grounds. Limited inexpensive dormitory-style overnight accommodations are available in the mission's retreat center. From the ocean, go east of I–5 on Route 76 then north on Rancho Del Oro Drive. ⊠ *4050 Mission Ave., Oceanside,* ☎ *760/757–3651,* WEB *www.sanluisrey.org.* ⌨ *$4.* ☉ *Daily 10–4:30.*

Oceanside Museum of Art, housed in the old City Hall, presents changing exhibits of local artwork and exhibitions loaned from major art museums. There's a gift shop and an art school two blocks south at 219 North Coast Highway.⊠ *704 Pier View Way, Oceanside,* ☎ *760/721–2787.* ⌨ *$3.* ☉ *Tues.–Sun. 10–4.*

Dining and Lodging

$$$ ✕ **A Taste of Europe.** French with a German accent is the theme at this comfortable little restaurant where candlelight, white table linens, and attentive service prevail. You can dine on such well-prepared entrées as rack of lamb Provençale, steak *au poivre vert* (with green pepper), or Wiener schnitzel. There's a good wine list featuring Californian and imported vintages. ⊠ *1733 S. Coast Hwy., Oceanside,* ☎ *760/722–7006. AE, D, DC, MC, V. Closed Mon. No lunch.*

$$–$$$$ ⌂ **Oceanside Marina Inn.** Of all the oceanfront lodgings in North County towns, this motel occupies the best location—a spit of land surrounded by water on all sides. All rooms have either ocean or harbor views. The rooms are unusually large and many have fireplaces and expansive balconies. A free boat shuttles you to the beach in summer. Continental breakfast is included. ⊠ *2008 Harbor Dr. N, Oceanside 92054,* ☎ *760/722–1561 or 800/252–2033,* FAX *760/439–9758,* WEB *www.omihotel.com. 64 suites. Kitchens, cable TV, pool, hot tub, sauna, laundry facilities. AE, MC, V.*

$–$$$ ⌂ **Marina Comfort Suites.** Convenient to I–5 and Route 76, this Mediterranean-style, all-suite hotel is close to the marina, the beach, and downtown Oceanside. A morning newspaper and Continental breakfast is included. ⊠ *888 N. Coast Hwy., Oceanside 92054,* ☎ *760/722–1904 or 888/574–7462,* FAX *760/722–1168. 64 suites. Fans, some in-room data ports, in-room hot tubs, microwaves, refrigerators, cable TV with movies, pool, gym, laundry service, laundry facilities, meeting room. AE, D, DC, MC, V.*

$–$$ ⌂ **Best Western Marty's Valley Inn.** This attractive family-owned motel, east of I–5, is a good choice for families. Rooms are ample with contemporary furniture. The hotel's La Mision Mexican restaurant is one of Oceanside's most popular eateries. Continental breakfast included. ⊠ *3240 E. Mission Ave., Oceanside 92054,* ☎ *760/757–7700 or 800/747–3529,* FAX *760/439–3311,* WEB *www.bwmartys.com. 111 rooms. Restaurant, in-room data ports, cable TV with movies, pool, health club, outdoor hot tub, business services, meeting rooms. AE, D, DC, MC, V.*

$ ⌂ **Guesthouse Inn & Suites.** Though close to I–5, rooms are fairly quiet. Those facing the Pacific are right above railroad tracks, so there may be the rumble of an occasional train passing, but the view is worth it. The hotel is close to the marina and convenient to Camp Pendleton. There's an on-site restaurant, The Flying Bridge, and a breakfast room, where a complimentary Continental breakfast is served. ⊠ *1103 N. Coast Hwy., Oceanside 92054,* ☎ *760/722–1904 or 800/914–2230,* FAX *760/722–1168,* WEB *www.guesthouseintl.com. 80 rooms. Restaurant, dining room, cable TV with movies, microwaves, refrigerators, pool. AE, D, DC, MC, V.*

Shopping

Oceanside Photo & Telescope (⊠ 1024 Mission Ave., Oceanside, ☎ 760/722–3348) is the place to pick up a telescope or binoculars to view San Diego County's dazzling night sky; call for information about stargazing parties the store holds regularly.

At **Coronet News Stand** (⊠ 111 S. Coast Hwy., Oceanside, ☎ 760/722–3233) you can pick up your hometown Sunday paper, an Italian fashion magazine, or an Asian financial journal. Popular with locals and Camp Pendleton Marines, Coronet's huge selection of national and international publications will stun you.

Pick up a bit of island flavor in a hand-carved tiki at **Bamboo 2 U** (⊠ 1015 S. Coast Hwy., Oceanside, ☎ 760/754–6996, WEB www.bamboo2u.com) on the Coast Highway. You can't miss it—it's the store with the grass thatched roof and the tikis in front. Inside, you'll find everything to do your home Hawaiian-style: sheets, furniture, dishes, the works. Bamboo opens at 10 AM everyday.

San Diego North Coast A to Z

To research prices, get advice from other travelers, and book travel arrangements, visit www.fodors.com.

AIR TRAVEL

McClellan Palomar Airport is run by the county of San Diego. America West Express and United Express operate flights between here and Los Angeles International Airport.

➤ AIRPORT INFORMATION: **McClellan Palomar Airport** (⊠ 2198 Palomar Airport Rd., Carlsbad, ☎ 760/431–4646).

BUS TRAVEL

The San Diego Transit District covers the city of San Diego up to Del Mar. The North County Transit District covers San Diego County from Del Mar north.

➤ BUS INFORMATION: **San Diego Transit District** (☎ 619/233–3004). The **North County Transit District** (☎ 800/266–6883).

CAR TRAVEL

Interstate 5 is the main freeway artery connecting San Diego to Los Angeles. Running parallel west of I–5 is Route S21, also known and sometime indicated as Highway 101, Old Highway 101, or Coast Highway 101, which never strays too far from the ocean.

TRAIN TRAVEL

Amtrak stops in Solana Beach and Oceanside. The last train leaves San Diego at about 7 each night (9 on Friday; the last arrival is at about midnight). Coaster operates commuter rail service between San Diego and Oceanside.

➤ TRAIN INFORMATION: **Amtrak** (☎ 760/722–4622 in Oceanside; 800/872–7245, WEB www.amtrakcalifornia.com). **Coaster** (Coast Express Regional Rail Service, ☎ 760/722–6283 or 800/262–7837, WEB www.sdcommute.com).

TOURS

Civic Helicopters gives whirlybird tours of the area along the beaches for about $90 per person per half hour. Barnstorming Adventures conducts open-cockpit vintage biplane excursions and military-style Top Dog air combat flights from McClellan Palomar Airport. Tours start at $98 per couple.

➤ Tour Companies: **Civic Helicopters** (✉ 2192 Palomar Airport Rd., Carlsbad, ☎ 760/438–8424). **Barnstorming Adventures** (☎ 760/438–7680 or 800/759–5667, WEB www.barnstorming.com).

VISITOR INFORMATION

➤ Contacts: **Carlsbad Convention and Visitors Bureau** (✉ 400 Carlsbad Village Dr., Carlsbad 92008, ☎ 760/434–6093 or 800/227–5722, WEB www.carlsbadca.org). **Greater Del Mar Chamber of Commerce** (✉ 1104 Camino del Mar, Del Mar 92014, ☎ 858/755–4844, WEB www.delmarchamber.org). **Oceanside Welcome Center** (✉ 928 North Coast Hwy., Oceanside 92054, ☎ 760/722–1534, WEB www.oceansidechamber.com). **San Diego North Convention and Visitors Bureau** (✉ 360 N. Escondido Blvd., Escondido 92025, ☎ 760/745–4741).

INLAND NORTH COUNTY

Rancho Bernardo, Escondido, Fallbrook, and Temecula

Long regarded as San Diego's beautiful backyard, replete with green hills, quiet lakes, and citrus and avocado groves, inland San Diego County is now one of the fastest-growing areas in southern California. Subdivisions, many containing palatial homes, now fill the hills and canyons around Escondido, Rancho Bernardo, and even extend north into Temecula, the wine-making area of southern Riverside County. Growth notwithstanding, the area still has such natural settings as the San Diego Wild Animal Park, Rancho Bernardo, and the Welk Resort Center.

Numbers in the margin correspond to points of interest on the San Diego North County map.

Rancho Bernardo

23 mi northeast of downtown San Diego on I–15.

Rancho Bernardo straddles a stretch of I–15 between San Diego and Escondido. Originally a suburban community where many wealthy retirees settled down, Rancho Bernardo is now home to a number of high-tech companies, the most notable of which is Sony. It is the location of the Rancho Bernardo Inn, one of San Diego's most delightful resorts. The town is also the home base of Ken Blanchard's Golf University of San Diego.

Dining and Lodging

$$$–$$$$ ✕ **Bernard'O.** The seasonal California-European menu consists of classic and innovative interpretations of French favorites such as rack of lamb roasted with pungent herbes de Provence, duck in orange–green peppercorn sauce, and such fresh fish selections as sea bass with a tasty ragout of white beans and balsamic vinegar. There's an enclosed patio, indoor and outdoor fireplaces, and an expanded, elegant dining room. ✉ *Village Shopping Center, 12457 Rancho Bernardo Rd., Rancho Bernardo,* ☎ *858/487–7171. AE, DC, MC, V. No lunch weekends.*

$$$–$$$$ ✕ **El Bizcocho.** Well-heeled locals have long rated this elegant restau-
★ rant at the Rancho Bernardo Inn tops for style and cuisine. The menu offers updated versions of classic entrées such as roasted rack of lamb, grilled chateaubriand carved tableside, medallions of veal with morel mushroom cream sauce, and grilled rib-eye steak with pinot noir sauce. For a little something different, try Maine lobster salad with Spanish red bell pepper mousse, or halibut poached in a lime and sea bean broth. A tasting menu for two includes a five-course dinner designed by chef Patrick Ponsaty, each course paired with an appropriate wine. The wine list has more than 500 selections, including rare vintages. ✉ *Rancho*

Bernardo Inn, 17550 Bernardo Oaks Pkwy., Rancho Bernardo, ☎ 858/675–8500. Jacket required. AE, D, DC, MC, V. No lunch.

$$–$$$$ ✕ **French Market Grill.** The Grill's stylish dark-wood dining room and the twinkling lights will help you forget that you're eating in a shopping center. Pasta and salads give a contemporary Italo-Californian accent to a menu whose dominant note is French. The fare changes with the seasons, but you can always count on expertly prepared fish, chicken, and meat. Lamb is a specialty. The service is cheerful and attentive, and the California and French wines are reasonably priced. ⊠ Ralph's Shopping Center, 15717 Bernardo Heights Pkwy., Rancho Bernardo, ☎ 858/485–8055. AE, DC, MC, V.

$–$$ ✕ **Spices Thai Cafe.** One of the North County's most stylish ethnic restaurants serves beautiful Thai dishes. The traditional pad Thai is a feast of shrimp, bean sprouts, bean curd, and noodles, and the seafood selections and salads are highly recommended. ⊠ 16441 Bernardo Center Dr., Rancho Bernardo, ☎ 858/674–4665. AE, DC, MC, V.

$$$$ 🔲 **Rancho Bernardo Inn.** This gem of a resort is on 265 oak-shaded
★ acres surrounded by a well-established residential community. The two-story, red-roof adobe buildings are complemented by bougainvillea-decked courtyards. Public areas are a collection of small sitting rooms where Spanish mission–style sofas and chairs invite you to linger with a good book. There are fireplaces everywhere, overstuffed furniture, and Oriental rugs on tile floors. Rooms inside are ample, but simply furnished and appointed with early California and Mexican art. ⊠ 17550 Bernardo Oaks Dr., Rancho Bernardo 92128, ☎ 858/675–8500 or 877/517–9342, FAX 858/675–8501, WEB www.ranchobernardoinn.com. 272 rooms, 15 suites. 2 restaurants, 2 bars, room service, in-room data ports, minibars, refrigerators, cable TV with movies, driving range, 18-hole golf course, 27-hole golf course, putting green, 12 tennis courts, 2 pools, 7 outdoor hot tubs, exercise equipment, sauna, spa, steam room, bicycles, volleyball, shops, children's programs, concierge, business services, meeting rooms. AE, D, DC, MC, V.

Shopping

A trip to **Bernardo Winery** (⊠ 13330 Paseo Del Verano, Norte, Rancho Bernardo, ☎ 858/487–1866, WEB www.bernardowinery.com) feels like traveling back to early California days; some of the vines on the former Spanish land grant property are over 100 years old. The winery was founded in 1889 and has been operated by the Rizzo family since 1928. Besides the wine-tasting room selling cold-pressed olive oil and other gourmet goodies, there's a fine café and ten shops. If you're lucky, the glassblowing artist will be working at the outdoor furnace. The winery is open daily 9–5; the shops are open Tuesday–Sunday 10–5.

Escondido

8 mi north of Rancho Bernardo on I–15, 31 mi northeast of downtown San Diego on I–15.

Escondido is a thriving, rapidly expanding residential and commercial city of more than 120,000 people.

The **California Center for the Arts,** an entertainment complex with two theaters, an art museum, and a conference center, presents operas, musicals, plays, dance performances, and symphony and chamber-music concerts. The museum, which focuses on 20th-century art, occasionally presents blockbuster exhibits such as the glass art of Dale Chihuly and photos by Ansel Adams, making a side trip worthwhile. ⊠ 340 N. Escondido Blvd., Escondido, ☎ 760/839–4100 or 800/988–4253 box office; 760/839–4120 museum, WEB www.artcenter.org. 🖅 Museum $5. ☉ Museum Tues.–Sat. 10–5, Sun. noon–5.

Deer Park Winery and Auto Museum is a branch of the well-known Napa Valley Deer Park Winery. Tastings are available. The museum contains a collection of vintage convertibles and other automobile memorabilia. There is also a gift shop–delicatessen and a picnic area. ✉ *29013 Champagne Blvd., 15 mi north of Escondido,* ☎ *760/749–1666,* WEB *www.deerparkwinery.com.* 🎫 *Museum $6.* ☉ *Daily 10–5.*

The **Escondido Municipal Gallery** showcases works by local artists. The Arts Bazaar gift shop carries locally crafted jewelry, blown glass, and textiles. ✉ *142 W. Grand Ave., Escondido,* ☎ *760/480–4101.* ☉ *Tues.–Sat. 11–4.*

Orfila Vineyards offers tours and tastings. The Rose Arbor has a picnic area and a gift shop with wine-related merchandise. ✉ *13455 San Pasqual Valley Rd., Escondido,* ☎ *760/738–6500 or 800/858–9463,* WEB *www.orfila.com.* ☉ *Daily 10–6.*

★ ☞ ❺ **San Diego Wild Animal Park** is an extension of the San Diego Zoo, a 35-minute drive south. The 1,800-acre preserve in the San Pasqual Valley is designed to protect endangered species of animals from around the world. Exhibit areas have been carved out of the dry, dusty canyons and mesas to represent the animals' natural habitats—North Africa, South Africa, East Africa, Heart of Africa, Australian Rain Forest, Asian Swamps, and Asian Plains.

The best way to see these preserves is on the 50-minute, 5-mi Wgasa Bushline Railway (included in the price of admission). As you pass in front of the large, naturally landscaped enclosures, you'll see animals bounding through prairies and mesas as they would in the wild. More than 3,000 animals of 450 species roam or fly above the expansive grounds. Predators are separated from prey by deep moats, but only the elephants, tigers, lions, and cheetahs are kept in isolation. Photographers with zoom lenses can get spectacular shots of zebras, gazelles, and rhinos (a seat on the right-hand side of the monorail is best for viewing). The trip is especially enjoyable in the early evening, when the heat has subsided and the animals are active and feeding. In summer the monorail travels through the park after dark, and sodium-vapor lamps highlight the active animals.

The park is as much a botanical garden as a zoo, and botanists collect rare and endangered plants for preservation. Unique gardens include cacti and succulents from Baja California, a bonsai collection, fuchsia display, native plants, protea, and water-wise plantings. The park sponsors a number of garden events throughout the year including the largest display of chrysanthemums on the West Coast and a spring orchid show.

The 1¼-mi-long **Kilimanjaro Safari Walk** winds through some of the park's hilliest terrain in the East Africa section, with observation decks overlooking the elephants and lions. A 70-ft suspension bridge spans a steep ravine, leading to the final observation point and a panorama of the entire park and the San Pasqual Valley.

The ticket booths at **Nairobi Village,** the park's center, are designed to resemble the tomb of an ancient king of Uganda. Animals in the **Petting Kraal** affectionately tolerate tugs and pats and are quite adept at posing for pictures with toddlers. At the **Congo River Fishing Village** 10,000 gallons of water pour each minute over a huge waterfall into a large lagoon. **Hidden Jungle,** an 8,800-square-ft glass house, houses creatures that creep, flutter, or just hang out in a tropical habitat. Gigantic cockroaches and bird-eating spiders share the turf with colorful butterflies and hummingbirds and oh-so-slow-moving two-toed

sloths. **Lorikeet Landing** holds 75 of the loud and colorful small par-
rots—you can buy a cup of nectar at the aviary entrance to induce them
to land on your hand. Along the trails of 32-acre **Heart of Africa** you
can travel in the footsteps of an early explorer through forests and low-
lands, across a floating bridge to a research station where an expert is
on hand to answer questions; finally you arrive at Panorama Point where
you capture an up-close-and-personal view of cheetahs, a chance to
feed the giraffes, and a distant glimpse of the expansive savanna where
rhinos, impalas, wildebeest, oryx, and beautiful migrating birds reside.
The Wild Animal Park, which conducts captive breeding programs to
save rare and endangered species, shows off one of its most successful
efforts, the California Condor, at the **Condor Ridge** exhibit—this
opened in 2000. The exhibit, perched like one of the ugly black vultures it features, occupies nearly the highest point in the park, and affords a sweeping view of the surrounding San Pasqual Valley. Also on
exhibit here is a herd of rare desert bighorn sheep.

Ravens, vultures, hawks, and a great horned owl perform throughout
the day at the **Bird Show Amphitheater.** All the park's animal shows
are entertainingly educational. The gift shops here offer wonderful merchandise, much of it limited-edition items. Rental camcorders, strollers,
and wheelchairs are available. Serious shutterbugs might consider joining one of the park's special photo caravans ($96–$116.50, including
admission). You can also camp overnight in the park in summer on a
Roar and Snore Campover ($105), take a Sunrise Safari in August, and
celebrate the holidays during the annual Festival of Lights. Also in summer, the railway travels through the park after dark, and sodium-
vapor lamps highlight the active animals. ⊠ *15500 San Pasqual Valley
Rd., Escondido. Take I–15 north to Via Rancho Pkwy. and follow signs
(6 mi),* ☎ *760/747–8702,* WEB *www.sandiegozoo.org/wap.* ⊠ *$25.95,
includes all shows and monorail tour; a $45 combination pass grants
entry, within 5 days of purchase, to both the San Diego Zoo and the
San Diego Wild Animal Park; parking $6. D, MC, V.* ☉ *Mid-June–
Labor Day, daily 9–8; Mid-Sept.–mid-June, daily 9–4.*

San Pasqual Battlefield State Historic Park and Museum commemorates an important moment in the Mexican-American War. On December
6, 1846, a contingent of Americans, including famous frontier scout
Kit Carson, suffered defeat by a group of Californios (Spanish-Mexi-
can residents of California). This was the Californios' most notable success during the war, but the Americans, with support from Commodore
Stockton in San Diego, regained control of the region. An historic battle reenactment is held every December. ⊠ *15808 San Pasqual Valley
Rd., Escondido,* ☎ *760/737–2201,* WEB *www.sanqpasqual.org.* ⊠
Free. ☉ *Weekends 10–5.*

Dining and Lodging

$$–$$$ ✕ **150 Grand Cafe.** The seasonal menu of this pretty restaurant show-
cases contemporary California-style dishes prepared with a European
flair. It's within walking distance of the California Center for the Arts.
⊠ *150 W. Grand Ave., Escondido,* ☎ *760/738–6868. AE, DC, MC,
V. Closed Sun.*

$$–$$$ ✕ **Vincent's Sirino's.** Here's an excellent choice for dining before at-
tending an event at the nearby California Center for the Arts. The simpler dishes are particularly recommended. Try the steamed mussels
followed by the grilled salmon with roasted garlic, the duck breast con-
fit, or the rack of lamb; good homemade bread accompanies them. The
wine list is serious, as are the desserts. The service is friendly and attentive. ⊠ *113 W. Grand Ave., Escondido,* ☎ *760/745–3835. AE, D,
MC, V. Closed Sun.–Mon. No lunch Sat.*

$$ ⚏ **Welk Resort Center.** This resort sprawls over 600 acres of rugged, oak-studded hillside. Built by band leader Lawrence Welk in the 1960s, the resort includes a hotel, time-share condominiums, and a recreation and entertainment complex. A museum displays Welk memorabilia, a theater presents Broadway-style musicals year-round, and there are many shops on the premises. Hotel rooms, decorated with a Southwestern flair, have golf-course views. ⊠ *8860 Lawrence Welk Dr., Escondido 92026,* ☎ *760/749–3000 or 800/932–9355,* FAX *760/749–6182,* WEB *www. welkresort.com. 137 rooms, 10 suites. In-room data ports, 3 restaurants, bar, grocery, cable TV, 6 pools, 7 hot tubs, 2 18-hole golf courses, 5 tennis courts, health club, shops, theater, children's programs, meeting room, travel services. AE, D, DC, MC, V.*

Shopping

Despite its urbanization, much of San Diego County remains rural; inland valleys and mountains support boutique farms that supply gourmet ingredients to the nation's finest restaurants. You can sample this bounty by stopping at one of the roadside produce stands that dot the countryside along Route 78, Route 76, and San Pasqual Valley Road; most are open on a seasonal basis.

Bates Nut Farm (⊠ 15954 Woods Valley Rd., Valley Center, ☎ 760/ 749–3333, WEB www.batesfarm.com) sells pecans, macadamia nuts, and almonds cultivated from a 100-acre farm. There are also picnic tables and a deli. In fall a 25-acre pumpkin patch produces squash weighing up to 200 pounds; there's a petting zoo with sheep, llamas, ponies, and emus. **Canterbury Gardens** (⊠ 2402 S. Escondido Blvd., Escondido, ☎ 760/746–1400) specializes in seasonal designer decorator items and giftware plus a year-round selection of Christmas ornaments and collectibles. Interior decorations and silk plants are all designed and crafted on premises. **Farm Stand** (⊠ San Pasqual Valley Rd., Escondido, ☎ 760/432–8912) sells fresh produce including luscious strawberries. **Rave Reviews** (⊠ 120 W. Grand Ave., Escondido, ☎ 760/ 743–0056) offers high-end vintage clothing and accessories from the 1940s, '50s, and '60s.

Palomar Mountain

❻ *35 mi northeast of Escondido on I–15 to Rte. 76 to Rte. S6, 66 mi northeast of downtown San Diego on Rte. 163 to I–15 to Rte. 76 to Rte. S6.*

Palomar Observatory, atop Palomar Mountain and home to the 200-inch Hale telescope, is the site of some of the most important astronomical discoveries of the 20th century. The small museum at the observatory contains photos of some of these discoveries and presents informative videos. A park with picnic areas surrounds the observatory. ⊠ *Rte. S6, north of Rte. 76, east of I–15; Palomar Mountain,* ☎ *760/742–2119,* WEB *www.astro.caltech.edu/palomarpublic.* ▱ *Free.* ☉ *Observatory for self-guided tours daily 9–4, except Dec. 24 and 25.*

You can take the scenic route down 6,140-ft Palomar Mountain by way of the **Palomar Plunge,** a 16-mi bike ride to the bottom (no pedaling required) conducted by Gravity Activated Sports (⊠ 16220 Rte. 76, Pauma Valley, ☎ 760/742–2294; ▱ $80).

Mission San Antonio de Pala, built in 1816, is a living remnant of the mission era and serves the local Native American community. In fact, it's the only original Spanish mission to continue with its purpose in serving Native American Indians. Displays in a small museum include artifacts from the original mission. ⊠ *Pala Mission Rd., off Rte. 76,*

6 mi east of I–15, Pala, ☎ 760/742–1600. ⌨ $2. ⊘ Museum and gift shop Wed.–Sun. 10–4.

Fallbrook

19 mi northwest of Escondido on I–15 to Mission Rd. (Rte. S13) to Mission Dr.

With 6,000 hillside acres planted, Fallbrook bills itself as the avocado capital of the world. Citrus and macadamia nuts are grown in the region, too. Historic Old Main Street, a few antiques malls, and agriculture are the attractions in this small walkable town. There's an Avocado Festival every April where you can sample great guacamole or even avocado ice cream.

Temecula

29 mi from Escondido, 60 mi from San Diego on I–15 north to Rancho California Rd. east.

Once an important stop on the Butterfield Overland Stagecoach route and a market town for the huge cattle ranches occupying the surrounding hillsides, Temecula (pronounced teh-*mec*-yoo-la) is southern California's only developed wine region. Premium wineries, most of which allow tasting for a small fee, can be found along Rancho California Road as it snakes through oak-studded hills. Temecula draws thousands of people to its Balloon and Wine Festival held in the spring. Hot-air-balloon excursions are a good choice year-round. **Grape Escape Balloon Adventure** (☎ 800/965–2122, WEB www.agrapeescape.com) has morning flights.

Thornton Winery (✉ 32575 Rancho California Rd., Temecula, ☎ 909/699–0099, WEB www.thorntonwine.com) produces several varieties of wine, including sparkling white wine; it offers weekend tours and daily tastings. **Callaway Vineyard & Winery** (✉ 32720 Rancho California Rd., Temecula, ☎ 909/676–4001) is best known for its Callalees chardonnay. Tastings, tours, and theme dinners and luncheons are all available, and there's a gift shop. **Maurice Car'rie Vineyard & Winery** (✉ 34225 Rancho California Rd., Temecula, ☎ 909/676–1711) has a tasting room, a gift shop, and a picnic area.

Once a hangout for cowboys, **Old Town Temecula** still looks the part. Park on Front Street and walk along the six-block stretch past the large 19th-century wooden buildings that line the streets; several antiques shops here specialize in local and Wild West memorabilia.

Temecula Valley Historic Museum, adjacent to Sam Hicks Memorial Park, displays a collection of writer Erle Stanley Gardner memorabilia including a sampling of his Perry Mason mystery novels. The museum also shows the early–Native American history of the Temecula Valley, Butterfield stage routes, and ranchero period. Docent tours are available. *✉ 28314 Mercedes St., Temecula, ☎ 909/694–6452. ⌨ $2 donation requested. ⊘ Tues.–Sat. 10–5, Sun. 1–5.*

The **Santa Rosa Plateau Ecological Reserve** provides a glimpse of what this countryside was like before the developers took over. Trails wind through oak forests and past vernal pools and rolling grassland. A visitor and operations center has interpretive displays and maps; some of the reserve's hiking trails begin here. *✉ Take I–15's Clinton Keith Rd. exit and head west 5 mi, Murrietta, ☎ 909/677–6951, WEB www.santarosaplateau.org. ⌨ $2. ⊘ Daily sunrise–sunset.*

Dining and Lodging

$$$–$$$$ ✕ **Cafe Champagne.** The Thornton Winery's airy country restaurant, whose big windows overlook the vineyards, serves contemporary cuisine. It's the best place to eat in a region not abounding in high-quality restaurants. ✉ *32575 Rancho California Rd., Temecula,* ☎ *909/699–0088. AE, D, DC, MC, V. No dinner Mon.*

$$$–$$$$ ⬚ **Temecula Creek Inn.** This upscale golf resort occupies a collection of low-slung, red-roof buildings on a hillside a short distance from the wine-touring area. Unusually large rooms are nicely appointed with double vanity areas and expansive windows revealing a tranquil golf-course view. Rooms, decorated in soft desert colors, contain interesting displays of Native American pottery, basket remnants, and antique tribal weavings. All have balconies or garden patios. ✉ *44501 Rainbow Canyon Rd., Temecula 92592,* ☎ *909/694–1000 or 877/517–1823,* FAX *909/676–3422,* WEB *www.temeculacreekinn.com. 80 rooms. Restaurant, refrigerators, pool, outdoor hot tub, gym, massage, driving range, 27-hole golf course, putting green, 2 tennis courts, hiking, bar, dry cleaning, meeting room. AE, D, DC, MC, V.*

$$–$$$ ⬚ **Loma Vista Bed and Breakfast.** This mission-style inn has tranquil views of vineyards, citrus groves, and gardens. One room has a fireplace and a whirlpool tub. A full breakfast, with champagne, is included. ✉ *33350 La Serena Way, Temecula 92592,* ☎ *909/676–7047. 10 rooms. Hot tub. MC, V.*

Inland North County A to Z

To research prices, get advice from other travelers, and book travel arrangements, visit www.fodors.com.

BUS TRAVEL

➤ Bus Information: **North County Transit District** (☎ 800/266–6883).

CAR TRAVEL

Escondido sits at the intersection of Route 78, which heads east from Oceanside, and I–15, the inland freeway connecting San Diego to Riverside, which is 30 minutes north of Escondido. Del Dios Highway winds from Rancho Santa Fe through the hills past Lake Hodges to Escondido. Route 76, which connects with Interstate 15 north of Escondido, veers east to Palomar Mountain. Interstate 15 continues north to Fallbrook and Temecula.

VISITOR INFORMATION

➤ Contacts: **Escondido Chamber of Commerce** (✉ 720 N. Broadway, Escondido 92025, ☎ 760/745–2125, WEB www.escondidochamber. org). **Fallbrook Chamber of Commerce** (✉ 233 E. Mission Rd., Suite A, Fallbrook 92028, ☎ 760/728–5845, WEB www.fallbrookca.org). **Rancho Bernardo Chamber of Commerce** (✉ 11650 Iberia Pl., Suite 220, San Diego, 92128, ☎ 858/487–1767, WEB www.ranchobernardochamber.com). **San Diego North Convention and Visitors Bureau** (✉ 360 N. Escondido Blvd., Escondido 92025, ☎ 760/745–4741). **Temecula Valley Chamber of Commerce** (✉ 27450 Ynez Rd., #124, Temecula, 92591, ☎ 909/676–5090, WEB www.temecula.org).

THE BACKCOUNTRY AND JULIAN

The Cuyamaca and Laguna mountains to the east of Escondido—sometimes referred to as the backcountry by county residents—are favorite weekend destinations for hikers, nature lovers, stargazers, and apple-pie fanatics. Most of the latter group head to Julian, a historic

SAN DIEGO COUNTY'S CASINO COUNTRY

SINCE THE STATE GRANTED twelve Native American tribes permission to operate casinos in greater San Diego, the county has become the undisputed casino capital of California. The casinos range from sprawling Las Vegas–style resorts, with big-name entertainment and golf courses, to small card rooms tucked away on rural crossroads. The three most central of these are described below followed by another four found on North County backroads. More are on their way. Many casinos offer bus transport, so call before visiting and save on gas. Also, note that the gambling age is 18 years and over.

Viejas Casino and Turf Club (✉ 5000 Willows Rd., Alpine, ☎ 619/445–5400, WEB www.viejas.com) is a massive entertainment/shopping complex with the largest casino in San Diego County. Viejas has 2,000 slot machines, plus blackjack, poker, bingo, pai gow, and off-track wagering. There are five restaurants and a cocktail lounge, and the Dream Catcher Showroom presents top-of-the-line entertainment. A Native American-theme factory outlet mall across from the casino has 57 shops, restaurants, and a landscaped amphitheater where evening shows are presented.

Barona (✉ 1000 Wildcat Canyon Rd., Lakeside, ☎ 619/443–2300, WEB www. barona.com) is a western-style resort with a casino, hotel, and golf course. It operates 2,000 video slot machines, 50 gaming tables, a bingo hall, and off-

track betting. There are three restaurants, plus a kiosk-filled food court, including a Krispy Kreme store. Adjacent is the 18-hole Barona Creek Golf Club.

The more compact **Sycuan Casino** (✉ 5469 Dehesa Rd., El Cajon, ☎ 619/445–8092, WEB www.sycuan.com) has video slot machines, Vegas-style card games, bingo, and off-track betting. You can dine at the Turf Club Restaurant.

Pala Casino (✉ 11154 Rte. 76, Pala 92059, ☎ 877/946–7252, WEB www. palacasino.com), San Diego's most elegant, has got it all: 2,000 slot and video machines, and 51 gaming tables for poker, pai gow, blackjack, and baccarat. Pala also offers no-smoking areas and a high-stakes casino. The casino rises over a bend in the San Luis Rey River amid stunning mountain scenery. Dine near a roaring fire in the Oak Room or outside by the river in the Pala Terrace. You'll find a gift shop, a deli, a lounge with live music, and an events center.

Valley View Casino (✉ 16300 Nyemii Pass Rd., Valley Center, ☎ 866/726–7277) has more than 750 slots, a dozen blackjack tables, and a 24-hour buffet. There's no entertainment or alcohol at this point, but a huge resort is in the works.

Tropically themed **Casino Pauma** (✉ 777 Pauma Reservation Rd., Pauma Valley, ☎ 760/742–2177) has 850 slot machines, 24 gaming tables, a café, and two bar-lounges.

mining town now better known for apples than for the gold once extracted from its hills. Nearby Cuyamaca Rancho State Park is full of well-maintained trails and picnic and camping areas.

The **Sunrise National Scenic Byway,** in the Cleveland National Forest, is the most dramatic approach to Julian—its turns and curves reveal amazing views of the desert from the Salton Sea all the way to Mexico. You can spend an entire day roaming these mountains; an early morning hike to the top of Garnet Peak (mile marker 27.8) is the best way to catch the view. Springtime wildflower displays are spectacular, particularly along Big Laguna Trail from Laguna Campground. There are picnic areas along the highway at Desert View and Pioneer Mail.

On summer weekends you can view the heavens through a 21-inch telescope in the **Mount Laguna Observatory** (⊠ Morris Ranch Rd., off Sunrise Scenic Byway, Mt. Laguna, ☎ 619/594–6182), which sits at an altitude of 6,100 ft. It's operated by San Diego State University at Mount Laguna.

Cuyamaca Mountains

An alternative route into the mountains is through **Cuyamaca Rancho State Park** (⊠ Rte. 79, 9 mi east of I–8, Descanso 92016, ☎ 760/765–0755, WEB www.cuyamaca.statepark.org). The park spreads over 24,677 acres of open meadows, forested mountains, and oak woodlands. Cuyamaca Peak rises to 6,512 ft. Oak and pine trees adorn the park's hills; small streams and meadows provide a quiet escape for nature lovers. In fall, the hillsides provide one of the most beautiful fall foliage displays in southern California, as native oak and poplar trees turn crimson and golden. There are 120 mi of hiking and nature trails, scenic picnic areas, campgrounds, and a small museum, and along the road you may spot the remains of a now-closed gold mine. For an inspirational desert view, stop at the lookout about 2 mi south of Julian on Route 79; on a clear day you can see several mountain ranges in hues ranging from pink to amber stepped back behind the Salton Sea.

Just beyond the eastern boundary of the park, 110-acre **Lake Cuyamaca** (⊠ 15027 Rte. 79, Julian 92037, ☎ 760/765–0515, WEB www. lakecuyamaca.org), open daily from 6 AM to dusk, is popular with anglers and boaters. Bait, tackle, rental boats, and motors are available. You can rent two lakeside condos, Rainbow Rendezvous and Raccoon Hollow, or check into the campground (first come, first served).

Dining

$ ✕ **Lake Cuyamaca Restaurant.** This tidy, lace-curtain lakefront café specializes in Austrian fare, highlights of which include a selection of schnitzels and wursts, plus several chicken and steak entrées. Austrian beers are are on tap. The restaurant, as well as the adjacent food market, are popular with anglers and locals. ⊠ *15027 Rte. 79., Julian,* ☎ *760/765–0070. AE, D, DC, MC, V.*

Julian and Santa Ysabel

62 mi from San Diego (to Julian), east on I–8 and north on Rte. 79.

Gold was discovered in the Julian area in 1869 and gold-bearing quartz a year later. More than $15 million worth of gold was taken from local mines in the 1870s. Today this mountain town retains some historic false-front buildings from its mining days. Many of the buildings along Julian's Main Street and the side streets date back to the gold rush period; others are reproductions. When gold and quartz became scarce the locals turned to growing apples and pears. During the fall harvest season you can buy fruit, sip cider, eat apple pie, and shop for antiques and collectibles. But spring is equally enchanting (and less congested), as the hillsides explode with wildflowers, lilacs, and peonies. More than 50 artists have studios tucked away in the hills surrounding Julian; they often show their work in local shops and galleries.

You can take an hour-long tour of an authentic Julian gold mine given by the **Eagle Mining Company.** A small rock shop and gold-mining museum are also on the premises. ⊠ *C St., 5 blocks east from center of Julian,* ☎ *760/765–0036.* ⊡ *$7.* ☉ *Daily 10–3, weather permitting.*

In Julian's heyday, mobs of goldminers invaded the tiny hamlet. When the mines played out, the goldminers left, leaving behind discarded mining tools and empty houses. Today the **Julian Pioneer Museum,** itself a 19th-century building, displays remnants of that time, including pioneer clothing, a collection of old lace, and old photographs of the town's historic buildings and mining structures. ⊠ *4th and Washington Sts.,* ☎ *760/765–0227.* ⊡ *$1.* ☉ *Apr.–Nov., daily 10–4; Dec.–Mar., weekends 10–4.*

The 1¼-mi trail through **Volcan Mountain Wilderness Preserve** passes through orchards, oak groves, and native manzanita to a panoramic viewpoint extending north all the way to Palomar Mountain. At the entrance you pass through gates designed by local artist James Hubbell, who is known for his ironwork, wood carving, and stained glass. ⊠ *From Julian take Farmer Rd. to Wynola Rd.; go east a few yards, and then north on Farmer Rd.,* ☎ *760/765–1065,* WEB *www.volcanmt.org.* ⊡ *Free.* ☉ *Open daily.*

The Santa Ysabel Valley, where three Native American tribes live, looks pretty much the way the backcountry appeared a century ago, with sweeping meadows surrounded by oak-studded hillsides. The Indians run cattle here and operate small farms. In recent years, the valley's beautiful pasturelands have been threatened by development. However, in 2000 the Nature Conservancy acquired large portions of the valley to set aside as a nature preserve. The village of **Santa Ysabel,** 7 mi west of Julian, has several interesting shops. Tiny **Mission Santa Ysabel** (⊠ Rte. 79, west of town of Santa Ysabel, ☎ 760/765–0810) is a late 19th-century adobe mission that continues to serve several local Native American communities.

Dining and Lodging

$–$$$ ✕ **Romano's Dodge House.** You can gorge on huge portions of antipasto, pizza, pasta primavera, sausage sandwiches, and seafood in a cozy, historic house. This is a casual, red-checkered tablecloth kind of place. ⊠ *2718 B St., Julian,* ☎ *760/765–1003. No credit cards. Closed Tues.*

$$ ✕ **Julian Grille.** The menu at this casual restaurant inside a historic home appeals to a variety of tastes, including vegetarian. Chicken dishes are popular, as are steaks and the smoked pork chops served with applesauce. Lunch options include good burgers, whopping sandwiches, and soups. There's tree-shaded outdoor dining, which is heated on cool evenings. ⊠ *2224 Main St., Julian,* ☎ *760/765–0173. AE, MC, V. No dinner Mon.*

$$ ✕ **Pine Hills Lodge Dinner Theater.** Weekend musical and comedy shows staged by the Pine Hills Players include a barbecue dinner with an all-you-can-eat salad bar for $30 per person. The historic theater was built as a gymnasium for world heavyweight champion Jack Dempsey. The lodge has a pub, which is popular with locals. ⊠ *2960 La Posada Way, Julian,* ☎ *760/765–1100. AE, MC, V.*

$ ✕ **Julian Tea and Cottage Arts.** Sample finger sandwiches, scones topped with whipped cream, and lavish sweets during afternoon tea inside an historic house. Sandwiches, soups, and other lunch items are also available. ✉ *2124 3rd St., Julian,* ☎ *760/765–0832. No dinner. AE, D, MC, V.*

$$$–$$$$ 🛏 **Orchard Hill Country Inn.** On a hill above town, this inn, comprising a lodge and five Craftsman-style cottages, has a sweeping view of the countryside. Inside are luxurious backcountry accommodations decorated with antiques and handcrafted quilts. The cottage suites have fireplaces, double whirlpool tubs, and wet bars, even private patios or balconies. Gather in the evening for wine and hors d'oeuvres in the Great Room, where a fire blazes in the stone fireplace. On weekends, an excellent dinner is available and a two-night stay is required. ✉ *Washington St., Julian 92036,* ☎ *760/765–1700 or 800/716–7242,* FAX *760/765–0290,* WEB *www.orchardhill.com. 10 rooms, 12 suites. Dining room, bar, lounge, some in-room hot tubs, some minibars, cable TV, in-room VCRs, hiking, meeting room; no smoking. AE, MC, V.*

$$–$$$ 🛏 **All Seasons Lodge.** A convenient stop along the highway through the Cuyamaca Mountains, this bed-and-breakfast offers simply furnished rooms. Large rooms, designed for two couples or families, have kitchens, private entrances, fireplaces, and hot tubs. The lodge is well suited for children; toys and videos are available. ✉ *569 K.Q. Ranch Rd., Julian 92036,* ☎ *760/765–4880 or 877/495–4880,* WEB *www.allseasonslodge. com. 6 rooms. Fans, kitchenettes, cable TV, in-room VCRs, some in-room hot tubs, hiking, library. AE, D, MC, V.*

$$ 🛏 **Julian Lodge.** This B&B in the center of town is a replica of a late 19th-century Julian hotel. The rooms and public spaces are furnished with antiques; on chilly days you can warm yourself at the large stove in the lobby. Complimentary breakfast is buffet style. ✉ *4th and C Sts., Julian 92036,* ☎ *760/765–1420 or 800/542–1420. 23 rooms. Dining room, cable TV, library, piano. AE, D, MC, V.*

Shopping

Julian and Santa Ysabel have a number of unique shops that are open weekends, but midweek hours vary considerably. In autumn locally grown apples, pears, nuts, and cider are sold at numerous fruit stands. The best apple variety produced here is a Jonagold, a hybrid of Jonathan and Golden Delicious.

Applewood & Company (✉ 2804 Washington St., Julian, ☎ 760/765–1185) carries an attractive selection of antiques, decorative accessories, and collectibles. The **Birdwatcher** (✉ 2775 B St., Julian, ☎ 760/765–1817) offers wild bird items, including birdhouses, birdseed, hummingbird feeders, plus bird-themed accessories such as jewelry, apparel, novelties, and guidebooks for serious birders. **Farmer's Mountain Vale Ranch** (✉ 4510 Rte. 78, Julian, ☎ 760/765–0188) sells apples, pears, and other locally grown produce. It has a small picnic area and aviary of exotic birds.

The **Julian Bell, Book and Candle** (✉ 2007 Main St., Julian, ☎ 760/765–2377 or 800/664–5851) displays an unusual collection of handcrafted candles and accessories. **Meyer Orchards** (✉ 3962 Rte. 78, Julian, ☎ 760/765–0233) carries different kinds of local apples, including a few heirloom varieties that do well in Julian's cold climate. **Once Upon a Time** (✉ Rte. 78 and Rte. 79, Santa Ysabel, ☎ 760/765–1695) comprises three tiny cottages, each devoted to antiques, florals, gifts, and Christmas decorations. **Santa Ysabel Art Gallery** (✉ Rte. 78 and Rte. 79, Santa Ysabel, ☎ 760/765–1676) shows watercolors, stained glass, sculptures, and other creations by local artists.

The Backcountry and Julian A to Z

To research prices, get advice from other travelers, and book travel arrangements, visit www.fodors.com.

CAR TRAVEL

A loop drive beginning and ending in San Diego is a good way to explore this area. You can take the Sunrise National Scenic Byway (sometimes icy in winter) from I–8 to Route 79 and return through Cuyamaca Rancho State Park (also icy in winter). If you're only going to Julian (a 75-minute trip from San Diego in light traffic), take either the Sunrise Byway or Route 79, and return to San Diego via Route 78 past Santa Ysabel to Ramona and Route 67; from here I–8 heads west to downtown.

VISITOR INFORMATION

➤ CONTACT: **Julian Chamber of Commerce** (⊠ 2129 Main St., Julian 92036, ☎ 760/765–1857, WEB www.julianca.com).

THE DESERT

In most spring seasons the stark desert landscape east of the Cuyamaca Mountains explodes with colorful wildflowers. The beauty of this spectacle, as well as the natural quiet and blazing climate, lures many tourists and natives each year to Anza-Borrego Desert State Park, less than a two-hour drive from central San Diego.

For hundreds of years the only humans to linger in the area were Native Americans from the Cahuilla and Kumeyaay tribes, who made their winter homes in the desert. It was not until 1774, when Mexican explorer Captain Juan Bautista de Anza first blazed a trail through the area seeking a shortcut from Sonora, Mexico, to San Francisco, that Europeans had their first glimpse of the oddly enchanting terrain.

The desert is best visited from October through May to avoid the extreme summer temperatures. Winter temperatures are comfortable, but nights (and sometimes days) are cold, so bring a warm jacket.

Numbers in the margin correspond to points of interest on the San Diego North County map.

Anza-Borrego Desert State Park

❼ *88 mi from downtown San Diego (to park border due west of Borrego Springs), east on I–8, north on Rte. 67, east on Rte. S4 and Rte. 78, north on Rte. 79, and east on Rtes. S2 and S22.*

Today more than 600,000 acres are included in the Anza-Borrego Desert State Park, making it the largest state park in the contiguous United States. It is also one of the few parks in the country where people can camp anywhere. No campsite is necessary; follow the trails and pitch a tent wherever you like. Rangers and displays at an excellent underground **Visitors Information Center** (⊠ 200 Palm Canyon Dr., Borrego Springs, ☎ 760/767–5311; 760/767–4684 wildflower hot line, WEB www.anzaborrego.statepark.org; ☉ Oct.–May, daily 9–5; June–Sept., weekends and holidays 9–5) can point you in the right direction.

Five hundred miles of paved and dirt roads traverse the park, and you are required to stay on them so as not to disturb the ecological balance. However, 28,000 acres have been set aside in the eastern part of the desert near Ocotillo Wells for off-road enthusiasts. General George S. Patton conducted field training in the Ocotillo area to prepare for the World War II invasion of North Africa.

Many of the park's sites can be seen from paved roads, but some require driving on dirt roads. Rangers recommend using four-wheel-drive vehicles when traversing dirt roads. Carry the appropriate supplies: shovel and other tools, flares, blankets, and plenty of water. Canyons are susceptible to flash flooding; inquire about weather conditions before entering.

Narrows Earth Trail is a short walk off Route 78, east of Tamarisk Grove, that reveals the many geologic processes involved in forming the canyons of the desert. Water, wind, and faulting created the commanding vistas along **Erosion Road,** a self-guided, 18-mi auto tour along Route S22. The **Southern Emigrant Trail** follows the route of the Butterfield Stage Overland Mail through the desert.

At **Borrego Palm Canyon,** a few minutes west of the Anza-Borrego Visitors Information Center, a 1½-mi trail leads to a small oasis with a waterfall and palms. The Borrego Palm Canyon campground is one of only two developed campgrounds with flush toilets and showers in the park. (The other is Tamarisk Grove Campground, at the intersection of Route 78 and Yaqui Pass Road; sites at both are $10, $16 with hookup at Borrego Palm Canyon.)

Geology students from all over the world visit the Fish Creek area of Anza-Borrego to explore a famous canyon known as **Split Mountain** (⊠ Split Mountain Rd., south from Rte. 78 at Ocotillo Wells), a narrow gorge with 600-ft perpendicular walls that was formed by an ancestral stream. Fossils in this area indicate that a sea covered the desert floor at one time. A 2-mi nature trail west of Split Mountain rewards hikers with a good view of shallow caves created by erosion.

Borrego Springs

31 mi from Julian, east on Rte. 78 and north on Rte. S3.

Long a quiet town with a handful of year-round residents, Borrego Springs is emerging as a laid-back destination for desert-lovers, where you can enjoy outdoor activities such as hiking, nature study, golf, tennis, horse-back riding, and mountain-bike riding from September through June when temperatures hover in the 80s and 90s. If winter rains cooperate, Borrego Springs puts on some of the best wildflower displays in the low desert.

Lodging

$$$$ ⊞ **La Casa del Zorro.** This lovely resort owned by San Diego's promi-
★ nent Copley family consists of a collection of casitas spotted around lushly landscaped grounds. You need walk only a few hundred yards from this low-key resort to be alone under the sky, and you may well see roadrunners crossing the highway. The resort is luxurious in every way, with accommodations ranging from ample standard rooms to private four-bedroom casitas with their own pools. Service is excellent. The elegant Continental restaurant puts on a good Sunday brunch. ⊠ *3845 Yaqui Pass Rd., Borrego Springs 92004,* ☎ *760/767–5323 or 800/824–1884,* FAX *760/767–5963,* WEB *www.lacasadelzorro.com. 4 rooms, 54 suites, 19 casitas. Restaurant, bar, some in-room hot tubs, minibars, cable TV, 3 pools, 6 tennis courts, putting green, Ping Pong, shuffleboard, health club, hair salon, 3 outdoor hot tubs, massage, bicycles, hiking, horseback riding, horseshoes, jogging, volleyball, children's programs, business services, meeting rooms, airport shuttle. AE, D, MC, V.*

$$ ⊞ **Borrego Springs Resort and Country Club.** This low-key resort is surrounded by expansive desert views, visible from every room. Simple furnishings are contemporary. Amenities include hair dryers and in-room coffeemakers. ⊠ *1112 Tilting T Dr., Borrego Springs 92004,*

☎ 760/767–5700 or 888/826–7734, FAX 760/767–5710, WEB *www. borregospringsresort.com. 100 rooms. Restaurant, bar, refrigerators, microwaves, cable TV, some kitchenettes, 2 pools, hot tub, 18-hole golf course, putting green, 6 tennis courts, gym, meeting room. AE, D, MC, V.*

$$ ⬚ **Palm Canyon Resort.** One of the largest properties around Anza-Borrego Desert State Park includes a hotel, an RV park, a restaurant, and recreational facilities. More upscale rooms have refrigerators and balconies or patios. ✉ *221 Palm Canyon Dr., Borrego Springs 92004,* ☎ *760/767–5341 or 800/242–0044,* FAX *760/767–4073,* WEB *www.pcresort. com. 60 rooms, 1 suite. Restaurant, bar, cable TV, 2 pools, 2 hot tubs, gym, shops, laundry facilities, meeting room. AE, D, DC, MC, V.*

Outdoor Activities and Sports

The 18-hole **Rams Hill Country Club** (☎ 760/732–5124) course is open to the public. The greens fee is $80–$105, which includes a mandatory cart. **Roadrunner Club** (☎ 760/767–5374) has an 18-hole par-3 golf course. The greens fee is $15.

OFF THE **OCOTILLO WELLS STATE VEHICULAR RECREATION AREA –** The sand dunes
BEATEN PATH and rock formations at this 42,000-acre haven for off-road enthusiasts are fun and challenging. Camping is permitted throughout the area, but water is not available. The only facilities are in the small town (really no more than a corner) of Ocotillo Wells. ✉ *Rte. 78, east from Borrego Springs Rd., Ocotillo Wells,* ☎ *760/767–5391.*

The Desert A to Z

To research prices, get advice from other travelers, and book travel arrangements, visit www.fodors.com.

BUS TRAVEL
The Northeast Rural Bus System connects Julian, Borrego Springs, Agua Caliente, and many other small communities with La Mesa, 15 mi east of downtown San Diego. No service on Sunday or Monday.
➤ BUS INFORMATION: The **Northeast Rural Bus System** (NERBS, ☎ 760/ 767–4287).

CAR TRAVEL
From downtown San Diego, take I–8 east to Route 67 north, to Route 78 east, to Route 79 north, to Routes S2 and S22 east.

VISITOR INFORMATION
➤ CONTACTS: **Anza-Borrego Desert State Park** (✉ 200 Palm Canyon Dr., Borrego Springs 92004, ☎ 760/767–5311, WEB www.anzaborrego. statepark.org). **Borrego Springs Chamber of Commerce** (✉ 622 Palm Canyon Dr., Borrego Springs 92004, ☎ 760/767–5555, WEB www. borregosprings.org). **State Park Reservations** (☎ 800/444–7275, WEB www.reserveamerica.com). **Wildflower Hotline** (☎ 760/767–4684).

9 TIJUANA AND PLAYAS DE ROSARITO

Since you've come as far as the southwesternmost city in the continental United States, take advantage of the opportunity and go "un poquito mas allá" (a bit farther) and experience Mexico. Only 18 mi south of San Diego lies Baja California, a 1,000-mi-long stretch of beaches, desert, and hills that has long been a refuge for Californians with an urge to swim, surf, fish, and relax in a country unlike their own.

By Maribeth
Mellin

SEPARATED FROM MAINLAND MEXICO by the Sea of Cortez, the
Baja California peninsula stretches 1,625 km (1,000 mi) from
Tijuana to Los Cabos. The desert landscape harbors isolated fishing retreats, Prohibition-era gambling palaces, world-class golf courses,
and one of the busiest international borders in the world. Adventur-
ers delight in kayaking alongside migrating gray whales, diving with
hammerhead sharks, and hiking to hidden cave paintings.

Tijuana, just 29 km (18 mi) south of San Diego at the international
border, is home to more than 2 million people, making it more popu-
lous than the entire remainder of the peninsula. It's also the most popular destination for day-trippers from San Diego, who come for the
souvenir shopping, sports events, and sophisticated Mexican dining.

On the Pacific Coast of *Baja Norte* (meaning north Baja), travelers stream
down thte Transpeninsular Highway (Highway 1) to the beach community of Rosarito (and Ensenada, 75 km [47 mi] south of Rosarito),
in search of a more laid back Mexico. Here, English is spoken as freely
as Spanish, and the dollar is as readily acccepted as the peso. Between
Baja's towns, the landscape is unlike any other, with cacti growing beside the sea, and stark mountains and plateaus rising against clear blue
skies.

You can visit Tijuana and Playas de Rosarito in one day. Begin by by-
passing Tijuana and heading straight for the toll road to Playas de Rosarito, about a 40-mi drive south. Stop at the Rosarito Beach Hotel for
breakfast, take a walk on the beach in front of the hotel, and check
out a few of the shops on Boulevard Benito Juárez.

If you finish lunch by mid-afternoon, you'll be able to reach Tijuana
by evening. Once in the city, park in a lot by Calle 2A, the road that
ties the highway to the border; walk up Calle 2A to Avenida Revolución, finish your souvenir shopping, and have dinner at a restaurant
on the way back to your car. It's smart to wait until after 7 to cross
the border, when rush-hour traffic has diminished.

Baja travelers have traditionally been adventurous, and the peninsula has
become a cult destination. Back in the days of Prohibition, the Hollywood
crowd learned the joy of having an international border so near, filming,
fishing, and building resorts in their newfound southern playground.
Baja's resort towns have become mainstream, but you can still find adventure and sublime solitude at the peninsula's hidden beaches and bays.

Pleasures and Pastimes

Dining
Baja's cuisine highlights food from the sea. Fresh fish, lobster, shrimp,
and abalone are particularly good. In both states, scores of restaurants
and kitchens serve great authentic Mexican seafood dishes. Beef, pork,
and local quail are also excellent, both grilled and marinated. Imported steak, lamb, and duck are popular in upscale places. Many restaurants serve regional Mexican cuisine, and plenty of spots throughout
the peninsula combine U.S. and Mexican flavors in tacos, burritos, burgers, and pizza.

Two dishes that originated in Baja have become standard fare in southern California. Lobster Puerto Nuevo–style (shellfish grilled or boiled
in oil and served with beans, rice, and tortillas) comes from the fishing settlement of the same name near Tijuana. Fish tacos (chunks of
deep-fried fish wrapped with condiments in a corn tortilla) are said to
have originated in the northern Baja town of San Felipe. Mexico's best

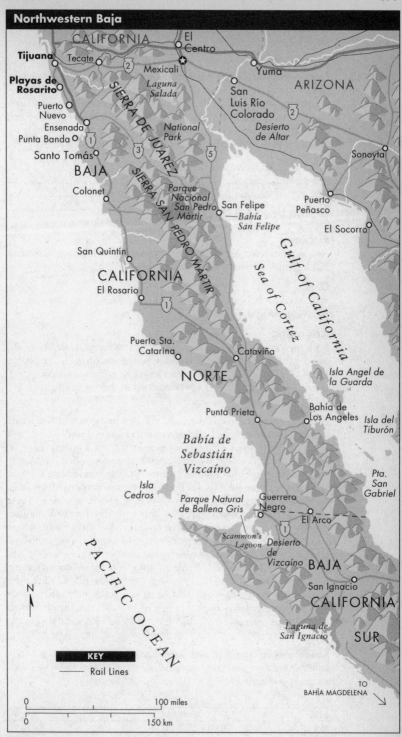

Northwestern Baja

CALIFORNIA
El Centro
Tijuana · Tecate
Playas de Rosarito
Mexicali
Laguna Salada
San Luis Río Colorado
Yuma
ARIZONA
Puerto Nuevo
Ensenada
Punta Banda
National Park
Desierto de Altar
Sonoyta
Santo Tomás
BAJA
Colonet
Parque Nacional San Pedro Mártir
San Felipe
Bahía San Felipe
Puerto Peñasco
El Socorro
SIERRA DE JUAREZ
SIERRA SAN PEDRO MÁRTIR
San Quintín
CALIFORNIA
El Rosario
Gulf of California
Sea of Cortez
Puerto Sta. Catarina
Cataviña
NORTE
Isla Angel de la Guarda
Punta Prieta
Bahía de Los Angeles
Isla del Tiburón
Bahía de Sebastián Vizcaíno
Isla Cedros
Pta. San Gabriel
Parque Natural de Ballena Gris
Guerrero Negro
El Arco
Scammon's Lagoon
Desierto de Vizcaíno
BAJA
San Ignacio
CALIFORNIA
SUR
PACIFIC OCEAN
Laguna de San Ignacio
N

KEY
— Rail Lines

0 — 100 miles
0 — 150 km

TO BAHÍA MAGDELENA

domestic wines are nurtured in the vineyards and wineries in the Santo Tomás and Guadalupe valleys outside Ensenada, and one of the country's most popular beers, Tecate, comes from the Baja Norte town of the same name.

Restaurants as a rule are low-key, except in Tijuana, where dining options range from *taquerías* (taco stands) to upscale Continental dining rooms. Dress is accordingly casual at nearly all Baja restaurants, and reservations are not required unless otherwise noted. Moderate prices prevail even in city restaurants, which can be surprisingly expensive. Some places add a 15% service charge to the bill.

CATEGORY	COST*
$$$	over $15
$$	$10–$15
$	under $10

per person for a main course at dinner

Fishing

Baja is considered one of the world's great sportfishing destinations. Fishing from Ensenada is best in summer and early fall.

Golf

With well-established courses in Tijuana, Rosarito, and Ensenada, Baja is growing in popularity among golfers.

Kayaking

Both the Pacific Ocean and the Sea of Cortez have isolated bays and coves ideal for kayaking. Some hotels and outfitters in Ensenada, Loreto, La Paz, and Los Cabos offer kayak rentals and excursions, and some U.S. companies offer kayaking trips to the Sea of Cortez.

Lodging

Baja lodging is mostly low-key, and you can find great deals at small, one-of-a-kind hostelries. Reservations are a must on holiday weekends; some hotels require a minimum two-night stay for a confirmed reservation. Several hotels in Baja have toll-free numbers that connect directly to the hotel; although the operator may answer in Spanish, there is usually someone who speaks English in the reservations office. Some hotels have fax numbers, although you may have to ask them to turn on the fax machine when you call. Many have Web sites or E-mail addresses you can use to confirm reservations. Ask for a confirmation, and print it out before you leave. A few of the out-of-the-way and budget-price hotels do not accept credit cards; some of the more lavish places add a 10%–20% service charge to your bill. Most properties also raise their rates for the December–April high season (and raise them even higher for the days around Christmas). Rates here are based on high-season standards. Expect to pay 25% less during the off-season. Many hotels offer midweek discounts of 30%–50% off the weekend rates; always ask about special promotions.

Several agencies in the United States book reservations at Baja hotels, condos, and time-share resorts, which may actually cost less than hotel rooms if you are traveling with a group of four or more.

CATEGORY	COST*
$$$$	over $160
$$$	$90–$160
$$	$50–$90
$	under $50

All prices are for a standard double room, excluding service charge and 12%–17% hotel occupancy tax.

Whale-Watching

Gray whales migrate to the Pacific coast of Baja from January through March, when whale-watching expeditions are available in Ensenada and other coastal towns.

TIJUANA

29 km (18 mi) south of San Diego.

Tijuana is the only part of Mexico many people see—a distorted view of the country's many cultures. Before the city became a gigantic recreation center for southern Californians, it was a ranch populated by a few hundred Mexicans. In 1911 a group of Americans invaded the area and attempted to set up an independent republic; they were quickly driven out by Mexican soldiers. When Prohibition hit the United States in the 1920s and the Agua Caliente Racetrack and Casino opened (1929), Tijuana boomed. Americans seeking alcohol, gambling, and more fun than they could find back home flocked across the border, spending freely and fueling the region's growth. Tijuana became the entry port for what some termed a "sinful, steamy playground" frequented by Hollywood stars and the idle rich.

Then Prohibition was repealed, Mexico outlawed gambling, and Tijuana's fortunes declined. Although the flow of travelers from the north slowed to a trickle for a while, Tijuana still captivated those in search of the sort of fun that was not allowed back home. Drivers heading into Baja's wilderness passed through downtown Tijuana, stopping along Avenida Revolución and its side streets for supplies and souvenirs.

When the toll highway to Ensenada was finished in 1967, travelers bypassed the city and tourism dropped again. But Tijuana began attracting residents from throughout Latin America. The city's population mushroomed from a mere 300,000 in 1970 to more than 2 million today. The city has spread into canyons and dry riverbeds, over hillsides, and onto ocean cliffs. As the government struggles to keep up with the growth and demand for services, thousands live without electricity, running water, or adequate housing in squatters' villages along the border. Crime is now a significant problem in Tijuana. Poverty is vast, and petty crime is on the rise. Moreover, the area has become headquarters for serious drug cartels, and violent crime—reaching the highest levels of law enforcement and business—is booming. You're unlikely to witness a shooting or some other frightening situation, but be mindful of your surroundings and guard your belongings.

City leaders, realizing that tourism creates jobs and bolsters Tijuana's fragile economy, are working hard to attract visitors. Avenida Revolución, the main street, is lined with tourist-oriented shopping arcades, restaurants, and bars. The city has an international airport; a fine cultural center that presents international music, dance, and theater groups; and deluxe high-rise hotels. The demand for high-end accommodations has increased with the growth of *maquiladoras* (foreign manufacturing plants). Although it's no longer considered just a bawdy border town, the city remains best known as a place for an intense, somewhat exotic day-long adventure.

Tijuana's tourist attractions have remained much the same throughout the century. The impressive El Palacio Frontón (Jai Alai Palace) no longer hosts jai alai games but is occasionally used as a concert venue. Some of Mexico's greatest bullfighters appear at the oceanfront and downtown bullrings, and an extraordinary number of places in town serve up good food and drinks.

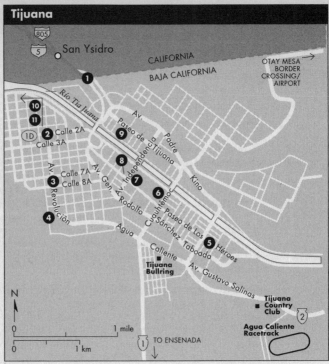

And then, of course, there's shopping. From the moment you cross the border, people will approach you or call out and insist that you look at their wares. If you drive, workers will run out from auto-body shops to place bids on new paint or upholstery for your car. All along Avenida Revolución and its side streets, shops sell everything from tequila to Tiffany-style lamps. Serious shoppers can spend a full day searching and bargaining for their items of choice. If you intend to buy food in Mexico, get the U.S. customs list of articles that are illegal to bring back so that your purchases won't be confiscated.

Exploring

Numbers in the margin correspond to points of interest on the Tijuana map

2 Avenida Revolución. This infamous strip, lined with shops and restaurants that cater to uninhibited travelers, has long been Tijuana's main tourism zone. Shopkeepers call out from their doorways, offering low prices for an assortment of garish souvenirs and genuine folk art treasures. Many shopping arcades open onto Avenida Revolución; inside the front doors are mazes of stands with low-priced pottery and other crafts.

8 Centro Cultural. The Cultural Center was designed by architects Manuel Rosen and Pedro Ramírez Vásquez, who also created Mexico City's famous Museum of Anthropology. The center's Museum of the Californias provides an excellent overview of the history, geography, and flora and fauna of Baja. Exhibits include replicas of several Baja missions and prehistoric cave paintings, along with a nearly full-size sailing ship filled with interactive exhibits for children. The Omnimax Theater, with its curved 180-degree screen, shows films on a rotating schedule; some are in English. Exhibitions on art and culture change frequently, and the center's stage hosts musical and dance performances by international groups. The bookstore has an excellent selection of Mexican history, culture, and arts, mostly in Spanish. ⊠ *Paseo de los Héroes and Av. Independencia, Zona Río,* ☎ *664/687–9600 or 664/ 684–1125.* ⌨ *Museum $2, museum and Omnimax Theater $4.* ☉ *Tues.–Fri. 10–6, weekends 10–8, closed Mon.*

④ L.A. Cetto Winery. Most of Baja's legendary wineries are in the Ensenada region, but Tijuana does have this branch of one of Mexico's finest wineries. You can tour the bottling plant, sample the excellent wines while watching a video on the winery's operations in the Guadalupe Valley, and spend as long as you like in the gift and wine shop, where prices are far lower than in regular liquor stores. ⊠ *Cañon Johnson 8151, at Av. Constitución Sur, Centro,* ☎ *664/685–3031 or 664/685– 1644.* ⌨ *$2 for tour and tasting 4 wines; $6 for tour and tasting 11 wines.* ☉ *Mon.–Sat. 10–5.*

⟲ ⑤ Mundo Divertido. This popular amusement park in the Río zone includes a miniature golf course, batting cages, bumper boats, go-carts, a roller coaster, and a video-game parlor. A food court with hot dogs, burgers, and tacos will keep the kids happy. Admission is free, and the rides cost just a few pesos. ⊠ *Paseo de los Héroes at Calle Velasco, Zona Río,* ☎ *664/634–3213 or 664/634–3214.* ☉ *Weekdays noon– 8:30, weekends 11–9:30.*

③ El Palacio Frontón (Jai Alai Palace). For many years, the magnificent Moorish-style Jai Alai Palace hosted fast-paced jai alai games. The sport has declined in popularity, however, and the Palacio is now occasionally used for boxing contests and concerts. ⊠ *Av. Revolución at Calle 7, Downtown,* ☎ *664/685–7833.*

⑩ Playas Tijuana. Along the oceanfront is this mix of modest and expensive residential neighborhoods, with a few restaurants and hotels. The isolated beaches are visited mostly by residents.

⑪ Plaza de Toros Monumental. The "Bullring by the Sea" sits at the northwest corner of the beach area near the U.S. border. The bullring is occasionally used for summer concerts.

⑦ Plaza Río Tijuana. The area's largest shopping complex has good restaurants, department stores, hundreds of shops, and the Cineopolis, a multiplex theater where several English-language films are usually shown. Shade trees and flowers line the sidewalks that lead from the shopping complex to the Cultural Center. ⊠ *Paseo de los Héroes, across from the Centro Cultural, Zona Río,* ☎ *664/684–0402.*

⑨ Pueblo Amigo. This entertainment center was built to resemble a colonial Mexican village, replete with stucco facades and tree-lined pathways leading to a domed gazebo. The complex includes a hotel, several restaurants and clubs, a huge grocery store, and a large branch of the Caliente Race Book, where gambling on televised races and sporting events is legal. It's more interesting for nightlife than daytime touring. ⊠ *Paseo de Tijuana between Puente Mexico and Av. Independencia, Zona Río.*

① San Ysidro Border Crossing. Locals and tourists jostle each other along the pedestrian walkway through the Viva Tijuana dining and shopping center and into the center of town. Artisans' stands line the walkway and adjoining streets, offering a quick overview of the wares to be found all over town.

⑥ Zona Río. The section that runs along Avenida Paseo de los Héroes, parallel to the dry Tia Juana River, is one of the city's main thoroughfares, with large statues of historical figures, including Abraham Lincoln. With its impressive **Centro Cultural,** several shopping complexes, fine restaurants, and fashionable discos, this part of town rivals Avenida Revolución for tourists' as well as locals' attention. A massive 10-story-high cathedral dedicated to the Virgin of Guadalupe is under construction in this neighborhood; when completed (construction is expected to take several years) it will surely be a city landmark. ⊠ *Paseo de los Héroes between Blvd. Sanchez Taboada and the border, Zona Río.*

Dining and Lodging

$$–$$$ ✕ **Señor Frog's.** Kitschy license plates, posters, and Mexican crafts cover the walls of this wildly popular restaurant where waiters encourage patrons to eat, drink, and sing along with the blaring music. Known for its barbecued ribs and chicken, the kitchen also prepares good Mexican standards such as tacos and carne asada. ⊠ *Pueblo Amigo, Paseo Tijuana between Puente México and Av. Independencia,* ☎ 664/682–4964. MC, V.

$$–$$$ ✕ **Villa Saverios.** Well-dressed Tijuanans savor exceptional pastas, gourmet pizzas, and unusual entrées in this elegant dining room reminiscent of a Mediterranean café. Starters include foie gras, carpaccio, sashimi, lobster taquitos, and tiny mesquite-grilled quail with a tamarind glaze. Canneloni is stuffed with eggplant, spinach, and mushrooms; duck is marinated with raspberry liqueur; and Calvados scents the sweetbreads. The menu is ambitious, the service attentive. ⊠ *Escuadrón 201 at Blvd. Sánchez Taboada, Zona Río,* ☎ 664/686–6502. AE, MC, V.

$$ ✕ **Cien Años.** Haute cuisine is featured in this gracious Spanish colonial–style restaurant with dishes including crêpes filled with *huitlacoche* (fungus that grows on corn), beet salad, shrimp with nopal cactus, and tender beef with avocado and cheese. Each has an unusual blend of flavors—tamarind, Mexican oregano, mango, poblano chilies—that distinguishes the taste of even the *queso fundido* (melted cheese wrapped in tortillas). ⊠ *Av. José María Velasco 1407, Zona Río,* ☎ 664/634–3039. MC, V.

$–$$ ✕ **El Faro de Mazatlán.** Fresh fish prepared simply is the hallmark of one of Tijuana's best seafood restaurants. This is the place to try ceviche, abalone, squid, and lobster without spending a fortune. Meals start with savory soup and crusty rolls. Frequented by professionals from nearby offices, the dining room is a peaceful spot for a long, leisurely lunch. Appetizers and soup are included in the price of the meal. ⊠ *Blvd. Sanchez Taboada 9542, Zona Río,* ☎ 664/684–8883. MC, V.

$–$$ ✕ **La Fonda de Roberto.** Roberto's is the best restaurant in Tijuana for traditional cuisine from the diverse culinary regions of Mexico. Try the *chiles en nogada* (chilies stuffed with raisins and meat and topped with cream and pomegranate seeds), meats with spicy *achiote* (a blend of seasonings) sauce, and many varieties of mole. Portions are small, so order liberally and share samples of many dishes. ⊠ *La Siesta Motel, Blvd. Cuauhtémoc Suroeste 2800, also called Old Ensenada Hwy., near Blvd. Agua Caliente, Agua Caliente,* ☎ 664/686–1601. MC, V.

$ ✕ **La Especial.** At the foot of the stairs leading to an underground shop-
★   ping arcade, this place serves up home-style Mexican cooking at low prices. The gruff, efficient waiters, decked out in black slacks and vests, shuttle platters of *carne asada* (grilled strips of marinated meat), enchiladas, and burritos, all with a distinctive flavor found only at this busy, cavernous basement dining room. ⊠ *Av. Revolucion 78, Centro,* ☎ 664/685–6654. *No credit cards.*

$$$$ ⌂ **Camino Real.** Elegant and fashionable, this modernistic purple and yellow hotel near the Centro Cultural is the most prestigious hotel in town. Business guests abound, but tourists also appreciate the plush rooms

decorated in browns and gold, an excellent restaurant, and the perfect location, though the lack of a swimming pool is a detraction. ✉ *Paseo de los Héroes 10305, Zona Río 22320,* ☎ *664/633–4000 or 800/722–6466,* FAX *664/633–4001,* WEB *www.tjcamino.com. 235 rooms, 15 suites. Restaurant, room service, gym, 2 bars, laundry service. AE, MC, V.*

$$$–$$$$ 🏨 **Grand Hotel.** The twin, mirrored towers of the hotel and a high-rise office building are Tijuana's most ostentatious landmarks. The hotel's atrium restaurant is a favorite lunch and Sunday brunch spot. The rooms could use modernization, but are large; ask for one with good views of the city. It's a good spot for business travelers and anyone looking for a touch of luxury. The hotel mall has an Internet café. ✉ *Blvd. Agua Caliente 4500, Zona Río 22420,* ☎ *664/681–7000,* FAX *664/681–7016. 422 rooms. Restaurant, 2 tennis courts, pool, gym, shops, nightclub, travel services. AE, MC, V.*

$$$ 🏨 **Fiesta Inn.** It's hard to resist this quirky hotel set between two boulevards on a landscaped island. The building stands beside the thermal spring for the 1920s-era Agua Caliente Spa. Today's rooms are modern and comfortable. The Vita Spa, with individual and couples' hot tubs fed from the healing spring, offers facials, massage, soothing mud wraps, and a cozy relaxation room. ✉ *Paseo de los Héroes 18818, Zona Río 22320,* ☎ *664/634–6901 or 800/343–7821,* FAX *664/634–6912,* WEB *www.fiestainn.com. 122 rooms, 5 suites. Restaurant, pool, spa. AE, MC, V.*

$$$ 🏨 **Lucerna.** Once one of the most charming hotels in Tijuana, the Lucerna is now showing its age. Still, the lovely gardens, large pool surrounded by palms, touches of tile work, and folk art lend the hotel a distinct Mexican character. ✉ *Paseo de los Héroes 10902, at Av. Rodríguez, Zona Río 22320,* ☎ *664/633–3900 or 800/582–3762,* FAX *664/634–2400,* WEB *www.hotel-lucerna.com.mx. 167 rooms, 11 suites. Restaurant, coffee shop, pool, nightclub, travel services. MC, V.*

$$ 🏨 **Bugambilias.** Proximity to the Tijuana airport makes this modest hotel a great find. The pink three-story building has motel-like rooms; suites have kitchenettes. The hotel offers free transportation to and from the Tijuana airport. ✉ *Av. Tijuana 1600, Otay Mesa 22450,* ☎ *664/623–7600 or 800/472–1153. 132 rooms, 9 suites. Restaurant, pool, gym, bar. MC, V.*

$$ 🏨 **La Villa de Zaragoza.** Some rooms in this brown stucco motel have kitchenettes, and all offer air-conditioning and cable TV. The location, near the Jai Alai Palace and around the corner from Avenida Revolución, is ideal. The neighborhood can be noisy, so it's best to choose a room at the back. The guarded parking lot is a major plus. The motel is used by tour groups, so book ahead for holidays and weekends. ✉ *Av. Madero 1120, Downtown 22000,* ☎ *664/685–1832,* FAX *664/685–1837. 66 rooms. Restaurant, free parking. MC, V.*

$ 🏨 **Hotel Nelson.** Were it better cared for, the Nelson's pale pink, five-story corner building might be considered a historic landmark. It feels like an older downtown inn, with a barber shop, somewhat noisy bar, and coffee shop on the ground floor. The rooms are serviceable and clean; the best have air-conditioning, heat, and cable TV. ✉ *Av. Revolución 721, Downtown 22000,* ☎ *664/685–4302,* FAX *664/685–4304. 92 rooms. Restaurant, bar, parking (fee). MC, V.*

Nightlife

Tijuana has toned down its Sin City image, but there are still plenty of raucous bars on Avenida Revolución. Locals, however, prefer the classier nightclubs in the Zona Río. Tijuana's discos usually have strict dress codes—no T-shirts, jeans, or sandals allowed.

Baby Rock (✉ Calle Diego Rivera 1482, Zona Río, ☎ 664/634–2404), an offshoot of a popular Acapulco disco, attracts a young, hip crowd. The **Hard Rock Cafe** (✉ Av. Revolución 520, between Calles 1 and 2, Downtown, ☎ 664/685–0206) has the same menu and decor as other branches of the ubiquitous club. This one, too, is popular with families and singles. Businessmen (there's a definite shortage of women here) favor **María Bonita** (✉ Camino Real hotel, Paseo de los Héroes 10305, Zona Río, ☎ 664/633–4000). Designed after the famed L'Opera bar in Mexico City, this small clublike tavern serves several brands of fine tequila along with beer and mixed drinks, and patrons are encouraged to play dominoes, chess, and card games at the tables. Tijuana has its own brand name beer, thanks to the Czech brewmaster at **Tijuana Brewery Company/La Cervecería** (✉ Blvd. Fundadores 2951, Downtown, ☎ 664/638–8662). The European-style pub serves only two drinks–Tijuana Clara and Tijuana Oscura, the light and dark beers brewed in the glassed-in brewery beside the bar. *Botanes,* or appetizers, include *chiles rellenos, queso fundido,* and smoked tuna; live music is offered some nights. The bar is a popular after-work spot, and is usually crowded by 7 PM. One of the hottest night spots with the fashionable set is **Zka** (✉ Blvd. Paseo de los Heroes, at Av. Diego Rivera, Zona Río, ☎ 664/634–7140). Dancers take a break from the action on the large disco floor by settling in on comfy couches in the quieter cocktail lounge.

Outdoor Activities and Sports

Bullfighting

Bullfights feature skilled matadors from throughout Mexico and Spain. Admission to bullfights varies, depending on the fame of the matador and the location of your seat—try for one in the shade. Fights are held at **El Toreo de Tijuana** (✉ Blvd. Agua Caliente, Zona Río, ☎ 664/686–1510) Sunday at 4:30, June through October. In July and August you can see bullfights at the **Plaza de Toros Monumental** (✉ Playas Tijuana area, Ensenada Hwy., Playas Tijuana, ☎ 664/685–2210) Sunday at 4:30.

Golf

The **Tijuana Country Club** (✉ Blvd. Agua Caliente, east of downtown, Zona Río, ☎ 664/681–7855) is open to the public. You can rent clubs, electric and hand carts, and caddies for the 18-hole course.

Shopping

The Avenida Revolución shopping area spreads across Calle 2 to the pedestrian walkway leading from the border. Begin by checking out the stands along the border-crossing walkway, comparing prices as you travel toward Avenida Revolución. You may find that the best bargains are closer to the border; you can pick up your piñatas and serapes on your way out of town. The traditional shopping strip is Avenida Revolución between Calles 1 and 8; it's lined with shops and arcades that display a wide range of crafts and curios. Bargaining is expected on the streets and in the arcades, but not in the finer shops.

Importaciones Sara (✉ Av. Revolución at Calle 4, Downtown, ☎ 664/688–0482), one of the best department stores in Tijuana, features a wide selection of imported perfumes and fine clothing at attractive prices. **La Piel** (✉ Av. Revolución between Calles 4 and 5, Downtown, ☎ 664/687–2398) has dependable quality in its leather jackets, backpacks, and luggage.

High-quality furnishings and art are tastefully displayed at **Mallorca** (✉ Calle 4 at Av. Revolución, Downtown, ☎ 664/688–8224). The

Mercado Hidalgo (⊠ Av. Independencia at Av. Sanchez Taboada, Downtown, two blocks south of Paseo de los Héroes) is Tijuana's municipal market, with rows of fresh produce, grains, herbs, some souvenirs, and the best selection of piñatas in Baja.

The **Mexicoach Terminal** (⊠ Av. Revolución between Calles 6 and 7, Downtown, ☎ 664/685–1470) is a one-stop center. **Plaza Fiesta** (⊠ Paseo de los Héroes, across from Plaza Río Tijuana, Zona Río) has a collection of boutiques, jewelry stores, and stained-glass shops, but the plaza has become a bit run down and not worth visiting unless you're in the neighborhood. The shops in **Plaza Revolución** (⊠ Calle 1 and Av. Revolución, Downtown) sell quality crafts. You can find great buys on fashionable clothing and shoes at **Plaza Río Tijuana** (⊠ Paseo de los Héroes, Zona Río).

Sanborns (⊠ Av. Revolución at Calle 8, Downtown, ☎ 664/688–1462) has beautiful crafts from throughout Mexico, an excellent bakery, and chocolates from Mexico City. The nicest folk-art store, **Tolán** (⊠ Av. Revolución between Calles 7 and 8, Downtown, ☎ 664/688–3637), carries everything from antique, carved wooden doors to tiny, ceramic miniature village scenes.

PLAYAS DE ROSARITO

29 km (18 mi) south of Tijuana.

For better or worse, Rosarito has seen a transformation during the past few decades. The one-time small seaside community, once part of the municipality of Tijuana, had been an overlooked suburb on the way to the port city of Ensenada. But as the roads improved—and particularly after the 1973 completion of Baja's Transpeninsular Highway—Rosarito began to flower. Rosarito is now a municipality separate from Tijuana and is self governed. Rosarito attracted considerable attention when 20th Century Fox built a permanent movie-production studio on the coastline south of town to film the mega-success *Titanic*. Today, the studio is home to an exciting theme park. Rosarito's leaders had hoped their town would become a cruise ship port, and funded construction of a long pier at the Rosarito Beach Hotel. The sea, however, is too rough and shallow for the ships, so the pier has become a bustling outdoor café.

Meanwhile, Rosarito's population, now about 110,000, has been growing steadily. The city's main drag, alternately known as the Old Ensenada Highway and Boulevard Benito Juárez, reflects the unrestrained growth and speculation that have both helped and harmed Rosarito. The street is packed with restaurants, bars, and shops in a jarring juxtaposition of building styles. Fortunately, the building boom has slowed and the town's boosters are attempting to beautify the boulevard.

Southern Californians have made Rosarito their weekend getaway, and the crowd is far from subdued. Surfers, swimmers, and sunbathers come here to enjoy the beach, which stretches from the power plant at the north end of town to about 8 km (5 mi) south. Horseback riding, jogging, and strolling are popular along this uninterrupted strand, where whales swim within viewing distance on their winter migration and dolphins and sea lions frequent the shoreline.

Rosarito has always attracted a varied group. These days it's made up of prosperous young Californians building villas and vacation developments, retired Americans and Canadians homesteading in gated communities, and an abundance of young adults seeking cheap food, drink, and an escape from supervision. It often seems that spring break is a year-round event here, with much of the action centered on the Festival Plaza hotel. The police do their best to control the revelers, but spring and summer weekend nights can be outrageously noisy. If you're here to relax in peace, choose a hotel room far from any bars or restaurants.

Hedonism and health get equal billing in Rosarito. Seafood is a favorite here, especially lobster, shrimp, and fish tacos, and visiting Americans eagerly cluster by watering holes for margaritas and beer. People cast off their inhibitions, at least to the degree permitted by local constables. A typical Rosarito day might begin with a breakfast of eggs, refried beans, and tortillas, followed by a few hours of horseback riding on the beach. Lying in the sun or browsing in shops takes care of midday. Siestas are imperative and are usually followed by more shopping, strolling, or sunbathing before a night of dinner and dancing.

Exploring

Rosarito has few historic or cultural attractions, beaches and bars being the main draws. Sightseeing consists of strolling along the beach or down **Boulevard Benito Juárez,** which runs parallel to it. An immense Pemex gasoline installation and electric plant anchor the northern end of Boulevard Juárez, which then runs along a collection of shopping arcades, restaurants, and motels. Nearly everyone stops at the Rosarito Beach Hotel, the town's landmark historic hotel. A wooden pier stretches over the ocean; on calm days, there's no better place to watch the sunset than from the hotel café tables along its glassed-in edges.

Museo Wa-Kuatay. Rosarito's history is illustrated in exhibits on the Kumiai Indians, the early missions, and ranching in the region at this small museum. The hours are inconsistent. ⊠ *Blvd. Juárez next to the Rosarito Beach Hotel,* ☎ *no phone.* ⊠ *Free.* ⊙ *Closed Tues.*

Foxploration. Fox Studios has expanded its operation to include a film-oriented theme park. Guests learn how films are made by visiting a set resembling a New York street scene, and another filled with props from *Titanic.* Exhibits on filming, sound and light effects, and animation are both educational and entertaining, and Fox's most famous films are shown in the large state-of-the-art theater. The park includes a children's playroom where kids can shoot thousands of foam balls out of air cannons, a food court with U.S. franchises including Subway and Starbucks, and a large retail area. ⊠ *Old Ensenada Hwy. Km 32.8, Popotla,* ☎ *661/614–9499,* WEB *www.foxploration.com.* ⊠ *$9–$12. Closed Tues.–Wed.*

Galería Giorgio Santini. Baja's finest painters and sculptors now have a worthwhile venue for their works, which are handsomely displayed in this architecturally stunning gallery. Stop by for a glass of wine or an espresso in the coffeeshop, and learn something about Baja's vibrant art scene. ⊠ *Old Ensenada Hwy. Km 40,* ☎ *661/614–1459,* WEB *www. giorgiosantini.com.* ⊠ *Free.* ⊙ *Closed Wed.*

Dining and Lodging

$–$$$ ✕ **El Nido.** A dark, wood-paneled restaurant with leather booths and a large central fireplace, this is one of the oldest eateries in Rosarito. Diners unimpressed with newer, fancier places come here for mesquite-grilled steaks and for grilled quail from the owner's farm in the Baja wine country. ⊠ *Blvd. Juárez 67,* ☎ *661/612–1430. MC, V.*

$–$$$ ✕ **El Patio.** Calm amid the bustle of the Festival Plaza complex, this tasteful, colonial-style restaurant is the best spot for a relaxed, authentic Mexican meal. Umbrella-covered tables are framed by soft-blue and azure walls, and the aromas of chilies, mole, and grilled meats spark the appetite. The menu favors dishes like savory grilled quail, shrimp crepes, and chicken with poblano sauce. The bar is peaceful as well—a good place to enjoy a cocktail away from the streetside crowds. ✉ *Festival Plaza, Blvd. Juárez,* ☎ *661/612–2950. AE, MC, V.*

$–$$ ✕ **La Leña.** The cornerstone restaurant of the Quinta Plaza shopping
★ center, La Leña is spacious and impeccably clean, with tables spread far enough apart for privacy. Try any of the beef dishes, especially the tender *carne asada* with tortillas and guacamole or the steak and lobster combo. ✉ *Quinta Plaza, Blvd. Juárez,* ☎ *661/612–0826. MC, V.*

$ ✕ **La Flor de Michoacán.** Michoacán-style carnitas, served with homemade tortillas, guacamole, and salsa, are featured at this rustic Rosarito landmark, established in 1950. The tacos, *tortas* (sandwiches), and tostadas are great. Takeout is available. ✉ *Blvd. Juárez 291,* ☎ *661/ 612–1858. No credit cards. Closed Wed.*

$ ✕ **Tacos El Yaqui.** For true downhome Mexican cooking, nothing beats this taco stand. Carne asada tacos wrapped in fresh corn tortillas are superb and the perfect fix for late-night munchies. The stand is clean and the cooks use purified water. ✉ *Calle de la Palma off Blvd. Juárez across from the Rosarito Beach Hotel,* ☎ *no phone. No credit cards.*

$$$–$$$$ ▥ **Rosarito Beach Hotel and Spa.** Charm rather than comfort is the main reason for staying here. The rooms in the oldest section have hand-painted wooden beams and heavy dark furnishings. Those in the tower have air-conditioning and a more modern pastel look. Reduced midweek rates and special packages are often available. The Casa Playa Spa offers treatments, exercise equipment, and hot tubs. ✉ *Blvd. Juárez, south end of town, (Box 430145, San Diego, CA 22710),* ☎ *661/612–1106 or 800/ 343–8582,* ℻ *661/612–1125,* ⓦⒺⒷ *www.rosaritobeachhotel.com. 180 rooms, 100 suites. 3 restaurants, tennis court, 2 pools, gym, spa, beach, bar, playground. MC, V.*

$$–$$$$ ✕▥ **Marriott Real Del Mar Residence Inn.** Golfers and escapists relish this all-suites hotel with faraway views of the sea. Accommodations have living rooms with vaulted brick ceilings, fireplaces, kitchens, and two double beds; some have one or two bedrooms. Greens fees at the on-site golf course are included in packages. Both restaurants attract diners from Tijuana and Rosarito for their fresh seafood and nouvelle Mexican preparations. ✉ *Ensenada toll road Km 19.5, 22710,* ☎ *661/ 631–3670 or 800/331–3131,* ℻ *661/631–3677,* ⓦⒺⒷ *www.realdelmar. com.mx. 75 suites. 2 restaurants, snack bar, 18-hole golf course, pool, gym, spa, bar. AE, MC, V.*

$–$$$ ✕▥ **Calafia.** This complex, a 10-minute car ride south of Rosarito, houses an eclectic array of attractions—all perched above the intractable sea. The walls are a nascent museum dedicated to the missionary conquests in Baja. The restaurant, with tables posed on cliffs over the crashing waves, features fresh seafood and creative Mexican cuisine. Hotel rooms are available in a variety of buildings and trailers packed tightly by the restaurant. The least expensive are in trailers near the highway. The best are right above the water. ✉ *Old Ensenada Hwy. Km 35.5,* ☎ *661/612–1581,* ℻ *661/612–0296,* ⓦⒺⒷ *www.calafia.com.mx. 52 rooms. Restaurant, bar, pool, beach. MC, V.*

$$$–$$$$ ▥ **Las Rocas.** This white hotel with blue-tile domes is the most romantic
★ in the area. All rooms have ocean views. The least expensive ones are small; others are larger and have fireplaces and microwaves. The pool and whirlpool seem to spill into the ocean. An excellent full spa offers state-of-the-art treatments at reasonable prices. Ask about spa packages and midweek specials. ✉ *Old Ensenada Hwy. Km 38.5, 22710,*

☎ 888/527–7622, ☎ FAX 661/612–2140, WEB *www.lasrocas.com 40 rooms, 34 suites. Restaurant, 2 pools, hot tub, spa, beach, 2 bars. AE, MC, V.*

$$–$$$ 🏨 **Festival Plaza.** Designed with unrestrained fun in mind, the motel-like rooms are in an eight-story building beside the road and bars. The casitas close to the beach are the quietest accommodations and have small hot tubs, living rooms with foldout couches, but no kitchen facilities. The 13 villas just south of Rosarito have full kitchens. The central courtyard serves as a concert stage, playground, and party headquarters. Discounted room rates are often available, especially in winter. ✉ *Blvd. Juárez 11, 22710,* ☎ *624/612–0842, 661/612–2950, or 800/453–8606,* FAX *661/612–0124,* WEB *www.festivalbaja.com. 217 rooms, 5 suites, 7 casitas, 13 villas. 4 restaurants, pool, 6 bars, dance club. AE, MC, V.*

$$ 🏨 **Brisas del Mar.** This roadside motel is especially good for families—the large pastel rooms comfortably accommodate four people. A few of the suites on the second story have hot tubs and ocean views; all have air-conditioning and TV. The motel is on the inland side of Boulevard Juárez, and traffic noise can be a problem. ✉ *Blvd. Juárez 22, 22710,* ☎ FAX *661/612–2547 or 888/871–3605,* WEB *www.hotelbrisas. com. 69 rooms, 2 suites. Coffee shop, pool, bar. AE, MC, V.*

$–$$ 🏨 **Los Pelicanos Hotel.** Guests return annually to their favorite rooms in this small hotel by the beach. Those without ocean views are inexpensive; rates are higher for rooms on the top floors. There's no pool, but the restaurant is a local favorite for sunset cocktails. ✉ *Calle Ebano 113, 22710,* ☎ FAX *661/612–0445. 39 rooms. Restaurant, bar. No credit cards.*

Nightlife and the Arts

Rosarito's many restaurants keep customers entertained with live music, piano bars, or *folklórico* (folk music and dance) shows, and the bar scene is hopping as well. Drinking-and-driving laws are stiff; the police will fine you no matter how little you've had. If you drink, take a cab or assign a designated driver. The police are also enforcing laws that prohibit drinking in the streets: confine your revelry to the bars.

The **Festival Plaza** (✉ Blvd. Juárez 11, ☎ 661/612–0842) has become party central for Rosarito's younger crowd and presents live concerts on the hotel's courtyard stage most weekends. In the hotel complex are **El Museo Cantina Tequila** (☎ 661/612–2950), dedicated to the art of imbibing tequila and stocked with more than 130 brands of the fiery drink—including the house rattlesnake tequila, said to be an aphrodisiac. Also at Festival Plaza, **Rock & Roll Taco** is a taco stand and boisterous bar with several sections, including an outdoor area backed by hotel rooms. It's the largest (and probably the most rambunctious) dancing and drinking hangout in town. **Papas and Beer** (✉ On the beach off Blvd. Juárez near Rosarito Beach Hotel, ☎ 661/612–0444) draws a young, energetic crowd for drinking and dancing on the beach and small stages. **Rene's Sports Bar** (✉ Carretera Transpeninsular Km 28, ☎ 661/612–1061) draws a somewhat quieter, older crowd; the restaurant isn't great, but a few pool tables, TVs broadcasting sporting events, and a convivial gaggle of gringos make the bar a great hangout. There's a lot going on at night at the **Rosarito Beach Hotel** (✉ Blvd. Juárez, ☎ 661/612–1106): live music at the ocean-view **Beachcomber Bar**; a Mexican Fiesta on Friday and Saturday nights; and occasional live bands and dances in the cavernous ballroom. **Señor Frog's** (✉ Blvd. Juárez 1 block north of the Festival Plaza) offers a raucous blend of tequila and loud music.

Outdoor Activities and Sports

Golf

The **Real del Mar Golf Club** (⊠ 18 km [11 mi] south of the border on Ensenada toll road, ☎ 661/631–3401) has 18 holes overlooking the ocean. Golf packages are available at some Rosarito Beach hotels.

Horseback Riding

You can hire horses at the north and south ends of Boulevard Juárez and on the beach south of the Rosarito Beach Hotel for $10 per hour. If you're a dedicated equestrian, ask about tours into the countryside, which can be arranged with the individual owners.

Surfing

The waves are particularly good at **Popotla** (Km 33), **Calafia** (Km 35.5), and **Costa Baja** (Km 36) on the Old Ensenada Highway.

Shopping

Shopping is far better in Rosarito than in most Baja cities, especially for pottery, wood furniture, and high-end household items favored by condo-owners in nearby expat clusters. Curio stands and open-air artisans' markets line Boulevard Juárez both north and south of town. Major hotels have shopping arcades with restaurants, taco stands, and some decent crafts stores.

Apisa (⊠ Blvd. Juárez 2400, ☎ 661/612–0125) is said to be the finest home-decor shop in town, and sells contemporary furnishings and iron sculptures from Guadalajara. The **Calimax** grocery store on Boulevard Juárez is a good place to stock up on necessities. **Casa la Carreta** (⊠ Old Ensenada Hwy. Km 29, ☎ 661/612–0502), one of Rosarito's best furniture shops, keeps expanding and is worth a visit just to see the wood-carvers shaping elaborate desks, dining tables, and armoires. **Casa Torres** (⊠ Rosarito Beach Hotel Shopping Center, Blvd. Juárez, ☎ 661/ 612–1008) carries a wide array of imported perfumes. There are several shops in this center by the hotel's parking lot, along with an Internet café. **Don Quijote Furniture** (⊠ Blvd. Juárez s/n, across from Quinta Plaza, ☎ no phone) is a great outlet for custom furnishings and wrought iron. Resembling a colonial church with its facade of hand-painted tiles, **La Misión** (⊠ Blvd. Juárez s/n, across from Ortega's, ☎ 661/612–1576) displays hand-carved chairs, tin lamps shaped like stars, and glazed pottery.

TIJUANA AND PLAYAS DE ROSARITO A TO Z

To research prices, get advice from other travelers, and book travel arrangements, visit www.fodors.com.

Addresses

The Mexican method of naming streets can be exasperatingly arbitrary, so **be patient when searching for street addresses.** Streets in the centers of many colonial cities (those built by the Spanish) are laid out in a grid surrounding the *zócalo* (main square) and often change names on different sides of the square. Other streets simply acquire a new name after a certain number of blocks. Numbered streets are usually designated *norte/sur* (north/south) or *oriente/poniente* (east/west) on either side of a central avenue. (Three of these are abbreviated: Nte., Ote., and Pte. Sur is spelled out.) In many cities, streets that have proper names, such as Avenida Benito Juárez, change names when they cross some other street—and only a map will show where one begins and the other ends. Blocks are often labeled numerically, according to distance from a chosen starting point, as in "la Calle de Pachuca," "2a Calle de Pachuca," etc. Many Mexican addresses have "s/n" for *sin número* (no number) after the street name. Similarly, many hotels give their address as "Old Ensenada Highway Km 30," which indicates that the property is at the 30th kilometer on the highway heading to Ensenada.

BUS TRAVEL

Greyhound serves the border from San Diego several times daily. Buses to San Diego and Los Angeles depart from the Greyhound terminal in Tijuana at Avenida Mexico at Madero. Mexicoach runs buses from the trolley depot and the large parking lot on the U.S. side of the border to its depot on Avenida Revolución. Buses also run from Tijuana to Rosarito several times daily.

The downtown bus station in Tijuana is at Calle 1a and Avenida Madero (☎ 664/686–9515). Most city buses at the border will take you downtown; look for the ones marked CENTRO CAMIONERA. To catch the bus back to the border from downtown, go to Calle Benito Juárez (also called Calle 2a) between Avenidas Revolución and Constitución. *Colectivos* (small vans often painted white with colored stripes) cover neighborhood routes in most Baja cities and towns. The destination is usually painted on the windshield; look for them on main streets.

Buses traveling to Rosarito stop at the Rosarito exit on the toll road where taxis wait to transport passengers to town. There is no official bus station here; check at the hotels for bus-schedule information.
➤ BUS INFORMATION: **Greyhound** (☎ 664/621–2951 or 664/686–0695 in Tijuana; 619/239–3266 in the U.S.; 800/231–2222). **Mexicoach** (☎ 664/685–1470; 619/428–9517 in the U.S., WEB www.mexicoach.com).
➤ BUS STATIONS: **Tijuana bus station** (✉ Calzada Lázaro Cárdenas and Blvd. Arroyo Alamar, Tijuana, ☎ 664/621–2982).

CAR RENTAL

Many U.S. car-rental companies do not allow you to drive their cars into Mexico. Avis permits its cars to go from San Diego into Baja as far as 724 km (450 mi) south of the border. Cars must be returned by the renter to San Diego, and you must declare your intention to take the car into Mexico and purchase Mexican auto insurance. Southwest Car Rentals allows its cars as far as Ensenada. You must purchase Mexican insurance when you rent the car. California Baja Rent-A-Car rents four-wheel-drive vehicles, convertibles, and sedans for use throughout Mexico (the only company to do this). If you plan to rent your car in Tijuana or San Diego and drop it in Los Cabos, be prepared to pay a hefty sum (up to $900) on top of the rental price.

The larger U.S. rental agencies have offices at the Tijuana International Airport (Aeropuerto Alberado Rodriguez), and Avis and Budget have offices in downtown Tijuana. California Baja Rent-A-Car has a fabulous fleet of vehicles you can drive all over Mexico. Vans, recreational vehicles, off-road four by fours, and regular sedans are all available.
➤ MAJOR AGENCIES: **Avis** (✉ Av. Agua Caliente 3310, Tijuana, ☎ 664/686–4004, 664/686–3718, or 800/331–1212). **Budget** (✉ Paseo de los Héroes 77, Tijuana, ☎ 664/634–3303). **California Baja Rent-A-Car** (✉ 9245 Jamacha Blvd., Spring Valley, CA 91977, ☎ 619/470–7368 or 888/470–7368).

CAR TRAVEL

The best way to tour Baja Norte is by car, although the driving can be difficult and confusing. If you're just visiting Tijuana, it's easiest to park on the U.S. side of the border and walk across.

From San Diego, U.S. 5 and I–805 end at the San Ysidro border crossing; Highway 905 leads from I–5 and I–805 to the Tijuana border crossing at Otay Mesa. U.S. 94 from San Diego connects with U.S. 188 to the border at Tecate, 57 km (35 mi) east of San Diego.

To head south into Baja from Tijuana, follow the signs for Ensenada Cuota, the toll road (also called Highway 1 and, on newer signs, the Scenic Highway) that runs south along the coast. There are two clearly marked exits for Rosarito, and one each for Puerto Nuevo, Bajamar, and Ensenada. The road is excellent, although it has some hair-raising curves atop the cliffs and is best driven in daylight (the stretch from Rosarito to Ensenada is one of the most scenic drives in Baja). Tollbooths accept U.S. and Mexican currency; tolls are usually just over $3. Rest rooms are available near toll stations. The alternative free road—Highway 1D or Ensenada Libre—has been vastly improved, but it's difficult for the first-timer to navigate.

Mexico Highway 2 runs east from Tijuana to Tecate and Mexicali. There are toll roads between Tijuana and Tecate and between Tecate and Mexicali. The 134-km (83-mi) journey from Tecate east to Mexicali on La Rumorosa, as the road is known, is as exciting as a roller-coaster ride, with the highway twisting and turning down steep mountain grades and over flat, barren desert.

If you're traveling only as far as Ensenada or San Felipe, you do not need a tourist card, unless you stay longer than 72 hours. If you know you'll be traveling south of Ensenada, you can get the form at the Mexican Customs Office. You must have Mexican auto insurance, available at agencies near the border.

The combination of overpopulation, lack of infrastructure, and heavy winter rains makes many of Tijuana's streets difficult to navigate by automobile. It's always best to stick to the main thoroughfares. There are parking lots along Avenida Revolución and at most major attractions. Most of Rosarito proper can be explored on foot, which is a good idea on weekends, when Boulevard Juárez has bumper-to-bumper traffic.
➤ CONTACT: **Mexican Customs Office** (✉ inside San Ysidro border crossing, ☏ 664/682–3439 or 664/684–7790).

CHILDREN IN MEXICO

Mexico has one of the strictest policies about children entering the country. All children, including infants, must have proof of citizenship (a birth certificate) for travel to Mexico. All children up to age 18 traveling with a single parent must also have a notarized letter from the other parent stating that the child has his or her permission to leave their home country. If the other parent is deceased or the child has only one legal parent, a notarized statement saying so must be obtained as proof. In addition, parents must now fill out a tourist card for each child over the age of 10 traveling with them.

EMBASSIES
➤ UNITED STATES: **U.S. Consulate** (✉ Tapachula 96, Tijuana, ☏ 664/681–7400).

EMERGENCIES

In an emergency anywhere in Baja Norte, dial **060** for the police, **066** for Red Cross, and **068** for the fire department. Tijuana operates a bilingual

Tourist Assistance Hot Line, and the city's Tourist Assistance Office takes calls on weekdays to help with tourist complaints and problems.

➤ CONTACTS: **Tourist Assistance Hot Line** (☎ 078). **Tourist Assistance Office** (☎ 664/688–0555).

ENTRY REQUIREMENTS

For stays of up to 180 days, Americans must prove citizenship through either a valid passport, certified copy of a birth certificate, or voter-registration card (the last two must be accompanied by a government-issue photo ID). Australians, Britons, and New Zealanders need a valid passport to enter Mexico. Canadians need only proof of citizenship to enter Mexico for stays of up to six months. For stays of more than 180 days, all U.S. citizens, even infants, need a valid passport to enter Mexico. Minors traveling with one parent need notarized permission from the absent parent.

If you're visiting for less than 72 hours or are not traveling past the 26–30-km (16–18-mi) checkpoint into the country's interior, you don't have to pay Mexico's $17 visitor fee (tourist card). You can get a tourist card at the Mexican Customs Office inside San Ysidro border crossing.

LODGING

Several companies specialize in arranging hotel reservations in northern Baja. Baja Information is one of the oldest and best agencies working with Baja hotels and tourism departments. Baja California Tours books hotel rooms in the cities and outlying areas. Mexico Condo Reservations books hotel and condo accommodations and represents La Pinta Hotels, a chain with several hotels on the peninsula.

➤ CONTACTS: **Baja California Tours** (✉ 7734 Herschel Ave., Suite O, La Jolla, CA 92037, ☎ 858/454–7166; 800/336–5454 in the U.S., FAX 858/454–2703, WEB www.bajatours.signonsandiego.com). **Baja Information** (✉ 6855 Friars Rd., Suite 26, San Diego, CA 92108, ☎ 619/298–4105; 800/522–1516 in CA, NV, AZ; 800/225–2786 elsewhere, FAX 619/294–7366). **Mexico Condo Reservations** (✉ 4420 Hotel Circle Ct., Suite 230, San Diego, CA 92108, ☎ 619/275–4500 or 800/262–9632, FAX 619/456–1350, WEB www.gobaja.com).

TELEPHONES

The country code for Mexico is 52. When calling a Mexico number from abroad, dial the country code and then all of the numbers listed for the entry.

In February 2002, Mexico implemented a national numbering program that entailed switching to a new 10-digit dialing plan. **Only 10-digit calls can be connected** throughout the country. From outside the country, you now dial the country code (52) followed by the 10-digit number. To convert any old number into a 10-digit number, use the converter at www.sprint.com/mexico/mexicodialplanchange.

To make an international call, **dial 00 before the country code, area code, and number.** When calling home, the country code for the U.S. and Canada is 1, the U.K. 44, Australia 61, New Zealand 64, and South Africa 27.

Directory assistance is 040 nationwide. For international assistance, dial 00 first for an international operator and most likely you'll get one that speaks English; tell the operator in what city, state, and country you require directory assistance, and he or she will connect you with directory assistance there.

TOURS AND PACKAGES

Baja California Tours (*See* Lodging) has comfortable, informative bus trips throughout northern Baja. Seasonal day and overnight trips focus on whale-watching, fishing, shopping, wineries, sports, dude ranches, and art and cultural events in Tijuana, Rosarito, Ensenada, and San Felipe.

TROLLEY TRAVEL

The San Diego Trolley travels from the Santa Fe Depot in San Diego, at Kettner Boulevard and Broadway, to within 100 ft of the border every 15 minutes from 5 AM to midnight. The 45-minute trip costs $3.

➤ CONTACT: **San Diego Trolley** (☎ 619/233–2004).

VISITOR INFORMATION

Baja tours, Mexican auto insurance, a monthly newsletter, and workshops are available through Discover Baja. Some of the smaller areas do not have offices. The excellent Baja California State Secretary of Tourism distributes information on the entire state.

➤ TOURIST INFORMATION: **Baja California State Secretary of Tourism** (✉ Paseo de los Héroes 10289, Tijuana, ☎ 664/634–6330, FAX 664/634–7157, WEB www.turismobc.gob.mx). **Discover Baja** (✉ 3089 Clairemont Dr., San Diego, CA 92117, ☎ 619/275–4225 or 800/727–2252, FAX 619/275–1836, WEB www.discoverbaja.com). **Mexican Customs Office** (✉ inside San Ysidro border crossing, ☎ 664/682–3439 or 664/684–7790). **Mexico Tourism Board** (☎ 800/446–3942) **Rosarito Tourist Board** (✉ Blvd. Juárez 907, Oceana Plaza Shopping Center, ☎ 624/612–0396 or 800/962–2252, WEB www.rosaritobch.com). **Tijuana Convention and Tourism Bureau** (✉ inside the San Ysidro border crossing, ☎ 664/683–1405; ✉ Av. Revolución between Calles 3 and 4, ☎ 664/684–0481 or 664/684–7790). **Tijuana Tourist Board** (✉ Paseo de los Héroes 9365-201, in the Zona Río, ☎ 664/684–0537 or 888/775–2417, WEB www.seetijuana.com).

INDEX

Fodor's Key to the Guides

America's guidebook leader publishes guides for every kind of traveler.
Check out our many series and find your perfect match.

Fodor's Gold Guides
America's favorite travel-guide series offers the most detailed insider reviews of hotels, restaurants, and attractions in all price ranges, plus great background information, smart tips, and useful maps.

Fodor's Road Guide USA
Big guides for a big country—the most comprehensive guides to America's roads, packed with places to stay, eat, and play across the U.S.A. Just right for road warriors, family vacationers, and cross-country trekkers.

COMPASS AMERICAN GUIDES
Stunning guides from top local writers and photographers, with gorgeous photos, literary excerpts, and colorful anecdotes. A must-have for culture mavens, history buffs, and new residents.

Fodor's CITYPACKS
Concise city coverage with a foldout map. The right choice for urban travelers who want everything under one cover.

Fodor's EXPLORING GUIDES
Hundreds of color photos bring your destination to life. Lively stories lend insight into the culture, history, and people.

Fodor's POCKET GUIDES
For travelers who need only the essentials. The best of Fodor's in pocket-size packages for just $9.95.

Fodor's To Go
Credit-card–size, magnetized color microguides that fit in the palm of your hand—perfect for "stealth" travelers or as gifts.

Fodor's FLASHMAPS
Every resident's map guide. 60 easy-to-follow maps of public transit, parks, museums, zip codes, and more.

Fodor's CITYGUIDES
Sourcebooks for living in the city: Thousands of in-the-know listings for restaurants, shops, sports, nightlife, and other city resources.

Fodor's AROUND THE CITY WITH KIDS
68 great ideas for family days, recommended by resident parents. Perfect for exploring in your own backyard or on the road.

Fodor's ESCAPES
Fill your trip with once-in-a-lifetime experiences, from ballooning in Chianti to overnighting in the Moroccan desert. These full-color dream books point the way.

Fodor's FYI
Get tips from the pros on planning the perfect trip. Learn how to pack, fly hassle-free, plan a honeymoon or cruise, stay healthy on the road, and travel with your baby.

Fodor's Languages for Travelers
Practice the local language before hitting the road. Available in phrase books, cassette sets, and CD sets.

Karen Brown's Guides
Engaging guides to the most charming inns and B&Bs in the U.S.A. and Europe, with easy-to-follow inn-to-inn itineraries.

Baedeker's Guides
Comprehensive guides, trusted since 1829, packed with A–Z reviews and star ratings.

At bookstores everywhere.   www.fodors.com/books